한국 인권문제

유엔 반응 및 동향 1

• 외교문서 비밀해제 - 한국 인권문제 14 •

한국 인권문제

유엔 반응 및 동향 1

한국학술정보

| 머리말

일제 강점기 독립운동과 병행되었던 한국의 인권운동은 해방이 되었음에도 큰 결실을 보지 못했다. 1950년대 반공을 앞세운 이승만 정부와 한국전쟁, 역시 경제발전과 반공을 내세우다 유신 체제에 이르렀던 박정희 정권, 쿠데타로 집권한 1980년대 전두환 정권까지, 한국의 인권은 이를 보장해야 할 국가와 정부에 의해 도리어 억압받고 침해되었다. 이런 배경상 근대 한국의 인권운동은 반독재, 민주화운동과 결을 같이했고, 대체로 국외에 본부를 둔 인권 단체나 정치로부터 상대적으로 자유로운 종교 단체에 의해 주도되곤 했다. 이는 1980년 5 · 18광주민주화운동을 계기로 보다 근적인 변혁을 요구하는 형태로 조직화되었고, 그 활동 영역도 정치를 넘어 노동자, 농민, 빈민 등으로 확대되었다. 이들이 없었다면 한국은 1987년 군부 독재 종식하고 절차적 민주주의를 도입할 수 없었을 것이다. 민주화 이후에도 수많은 어려움이 있었지만, 한국의 인권운동은 점차 전문적이고 독립된 운동으로 분화되며 더 많은 이들의 참여를 이끌어냈고, 지금까지 많은 결실을 맺을 수 있었다.

본 총서는 1980년대 중반부터 1990년대 초반까지, 외교부에서 작성하여 30여 년간 유지했던 한국 인권문제와 관련한 국내외 자료를 담고 있다. 6월 항쟁이 일어나고 민주화 선언이 이뤄지는 등 한국 인권운동에 많은 변화가 있었던 시기다. 당시 인권문제와 관련한 국내외 사안들, 각종 사건에 대한 미국과 우방국, 유엔의 반응, 최초의 한국 인권보고서 제출과 아동의 권리에 관한 협약 과정, 유엔인권위원회 활동, 기타 민주화 관련 자료 등 총 18권으로 구성되었다. 전체 분량은 약 9천여 쪽에 이른다.

2024년 3월

한국학술정보(주)

| 일러두기

· 본 총서에 실린 자료는 2022년 4월과 2023년 4월에 각각 공개한 외교문서 4,827권, 76만 여 쪽 가운데 일부를 발췌한 것이다.

· 각 권의 제목과 순서는 공개된 원본을 최대한 반영하였으나, 주제에 따라 일부는 적절히 변경하였다.

· 원본 자료는 A4 판형에 맞게 축소하거나 원본 비율을 유지한 채 A4 페이지 안에 삽입하였다. 또한 현재 시점에선 공개되지 않아 '공란'이란 표기만 있는 페이지 역시 그대로 실었다.

· 외교부가 공개한 문서 각 권의 첫 페이지에는 '정리 보존 문서 목록'이란 이름으로 기록물 종류, 일자, 명칭, 간단한 내용 등의 정보가 수록되어 있으며, 이를 기준으로 0001번부터 번호가 매겨져 있다. 이는 삭제하지 않고 총서에 그대로 수록하였다.

· 보고서 내용에 관한 더 자세한 정보가 필요하다면, 외교부가 온라인상에 제공하는 『대한민국 외교사료요약집』 1991년과 1992년 자료를 참조할 수 있다.

차례

정 리 보 존 문 서 목 록					
기록물종류	일반공문서철	등록번호	2014050031	등록일자	2014-05-14
분류번호	734.3	국가코드		보존기간	30년
명 칭	UNCSDHA(유엔사회개발인도문제센터), 1984				
생 산 과	국제연합과	생산년도	1984~1984	담당그룹	
내용목차					

0001

주 오 스 트 리 아 대 사 관

오지리(정)743-529 1984. 5 . 7 .

수신 : 외무부 장관

참조 : 국제기구조약국장

제목 : 유엔 사회 문제 자료 요청

UN 당국으로 부터 범세계적인 해외 이주 노동자 및 가족 문제 연구와 관련 별첨과 같이 자료 요청이 있으니 검토 회시 바랍니다.

첨부 : SD 2091/1

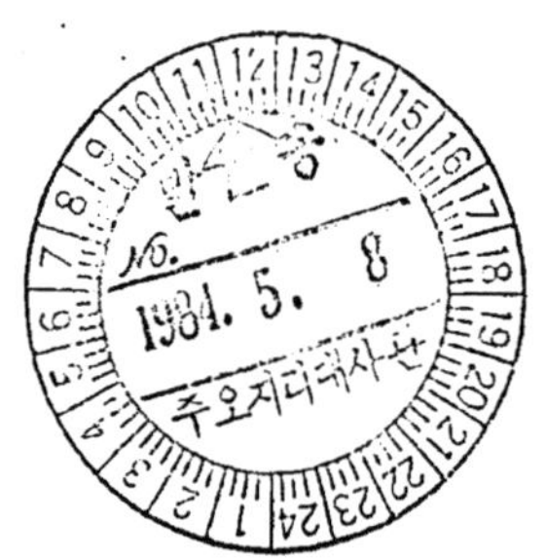

주 오 스 트 리 아 대 사

0002

결 재	외 무 부		지시사항	
	접수번호	제 28527 호		
과	접수일자	1984. 5. 11		
자	처리과		198 년 월 일 까지 처리할것	

0003

UNITED NATIONS NATIONS UNIES

VIENNA INTERNATIONAL CENTRE
P.O. BOX 500, A-1400 VIENNA, AUSTRIA
TELEPHONE: 26 310 TELEGRAPHIC ADDRESS: UNATIONS VIENNA TELEX: 135612

REFERENCE: SD 2092/1

2 May 1984

Sir,

In accordance with Economic and Social Council resolutions 1981/21 and 1983/16, copies of which are enclosed, the Centre for Social Development and Humanitarian Affairs is undertaking a global study on the social situation of migrant workers and their families.

In this study an attempt will be made to assess the present position of migrant workers and their families with special reference to their social needs and problems resulting from certain significant changes, brought about by the economic crisis, in the conditions of international migration of labour over the past ten years. Among the most important developments in this field, in our view, are the following: (a) stoppage of, or significant reduction in, the traditional movements of workers introduced by major receiving countries; (b) continuation of return of migrant workers to their countries of origin; (c) profound change in the character and scale of labour migration to the high-income oil-exporting countries in the Middle East; and (d) increase in the periods of residence of migrants in host countries.

His Excellency
The Permanent Observer of the Republic of Korea
to the United Nations
5th Floor
866 United Nations Plaza
New York, N.Y. 10017

0004

In order to be able to determine how these developments have affected the situation of migrant workers and their families, we need information from Member States. In this connection, we would like to refer to operative paragraph 2 of Economic and Social Council resolution 1981/21, in which Member States are invited "to present existing research findings and governmental reports to the Secretary-General so as to obtain an over-all view of the situation of migrant workers and their families".

We are particularly interested in obtaining information on the numbers of migrant workers and their family members in receiving countries; the characteristics of migrant workers in terms of their skills, age, and sex, and the duration of their stay in the country of employment; the position of migrant workers and their family members in the labour market; the legal and socio-economic status of migrants; conditions of their adaptation to, and integration into, the host society; ways in which the needs of the migrants' families remaining at home are met; and reintegration of returning migrants in sending countries.

We should be most grateful if you would request the appropriate governmental bodies of your country to let us have this information as soon as possible, but not later than the end of June 1984.

Accept, Sir, the assurances of my highest consideration.

Leticia R. Shahani
Assistant Secretary-General
for Social Development and
Humanitarian Affairs

0005

14th plenary meeting
26 May 1983

Resolution 1983/16. Welfare of migrant workers and their families

The Economic and Social Council,

Recalling its resolutions 1926 (LVII) of 6 May 1975, 1979/12 of 9 May 1979 and 1981/21 of 6 May 1981,

Having taken note of the report of the Secretary-General on pertinent regulations concerning the welfare of migrant workers and their families, 25/

Concerned at the fact that bilateral agreements concluded between labour-employing and labour-supplying countries, as well as national legislative and administrative provisions, do not completely exclude the possibility of practices that discriminate against migrant workers and members of their families, particularly with regard to living conditions and access to national systems of social services,

Conscious of the fact that the social situation of migrant workers and their families has deteriorated as a result of present unfavourable economic trends,

Recognizing the need for further efforts to improve the welfare of migrant workers and their families,

1. Expresses its general agreement with respect to the need for action at the national, regional and international levels to improve the welfare of migrant workers and their families;

2. Reaffirms the need for full implementation of the principle of equal treatment for migrants and their families, in accordance with ratified international agreements, particularly with regard to their living conditions and access to national systems of social services;

3. Affirms the need for concerted action by the Governments of both labour-employing and labour-supplying countries to harmonize existing bilateral and multilateral agreements on migrant workers, to extend the coverage of services and benefits provided for them and their families and to eliminate provisions that are either discriminatory or contradictory;

4. Requests the Secretary-General to take the necessary steps to ensure the effective co-operation of intergovernmental organizations, specialized agencies and organs of the United Nations system with a view to affirming the rights of migrants and their families and ensuring their full implementation, in accordance with Economic and Social Council resolution 1926 B (LVII);

5. Welcomes the progress made by the Working Group on the Drafting of an International Convention on the Protection of the Rights of All Migrant Workers and Their Families, established in accordance with General Assembly resolution 34/172 of 17 December 1979;

6. Requests the Secretary-General to use the information received from Member States pursuant to paragraph 2 of Economic and Social Council resolution 1981/21 to prepare, in co-operation with the specialized agencies and other organizations concerned, a report on the situation of migrant workers and their families in which the needs and problems emerging as a result of the changing conditions of international migration will be fully taken into account, and to submit that report to the Commission for Social Development at its twenty-ninth session.

0006

1981/21. Welfare of migrant workers and their families

The Economic and Social Council,

Recalling its resolutions 1926 (LVII) of 6 May 1975 and 1979/12 of 9 May 1979,

Conscious of the fact that in certain regions the problems of migrant workers are becoming more serious as a result of current economic trends and related social and cultural issues,

Concerned about the fact that, despite the efforts of Member States and international organizations, migrant workers and their families are, to a great extent, not always able to enjoy all the benefits of the application of the basic principle of equality of opportunity and treatment with regard to their working and living conditions,

Noting that the social provisions of bilateral agreements concluded between labour-employing and labour-supplying countries are often limited to general statements,

Taking into account the conventions and recommendations of the International Labour Organisation concerning migration for employment, migrant workers, migration in abusive conditions and the promotion of equality of opportunity for the treatment of workers,

Recognizing the need for further efforts to improve the welfare of migrant workers and their families as well as the preservation of their identity,

Recalling the World Population Plan of Action,[33] adopted by the World Population Conference, in which, *inter alia*, both labour-employing and labour-supplying countries were urged, if they had not yet done so, to conclude bilateral or multilateral agreements which would protect and assist migrant workers and safeguard the interests of the countries concerned,

1. *Reaffirms* the need for the United Nations to consider the situation of migrant workers in an interrelated manner, bearing in mind that the principle of equality of treatment extends to include the living conditions of migrant workers and their families, particularly with regard to housing, health, education and cultural and social welfare;

2. *Invites* Member States to present existing research findings and governmental reports to the Secretary-General so as to obtain an over-all view of the situation of migrant workers and their families;

3. *Welcomes* the progress made by the Working Group on the Drafting of an International Convention on the Protection of the Rights of All Migrant Workers and Their Families, established in accordance with General Assembly resolution 34/172 of 17 December 1979;

4. *Requests* the Secretary-General to include in the programme budget for 1982-1983 studies on the questions concerned with the welfare of migrant workers and their families, and to undertake those studies in a comprehensive manner to include common recommendations;

5. *Also requests* the Secretary-General to ensure, taking into account the views of the Governments and organizations concerned, that the reports requested in Economic and Social Council resolutions 1926 (LVII) and 1979/12 shall be presented to the Commission for Social Development at its twenty-eighth session;

6. *Recommends* the inclusion of the question of the welfare of migrant workers and their families in the agenda of the twenty-eighth session of the Commission for Social Development to permit an exchange of views and to promote further attention to this specific group.

II

기 안 용 지

분류기호 문서번호	국연 731-	(전화번호)	전 결 규 정 조 항 전결사항
처리기간		장 관	
시행일자	84. 5. 17.		
보존연한			

보조기관			협조
국 장	전결		
과 장			
기안책임자	김 봉 현	국제연합과	

경 유 수 신 참 조	노동부장관 직업안정국장	1984. 5. 18 외무부 019483	통제	검열 1984. 5. 18 통제관
제 목	자료요청			

유엔사무국(사회개발 및 인도문제 센터)은 유엔경제사회이사회 결의 1981/21 및 1983/16에 따라 아국에 거주하는 외국인 노동자 및 그 가족에 관한 자료를 별첨과 같이 요청하여 왔으니 84. 6. 18.한 당부로 송부하여 주시기바랍니다.

첨 부 : 사회개발 및 인도문제센터 사무차장 서한사본 및 경제사회이사회 결의. 끝.

정서

관인

발송

0008

1205-25(2-1)A(갑) 1981. 12. 18승인

정직 질서 창조

190㎜×268㎜(인쇄용지2급60g/㎡) 조 달 청(1,500,000매 인 쇄)

김석

노 동 부

고대 1456-12100 (633-8223) 1984. 5. 25.

수신 외무부장관

참조 국제기구조약국장

제목 자료 요청 회신

1. 관련 : 국연 731-019483(84.5.17)

2. 귀부에서 요청하신 아국 거주 외국인 근로자 및 그 가족에 관한 자료는 법무부 출입국관리국에서 관장하고 있음을 통보하오니 양지하시기 바랍니다. 끝.

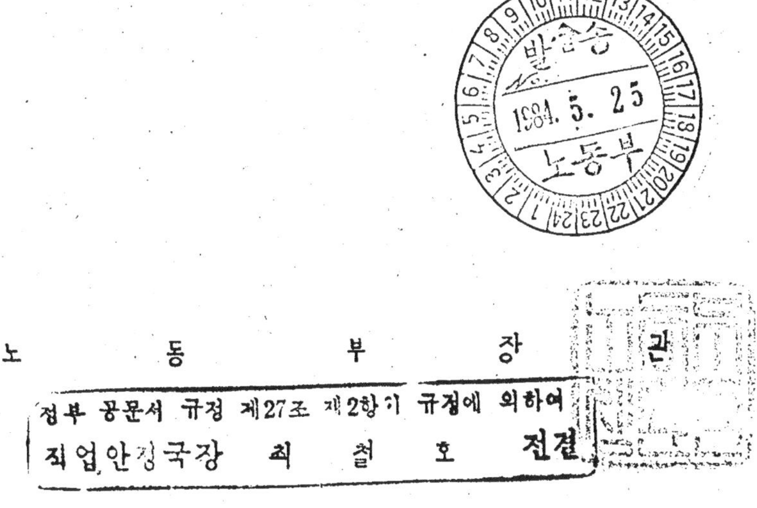

노 동 부 장 관

정부 공문서 규정 제27조 제2항에 의하여
직업안정국장 최 철 호 전결

0009

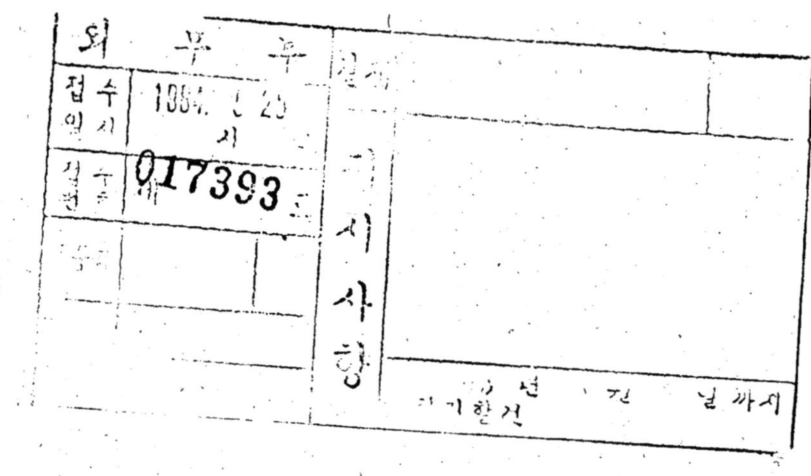

0010

기 안 용 지

분류기호 문서번호	국연 731-	(전화번호)	전결규정 조 항 전결사항
처리기간		장 관	
시행일자	84. 5. 28.		
보존연한			

보조기관			협조	
국 장	전결			
과 장				
기안책임자	김봉현	국제연합과		

경 유 수 신 참 조	법무부장관 출입국관리국장	발신 1984. 5. 29 외무부 020611	통제 검인 1984. 5. 29 통제관
제 목	자료요청		

유엔사무국(사회개발 및 인도문제센터)은 유엔경제사회이사회 결의 1981/21 및 1983/16에 따라 아국에 거주하는 외국인 노동자 및 그 가족에 관한 자료를 별첨과 같이 요청하여 왔으니 84. 6. 18. 한 당부로 송부하여 주시기바랍니다.

첨 부 : 사회개발 및 인도문제센터 사무차장 서한사본 및 경제사회이사회 결의. 끝.

정서 관인 발송

0011

1205-25(2-1) A (갑)
1981. 12. 18승인

정직 질서 창조

190mm×268mm (인쇄용지 2급 60g/m²)
조 달 청(1,500,000매 인 쇄)

주 국 련 대 표 부

주국련 731- 520 1984. 6. 1.

수신 : 장 관

참조 : 국제기구조약국장

제목 : 해외이주노동자에 관한 자료 요청

사무국은 ECOSOC 결의 1981/21 및 1983/16에 따라 해외이주노동자 (Migrant Workers)에 대한 각국 정부의 자료를 별첨과 같이 요청하여 왔읍니다.

첨 부 : 상기 서한 및 ECOSOC 결의 1981/21, 1983/16 각 1부. 끝.

주 국 련 대

0012

<table>
<tr><td>결 재</td><td colspan="3">외 무 부</td><td rowspan="3">지
시
사
항</td><td></td></tr>
<tr><td></td><td>접수
번호</td><td colspan="2">제 83799 호</td><td></td></tr>
<tr><td>주 무 과</td><td>접수
일자</td><td colspan="2">1984. 6. 94</td><td></td></tr>
<tr><td></td><td rowspan="2">위
임
근
거</td><td colspan="2" rowspan="2"></td><td colspan="2">198 년 월 일</td></tr>
<tr><td>담 당 자</td><td colspan="2">까지 처리할것</td></tr>
</table>

0013

UNITED NATIONS NATIONS UNIES

VIENNA INTERNATIONAL CENTRE

P.O. BOX 500, A-1400 VIENNA, AUSTRIA

TELEPHONE: 26 310 TELEGRAPHIC ADDRESS: UNATIONS VIENNA TELEX: 135612

REFERENCE: SD 2092/1 2 May 1984

Sir,

In accordance with Economic and Social Council resolutions 1981/21 and 1983/16, copies of which are enclosed, the Centre for Social Development and Humanitarian Affairs is undertaking a global study on the social situation of migrant workers and their families.

In this study an attempt will be made to assess the present position of migrant workers and their families with special reference to their social needs and problems resulting from certain significant changes, brought about by the economic crisis, in the conditions of international migration of labour over the past ten years. Among the most important developments in this field, in our view, are the following: (a) stoppage of, or significant reduction in, the traditional movements of workers introduced by major receiving countries; (b) continuation of return of migrant workers to their countries of origin; (c) profound change in the character and scale of labour migration to the high-income oil-exporting countries in the Middle East; and (d) increase in the periods of residence of migrants in host countries.

His Excellency
The Permanent Observer of the Republic of Korea
to the United Nations
5th Floor
866 United Nations Plaza
New York, N.Y. 10017

0014

In order to be able to determine how these developments have affected the situation of migrant workers and their families, we need information from Member States. In this connection, we would like to refer to operative paragraph 2 of Economic and Social Council resolution 1981/21, in which Member States are invited "to present existing research findings and governmental reports to the Secretary-General so as to obtain an over-all view of the situation of migrant workers and their families".

We are particularly interested in obtaining information on the numbers of migrant workers and their family members in receiving countries; the characteristics of migrant workers in terms of their skills, age, and sex, and the duration of their stay in the country of employment; the position of migrant workers and their family members in the labour market; the legal and socio-economic status of migrants; conditions of their adaptation to, and integration into, the host society; ways in which the needs of the migrants' families remaining at home are met; and reintegration of returning migrants in sending countries.

We should be most grateful if you would request the appropriate governmental bodies of your country to let us have this information as soon as possible, but not later than the end of June 1984.

Accept, Sir, the assurances of my highest consideration.

L. Shahani

Leticia R. Shahani
Assistant Secretary-General
for Social Development and
Humanitarian Affairs

0015

14th plenary me[illegible]
6 May [illegible]

1981/21. Welfare of migrant workers and their families

The Economic and Social Council,

Recalling its resolutions 1926 (LVII) of 6 May 1975 and 1979/12 of 9 May 1979,

Conscious of the fact that in certain regions the problems of migrant workers are becoming more serious as a result of current economic trends and related social and cultural issues,

Concerned about the fact that, despite the efforts of Member States and international organizations, migrant workers and their families are, to a great extent, not always able to enjoy all the benefits of the application of the basic principle of equality of opportunity and treatment with regard to their working and living conditions,

Noting that the social provisions of bilateral agreements concluded between labour-employing and labour-supplying countries are often limited to general statements,

Taking into account the conventions and recommendations of the International Labour Organisation concerning migration for employment, migrant workers, migration in abusive conditions and the promotion of equality of opportunity for the treatment of workers,

Recognizing the need for further efforts to improve the welfare of migrant workers and their families as well as the preservation of their identity,

Recalling the World Population Plan of Action,[33] adopted by the World Population Conference, in which, *inter alia*, both labour-employing and labour-supplying countries were urged, if they had not yet done so, to conclude bilateral or multilateral agreements which would protect and assist migrant workers and safeguard the interests of the countries concerned,

1. *Reaffirms* the need for the United Nations to consider the situation of migrant workers in an interrelated manner, bearing in mind that the principle of equality of treatment extends to include the living conditions of migrant workers and their families, particularly with regard to housing, health, education and cultural and social welfare;

2. *Invites* Member States to present existing research findings and governmental reports to the Secretary-General so as to obtain an over-all view of the situation of migrant workers and their families;

3. *Welcomes* the progress made by the Working Group on the Drafting of an International Convention on the Protection of the Rights of All Migrant Workers and Their Families, established in accordance with General Assembly resolution 34/172 of 17 December 1979;

4. *Requests* the Secretary-General to include in the programme budget for 1982-1983 studies on the questions concerned with the welfare of migrant workers and their families, and to undertake those studies in a comprehensive manner to include common recommendations;

5. *Also requests* the Secretary-General to ensure, taking into account the views of the Governments and organizations concerned, that the reports requested in Economic and Social Council resolutions 1926 (LVII) and 1979/12 shall be presented to the Commission for Social Development at its twenty-eighth session;

6. *Recommends* the inclusion of the question of the welfare of migrant workers and their families in the agenda of the twenty-eighth session of the Commission for Social Development to permit an exchange of views and to promote further attention to this specific group.

0016

14th plenary meeting
26 May 1983

Resolution 1983/16. Welfare of migrant workers and their families

The Economic and Social Council,

Recalling its resolutions 1926 (LVII) of 6 May 1975, 1979/12 of 9 May 1979 and 1981/21 of 6 May 1981,

Having taken note of the report of the Secretary-General on pertinent regulations concerning the welfare of migrant workers and their families, 25/

Concerned at the fact that bilateral agreements concluded between labour-employing and labour-supplying countries, as well as national legislative and administrative provisions, do not completely exclude the possibility of practices that discriminate against migrant workers and members of their families, particularly with regard to living conditions and access to national systems of social services,

Conscious of the fact that the social situation of migrant workers and their families has deteriorated as a result of present unfavourable economic trends,

Recognizing the need for further efforts to improve the welfare of migrant workers and their families,

1. Expresses its general agreement with respect to the need for action at the national, regional and international levels to improve the welfare of migrant workers and their families;

2. Reaffirms the need for full implementation of the principle of equal treatment for migrants and their families, in accordance with ratified international agreements, particularly with regard to their living conditions and access to national systems of social services;

3. Affirms the need for concerted action by the Governments of both labour-employing and labour-supplying countries to harmonize existing bilateral and multilateral agreements on migrant workers, to extend the coverage of services and benefits provided for them and their families and to eliminate provisions that are either discriminatory or contradictory;

4. Requests the Secretary-General to take the necessary steps to ensure the effective co-operation of intergovernmental organizations, specialized agencies and organs of the United Nations system with a view to affirming the rights of migrants and their families and ensuring their full implementation, in accordance with Economic and Social Council resolution 1926 B (LVII);

5. Welcomes the progress made by the Working Group on the Drafting of an International Convention on the Protection of the Rights of All Migrant Workers and Their Families, established in accordance with General Assembly resolution 34/172 of 17 December 1979;

6. Requests the Secretary-General to use the information received from Member States pursuant to paragraph 2 of Economic and Social Council resolution 1981/21 to prepare, in co-operation with the specialized agencies and other organizations concerned, a report on the situation of migrant workers and their families in which the needs and problems emerging as a result of the changing conditions of international migration will be fully taken into account, and to submit that report to the Commission for Social Development at its twenty-ninth session.

0017

기 안 용 지

분류기호 문서번호	국연 731-	(전화번호)	전결규정 조 항 전결사항
처리기간	16777	장 관	
시행일자	1984. 6. 19.		
보존연한			
보조기관	과 장 전결		협조
기안책임자	김주석	국제연합과	
경유 수신 참조	주유엔, 주오지리 대사	발송 1984. 6. 20 외무부	통제 1984. 6. 19 통제관
제 목	해외이주 노동자에 관한 사료		

대 : 주국련 731-520 (84.6.1)

오지리(정) 743-529 (84.5.7)

대호 관계부처에 해당 자료가 없다고 하니 참고하시기 바랍니다. 끝.

정서 / 관인 / 발송

0018

1205-25(2-1) A(갑)
1981. 12. 18승인

정직 질서 창조

190mm×268mm(인쇄용지 2급 60g/㎡)
조 달 청(1,500,000매 인쇄)

주 오 스 트 리 아 대 사 관

3
7

오지리(정)743- 183 1984. 9 . 19 .

수신 : 외무부 장관

참조 : 국제기구조약국장

제목 : 유엔 사회개발 인도 문제 센터(CSDHA)

당지 유엔 사회개발 인도 문제 센터(CSDHA)에서 배포한 제39차 유엔총회 관련 동 센터 소관 업무 등에 관한 자료를 별첨 송부하오니 참고 바랍니다.

첨부 : 상기 자료 1부.

주 오 스 트 리 아 대 사

0019

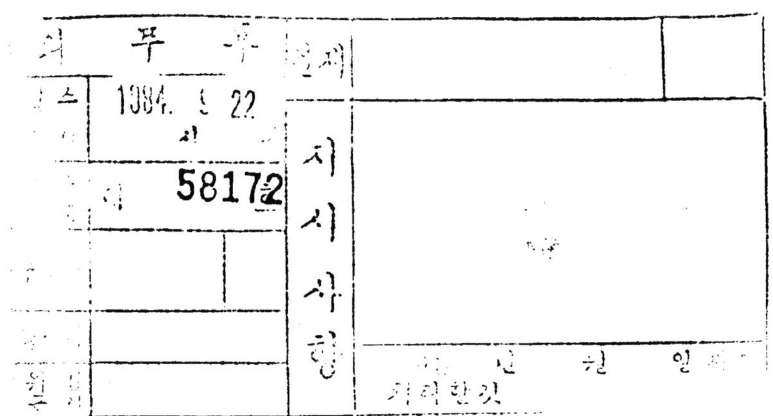
외 무 부
1984. 9. 22
58172
지시사항

0020

CENTRE FOR SOCIAL DEVELOPMENT AND HUMANITARIAN AFFAIRS

Meeting of Permanent Representatives

Thursday, 27 September 1984 from 3.30 - 5.00 p.m. in the UNIDO Board Room 4th floor

0021

Centre for Social Development and Humanitarian Affairs

Documents submitted by CSDHA for the 39th session of the General Assembly

Item No.	Title of Document
80 (k)	Report of the Secretary-General on the World Survey on the Role of Women in Development (Res. 36/74)
85	International Youth Year: Participation, Development, Peace, Report of the Secretary-General (Res. 38/22)
89 *	Policies and programmes relating to Youth: Report of the Secretary-General (Res. 38/26)
90	Question of Aging: Report of the Secretary-General (Res. 38/27)
91	Implementation of the World Programme of Action concerning Disabled Persons: Report of the Secretary-General (Res. 37/53 and 38/28)
93 (a)	Note by the Secretary-General on national experience in improving the situation of women in rural areas
93 (b) **	Report of the Commission on the Status of Women Acting as the Preparatory Body for the World Conference to Review and Appraise the Achievements of the UN Decade for Women: Equality, Development and Peace on its second session.

---

* This item is combined with item 85.

** Submitted as an annex to the Report of the Economic and Social Council, 1984

0022

Item No.	Title of Document
93 (c)	Report of the Secretary-General on the continuation of the activities of the Voluntary Fund for the United Nations Decade for Women beyond the Decade
93 (c)	Report of the Secretary-General on the substantive and financial implications and proposals for the timing and modalities for a relocation of the Voluntary Fund for the UN Decade for Women within the Centre for Social Development and Humanitarian Affairs
93 (c)	Report of the Secretary-General on the management of the Voluntary Fund for the UN Decade for Women and on the progress of its activities
94 (a)	Reports of the Committee on the Elimination of Discrimination against Women on its second and third sessions
94 (b)	Status of the Convention on the Elimination of All Forms of Discrimination Against Women: Report of the Secretary-General

0023

ANNOTATED PRELIMINARY LIST OF ITEMS, RELATED TO CSDHA, TO BE INCLUDED IN THE PROVISIONAL AGENDA OF THE THIRTY-NINTH SESSION OF THE GENERAL ASSEMBLY

0024

80 (k) Effective mobilization and integration of women in development

At its thirtieth session, in 1975, the General Assembly requested the Secretary-General to prepare a preliminary report on the extent to which women participated in agriculture, industry, trade and science and technology, with a view to making recommendations on ways and means of increasing and upgrading the participation of women therein (resolution 3505 (XXX)).

At its thirty-first session, the General Assembly urged Member States to implement the recommendations in resolution 3505 (XXX); and requested the Secretary-General to prepare a comprehensive report for submission to the Assembly at its thirty-third session (resolution 31/175).

At its thirty-third session, the General Assembly requested organizations of the United Nations system to prepare development-oriented studies relevant to their programmes of work, focusing on the impact of policies aimed at the effective mobilization and integration of women in the development process, on the overall development of their countries, with special emphasis on the developing countries, and on ways of promoting such policies; and requested the Secretary-General on the basis of these studies to submit a comprehensive report to the Assembly at its thirty-fourth session (resolution 33/200).

At its thirty-fourth session, the General Assembly noted with regret that it had not been possible for the Secretary-General to submit the comprehensive report requested in resolution 33/200; urged the United Nations agencies that had not already done so to submit to the Secretary-General without delay the information called for in resolution 33/200; and requested the Secretary-General to submit the comprehensive report to the Assembly at its thirty-fifth session (resolution 34/204).

At its thirty-fifth session, the General Assembly noted the report of the Secretary-General (A/35/82) and requested the Secretary-General to submit a report to the Assembly at its thirty-sixth session on the implementation of paragraph 1 of resolution 34/204 on the role of the relevant United Nations agencies and organizations in assisting Governments in the implementation of the provisions on the integration of women in rural development; and further requested the Secretary-General to prepare a comprehensive and detailed outline for an interdisciplinary and multisectoral world survey on the role of women in overall development, taking into account the relevant recommendations of the World Conference of the United Nations Decade for Women as well as the results of the relevant United Nations conferences on development issues, and to report thereon to the Assembly at its thirty-sixth session (resolution 35/78).

At its thirty-sixth session, the General Assembly, taking note of the Secretary-General's report on a comprehensive outline of a world survey on the role of women in development (A/36/590), made a number of recommendations on the focus of the survey; and requested the Secretary-General to submit a progress report to the Assembly at its thirty-seventh session and to submit the survey in its final form to the Assembly at its thirty-ninth session (resolution 36/74). At the same session, the Assembly took note of the other reports submitted under the item (decision 36/422).

/...

0025

At its thirty-seventh session, the General Assembly took note of the report of the Secretary-General on the progress made in the world survey on the role of women in development (decision 37/449).

At its thirty-eighth session, 124/ the General Assembly took note of the report of the Second Committee (A/38/702/Add.9) (decision 38/443).

At its thirty-ninth session, the General Assembly will have before it the report of the Secretary-General called for under resolution 36/74.

0026

85. <u>International Youth Year: Participation, Development, Peace: report of the Secretary-General</u>

At its thirty-second session, in 1977, the General Assembly requested the Secretary-General to prepare a report containing the views of Member States on the proclamation of an international youth year (resolution 32/134).

At its thirty-third session, the General Assembly decided to proclaim an International Youth Year and to designate the most suitable period for its celebration, as well as the ways and means for its observance, at its thirty-fourth session (resolution 33/7).

At its thirty-fourth session, the General Assembly decided to designate 1985 as International Youth Year: Participation, Development, Peace; and decided to establish an Advisory Committee for the International Youth Year, to be composed of 23 Member States appointed by the Chairman of the Third Committee on the basis of equitable geographical distribution (resolution 34/151).

In May 1980, the Chairman of the Third Committee informed the Secretary-General (A/34/855, para. 2) that disagreement among the regional groups on the distribution of seats had prevented him from appointing the 23 members of the Advisory Committee.

At its thirty-fifth session, the General Assembly decided that the Advisory Committee should be composed of representatives of the 24 Member States listed in the note by the Secretary-General of 17 June 1980 (A/34/855), on the clear understanding that that should not be regarded as setting a precedent in the establishment of similar bodies in the future (decision 35/318). As a result, the Advisory Committee is composed of the following 24 Member States:

Algeria, Chile, Costa Rica, Democratic Yemen, Germany, Federal Republic of, Guatemala, Guinea, Indonesia, Ireland, Jamaica, Japan, Lebanon, Morocco, Mozambique, Netherlands, Nigeria, Norway, Poland, Romania, Rwanda, Sri Lanka, Union of Soviet Socialist Republics, United States of America and Venezuela.

At the same session, the General Assembly requested the Secretary-General to convene three sessions of the Advisory Committee in the period 1981-1985 so that it might formulate, for consideration by the Assembly, a specific programme of measures and activities to be undertaken prior to and during the Year on the basis of the Secretary-General's draft programme (resolution 35/126).

At its thirty-sixth session, the General Assembly endorsed the specific Programme of Measures and Activities to be undertaken prior to and during the Year, as adopted by the Advisory Committee and contained in its report (A/36/215, annex);

/...

0027

requested the Secretary-General to submit to the Assembly at its thirty-seventh session, through the Advisory Committee, a progress report on the implementation of the specific Programme of Measures and Activities (resolution 36/28); and requested the Advisory Committee to ensure that, in the context of the preparations for the Year, systematic and continuous attention would be given to the efforts aimed at the promotion of human rights and their enjoyment by youth, particularly the right to education and vocational training and to work, with a view to resolving the problem of youth unemployment (resolution 36/29).

At its thirty-seventh session, the General Assembly, inter alia, endorsed the recommendations made by the Advisory Committee for the further implementation of the Specific Programme of Measures and Activities to be undertaken prior to and during the Year (A/37/348, annex); requested the Secretary-General to continue to take the necessary measures to ensure the proper co-ordination of the implementation and follow-up to the Specific Programme of Measures and Activities, including the provision of information, and to submit a report to the Assembly at its thirty-eighth session (resolution 37/48); and requested the Advisory Committee to give full attention to resolution 36/29 and to all relevant international human rights instruments in the preparation and in the course of the Year, in particular in elaborating its recommendations concerning the Year (resolution 37/49).

At its thirty-eighth session, 138/ the General Assembly, inter alia, commended the five regional meetings devoted to the International Youth Year held during 1983 and requested the Secretary-General to bring the regional plans of action and the recommendations adopted by the regional meetings to the notice of all States with a view to their implementation; requested the Secretary-General to use all means at his disposal, within the existing resources, to ensure the implementation and follow-up of the Specific Programme of Measures and Activities, including the provision of information; requested the Advisory Committee, at its third session, to make every effort to implement tasks entrusted to it by the decisions of the Assembly and by recommendations of the five regional meetings and to submit the report on its third session to the Assembly at its thirty-ninth session with practical proposals on specific ways and means for the observance, in 1985, of the Year in an appropriate organizational framework within the United Nations; and appealed to all States, to international governmental and non-governmental organizations and to the public to make generous voluntary contributions to supplement funds provided under the regular budget of the United Nations for the costs of the Specific Programme of Measures and Activities (resolution 38/22).

138/ References for the thirty-eighth session (agenda item 84):

(a) Report of the Secretary-General: A/38/460 and Add.1;

(b) Report of the Third Committee: A/38/571;

(c) Resolutions 38/22 and 38/23;

(d) Meetings of the Third Committee: A/C.3/38/SR.18-20, 22-29 and 31-33;

(e) Plenary meeting: A/38/PV.66.

/...

0028

At the same session, the General Assembly, *inter alia*, called upon all States, all governmental and non-governmental organizations and the interested bodies of the United Nations and specialized agencies to pay continuous attention to the implementation of resolutions 36/29 and 37/49 relating to efforts and measures aimed at the promotion of human rights and their enjoyment by youth, particularly the right to education and vocational training and to work, with a view to resolving the problem of youth unemployment; requested the Advisory Committee for the International Youth Year to give full attention to resolutions 36/29 and 37/49 and to all relevant international human rights instruments in the preparation for and in the course of the Year; and invited national co-ordinating committees or other organs of co-ordination for the Year to give appropriate priority in activities to be undertaken prior to and during the Year to the implementation and the enjoyment by youth of human rights, particularly the right to education and to work (resolution 38/23).

At the thirty-ninth session, the General Assembly will have before it the report of the Secretary-General called for under resolution 38/22.

89. Policies and programmes relating to youth: report of the Secretary-General

At its thirty-fifth session, in 1980, the General Assembly requested the Secretary-General, in co-operation with the relevant bodies of the United Nations system, including the regional commissions, to report to the Assembly at its thirty-sixth session on the progress achieved in the implementation of the adopted guidelines for the improvement of the channels of communication between the United Nations and youth and youth organizations and to promote that implementation at the international, regional and national levels; and further requested the Secretary-General, taking into account the views expressed by Governments either in their replies or in their statements before the Assembly, to submit to the Assembly at its thirty-sixth session, for adoption, proposals for additional guidelines, consistent with those already adopted by the Assembly in its resolution 32/135, and on the basis of the draft additional guidelines contained in the annex to resolution 34/163, as well as the suggestions of the Secretary-General in his reports to the Assembly at its thirty-third, thirty-fourth and thirty-fifth sessions (A/33/261, A/34/199, A/35/503) (resolution 35/139).

At its thirty-sixth session, the General Assembly adopted the additional guidelines for the improvement of the channels of communication between the United Nations and youth and youth organizations set forth in the annex to the resolution; and requested the Advisory Committee for the International Youth Year (see item 85) to promote the implementation of the additional guidelines, together with the guidelines adopted in resolution 32/135, during the preparation for and celebration of the Year (resolution 36/17).

At its thirty-seventh session, the General Assembly, inter alia, requested Member States, specialized agencies and other intergovernmental organizations to promote further implementation of the guidelines adopted in Assembly resolution 32/135 and the additional guidelines adopted in its resolution 36/17; and invited Member States, specialized agencies, regional commissions, intergovernmental organizations and non-governmental youth organizations to communicate and further promote the guidelines and additional guidelines for the improvement of channels of communication between the United Nations and youth and youth organizations and to offer additional suggestions for their further development (resolution 37/50).

At its thirty-eighth session, 142/ the General Assembly requested the

---

142/ References for the thirty-eighth session (agenda item 88):

(a) Report of the Secretary-General: A/38/339;

(b) Report of the Third Committee: A/38/573;

(c) Resolution 38/26;

(d) Meetings of the Third Committee: A/C.3/38/SR.18-20, 22-29 and 31-33;

(e) Plenary meeting: A/38/PV.66.

/...

0030

Secretary-General to continue to give full co-operation and support to inter-agency co-operation and co-ordination in promotional and information activities within the context of the International Youth Year; called upon Member States, specialized agencies and other intergovernmental organizations, in co-operation with youth and with youth organizations in consultative status with the Council and other youth organizations concerned, to continue to promote actively the full and effective implementation of the guidelines and additional guidelines adopted in Assembly resolutions 32/135 and 36/17; requested the Advisory Committee for the International Youth Year at its third session to monitor and evaluate the measures taken with respect to the implementation of the guidelines and to make recommendations for the full and effective implementation and the further elaboration of the guidelines as an integral part of the preparation for, observance of and follow-up to the Year; and decided to review at its thirty-ninth session the question of the channels of communication between the United Nations and youth and youth organizations, on the basis of the report of the Advisory Committee (resolution 38/26).

At the thirty-ninth session, the General Assembly will have before it the report of the Secretary-General called for under resolution 38/26.

90. Question of aging: report of the Secretary-General

The item entitled "Question of the elderly and the aged" was included in the agenda of the twenty-fourth session of the General Assembly, in 1969, at the request of Malta (A/7644) and was considered at its twenty-sixth, twenty-eighth and thirty-second sessions (resolutions 2842 (XXVI), 3137 (XXVIII), 32/131 and 32/132).

At its thirty-third session, the General Assembly decided to organize, in consultation with Member States, specialized agencies and the organizations concerned, a World Assembly on the Elderly in 1982 (resolution 33/52).

At its thirty-fourth session, the General Assembly requested the Secretary-General to submit a progress report to the Economic and Social Council in 1981, through the Commission for Social Development, and to report to the Assembly at its thirty-sixth session (resolution 34/153).

At its thirty-fifth session, the General Assembly adopted the recommendations of the Economic and Social Council contained in its resolution 1980/26; decided to change the name of the World Assembly on the Elderly to the World Assembly on Aging in view of the interrelatedness of the issues of aging individuals and the aging of populations as defined by the Secretary-General's programme; requested the Secretary-General to establish a voluntary fund for the World Assembly; and requested the Secretary-General to prepare a progress report on the preparations for the World Assembly, including the report of the Advisory Committee for the World Assembly on Aging, to be considered under this item (resolution 35/129).

At its thirty-sixth session, the General Assembly invited Member States to consider designating in their respective countries a "Day for the Aging"; requested the Secretary-General to use the United Nations Trust Fund for the World Assembly on Aging to encourage further interest in the field of aging among developing

/...

0031

countries, particularly the least developed among them within the context of the World Assembly; and requested the Secretary-General to strengthen, within the limits of existing resources and voluntary contributions, activities in the field of aging in co-operation with the organizations concerned (resolution 36/20).

At its thirty-seventh session, the General Assembly, inter alia, took note of the report of the World Assembly on Aging, held at Vienna from 26 July to 6 August 1982 (A/CONF.113/31); endorsed the Vienna International Plan of Action on Aging contained in the report and adopted by consensus at the World Assembly; called upon Governments to make continuous efforts to implement the principles and recommendations contained in the Plan of Action in accordance with their national structures, needs and objectives; requested the Secretary-General to strengthen the international network of existing information, research and training centres in the field of aging in order to encourage and facilitate the exchange of knowledge, skills and experience, as well as technical co-operation among countries within the various regions; requested the Secretary-General to continue to use the United Nations Trust Fund to meet the rapidly increasing needs of the aging in the developing countries, in particular in the least developed countries; appealed to Member States to make voluntary contributions to the Trust Fund; requested the Economic and Social Council, through the Commission for Social Development, to review the implementation of the Plan of Action every four years, beginning in 1985, and to transmit its findings to the Assembly; and requested the Secretary-General to report to the Assembly at its thirty-eighth session on the progress achieved in implementing and following up the Plan of Action and to include in his report an account of project activities financed by the Trust Fund (resolution 37/51).

At its thirty-eighth session, 143/ the General Assembly, inter alia, called upon Governments to continue to make efforts to implement the principles and recommendations contained in the Vienna International Plan of Action on Aging in accordance with the economic, social and cultural circumstances of each country; requested the Secretary-General to continue to promote the Trust Fund for Aging, to continue his information exchange activities, to ensure that the question of aging was considered at the International Conference on Population, to promote joint activities in the field of aging and youth, especially during International Youth Year, and to bring the question of older women to the attention of the preparatory

---

143/ References for the thirty-eighth session (agenda item 89):

(a) Report of the Secretary-General: A/38/470;

(b) Report of the Third Committee: A/38/574;

(c) Resolution 38/27;

(d) Meetings of the Third Committee: A/C.3/38/SR.18-20, 22-29 and 31-33;

(e) Plenary meeting: A/38/PV.66.

/...

0032

body for the World Conference to Review and Appraise the Achievements of the United Nations Decade for Women in 1985 for its consideration; urged the United Nations Fund for Population Activities to continue its assistance in the field of aging; invited the regional commissions to review the objectives of the Plan of Action and contribute to their realization and to organize and conduct the regional periodic review and appraisal of the Plan in co-ordination with that at the international level; invited the specialized agencies and other intergovernmental and non-governmental organizations concerned to continue to be actively involved in the implementation of the Plan of Action; and requested the Secretary-General to report to the Assembly at its thirty-ninth session (resolution 38/27).

At the thirty-ninth session, the General Assembly will have before it the report of the Secretary-General called for under resolution 38/27.

91. <u>Implementation of the World Programme of Action concerning Disabled Persons: report of the Secretary-General</u>

At its thirty-first session, in 1976, the General Assembly proclaimed 1981 International Year for Disabled Persons with the theme "Full participation" (resolution 31/123).

At its thirty-second session, the General Assembly decided to establish the Advisory Committee for the International Year for Disabled Persons; and appealed to Member States to make in due time generous voluntary contributions for the Year (resolution 32/133).

At its thirty-third session, the General Assembly decided to increase the membership of the Advisory Committee from 15 to 23 Member States (resolution 33/170).

At its thirty-fourth session, the General Assembly approved the recommendations of the Advisory Committee (A/34/158 and Corr.1) and adopted them as a Plan of Action for the Year; and decided to expand the theme of the Year to "Full participation and equality"; and appealed for further voluntary contributions for the Year (resolution 34/154). At the same session, the Assembly agreed to a change in the designation of the Year, which was henceforth to be known in English as the International Year of Disabled Persons.

At its thirty-fifth session, the General Assembly continued its consideration of the item (resolution 35/133).

At its thirty-sixth session, the General Assembly, requested the Secretary-General to convene in 1982 a meeting of the Advisory Committee to finalize the draft World Programme of Action concerning Disabled Persons; and requested the Advisory Committee to consider at its fourth session the advisability of proclaiming the period 1983-1992 as the United Nations Decade of Disabled Persons and to submit its views to the Assembly at its thirty-seventh session; (resolution 36/77).

/...

0033

At its thirty-seventh session, the General Assembly, inter alia, adopted the World Programme of Action concerning Disabled Persons contained in recommendation 1 (IV) of the report of the Advisory Committee; called upon all Member States, all non-governmental organizations concerned and organizations of disabled persons and, through a reallocation of existing resources, called also upon all organs, organizations and agencies of the United Nations system to ensure early implementation of the World Programme of Action; and decided to evaluate at its forty-second session, with the help of the Secretary-General, the implementation of the World Programme of Action (resolution 37/52); requested the Secretary-General, in consultation with Governments, to examine the need and possibility of continuing the Trust Fund for the International Year of Disabled Persons for the purpose of assisting Governments, at their request, in the implementation of the World Programme of Action and to submit a report thereon to the Assembly at its thirty-eighth session; proclaimed the period 1983-1992 United Nations Decade of Disabled Persons as a long-term plan of action; and requested the Secretary-General to report to the Assembly at its thirty-ninth session on the implementation of the World Programme of Action (resolution 37/53).

At its thirty-eighth session, 144/ the General Assembly, inter alia, recognized the desirability of the continuation of the Trust Fund for the International Year of Disabled Persons throughout the United Nations Decade of Disabled Persons; decided that the Trust Fuynd should continue its activities pending a report by the Secretary-General to the Assembly at its thirty-ninth session; requested the Secretary-General to take the necessary steps to strengthen the Trust Fund; appealed to Governments and private sources for continuing generous voluntary contributions to the Trust Fund; called upon all Member States, all non-governmental organizations concerned and organizations of disabled persons and all organs, organizations and bodies of the United Nations system to continue to ensure the early implementation of the World Programme of Action; and requested the Secretary-General to include in his reports to the Assembly on the implementation of the World Programme of Action a section on the activities of the Trust Fund (resolution 38/28).

At the thirty-ninth session, the General Assembly will have before it the report of the Secretary-General called for under resolutions 37/53 and 38/28.

144/ References for the thirty-eighth session (agenda item 90):

(a) Report of the Secretary-General: A/38/506;

(b) Report of the Third Committee: A/38/575;

(c) Resolution 38/28;

(d) Meetings of the Third Committee: A/C.3/38/SR.18-20, 22-29 and 31-33;

(e) Plenary meeting: A/38/PV.66.

/...

0034

93. United Nations Decade for Women: Equality, Development and Peace

(a) Implementation of the Programme of Action for the Second Half of the United Nations Decade for Women: report of the Secretary-General

At its twenty-seventh session, in 1972, the General Assembly proclaimed 1975 International Women's Year (resolution 3010 (XXVII)).

At its fifty-sixth session, in 1974, the Economic and Social Council requested the Secretary-General to convene an international conference during the Year and recommended that the proposals and recommendations of the conference should be examined by the Assembly at its thirtieth session (resolution 1851 (LVI)).

At its thirtieth session, the General Assembly took note of the report of the World Conference of the International Women's Year, held at Mexico City from 19 June to 2 July 1975 (E/CONF.66/34); endorsed the proposals of the Declaration of Mexico on the Equality of Women and Their Contribution to Development and Peace, the World Plan of Action, the regional plans of action, and related resolutions; proclaimed the period from 1976 to 1985 United Nations Decade for Women: Equality, Development and Peace; and decided to convene a world conference in 1980, at the mid-term of the Decade (resolution 3520 (XXX)).

At its thirty-second session, the General Assembly requested the Commission on the Status of Women to consider, as a contribution to the preparation of the World Conference of the United Nations Decade for Women, the elaboration of a draft declaration on the participation of women in the struggle for the strengthening of international peace and security and against colonialism, racism, racial discrimination, foreign aggression and occupation and all forms of foreign domination and to report to the Economic and Social Council at its sixty-fourth session (resolution 32/142).

At its thirty-third and thirty-fourth sessions, the General Assembly decided on a number of arrangements for the Conference (resolutions 33/185, 33/189 to 33/191 and 34/160 to 34/162).

At its thirty-fifth session, the General Assembly took note with satisfaction of the report of the Conference, held at Copenhagen from 14 to 30 July 1980 (A/CONF.94/35); endorsed the Programme of Action for the Second Half of the United Nations Decade for Women, as adopted at the Conference; urged Governments, organizations of the United Nations system and intergovernmental and non-governmental organizations to take appropriate measures to implement the Programme of Action and other relevant resolutions and decisions at the national, regional and international levels; and requested the Secretary-General to consider appropriate measures to enable the Commission on the Status of Women to discharge the functions assigned to it for the implementation of the World Plan of Action for the Implementation of the Objectives of the International Women's Year and the Programme of Action for the Second Half of the United Nations Decade for Women and requested him to take immediate action to strengthen the Centre for Social Development and Humanitarian Affairs (resolution 35/136). At the same session, the Assembly requested the Secretary-General to seek the views of the Governments of

/...

0035

Member States on a draft declaration entitled "Draft Declaration on the Participation of Women in the Struggle for the Strengthening of International Peace and Security and against Colonialism, Apartheid, All Forms of Racism and Racial Discrimination, Foreign Aggression, Occupation and All Forms of Foreign Domination" and to report to the Assembly at its thirty-sixth session (decision 35/249).

(181) At its thirty-sixth session, the General Assembly called upon Governments to continue taking the measures necessary for achieving substantial progress in the implementation of the relevant recommendations of the Programme of Action with a view to ensuring equal participation by women as agents and beneficiaries in all sectors and at all levels of the development process; and requested the Economic and Social Council, at its first regular session of 1982, to consider the implementation of the Programme of Action, giving high priority in this regard to the report of the Commission on the Status of Women (resolution 36/126). At the same session, the Assembly adopted resolutions on the consideration within the United Nations of questions concerning the role of women in development (resolution 36/127) and equal rights to work (resolution 36/130) and decided to request the Secretary-General to seek further comments from Member States on the draft Declaration on the Participation of Women in the Struggle for the Strengthening of International Peace and for the Solution of Other Vital National and International Problems and to submit a report based on their comments as well as on the proposals submitted so far, with a view to ensuring the early adoption of the draft Declaration during the thirty-seventh session (decision 36/428).

At its thirty-seventh session, the General Assembly, inter alia, called upon the Secretary-General to encourage specialized agencies and regional commissions which had not yet done so to develop a comprehensive policy regarding the concerns of women, both as participants and as beneficiaries, in technical co-operation and development activities and to develop a strategy to ensure that women were an integral part of these activities; and requested the Secretary-General to submit a progress report to the Assembly at its thirty-eighth session on the implementation of the Programme of Action for the Second Half of the United Nations Decade for Women (A/37/458 and Add.1); noted with satisfaction the contribution made by the Voluntary Fund for the United Nations Decade for Women to the implementation of the Programme of Action; noted with satisfaction the commencement of the work of the International Research and Training Institute for the Advancement of Women; and requested the Secretary-General to report to the Assembly at its thirty-eighth session (resolution 37/58).

Also at the same session, the General Assembly requested the Secretary-General to prepare, within the framework of the integrated reporting system on the status of women, a comprehensive report containing the observations and comments received from Governments on national experience in improving the situation of women in rural areas; and further requested the Secretary-General to submit the report to the Assembly at its thirty-ninth session, through the Commission on the Status of Women and the Economic and Social Council (resolution 37/59); called upon all Member States, by the end of the Decade in 1985, to make special efforts to nominate and appoint women, on an equal basis with men and taking due account of the same professional criteria, to decision-making positions in those national and international bodies in which they were not equitably represented; and called upon

/...

0036

the Secretary-General and the executive heads of the specialized agencies and other organizations of the United Nations system to make, by the end of the Decade, increased efforts to select and appoint women, in accordance with Article 101 of the Charter of the United Nations, to decision-making positions in the Secretariat and in the organs and agencies of the United Nations system (resolution 37/61); and solemnly proclaimed the Declaration on the Participation of Women in Promoting International Peace and Co-operation (resolution 37/63).

At its thirty-eighth session, 146/ the General Assembly called upon the Secretary-General to disseminate widely the Declaration on the Participation of Women in Promoting International Peace and Co-operation in the six official languages of the United Nations; invited all Governments to take the necessary measures to ensure wide publicity for the Declaration; requested the Secretary-General to bring the Declaration to the attention of the appropriate specialized agencies, including the United Nations Educational, Scientific and Cultural Organization, the International Labour Organisation, the World Health Organization and other appropriate bodies within the United Nations system, for the consideration of measures to implement the Declaration; requested the Commission on the Status of Women to consider what measures might be necessary in order to implement the Declaration and to report, through the Economic and Social Council, to the Assembly at its thirty-ninth session; and decided to consider at its thirty-ninth session the report of the Commission on the Status of Women under the item entitled "United Nations Decade for Women: Equality, Development and Peace" (resolution 38/105).

146/ References for the thirty-eighth session (agenda item 91):

(a) Reports of the Secretary-General:

(i) Implementation of the Programme of Action for the Second Half of the United Nations Decade for Women: A/38/146;

(ii) Voluntary Fund for the United Nations Decade for Women: A/38/530;

(b) Note by the Secretary-General: A/C.3/38/2 and Add.1;

(c) Report of the Third Committee: A/38/681;

(d) Report of the Fifth Committee: A/38/736;

(e) Resolutions 38/105 to 38/108;

(f) Meetings of the Third Committee: A/C.3/38/SR.30-38, 53 and 55-59;

(g) Meeting of the Fifth Committee: A/C.5/38/SR.65;

(h) Plenary meeting: A/38/PV.100.

/...

0037

At the same session, the General Assembly urged Member States to take all appropriate humane measures, including legislation, to combat prostitution, exploitation of the prostitution of others and all forms of traffic in persons; appealed to Member States to provide special protection to victims of prostitution through measures including education, social guarantees and employment opportunities for those victims with a view to their rehabilitation; requested the Economic and Social Council, the Commission on Human Rights, the Commission on the Status of Women, the regional commissions and other concerned bodies of the United Nations system to devote greater attention to the problem of prostitution and the means for its prevention; and requested the Economic and Social Council to consider these questions at its first regular session of 1985, together with the reports requested by the Council in its resolution 1983/30, and to transmit its comments to the Assembly at its fortieth session (resolution 38/107).

At the thirty-ninth session, the General Assembly will have before it a note by the Secretary-General (A/39/58-E/1984/5).

(b) Preparations for the World Conference to Review and Appraise the Achievements of the United Nations Decade for Women

At its thirty-fifth session, in 1980, the General Assembly decided to convene in 1985, at the conclusion of the United Nations Decade for Women, a World Conference to Review and Appraise the Achievements of the United Nations Decade for Women (resolution 35/136).

At its thirty-sixth session, the General Assembly requested the Commission on the Status of Women, at its session to be held in 1982, to give priority to the question of the preparations for the Conference (resolution 36/126).

At its first regular session of 1982, the Economic and Social Council decided that the Commission on the Status of Women should be the preparatory body for the Conference and should operate on the basis of consensus, and invited the widest possible participation by Member States in the deliberations of the preparatory body; and decided also to recommend to the General Assembly that the Advancement of Women Branch of the Centre for Social Development and Humanitarian Affairs should serve as the secretariat of the preparatory body, as well as of the Conference (resolution 1982/26).

At its thirty-seventh session, the General Assembly endorsed Economic and Social Council resolution 1982/26 on the preparations for the Conference, to be held in 1985; welcomed the decision of the Council that the Commission on the Status of Women should be the preparatory body for the Conference and that it should operate on the basis of consensus; and decided to consider at its thirty-eighth session the recommendations of the Council on this matter together with the observations, if any, of the Secretary-General (resolution 37/60).

At its first regular session of 1983, the Economic and Social Council took note of the report of the Commission on the Status of Women Acting as the Preparatory Body for the World Conference to Review and Appraise the Achievements of the United Nations Decade for Women on its first session (A/CONF.116/PC/9 and Corr.1) and decided to endorse the recommendations contained therein and to

/...

0038

transmit the report to the General Assembly for consideration at its thirty-eighth session (decision 1983/132). At the same session, the Council decided that the programme budget implications (A/CONF.116/PC/9/Add.1) of those recommendations should be revised to adequately reflect the views expressed by delegations at the first session of the Commission Acting as the Preparatory Body and at the first regular session of 1983 of the Council, and requested the Secretary-General to submit those revised proposals to the Assembly at its thirty-eighth session (decision 1983/131).

At its thirty-eighth session, 146/ the General Assembly decided to accept with appreciation the offer of the Government of Kenya to act as host at Nairobi, in 1985, to the World Conference to Review and Appraise the Achievements of the United Nations Decade for Women; took note of the report of the Commission on the Status of Women on the work of its first session as the preparatory body for the Conference; endorsed the recommendations contained in the report of the Commission; considered that, within the framework of agenda item 7 of the provisional agenda proposed by the Commission at its first session as the preparatory body for the Conference, particular attention would be paid to the problems of women in Territories under racist colonial rule and in Territories under foreign occupation, on the basis of appropriate documentation from the international conferences on women, held at Mexico City and Copenhagen, with the theme equality, development and peace; and welcomed the decision of the Economic and Social Council, in its resolution 1983/28, to invite non-governmental organizations to participate in the preparations for the Conference (resolution 38/108).

At the thirty-ninth session, no advance documentation is expected under this item.

(c) Voluntary Fund for the United Nations Decade for Women: report of the Secretary-General

At its thirtieth session, in 1976, the General Assembly decided that the voluntary fund for the International Women's Year, established by Economic and Social Council resolution 1850 (LVI), should be extended to cover the period of the United Nations Decade for Women (A/10034, p. 100, "Other decisions", items 75 and 76).

At its thirty-first session, the General Assembly set forth the criteria for the use of the Voluntary Fund for the United Nations Decade for Women; requested the Secretary-General to report annually thereon; and requested the President of the Assembly to select five Member States, each of which should appoint a representative to serve, for a three-year period, on a Consultative Committee on the Fund to advise the Secretary-General on the use of the Fund (resolution 31/133). At present, the Consultative Committee on the Voluntary Fund for the United Nations Decade for Women is composed of the following Member States, whose term of office will expire on 31 December 1986: German Democratic Republic, India, Jamaica, Kenya and Norway (decision 37/326).

At its thirty-second to thirty-fifth sessions, the General Assembly continued its consideration of this question (resolutions 32/141, 33/188, 34/156 and 35/137).

/...

0039

At its thirty-sixth session, the General Assembly decided that the Fund should continue its activities beyond the Decade; requested the Secretary-General to invite the views of Member States on how best the Fund could continue its activities beyond the Decade and to submit a report thereon to the Assembly at its thirty-ninth session; and requested him to report on the substantive and financial implications and his proposals for the timing and modalities of a relocation of the Fund within the Centre for Social Development and Humanitarian Affairs in order to enable Member States to take decision in the matter (resolution 36/129).

At its thirty-seventh session, the General Assembly continued its consideration of this question (resolution 37/62).

At its thirty-eighth session, 146/ the General Assembly took note with satisfaction of the recommendations of the Consultative Committee for the Voluntary Fund for the United Nations Decade for Women at its thirteenth and fourteenth sessions (A/38/530, sect. V); expressed its concern that the quesion of senior women's programme officers posts at the regional commissions was still unresolved and that lack of progress in this regard was seriously impeding work on the women's programmes in several regions; urged the Secretary-General, in consultation with the executive secretaries of the regional commissions, to give priority to solving the question of senior women's programme officers and to take urgently appropriate measures to ensure that all temporary and permanent senior women's programme officers posts at the regional commissions should be continued within the regular budget resources available to them; noted with satisfaction the continuing increase in the number of projects submitted to and financed by the resources of the Fund and their contribution to promoting the involvement of women in development; considered that the Fund had a unique contribution to make in the technical assistance field to the implementation of the goals of the United Nations Decade for Women; stressed that the Fund had a unique contribution to make to the achievement of the goals of the Third United Nations Development Decade, and even beyond it; expressed its appreciation for the voluntary support given to the Fund by Member States, national committees for the Fund, national United Nations associations and other non-governmental organizations; noted with concern that contributions to the Fund had not been sufficient to enable it to take up all the worthwhile projects submitted to it; noted that contributions by Governments had a vital role to play in maintaining and increasing the financial viability and effectiveness of the work of the Fund; urged Governments, accordingly, to continue and increase, where possible, their contributions to the Fund and called upon those Governments that had not yet done so to consider contributing to the Fund; decided that, when considering the reports of the Secretary-General to be submitted to the Assembly at its thirty-ninth session pursuant to Assembly resolution 36/129, all possible options for continuing the Fund's activities beyond the end of the Decade would be reviewed in depth; requested that the results of the forward-looking assessment that was being undertaken on the activities assisted by the Fund be reflected in the reports of the Secretary-General on the Fund to be submitted to the Assembly at its thirty-ninth session; took note with appreciation of the measures taken by the Secretary-General, in response to its resolution 37/62, to improve and streamline the administration of the Fund; commended the United Nations Development Programme on its continuing technical and resource assistance to the Fund; and requested the Secretary-General to continue to report annually on the

/...

0040

management of the Fund and on the progress of its activities and to include in his report to the Assembly at its thirty-ninth session information on the implementation of measures taken in response to the problem of ensuring the continuation of all temporary and permanent senior women's programme officers posts at the regional commissions within regular budget resources available to them and to continue, on an annual basis, to include the Fund as one of the programmes of the United Nations Pledging Conference for Development Activities (resolution 38/106).

At the thirty-ninth session, the General Assembly will have before it the following reports of the Secretary-General:

(a) The continuation of the activities of the Voluntary Fund beyond the Decade, called for in paragraph 6 of resolution 36/129;

(b) The relocation of the Voluntary Fund, called for in paragraph 7 of resolution 36/129;

(c) The management of the Voluntary Fund, called for under resolution 38/106.

94. Elimination of all forms of discrimination against women

(a) Report of the Committee on the Elimination of Discrimination against Women

At its thirty-fourth session, in 1979, the General Assembly adopted the Convention on the Elimination of All Forms of Discrimination against Women, in which it called for the establishment of a Committee on the Elimination of Discrimination against Women which would consist, at the time of entry into force of the Convention, of 18 and, after ratification of or accession to the Convention by the thirty-fifth State Party, of 23 experts, elected for a term of four years. In accordance with article 21 of the Convention, the Committee shall, through the Economic and Social Council, report annually to the Assembly on its activities and may make suggestions and general recommendations based on the examination of reports and information received from the States Parties (resolution 34/180).

The first session of the Committee was held at Vienna from 18 to 22 October 1982. The second and third sessions were held from 1 to 12 August 1983 and from 26 March to 6 April 1984, respectively. In accordance with article 17 of the Convention, the Secretary-General convened on 9 April 1984 the second meeting of the States Parties to the Convention for the purpose of electing 11 members to the Committee. At present, the Committee is composed of the following members:

Ms. Desirée P. Bernard (Guyana)*

Ms. Aleksandra Pavlovna Biryukova (Union of Soviet Socialist Republics)**

Ms. Marie Caron (Canada)*

Ms. Irene R. Cortes (Philippines)**

Ms. Farida Abou El-Fetouh (Egypt)**

/...

0041

Ms. Elizabeth Evatt (Australia)*

Ms. Aida González Martínez (Mexico)*

Ms. Luvsandanzangyn Ider (Mongolia)**

Ms. Zagorka Ilić (Yugoslavia)**

Ms. Vinitha Jayasinghe (Sri Lanka)**

Ms. Chryssanthi Laiou-Antoniou (Greece)*

Ms. Raquel Macedo de Sheppard (Uruguay)**

Ms. Guan Minqian (China)**

Ms. Maria Margarida de Rego da Costa Salema Moura Ribeiro (Portugal)*

Ms. Alma Montenegro de Fletcher (Panama)*

Ms. Landrada Mukayiranga (Rwanda)**

Ms. Edith Oeser (German Democratic Republic)*

Ms. Vesselina Peytcheva (Bulgaria)**

Ms. Maria Regent-Lechowicz (Poland)**

Ms. Kongit Sinegiorgis (Ethiopia)*

Ms. Lucy Smith (Norway)*

Ms. Esther Veliz de Villalvilla (Cuba)*

Ms. Margareta Wadstein (Sweden)*

---

* Term of office expires in 1988.

** Term of office expires in 1986.

At its thirty-eighth session, 147/ the General Assembly, *inter alia*, took note

---

147/ References for the thirty-eighth session (agenda item 92):

(a) Report of the Committee on the Elimination of Discrimination against Women: Supplement No. 45 (A/38/45);

(b) Report of the Secretary-General: A/38/378;

(c) Report of the Third Committee: A/38/682;

(d) Resolution 38/109;

(e) Meetings of the Third Committee: A/C.3/38/SR.30-38, 53 and 55-59;

(f) Plenary meeting: A/38/PV.100.

/...

0042

of the report of the Committee on its first session (resolution 38/109) (see also discussion of sub-item (b) below).

At the thirty-ninth session, the General Assembly will have before it the report of the Committee on the Elimination of Discrimination against Women on its second and third sessions, Supplement No. 45 (A/39/45).

(b) Status of the Convention on the Elimination of All Forms of Discrimination against Women: report of the Secretary-General

At its thirty-fourth session, in 1979, the General Assembly adopted and opened for signature, ratification and accession the Convention on the Elimination of All Forms of Discrimination against Women; and expressed the hope that it would be signed and ratified or acceded to without delay and would come into force at an early date (resolution 34/180).

At its thirty-fifth session, the General Assembly expressed great satisfaction that, since its adoption by the Assembly in December 1979, 79 Member States had signed the Convention; and noted with appreciation that nine Member States had acceded to or ratified the Convention (resolution 35/140).

At its thirty-sixth session, the General Assembly welcomed with great satisfaction the fact that the Convention had entered into force on 3 September 1981; and invited all States which had not yet done so to become parties to the Convention by ratifying or acceding to it (resolution 36/131).

At its thirty-seventh session, the General Assembly noted with appreciation that an increasing number of Member States had ratified or acceded to the Convention; noted further that an important number of Member States had signed the Convention; welcomed the election of 23 members of the Committee on the Elimination of Discrimination against Women; and requested the Secretary-General to submit to the Assembly at its thirty-eighth session a report on the status of the Convention (resolution 37/64).

At its thirty-eighth session, 147/ the General Assembly, having taken note of the report of the Secretary-General (A/38/378), noted with appreciation the increasing number of Member States that had ratified or acceded to the Convention; invited States that had not yet done so to become parties to the Convention by ratifying or acceding to it; welcomed the fact that the Committee had successfully started its work and, *inter alia*, had adopted general guidelines regarding the form and contents of reports received from States parties under article 18 of the Convention; and requested the Secretary-General to submit to the Assembly at its thirty-ninth session a report on the status of the Convention (resolution 38/109).

At the thirty-ninth session, the General Assembly will have before it the following documents:

(a) Report of the Committee on the Elimination of Discrimination against Women: Supplement No. 45 (A/39/45);

(b) Report of the Secretary-General called for under resolution 38/109.

/...

0043

RELEVANT RESOLUTIONS

0044

Taking note of Economic and Social Council resolution 1981/69 C of 24 July 1981 on renewable sources of energy for human settlements,

Taking note, in this connection, of the *Report of the United Nations Conference on New and Renewable Sources of Energy*,[22] held at Nairobi from 10 to 21 August 1981,

1. *Welcomes* the contributions made by the United Nations Centre for Human Settlements (Habitat) to the preparations for and success of the United Nations Conference on New and Renewable Sources of Energy;

2. *Requests* the Executive Director of the United Nations Centre for Human Settlements to take the appropriate steps for the implementation of those recommendations of the United Nations Conference on New and Renewable Sources of Energy which are within the mandate of the Centre.

84th plenary meeting
4 December 1981

C

Mobilization of financial resources for the United Nations Centre for Human Settlements (Habitat)

The General Assembly,

Recalling its resolution 35/77 D of 5 December 1980, in which it urgently appealed to all States and appropriate financial institutions to make or to increase their voluntary contributions to the United Nations Habitat and Human Settlements Foundation in support of the activities of the United Nations Centre for Human Settlements (Habitat),

Noting the continued need for financial resources for the full implementation of the projected activities of the Centre under the work programme for the biennium 1982-1983 and the draft medium-term plan for the period 1984-1989 approved by the Commission on Human Settlements at its fourth session,[23]

Taking note of Economic and Social Council resolution 1981/69 A of 24 July 1981, in particular paragraphs 4 and 5 thereof which refer to the need for adequate financing for the projected activities of the Centre,

Expressing its appreciation to those Governments that have so far made financial contributions to the activities of the Centre,

Reiterates its urgent appeal to Member States to contribute and, if possible, to increase their contributions to the United Nations Habitat and Human Settlements Foundation in support of the activities of the United Nations Centre for Human Settlements (Habitat) and appeals to those that have not yet contributed, particularly developed countries and other countries in a position to do so, also to make voluntary contributions.

84th plenary meeting
4 December 1981

36/73. Living conditions of the Palestinian people

The General Assembly,

Recalling the Vancouver Declaration on Human Settlements, 1976,[24] and the relevant recommendations for national action[25] adopted by Habitat: United Nations Conference on Human Settlements,

Recalling also resolution 3, entitled "Living conditions of the Palestinians in occupied territories", contained in the recommendations for international co-operation adopted by Habitat: United Nations Conference on Human Settlements,[26] and Economic and Social Council resolutions 2026 (LXI) of 4 August 1976 and 2100 (LXIII) of 3 August 1977,

Recalling further its resolutions 3236 (XXIX) and 3237 (XXIX) of 22 November 1974, 31/110 of 16 December 1976, 32/171 of 19 December 1977, 33/110 of 18 December 1978, 34/113 of 14 December 1979 and 35/75 of 5 December 1980,

1. *Takes note* of the report of the Secretary-General on the living conditions of the Palestinian people;[27]

2. *Denounces* Israel for refusing to allow the Group of Experts on the Social and Economic Impact of the Israeli Occupation on the Living Conditions of the Palestinian People in the Occupied Arab Territories[28] to visit the Palestinian territories occupied by Israel;

3. *Condemns* Israel for the deteriorating living conditions of the Palestinian people in the occupied Palestinian territories;

4. *Affirms* that the elimination of the Israeli occupation is a prerequisite for the social and economic development of the Palestinian people in the occupied Palestinian territories;

5. *Recognizes* the need for a comprehensive report on the deterioration of the social and economic conditions of the Palestinian people in the occupied Palestinian territories;

6. *Requests* the Secretary-General to prepare a comprehensive and analytical report on the deteriorating living conditions of the Palestinian people in the occupied Palestinian territories and to submit it to the General Assembly at its thirty-seventh session, through the Economic and Social Council;

7. *Also requests* the Secretary-General, in preparing the above-mentioned report, to consult and co-operate with the Palestine Liberation Organization, the representative of the Palestinian people.

84th plenary meeting
4 December 1981

36/74. Comprehensive outline of a world survey on the role of women in development

The General Assembly,

Recalling its resolutions 3201 (S-VI) and 3202 (S-VI) of 1 May 1974, containing the Declaration and the Programme of Action on the Establishment of a New International Economic Order, 3281 (XXIX) of 12 December 1974, containing the Charter of Economic Rights and Duties of States, and 3362 (S-VII) of 16 September 1975 on development and international economic co-operation,

Recalling also its resolution 35/56 of 5 December 1980, the annex to which contains the International Development Strategy for the Third United Nations Development Decade,

Recalling further the provisions concerning the participation of women in development contained in the documents adopted at the World Conference of the United Nations

[22] United Nations publication, Sales No. E.81.I.24.

[23] *Official Records of the General Assembly, Thirty-sixth Session, Supplement No. 8* (A/36/8), annex I, decisions 4/17 and 4/18.

[24] *Report of Habitat: United Nations Conference on Human Settlements, Vancouver, 31 May-11 June 1976* (United Nations publication, Sales No. E.76.IV.7 and corrigendum), chap. I.

[25] *Ibid.*, chap. II.

[26] *Ibid.*, chap. III.

[27] A/36/260 and Add.1-3.

[28] For the report of the Group of Experts, see A/35/533 and Corr.1, annex I.

0045

Decade for Women: Equality, Development and Peace,[29]

Recalling its resolution 35/78 of 5 December 1980 on the effective mobilization and integration of women in development, in which it, *inter alia*, called for the preparation of a comprehensive and detailed outline for an interdisciplinary and multisectoral world survey on the role of women in over-all development,

Bearing in mind the International Development Strategy for the Third United Nations Development Decade, in particular the special provisions relating to the integration of women in over-all development with a view to securing women's equal participation both as agents and as beneficiaries in all sectors and at all levels of the development process,

Taking note of the report of the Secretary-General on a comprehensive outline of a world survey on the role of women in development,[30]

1. *Emphasizes* the need for a multisectoral and interdisciplinary survey on the role of women in development;

2. *Recommends* that the survey should analyse the role of women in relation to key developmental issues as envisaged in the International Development Strategy for the Third United Nations Development Decade, focusing in particular on trade, agriculture, industry, energy, money and finance, and science and technology;

3. *Further recommends* that, in its analysis, the survey should cover:

(*a*) The present role of women as active agents of development in each sector;

(*b*) An assessment of the benefits accruing to women as a result of their participation in development, namely, income, conditions of work, and decision-making;

(*c*) Ways and means of improving women's role as agents and beneficiaries of development at the national, regional and international levels;

(*d*) The potential impact of such improvements on the achievement of over-all development goals;

4. *Invites* the Secretary-General, in preparing the survey, to give due attention to the problems and requirements of women in every region and to the contribution of women to the achievement of goals of self-reliance and to economic and technical co-operation among developing countries;

5. *Calls upon* the Secretary-General to include in the survey an overview analysing interrelationships among key developmental issues with regard to women's current and future roles in development with a view to providing a basis for future action for women's effective mobilization and integration in development;

6. *Requests* the Secretary-General to prepare the survey in close collaboration and co-operation with the appropriate organizations of the United Nations system and with contributions from all organs and organizations concerned of the United Nations system, including the regional commissions and the International Research and Training Institute for the Advancement of Women, as well as national institutions having expertise on this subject;

7. *Further requests* the Secretary-General to submit a progress report on the preparation of the survey to the General Assembly at its thirty-seventh session and to submit the survey in its final form to the Assembly at its thirty-ninth session.

84th plenary meeting
4 December 1981

[29] See *Report of the World Conference of the United Nations Decade for Women: Equality, Development and Peace, Copenhagen, 14 to 30 July 1980* (United Nations publication, Sales No. E.80.IV.3 and corrigendum), chap. I.

[30] A/36/590.

36/75. United Nations Institute for Training and Research

The General Assembly,

Recalling its resolutions 3201 (S-VI) and 3202 (S-VI) of 1 May 1974, containing the Declaration and the Programme of Action on the Establishment of a New International Economic Order,

Recalling its resolution 3281 (XXIX) of 12 December 1974, containing the Charter of Economic Rights and Duties of States,

Recalling also its resolution 3362 (S-VII) of 16 September 1975 on development and international economic co-operation,

Recalling further its resolutions 35/53 A and B of 5 December 1980 on the United Nations Institute for Training and Research,

Acknowledging the value of the research and the studies on the future undertaken by the United Nations Institute for Training and Research,

Recognizing the role of the United Nations Institute for Training and Research in assisting, through training and other services within its mandate, members of permanent missions to the United Nations and other national officials concerned with the work of the United Nations,

1. *Takes note* of the report of the Executive Director of the United Nations Institute for Training and Research[31] and of his introductory statement on 2 October 1981;[32]

2. *Welcomes* the emphasis on, and urges the continuation of, the concentration of the work of the United Nations Institute for Training and Research in the sphere of economic and social training and research and the inclusion of specific projects on the problems that exist in the areas identified by the General Assembly at its sixth and seventh special sessions and in the relevant decisions adopted by the Assembly at its twenty-ninth and subsequent sessions, taking into consideration the statements on the programme of work of the Institute made at the present session;

3. *Calls upon* the Executive Director of the United Nations Institute for Training and Research to continue to rationalize the activities of the Institute and, in this context, to seek further co-ordination of its research programme with similar activities of other institutions, within and outside the United Nations system, and to continue to present research results, as far as possible, in a manner relevant to policy making;

4. *Welcomes also*, in accordance with General Assembly resolution 35/53 B, the steps taken so far by the United Nations Institute for Training and Research to enhance its effectiveness, to reduce its costs and to increase its resources, and calls upon the Institute to organize its programme of work and activities and to adjust its administrative costs so as to ensure that, as from 1982, estimated expenditure does not exceed estimated revenue;

5. *Urges* all States that have not yet contributed to the United Nations Institute for Training and Research to do so, and calls upon all donor countries, especially those that are not contributing at a level commensurate with their capacity, to increase their voluntary contributions in order to meet the needs of the Institute.

84th plenary meeting
4 December 1981

[31] *Official Records of the General Assembly, Thirty-sixth Session, Supplement No. 14* (A/36/14 and Corr.1.)

[32] *Ibid., Thirty-sixth Session, Second Committee*, 6th meeting, paras. 28-37.

0046

38/22. International Youth Year: Participation, Development, Peace

Date: 22 November 1983 Meeting: 66
Adopted without a vote Report: A/38/571

The General Assembly,

Recalling its resolutions 34/151 of 17 December 1979, 35/126 of 11 December 1980, 36/28 of 13 November 1981 and 37/48 of 3 December 1982,

Recognizing the profound importance of the direct participation of youth in shaping the future of mankind and the valuable contribution that youth can make in the implementation of the new international economic order based on equity and justice,

Considering it necessary to disseminate among youth the ideals of peace, respect for human rights and fundamental freedoms, human solidarity and dedication to the objectives of progress and development,

67/ Report of the Second World Conference to Combat Racism and Racial Discrimination, Geneva, 1-12 August 1983, (United Nations publication, Sales No. E.83.XIV.4 and corrigendum).

0047

Convinced of the imperative need to harness the energies, enthusiasms and creative abilities of youth to the tasks of nation-building, the struggle for self-determination and national independence, in accordance with the Charter of the United Nations, and against foreign domination and occupation, for the economic, social and cultural advancement of peoples, the implementation of the new international economic order, the preservation of world peace and the promotion of international co-operation and understanding,

Emphasizing again that the United Nations should give more attention to the role of young people in the world of today and to their demands for the world of tomorrow,

Recalling the topicality of assessing the needs and aspirations of youth, and reaffirming the importance of current and projected United Nations activities designed to increase the opportunities for youth and for its active participation in national development activities,

Believing that it is urgently desirable to intensify the efforts of all States in carrying out specific programmes concerning youth and to improve the activities of the United Nations and the specialized agencies in the field of youth, including youth exchanges in the cultural, sporting and other fields,

Reaffirming the importance of better co-ordination of efforts in dealing with specific problems confronting young people and in examining the manner in which those problems are being treated by the specialized agencies and by various United Nations bodies,

Aware of the valuable contribution which the United Nations Educational, Scientific and Cultural Organization is making to the promotion of international co-operation in the field of youth,

Convinced that the preparation and observance in 1985 of the International Youth Year under the motto "Participation, Development, Peace" will offer a useful and significant opportunity for drawing attention to the situation and specific needs and aspirations of youth, for increasing co-operation at all levels in dealing with youth issues, for undertaking concerted action programmes in favour of youth and for involving young people in the study and resolution of major national, regional and international problems,

Confident that the International Youth Year will serve to mobilize efforts at the local, national, regional and international levels in order to promote the best educational, professional and living conditions for young people, to ensure their active participation in the overall development of society and to encourage the preparation of new national and local policies and programmes in accordance with each country's experience, conditions and priorities,

Recognizing that the preparation and observance of the International Youth Year will contribute to the reaffirmation of the goals of the new international economic order and to the implementation of the International Development Strategy for the Third United Nations Development Decade, 68/

Recalling also in this connection its decision 35/424 of 5 December 1980 and Economic and Social Council resolution 1980/67 of 25 July 1980 on the question of guidelines for international years and anniversaries,

Aware that, for the International Youth Year to be successful and to maximize its impact and practical efficiency, adequate preparation and the widespread support of Governments, all specialized agencies, international intergovernmental and non-governmental organizations and the public will be required,

Recognizing the important role of the United Nations bodies, specialized agencies and regional commissions in promoting international co-operation in the field of youth and the necessity of strengthening their role in the effective implementation of the specific Programme of Measures and Activities to be undertaken prior to and during the International Youth Year, 69/

68/ General Assembly resolution 35/56, annex.

69/ A/36/215, annex, sect. IV, decision 1 (I).

0048

1. Takes note of the report of the Secretary-General on the implementation of its resolution 37/48; 70/

2. Commends the five regional meetings devoted to the International Youth Year held during 1983 and requests the Secretary-General to bring the regional plans of action and the recommendations adopted by the regional meetings to the notice of all States with a view to their implementation; 71/

3. Invites again all States that have not already done so to set up national co-ordinating committees or other forms of co-ordination for the International Youth Year;

4. Stresses again the importance of active and direct participation of youth organizations in the activities organized at the local, national, regional and international levels for the preparation and observance of the International Youth Year;

5. Requests the Secretary-General to use all means at his disposal, within the existing resources, to ensure the implementation and follow-up of the specific Programme of Measures and Activities, 72/ including the provision of information;

6. Decides that the third session of the Advisory Committee for the International Youth Year shall be convened at Vienna from 2 to 11 April 1984;

7. Requests the Advisory Committee to make all efforts for the implementation of tasks entrusted to it by the decisions of the General Assembly and by recommendations of the five regional meetings devoted to the International Youth Year and to submit the report on its third session to the General Assembly at its thirty-ninth session with practical proposals on specific ways and means for observance, in 1985, of the Year in an appropriate organizational framework within the United Nations;

8. Requests the Secretary-General to continue to take concrete measures, within the existing resources, through all the communications media at his disposal, to give widespread publicity to the activities of the United Nations system in the field of youth and to increase the dissemination of information on youth;

9. Welcomes the voluntary contributions made until now for the International Youth Year, expresses its appreciation to all contributors and again appeals to all States, to international governmental and non-governmental organizations and to the public to make in due time generous voluntary contributions to supplement funds provided under the regular budget of the United Nations for the costs of the specific Programme of Measures and Activities and requests the Secretary-General to take all appropriate measures for obtaining such voluntary contributions;

10. Decides to include in the provisional agenda of its thirty-ninth session the item entitled "International Youth Year: Participation, Development, Peace" and to grant it high priority.

38/26. Channels of communication between the United Nations and youth and youth organizations

Date: 22 November 1983 Meeting: 66
Adopted without a vote Report: A/38/573

The General Assembly,

Recalling its resolution 32/135 of 16 December 1977 and 36/17 of 9 November 1981, in which it adopted guidelines for the improvement of the channels of communication between the United Nations and youth and youth organizations, and 37/50 of 3 December 1982,

Bearing in mind the importance of the existence of effective channels of communication between the United Nations and youth and youth organizations for the proper information of young people and their effective participation in the work of th nited Nations and the specialized agencies at the national, regional and international levels,

Taking note of the report of the Secretary-General, 83/

Also taking note of the efforts in inter-agency co-operation to promote and strengthen channels of communication between the United Nations and youth and youth organizations within the context of the International Youth Year,

Convinced that the existence and proper functioning of channels of communication between the United Nations and youth and youth organizations form a basic prerequisite of the active involvement of young people and thus of the successful preparation for, celebration of and follow-up to the International Youth Year at all levels,

1. Requests the Secretary-General to continue to give full co-operation and support to inter-agency co-operation and co-ordination in promotional and information activities within the context of the International Youth Year;

2. Calls upon Member States, specialized agencies and other intergovernmental organizations, in co-operation with youth and youth organizations in consultative status with the Economic and Social Council and other youth organizations concerned, to continue to promote actively the full and effective implementation of the guidelines and additional guidelines adopted in General Assembly resolutions 32/135 and 36/17, in particular through informing young people of relevant policies and programmes and encouraging them to participate in the preparation and implementation of these policies and programmes;

3. Requests the Advisory Committee for the International Youth Year at its third session to monitor and evaluate the measures taken with respect to the implementation of the guidelines on the basis of the relevant reports of the Secretary-General and other relevant information provided to it, and to make recommendations for the full and effective implementation and the further elaboration of the guidelines as an integral part of the preparation for, celebration of and follow-up to the International Youth Year;

4. Decides to review the question of the channels of communication between the United Nations and youth and youth organizations at its thirty-ninth session on the basis of the report of the Advisory Committee for the International Youth Year.

38/27. Question of aging

Date: 22 November 1983 Meeting: 66
Adopted without a vote Report: A/38/574

The General Assembly,

Reaffirming its resolution 37/51 of 3 December 1982, in which it endorsed the International Plan of Action on Aging adopted by the World Assembly on Aging, 84/ held at Vienna from 26 July to 6 August 1982, and called upon Governments and the Secretary-General to make continuous efforts to implement the principles and recommendations of the Plan,

83/ A/38/339.

84/ Report of the World Assembly on Aging (United Nations publication, Sales No. E.82.I.16), chap. VI.A.

0050

Recalling Economic and Social Council resolution 1981/87 of 25 November 1981, in which the Council decided to convene in 1984 an International Conference on Population, 85/ and also recalling the Vienna International Plan of Action on Aging, 86/ which acknowledges that aging is a population issue that affects development and requires increasing international assistance and co-operation,

Recognizing the significant contributions of the World Assembly on Aging and the United Nations Trust Fund for Aging in the promotion and strengthening of international co-operation in this field,

Conscious of the positive response of many countries to the World Assembly on Aging and the recommendations of the Plan of Action and of the need to provide national authorities, at their request, with assistance in their efforts to implement the Plan,

Noting with satisfaction that many Governments have retained or established national mechanisms to facilitate the planning, implementation and co-ordination of the activities recommended by the Plan of Action,

Recognizing the role played by the United Nations and the specialized agencies through their efforts in the field of aging and the need to strengthen this role, especially at the regional level, in order to ensure the implementation of the Plan of Action and the systematic and efficient functioning of the technical advisory and co-ordination services of the United Nations,

Acknowledging the role played by the international network of existing information, research and training centres in exchanging information and experience at the international level and in stimulating progress and encouraging the adoption of measures to respond to the economic and social implications of the aging of populations and to meet the needs of older persons,

Noting that the Plan of Action recognizes the relationship between aging and youth, particularly as it relates to intergenerational matters,

Recognizing that women have a longer life expectancy than men and that they will increasingly constitute a majority of the older population,

1. *Takes note* of the report of the Secretary-General on the question of aging; 87/

2. *Affirms* that the question of aging should be considered in the context of economic development, political, social and cultural systems and social values and changes;

3. *Calls upon* Governments to continue to make efforts to implement the principles and recommendations contained in the Vienna International Plan of Action on Aging in accordance with the economic, social and cultural circumstances of each country;

4. *Invites* Governments to retain or establish, in a suitable form, mechanisms at the national level to promote the implementation of the Plan of Action;

5. *Urges* the Secretary-General to continue his efforts to ensure the effective implementation and follow-up action to the Plan of Action and to maintain the impetus generated by the Trust Fund for Aging at the national, regional and international levels;

6. *Requests* the Secretary-General to continue to promote the Trust Fund so as to assist countries in formulating and implementing policies and programmes for aging;

7. *Requests* the Secretary-General to continue his information exchange activities through, *inter alia*, the international network of existing information, research and training centres and to convene, using voluntary contributions, meetings of the members of this network, as appropriate, to strengthen these activities and to promote technical co-operation among developing countries;

85/ See General Assembly resolution 38/148 of 19 December 1983 in part IV of this release.

86/ *Report of the World Assembly on Aging* (United Nations publication, Sales No. E.82.I.16), chap. VI.A.

87/ A/38/470.

0051

8. Urges the Secretary-General to include advisory services to developing countries that request them in technical co-operation programmes to the extent feasible under the funding of those programmes;

9. Requests the Secretary-General to ensure, as requested by the Plan of Action that the question of the aging of populations is brought to the attention of the appropriate United Nations bodies responsible for the preparation of the International Conference on Population and that the question of aging will be considered under the appropriate agenda items of the Conference itself;

10. Also requests the Secretary-General to continue to promote, in co-operation with the national committees concerned, joint activities in the field of aging and youth, particularly as they relate to intergenerational matters, especially during the International Youth Year;

11. Further requests the Secretary-General to examine the gender-based difference in longevity and the impact of the increasing number and proportion of older women on living arrangements, income, health care and other support systems, and to bring the question of older women to the attention of the preparatory body for the World Conference to Review and Appraise the Achievements of the United Nations Decade for Women in 1985 for its consideration;

12. Urges the United Nations Fund for Population Activities, in co-operation with all organizations for international population assistance, to continue its assistance, within its mandate, in the field of aging, particularly in developing countries;

13. Invites the regional commissions to review the objectives of the Plan of Action and contribute to their realization and to organize and conduct the regional periodic review and appraisal of the Plan in co-ordination with that at the international level;

14. Also invites the specialized agencies and other intergovernmental and non-governmental organizations concerned to continue to be actively involved, in a co-ordinated manner, in the implementation of the Plan of Action;

15. Requests the Secretary-General to submit to the General Assembly at its thirty-ninth session a report on the measures taken to implement the present resolution;

16. Decides to include in the provisional agenda of its thirty-ninth session the item

0052

37/53. Implementation of the World Programme of Action concerning Disabled Persons

Date: 3 December 1982 | Meeting: 90
Adopted without a vote | Report: A/37/632

The General Assembly,

Recalling its resolutions 31/123 of 16 December 1976, by which it proclaimed the year 1981 International Year of Disabled Persons, 32/133 of 16 December 1977, by which it established the Advisory Committee for the International Year of Disabled Persons, 33/170 of 20 December 1978, 34/158 of 17 December 1979, in which it, *inter alia*, decided to expand the theme of the International Year of Disabled Persons to "Full participation and equality", 35/133 of 13 December 1980, 36/77 of 8 December 1981 and 37/52 of 3 December 1982, in which it adopted the World Programme of Action concerning Disabled Persons, 50/

47/ IYDP/SYMP/L.2/Rev.1.

48/ A/37/351/Add.1 and Add.1/Corr.1.

49/ *Ibid.*, para. 99.

50/ A/37/351/Add.1 and Add.1/Corr.1, para.99.

0053

Recognizing that the International Year of Disabled Persons contributed to the acceptance by the community of the right of disabled persons to participate fully in the social life and development of their societies and to enjoy living conditions equal to those of their fellow citizens,

Convinced that the International Year of Disabled Persons gave a genuine and meaningful impetus to activities related to equalization of opportunities for disabled persons, as well as prevention and rehabilitation at all levels,

Expressing its appreciation to the Advisory Committee for the International Year of Disabled Persons for its work, in particular for its contribution to the formulation of the World Programme of Action concerning Disabled Persons,

Expressing its satisfaction with the efforts of Member States during the International Year of Disabled Persons to improve the conditions and well-being of disabled persons and their willingness to involve disabled persons and their organizations in all matters of concern to them,

Also expressing its satisfaction with the initiatives taken by the specialized agencies and other organs and organizations of the United Nations system, non-governmental organizations and, in particular, organizations of disabled persons,

Encouraged by the emergence of organizations of disabled persons in all parts of the world and their positive influence on the image and condition of persons with a disability,

Having considered with appreciation the Vienna Affirmative Action Plan adopted by the World Symposium of Experts on Technical Co-operation among Developing Countries and Technical Assistance in Disability Prevention and Rehabilitation, 51/ which emphasized that, in developing countries, efforts to prevent disabilities should be intensified and standards of rehabilitation for disabled persons should be as high as possible,

Noting in particular the results of the meetings organized for the International Year of Disabled Persons by the regional commissions, which stressed the need for more efficient technical co-operation at the regional and subregional levels in the training of rehabilitation personnel, the production of prosthetic appliances and aids using locally available resources and also stressed the need for an interregional exchange of experience in the elaboration of national programmes for the development of such services, 52/

Stressing that the primary responsibility for promoting effective measures for prevention of disability, rehabilitation and the realization of the goals of full participation and equality of disabled persons rests with the individual countries and that in this regard international co-operation is highly desirable and should be directed to assisting and supporting national efforts,

Believing that, in addition to national programmes, an effective implementation of the World Programme of Action would be assisted by activities at the international level by the organs, organizations and agencies of the United Nations system, the non-governmental organizations and the organizations of disabled persons,

Recognizing that such activities will be difficult to finance at the present time and that every effort must be made to reallocate existing budgets within the United Nations system,

1. *Requests* the Secretary-General to assist in the early implementation of the World Programme of Action concerning Disabled Persons by ensuring its wide distribution and promotion;

2. *Requests* Member States to develop plans related to the equalization of opportunities for disabled persons, as well as to prevention and rehabilitation, and thereby ensure early implementation of the World Programme of Action concerning Disabled Persons;

51/ IYDP/SYMP/L.2/Rev.1.

52/ See A/37/351 and Corr.1.

0054

3. Requests all organs, organizations and agencies of the United Nations system to formulate and undertake measures within their sphere of competence, through a reallocation of existing resources, to ensure early implementation of the World Programme of Action concerning Disabled Persons and requests, in particular, the regional commissions to implement suitable programmes, on the understanding that effective consultation and co-ordination between the various bodies is essential;

4. Requests the Secretary-General to establish interorganizational task forces as recommended by the Advisory Committee for the International Year of Disabled Persons at its third and fourth sessions in order to implement support services, as embodied in paragraph 17 of General Assembly resolution 36/77, within the existing arrangements for interagency co-ordination in order to support national and regional activities in the developing regions in the fields of prevention, rehabilitation and equalization of opportunities;

5. Encourages the Secretary-General to find the means to provide the Centre for Social Development and Humanitarian Affairs of the Secretariat with the necessary resources to enable it to ensure follow-up to the International Year of Disabled Persons and to facilitate the implementation of the World Programme of Action concerning Disabled Persons;

6. Requests the Secretary-General to continue the consultative services to Member States concerning the design of national programmes for the prevention of disability, rehabilitation and equalization of opportunities for disabled persons and to develop a practical check list dealing with the equalization of opportunities for disabled persons which could be used by consultants in discussion with Governments of Member States, and to compile and distribute information on available technical and financial resources to assist developing countries in the prevention of disability, rehabilitation and equalization of opportunities;

7. Further requests the Secretary-General to continue to give appropriate priority to activities within the programmes for disabled persons with regard to organizations of disabled persons;

8. Again urges all organs, organizations and agencies of the United Nations system to undertake new measures or expedite those already under way to improve employment opportunities for disabled persons within these bodies at all levels and to improve access to their buildings and facilities and to their information sources, and requests the Secretary-General to submit a report on these measures to the General Assembly at its thirty-ninth session;

9. Requests the Secretary-General, in consultation with Governments, to examine the need and possibility of continuing the Trust Fund for the International Year of Disabled Persons for the purpose of assisting Governments, at their request, in the implementation of the World Programme of Action concerning Disabled Persons and to submit a report thereon to the General Assembly at its thirty-eighth session;

10. Requests all Governments in a position to do so, the United Nations Development Programme and all relevant United Nations organs, organizations and agencies to assist Governments of developing countries, at their request, in the formulation of national policies and programmes for disabled persons;

11. Proclaims the period 1983-1992 United Nations Decade of Disabled Persons as a long-term plan of action, on the understanding that no additional resources from the United Nations system will be needed for this purpose, and encourages Member States to utilize this period as one of the means to implement the World Programme of Action concerning Disabled Persons;

12. Encourages Governments to proclaim national days for the disabled;

13. Urges international organizations and funding bodies to give higher priority to human resources development, in particular to training activities in the fields of prevention and rehabilitation and to enhance the equalization of opportunities and the participation of disabled persons;

14. Requests the organizations of the United Nations system to recognize the needs of disabled persons in their activities relating to the International Youth Year and in international and regional congresses and meetings that they sponsor;

0055

15. Requests the World Health Organization, in the light of the experience of the International Year of Disabled Persons, to review its definitions of impairment, disability and handicap in consultation with organizations of disabled persons and other appropriate bodies;

16. Requests the Secretary-General to explore the possibility of convening in 1987 a meeting of experts, consisting largely of disabled persons, to prepare a report that would enable the Secretary-General to help the General Assembly at its forty-second session to evaluate the implementation of the World Programme of Action concerning Disabled Persons as provided for in paragraph 3 of resolution 37/52;

17. Requests the Secretary-General to report to the General Assembly at its thirty-ninth session on the implementation of the World Programme of Action concerning Disabled Persons.

0056

38/28. World Programme of Action concerning Disabled Persons

Date: 22 November 1983 | Meeting: 66
Adopted without a vote | Report: A/38/575

The General Assembly,

Recalling its resolutions 32/133 of 16 December 1977 and 34/154 of 17 December 1979, by which it appealed to Member States to make generous voluntary contributions to the International Year of Disabled Persons,

Recalling also its resolution 36/77 of 8 December 1981, by which it welcomed the contributions made by Governments and private sources to the United Nations Trust Fund for the International Year of Disabled Persons and appealed for further voluntary contributions which would facilitate the follow-up to the Year,

Deeply concerned that no less than 500 million persons are estimated to suffer from disability of one form or another, of whom 400 million are estimated to be in developing countries,

Convinced that the International Year of Disabled Persons gave a genuine and meaningful impetus to activities related to the equalization of opportunities for disabled persons, as well as prevention and rehabilitation at all levels,

0057

Noting the emergence of organizations of disabled persons in all parts of the world and their positive influence on the image and condition of persons with a disability,

Desirous of ensuring effective follow-up to the International Year of Disabled Persons and aware that, if this is to be achieved, Member States, organs, organizations and agencies of the United Nations system, non-governmental organizations and organizations of disabled persons must therefore be encouraged to continue the activities already undertaken and to initiate new programmes and activities,

Stressing that the primary responsibility for promoting effective measures for the prevention of disability, rehabilitation and the realization of the goals of "full participation" of disabled persons in social life and development and of "equality" rests with individual countries and that international action should be directed towards assisting and supporting national efforts in this regard, such as consultative services in designing national plans and programmes in the field of disability prevention, rehabilitation and the equalization of opportunities for persons with disabilities,

Reiterating its appreciation to the Advisory Committee for the International Year of Disabled Persons for its work, in particular for its contribution to the formulation of the World Programme of Action concerning Disabled Persons, 88/

Recalling its resolution 37/52 of 3 December 1982, by which it adopted the World Programme of Action concerning Disabled Persons, which, in paragraph 157, states that the Trust Fund established by the General Assembly for the International Year of Disabled Persons should be used to meet requests for assistance from developing countries and organizations of disabled persons and to further the implementation of the World Programme of Action, and, in paragraph 158, indicates that, in general, there is a need to increase the flow of resources to developing countries to implement the objectives of the World Programme of Action, that, therefore, the Secretary-General should explore new ways and means of raising voluntary funds and take the necessary follow-up measures for mobilizing resources, and that voluntary contributions from Governments and from private sources should be encouraged,

Recalling further its resolution 37/53 of 3 December 1982, by which it proclaimed the period 1983-1992 United Nations Decade of Disabled Persons as a long-term plan of action, on the understanding that no additional resources from the United Nations system would be needed for this purpose, and encouraged Member States to utilize this period as one of the means to implement the World Programme of Action concerning Disabled Persons,

Concerned that developing countries are experiencing increasing difficulties in mobilizing adequate resources for meeting pressing needs in the field of disability prevention, rehabilitation and equalization of opportunities for the millions of persons with disabilities in the face of pressing demands from other high-priority sectors concerned with basic needs,

Convinced that the United Nations Decade of Disabled Persons should give a strong impetus to the implementation of the World Programme of Action concerning Disabled Persons and to a broader understanding of its importance,

Noting Economic and Social Council resolution 1983/19 of 26 May 1983, in which the Secretary-General was requested to monitor and support the implementation of the World Programme of Action concerning Disabled Persons by enlisting extrabudgetary resources,

Noting with great appreciation the many generous voluntary contributions and pledges already made by Governments, organizations and individuals,

Noting also with appreciation the report of the Secretary-General on the results achieved so far by the United Nations Trust Fund for the International Year of Disabled Persons during the year and its follow-up, 89/

Recognizing that the Trust Fund for the International Year of Disabled Persons is an important instrument for the implementation of the World Programme of Action concerning Disabled Persons,

---

88/ A/37/351/Add.1 and Add.1/Corr.1, annex.

89/ A/38/508.

0058

1. Recognizes the desirability of the continuation of the Trust Fund for the International Year for Disabled Persons throughout the United Nations Decade of Disabled Persons for the benefit of disabled persons, particularly those in developing countries;

2. Decides that the Trust Fund for the International Year of Disabled Persons should continue its activities pending a report by the Secretary-General to the General Assembly at its thirty-ninth session, which should include recommendations for the further implementation of the World Programme of Action concerning Disabled Persons, the funding of such activities by voluntary contributions, the possible terms of reference of a trust fund for the United Nations Decade of Disabled Persons, the implementation of the provisions contained in Assembly resolution 36/77 concerning the organization of support services for technical co-operation in favour of disabled persons, as well as the organization of task forces mentioned in Assembly resolution 37/53;

3. Stresses the need that the administration of the Trust Fund should continue to be carried out as an integral part of the substantive responsibilities for disability matters discharged by the United Nations Secretariat;

4. Recommends that the resources of the Trust Fund should be geared, within the framework of the United Nations Decade of Disabled Persons, towards the implementation of the World Programme of Action concerning Disabled Persons and towards helping persons with disabilities to organize themselves, towards assisting in implementing support and consultative services for technical co-operation and inter-organizational task forces, as mentioned in resolutions 36/77 and 37/53, and towards strengthening the activities of the regional commissions in the field of disability prevention and the advancement of persons with disabilities;

5. Requests the Secretary-General to undertake the necessary steps to strengthen the Trust Fund and to enlist to this effect extrabudgetary resources as indicated in paragraph 158 of the World Programme of Action concerning Disabled Persons;

6. Appeals to Governments and private sources for continuing generous voluntary contributions to the Trust Fund;

7. Calls upon all Member States, all non-governmental organizations concerned and organizations of disabled persons and calls also upon all organs, organizations and agencies of the United Nations system, through a reallocation of existing resources, to continue to ensure the early implementation of the World Programme of Action concerning Disabled Persons;

8. Requests the Secretary-General to include in his reports to the General Assembly on the implementation of the World Programme of Action concerning Disabled Persons a section on

0059

38/105. Participation of women in promoting international peace and co-operation

Date: 16 December 1983 Meeting: 100
Adopted without a vote Report: A/38/681

The General Assembly,

Reaffirming its resolution 37/63 of 3 December 1982, in which it proclaimed the Declaration on the Participation of Women in Promoting International Peace and Co-operation,

Believing that further efforts are required to eliminate discrimination against women in all its forms and in every field of human endeavour,

Wishing to encourage the active participation of women in promoting international peace and security and co-operation,

Conscious of the need to implement the provisions of the Declaration,

Desiring that publicity be given to the Declaration,

1. *Calls upon* the Secretary-General to disseminate widely the Declaration on the Participation of Women in Promoting International Peace and Co-operation in the six official languages of the United Nations;

2. *Invites* all Governments to take the necessary measures to ensure wide publicity for the Declaration;

3. *Requests* the Secretary-General to bring the Declaration to the attention of the appropriate specialized agencies, including the United Nations Educational, Scientific and Cultural Organization, the International Labour Organisation, the World Health Organization and other appropriate bodies within the United Nations system for the consideration of measures to implement the Declaration;

4. *Requests* the Commission on the Status of Women to consider what measures may be necessary in order to implement the Declaration and to report through the Economic and Social Council to the General Assembly at its thirty-ninth session;

5. *Decides* to consider at its thirty-ninth session the report of the Commission on the Status of Women under the item entitled "United Nations Decade for Women: Equality, Development and Peace" together with the preparations for the World Conference to Review and Appraise the Achievements of the United Nations Decade for Women in 1985.

0060

38/107. Prevention of prostitution

Date: 16 December 1983 Meeting: 100
Vote: 121-0-25 (recorded) Report: A/38/681

The General Assembly,

Reaffirming the objectives of the United Nations Decade for Women: Equality, Development and Peace,

Taking into account the resolutions, declarations, conventions and recommendations of the United Nations and the specialized agencies and international conferences designed to eliminate all forms of discrimination against women, as well as those relating to the suppression of traffic in persons and the exploitation of the prostitution of others, including Economic and Social Council resolution 1983/30 of 26 May 1983,

Convinced of the importance of the full integration of women in the social, political and economic activities of their community,

Bearing in mind the essential role of women in the welfare of the family and the development of society,

Considering that prostitution and the accompanying evil of the traffic in persons for the purpose of prostitution are incompatible with the dignity and worth of the human person and endanger the welfare of the individual, the family and the community,

Further considering that women and children are still all too often victims of physical abuse and sexual exploitation,

Mindful that the prevailing economic and social conditions are largely responsible for the continued existence of the social problems of prostitution and traffic in persons,

1. *Urges* Member States to take all appropriate humane measures, including legislation, to combat prostitution, exploitation of the prostitution of others and all forms of traffic in persons;

2. *Appeals* to Member States to provide special protection to victims of prostitution through measures including education, social guarantees, employment opportunities for those victims with a view to their rehabilitation;

3. *Requests* the Economic and Social Council, the Commission on Human Rights, the Commission on the Status of Women, the regional commissions and other concerned bodies of the United Nations system to devote greater attention to the problem of prostitution and the means for its prevention;

4. *Requests* the Economic and Social Council to consider this question at its first regular session of 1985, together with the reports requested in Council resolution 1983/30, and to transmit its comments to the General Assembly at its fortieth session.

175/ A/38/530, sect. II, paras. 11-12.

0061

RECORDED VOTE ON RESOLUTION 38/107:

In favour: Afghanistan, Albania, Algeria, Angola, Argentina, Bahamas, Bahrain, Bangladesh, Belize, Benin, Bhutan, Bolivia, Botswana, Brazil, Bulgaria, Burma, Burundi, Byelorussia, Cape Verde, Central African Republic, Chad, Chile, China, Colombia, Congo, Costa Rica, Cuba, Cyprus, Czechoslovakia, Democratic Kampuchea, Democratic Yemen, Djibouti, Dominica, Dominican Republic, Ecuador, Egypt, El Salvador, Equatorial Guinea, Ethiopia, Fiji, Gabon, German Democratic Republic, Ghana, Grenada, Guatemala, Guinea, Guinea-Bissau, Guyana, Haiti, Honduras, Hungary, India, Indonesia, Iran, Iraq, Ivory Coast, Jamaica, Japan, Jordan, Kenya, Kuwait, Lao People's Democratic Republic, Lebanon, Lesotho, Libya, Madagascar, Malawi, Malaysia, Maldives, Mali, Malta, Mauritania, Mauritius, Mexico, Mongolia, Morocco, Mozambique, Nepal, Nicaragua, Niger, Oman, Pakistan, Panama, Papua New Guinea, Paraguay, Peru, Philippines, Poland, Qatar, Romania, Rwanda, Saint Lucia, Sao Tome and Principe, Saudi Arabia, Sierra Leone, Singapore, Somalia, Sri Lanka, Sudan, Suriname, Swaziland, Syria, Thailand, Togo, Turkey, Uganda, Ukraine, USSR, United Arab Emirates, United Republic of Cameroon, United Republic of Tanzania, Upper Volta, Uruguay, Vanuatu, Venezuela, Viet Nam, Yemen, Yugoslavia, Zaire, Zambia, Zimbabwe.

Against: None.

Abstaining: Australia, Austria, Belgium, Canada, Denmark, Finland, France, Federal Republic of Germany, Greece, Iceland, Ireland, Italy, Liberia, Luxembourg, Netherlands, New Zealand, Nigeria, Norway, Portugal, Seychelles, Spain, Sweden, Trinidad and Tobago, United Kingdom, United States.

Absent: Antigua and Barbuda, Barbados, Comoros, Gambia, Israel, Saint Christopher and Nevis, Saint Vincent, Samoa, Senegal, Solomon Islands, Tunisia.

0062

objectives of the International Development Strategy for the Third United Nations Development Decade,[103]

1. *Insists* on the urgency of assuring the prompt establishment of the International Research and Training Institute for the Advancement of Women in the host country;

2. *Reiterates* the guidelines set out in Economic and Social Council resolution 1998 (LX) of 12 May 1976 regarding the activities of the Institute, in particular the need for close collaboration with the regional centres and institutes which have similar objectives;

3. *Underlines* the importance of the contributions of the Institute to the work of all United Nations bodies, agencies and institutions involved with the advancement of women, in particular the Centre for Social Development and Humanitarian Affairs of the Secretariat;

4. *Urges* all Governments to consider contributing financially to the United Nations Trust Fund for the International Research and Training Institute for the Advancement of Women or co-operating in other ways with the Institute in order to assure its regular and effective financing so that it can plan the expansion of its programmes;

5. *Requests* the regional commissions, the specialized agencies and other organs and bodies of the United Nations system to co-operate fully with the Institute in their respective fields of competence.

97th plenary meeting
14 December 1981

36/129. Voluntary Fund for the United Nations Decade for Women

The General Assembly,

Recalling its resolution 3520 (XXX) of 15 December 1975, by which it proclaimed the period from 1976 to 1985 United Nations Decade for Women: Equality, Development and Peace,

Recalling its decision of 15 December 1975 to extend the activities of the Voluntary Fund for the International Women's Year so as to cover the period of the Decade,

Recalling its resolution 31/133 of 16 December 1976, containing the criteria and arrangements for the management of the Fund,

Recalling its resolution 32/138 of 16 December 1977,

Recalling also its resolution 34/156 of 17 December 1979, in which it expressed the desire to see the activities developed by the Fund continued beyond the United Nations Decade for Women and decided to review at its thirty-sixth session the decision regarding the location of the Fund in New York,

Recalling further Economic and Social Council resolution 1980/3 of 16 April 1980,

Bearing in mind its resolution 35/136 of 11 December 1980, in which it endorsed the Programme of Action for the Second Half of the United Nations Decade for Women,[102]

Conscious that the Fund is intended to supplement, through financial and technical support, the activities for implementing the goals for the United Nations Decade for Women: Equality, Development and Peace,

Noting with appreciation the effective management and continuing expansion of the Fund's activities and the co-operation extended by the relevant organs of the United Nations, including the United Nations Development Programme, the United Nations Children's Fund and the regional commissions,

Reaffirming the role of the Centre for Social Development and Humanitarian Affairs of the Secretariat as the focal point for inter-agency co-operation towards the implementation of the Programme of Action,

Noting with appreciation the support given by the Fund to projects in the developing countries,

Noting also with appreciation the report of the Secretary-General on the future of the Fund,[104]

1. *Notes with satisfaction* the decisions of the Consultative Committee on the Voluntary Fund for the United Nations Decade for Women during its ninth and tenth sessions;[105]

2. *Expresses its appreciation* for the voluntary contributions pledged by Member States and urges them to contribute or increase their contributions to the Fund;

3. *Decides* that the Fund should continue its activities beyond the United Nations Decade for Women;

4. *Stresses* the importance of the contributions of the Fund towards the realization of the goals and objectives of the United Nations Decade for Women;

5. *Stresses also* the interrelationship of the Voluntary Fund with the Advancement of Women Branch of the Centre for Social Development and Humanitarian Affairs of the Secretariat;

6. *Requests* the Secretary-General to invite the views of Member States on how best the Fund can continue its activities beyond the Decade and to submit a report thereon to the General Assembly at its thirty-ninth session;

7. *Requests also* the Secretary-General, taking into account the views expressed by Member States on this matter, to submit to the General Assembly at its thirty-ninth session a report on the substantive and financial implications of, and his proposals for the timing and modalities for, a relocation of the Fund within the Centre for Social Development and Humanitarian Affairs of the Secretariat in order to enable Member States to take a decision in the matter.

97th plenary meeting
14 December 1981

36/130. Equal rights to work

The General Assembly,

Recalling its resolution 34/155 of 17 December 1979, in which it called upon Governments to take steps to ensure the effective participation of women in the decision-making process with respect to foreign policy and international economic and political co-operation, including steps to ensure that they have equal access to diplomatic functions and that they are represented in the United Nations and other international organizations,

Recalling also its resolutions 33/184 of 29 January 1979 and 34/159 of 17 December 1979, in which it recommended that States should envisage in their policies all appropriate measures to create necessary conditions which will enable women to participate in work on an equal footing with men,

Noting that in some countries legal and administrative regulations hamper the possibilities of accompanying spouses of members of diplomatic missions or consular posts and of staff members of intergovernmental organizations to work,

Concerned that women continue to be under-represented in the professional staffs of international organizations, in-

[103] Resolution 35/56, annex.

[104] A/36/647 and Corr.1.

[105] *Ibid.*, para. 13.

0063

38/106. Voluntary Fund for the United Nations Decade for Women

Date: 16 December 1983 Meeting: 100
Adopted without a vote Report: A/38/681

The General Assembly,

Recalling its resolution 31/133 of 16 December 1976, containing the criteria and arrangements for the management of the Voluntary Fund for the United Nations Decade for Women,

Recalling also its resolution 36/129 of 14 December 1981, in which it decided that the Fund should continue its activities beyond the United Nations Decade for Women: Equality, Development and Peace,

Recalling further its resolution 37/62 of 3 December 1982 and, in particular, its view that the appointment of senior women's programme officers at the regional commissions represents a valuable contribution to the implementation of the goals of the Decade,

Reaffirming that women's affairs should be approached and dealt with as an integral part of overall policies and programmes in the field of social and economic development,

0064

Noting with appreciation the effective management and continuing expansion of the Fund's activities and the co-operation extended by relevant bodies of the United Nations - including the United Nations Children's Fund, the United Nations Development Programme and the regional commissions - and non-governmental organizations,

Welcoming the contributions made by Member States and non-governmental organizations towards the implementation of the goals of the Decade,

Noting with appreciation the report of the Secretary-General on the activities of the Fund, 172/

1. *Notes with satisfaction* the recommendations of the Consultative Committee for the Voluntary Fund for the United Nations Decade for Women during its thirteenth and fourteenth sessions, 173/ referred to in the report of the Secretary-General;

2. *Expresses its concern* that the question of senior women's programme officers posts at the regional commissions is still unresolved and that lack of progress in this regard is seriously impeding the work with the women's programmes in several regions;

3. *Urges* the Secretary-General, in consultation with the executive secretaries of the regional commissions, to give priority to solving the question of senior women's programme officers and to take urgently appropriate measures to ensure that all temporary and permanent senior women's programme officers posts should be continued at the regional commissions within regular budget resources available to them;

4. *Notes with satisfaction* the continuing increase in the number of projects submitted to and financed by the resources of the Fund and their contribution to promoting the involvement of women in development;

5. *Considers* that the Fund has a unique contribution to make in the technical assistance field to the implementation of the goals of the United Nations Decade for Women: Equality, Development and Peace;

6. *Stresses* that the Fund has a unique contribution to make to the achievement of the goals of the Third United Nations Development Decade, 174/ and even beyond it;

7. *Expresses its appreciation* for the voluntary support to the Fund by Member States, national committees for the Fund, national United Nations associations and other non-governmental organizations;

8. *Notes with concern* that contributions to the Fund have not been sufficient to enable it to take up all the deserving projects submitted to it;

9. *Notes* further that contributions by Governments have a vital role to play in maintaining and increasing the financial viability and effectiveness of the work of the Fund;

10. *Urges*, accordingly, Governments to continue and increase, where possible, their contributions to the Fund and calls upon those Governments that have not yet done so to consider contributing to the Fund;

11. *Decides* that, when considering the reports of the Secretary-General to be submitted at the thirty-ninth session pursuant to General Assembly resolution 36/129, all possible options for continuing the Fund's activities beyond the end of the Decade will be reviewed in depth;

12. *Requests* that the results of the forward-looking assessment that is being undertaken on the activities assisted by the Fund be reflected in the reports of the Secretary-General on the Fund to be submitted to the General Assembly at its thirty-ninth session;

13. *Takes note with appreciation* of the measures taken by the Secretary-General in response to its resolution 37/62 to improve and streamline the administration of the Fund;

172/ A/38/530.

173/ *Ibid.*, sect. V.

174/ See General Assembly resolution 35/56, annex.

0065

14. Commends the United Nations Development Programme on its continuing technical and resource assistance to the Fund; 175/

15. Requests the Secretary-General:

(a) To continue to report annually on the management of the Fund and on the progress of its activities and to include in his report to the General Assembly at its thirty-ninth session information on implementation of the measures taken in response to operative paragraph 3 above;

(b) To continue to include the Fund, on an annual basis, as one of the programmes of the United Nations Pledging Conference for Development Activities.

0066

38/109. Elimination of all forms of discrimination against women

Date: 16 December 1983 Meeting: 100
Adopted without a vote Report: A/38/682

The General Assembly

Considering that one of the purposes of the United Nations, as stated in Articles 1 and 55 of the Charter, is to promote universal respect for human rights and fundamental freedoms without distinction of any kind, including distinction as to sex,

Affirming that women and men should, on the basis of equality, participate in and contribute to the social, economic and political processes of development and should share equally in improved conditions of life,

Recalling its resolution 34/180 of 18 December 1979, by which it adopted the Convention on the Elimination of All Forms of Discrimination against Women,

Recalling also its resolutions 35/140 of 11 December 1980, 36/131 of 14 December 1981 and 37/64 of 3 December 1982, as well as Economic and Social Council resolution 1983/1 of 17 May 1983,

Having noted the report of the Secretary-General on the status of the Convention, 186/

Having considered the report of the Committee on the Elimination of All Forms of Discrimination against Women on its first session, 187/

186/ A/38/378.

187/ Official Records of the General Assembly, Thirty-eighth Session, Supplement No. 45 (A/38/45).

0067

1. Notes with appreciation the increasing number of Member States that have ratified or acceded to the Convention on the Elimination of All Forms of Discrimination against Women;

2. Invites States that have not yet done so to become parties to the Convention by ratifying or acceding to it;

3. Takes note of the report of the Committee on the Elimination of All Forms of Discrimination against Women on its first session;

4. Welcomes the fact that the Committee on the Elimination of All Forms of Discrimination against Women has successfully started its work and, inter alia, has adopted general guidelines regarding the form and contents of reports received from States parties under article 18 of the Convention; 188/

5. Requests the Secretary-General to submit to the General Assembly at its thirty-ninth session a report on the status of the Convention.

0068

정 리 보 존 문 서 목 록					
기록물종류	일반공문서철	등록번호	2020020018	등록일자	2020-02-04
분류번호	734.21	국가코드		보존기간	영구
명 칭	유엔 인권위원회, 제47차. Geneva, 1991.1.28-3.8				
생 산 과	국제연합과	생산년도	1990~1991	담당그룹	
내용목차	* 수석대표 : 박영우 주제네바 대사대리(옵서버대표단)				

0001

'소득은 정당하게, 소비는 알뜰하게'

주 인 도 대 사 관

인도(정)20270- 846 1990.11.30

수신 : 외무부장관

참조 : 국제기구조약국장

제목 : 세네갈, 아국의 유엔협조 사의표시

당지주재 세네갈 대사 (Ahmed El Mansour Diop)는 최근 유엔인권위원회에 자국인인 Mr. Birame N 'diaye가 동 위원회 위원으로 선출되었다 하고, 동 선출과정에서 아측이 협조하여 준데 대하여 사의를 표시하면서, 동 사의를 아국정부에게 적의 전달하여 줄 것을 요망하여 왔음을 보고드립니다. 끝.

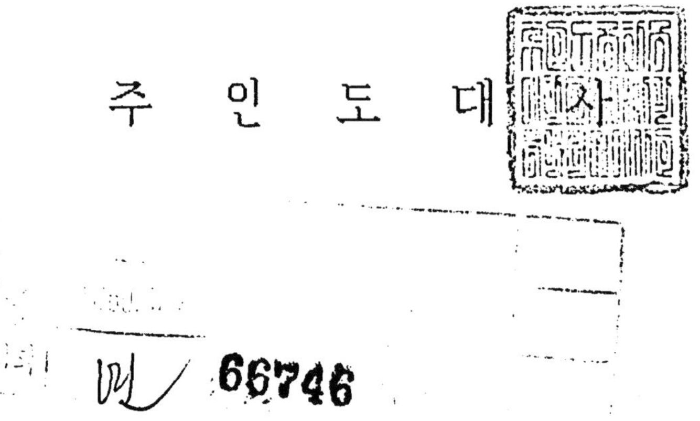

주 인 도 대 사

0002

OFFICE DES NATIONS UNIES À GENÈVE

CENTRE POUR LES DROITS DE L'HOMME

UNITED NATIONS OFFICE AT GENEVA

CENTRE FOR HUMAN RIGHTS

Téléfax: (022) 733 98 79
Télégrammes: UNATIONS, GENÈVE
Télex: 28 96 96
Téléphone: 734 60 11 731 02 11

Palais des Nations
CH-1211 GENÈVE 10

RÉF. N°: G/SO 214 (12-2)
(à rappeler dans la réponse)

The Secretary-General of the United Nations presents his compliments to the Minister for Foreign Affairs of the Republic of Korea and has the honour to draw the attention of His Excellency's Government to Commission on Human Rights resolution 1990/38 of 6 March 1990, entitled "Question of a draft body of principles and guarantees for the protection of mentally-ill persons and for the improvement of mental health care". A copy of the resolution is attached.

The Commission on Human Rights in that resolution decided to make available, prior to the forty-seventh session of the Commission, appropriate meeting time for the Working Group on the subject.

The Economic and Social Council, in its resolution 1990/37 of 25 May 1990, authorized an open-ended working group on the question to meet for a period of two weeks prior to the forty-seventh session of the Commission.

After consultations with interested delegations and participants, the Secretary-General wishes to inform you that the Working Group will hold this session from 29 October to 9 November 1990.

19 September 1990

0003

COMMISSION ON HUMAN RIG—

RESOLUTION 1990/38 OF 6 MARCH 1990

Question of a draft body of principles and guarantees for the protection of mentally-ill persons and for the improvement of mental health care

The Commission on Human Rights,

Recalling its resolution 10 A (XXXIII) of 11 March 1977, by which it requested the Sub-Commission on Prevention of Discrimination and Protection of Minorities to study the question of the protection of persons detained on the grounds of mental ill-health, with a view to formulating guidelines,

Recalling also its resolution 1989/40 of 6 March 1989,

Taking note of Economic and Social Council resolution 1989/76 of 24 May 1989, by which the Council authorized an open-ended working group of the Commission to examine, revise and simplify as necessary the draft body of principles and guarantees submitted by the Sub-Commission with a view to submitting it to the Commission at its forty-sixth session,

Noting with appreciation the comments submitted to the Secretary-General on the draft body of principles and guarantees by Governments, specialized agencies, in particular the World Health Organization, and non-governmental organizations (E/CN.4/1990/53 and Add.1-4), and their participation in the open-ended Working Group on the Question of the Draft Body of Principles and Guarantees for the Protection of Mentally-Ill Persons and for the Improvement of Mental Health Care,

Noting with satisfaction the progress made by the Working Group during its meeting prior to the forty-sixth session of the Commission,

Noting also the view of the Working Group that there is a reasonable expectation that its task could be completed within an acceptable time-scale if it were authorized to meet for a further session of two weeks before the forty-seventh session of the Commission and were then mandated to pursue its work in the same manner as before,

1. Takes note of the report of the Working Group on the Question of the Draft Body of Principles and Guarantees for the Protection of Mentally-Ill Persons and for the Improvement of Mental Health Care (E/CN.4/1990/31);

2. Decides to make available, prior to the forty-seventh session of the Commission, appropriate meeting time for the Working Group;

3. Invites the Working Group to pursue its work at that meeting in the same manner as before;

4. Recommends the following draft resolution to the Edonomic and Social Council for adoption:

0004

The Economic and Social Council,

Recalling Commission on Human Rights resolution 1990/38 of 6 March 1990,

1. Authorizes an open-ended working group of the Commission on Human Rights to meet for a period of two weeks prior to the forty-seventh session of the Commission, in order to continue the examination, revision and simplification of a draft body of principles and guarantees for the protection of mentally-ill persons and for the improvement of mental health care, for submission to the Commission at its forty-seventh session;

2. Requests the Secretary-General to extend all facilities to the Working Group on the Question of the Draft Body of Principles and Guarantees for the Protection of Mentally-Ill Persons and for the Improvement of Mental Health Care for its meeting prior to the forty-seventh session of the Commission, and to prepare and transmit to the Working Group a working paper covering the articles that remain to be discussed and taking account of the comments and suggestions made by Governments, specialized agencies and non-governmental organizations.

0005

원 본

외 무 부

종 별 :

번 호 : UNW-2700 일 시 : 90 1205 1900

수 신 : 장 관(국연)

발 신 : 주 유엔 대사

제 목 : 제45차 총회(3위)(22)

1. 제3위는 12.3-5.간 의제 12 (ECOSOC 보고서), 의제 108 (마약퇴치 국제협력), 의제 110 (정기적 공정한 선거) 관련 잔여 결의안 채택을 완료하고 제45차 총회 3위 업무를 종결함.

2.볼리비아는 12.3. 회의 초두에 G-77 을 대표하여 인권위원회 (COMMISSION ON HUMAN RIGHTS) 의 10개의석 증대가 아프리카 4석, 아시아 3석, 중남미 3석으로 구성되며 신규 위원선거가 명년 ECOSOC정기회기시 개최될 것이라고 밝힘.

3.채택된 결의안

가.유엔 인권센터 활동(L.72/REV.1)

- 추가 구두 수정안을 표결없이 채택(12.3)

나.피점령 쿠웨이트내 인권(L.90):12.3.

- 표결결과:132-1 (이락)-1(잠비아)

-요지: 쿠웨이트인 및 제3국인에 대한 이락 당국의 인권 탄압조치 규탄및 이락에 대한 국제법 준수촉구, 인권위원회 심의요청

- 동 표결에 앞서 이락대표가 제3위가 여사한 결의안을 채택할 헌장상 권한이 있는지 법적의견을 문의한바, 의장은 법률국의 의견을 토대로 권한이 있다고 답변함.

- 이락대표는 동 결의안이(1) 정치적 목적으로 이용되고 있고,(2)사실을 왜곡하고있으며, (3)안보리 심의중인 사항을 총회가 심의할수 없도록 규정한 헌장 12조를 위반하고있으며 (4) 이스라엘의 아랍영토 점령 사실로부터 관심을 전환시키려는 의도이며 ,(5) 유엔의 경제제재가 이락국민에게 가한 비인도적 처사를 외면하고 있고, (6) 현재 추진중인 대화를 통한 평화추구 노력을 저해한다고 역설함.

- 예멘은 동 결의안이 인권신장을 위한 법적조치보다는 정치적 고려에 기초하고 있다는 이유로 표결에 불참입장 표명

국기국

PAGE 1 90.12.06 10:23 WG

외신 1과 통제관

0006

다.마약퇴치 국제협력 (L.43/REV.1): 표결없이채택 (12.3.)

라.정기적 공정한 선거를 위한 유엔의 지원관련 서방측 결의안 (L.56), 쿠바수정안 (L.96) 및 미국의 재수정안 (L.99)

0. 표결결과(12.3.)

- 미국 재수정안 (L.99):82-18 (중국, 쿠바, 미얀마등)-18

- L.99 로 수정된 쿠바 수정안 (L.96):120-0-9 (중국, 인도등)

- L.99 및 L.96 으로 수정된 서방측 결의안 (L.56):106-9 (중국, 쿠바, 이란, 미얀마 등)-12

- 상기 L.56 문안전체 표결에 앞서 쿠바 요청에 따라 L.56 전문 8항 (96-11-12), 본문 10항 (85-12-15), 본문 11항(88-12-14)을 조항별 표결로 채택

0.토의경과

- 콜롬비아, 페루, 에쿠아돌, 중국, 멕시코, 쿠바, 짐바브웨등은 미국측 수정안 표결전 발언을 통해 (1) 선거제도는 각국의 주권에 속하는 국내문제로서 간섭해서 안되며 (2)유엔의 선거지원 대상이 탈식민 또는 분쟁해결의 경우에 한하며 (3) 잠정적 (AD HOC)이어야하며 (4) 해당국의 특별한 요청에 의거, 사안별로 처리되어야하며 (5)외부의 모델을 강요해서는 안되며 (6)동 결의안 통과로 선거지원이 제도화 될 경우 남용내지 나쁜선례 를 구성할것이라는 이유를 들어 반대내지 기권입장을 표명

- 이태리 (EC 대표), 폴란드, 독일, 소련, 브라질등은 동 결의안이 각국의 선거제도 선택에 관한 주권존중및 해당국의 요청에 근거하고 있는등 상기 반대 논거를 충분히 반영한 것이라는 점을 역설하였으며 파나마, 니카라과등은 자국에 대한 지원 사례를 예시하며 선거지원의 유용성을 강조함.

마.선거과정에 있어서의 국내문제 불간섭 (L.59: 쿠바등 6개국):12.4.

- 표결결과:94-32 (미, 영, EC, 일본등)- 7 (소련, 자이르등)

-이태리는 표결전 발언을 통해 동 결의안이 유엔헌장의 원칙을 원용하므로써 자유.공정선거권리를 저해할 것이므로 반대한다는 입장을, 파나마는 동 결의안이 기 채택된 L.56 과양립하지 않는다는 이유에서 반대한다는 입장을 표명

바.유엔 마약관련 부서 통합결의안 (L.44), 동수정안 (L.45: 우간다), 및 유엔 아프리카 범죄예방 연구소지원 (L.102: 스웨덴):12.4.

- 비공식 협의에서 사전 합의를 토대로 L.102 를 표결없이 채택하고 L.45 를 철회하였으며 이어 L.44 를 표결없이 채택함.

PAGE 2

0007

-내용:기존 마약관련 3개 유엔 부서를 하나로 통합 (UNIDCP: 비엔나 소재) 하고 유엔사무차장으로보함.

사.이란내 인권상황(L.93/REV.1):12.4

- 서방측 및 이란의 사전 협의에 따른 문안 타협결과를 토대로 표결없이 채택

아.국내문제 불간섭을 통한 인권분야 협력강화 (L.82 및 동 REV.1: 쿠바) 와 이에대한 서방측 수정안 (L.101) 간의 타협안으로 쿠바는 서방측안을 반영한 재수정안 (L.82/REV.2) 을 제출, 표결없이 채택되고 L.101수정안은 철회됨.

-동 결의안은 제목에서 '국내문제 불간섭'대신 '비선택성, 공정성, 객관성' 을 통한 인권분야 유엔조치 강화로 수정하고, 본문 내용을 유엔헌장, 인권선언및 인권규약, 기채택총회 결의안 문안 내용을 대폭 반영하므로써 유엔의 인권문제 관여가 국내문제 간섭이라는 인상을 대폭감소시킴.

- 미국, 이태리, 뉴질랜드등은 헌장 및 인권규약상의 의무를 모든 회원국이 준수해야한다는점과 유엔의조치가 국내문제 불간섭이 아니라는 전제하에 결의안 채택에 반대하지 않았다는 입장표명

자.제3위 업무합리화에 관한 실무그룹 보고서 (L.100) 및 동결의안 L.103 을 표결없이 채택함.

4.상기 결의안 채택후 관례에 따라 각 지역그룹 대표의 발언을 청취하고 폐회함.끝

(대사 현홍주-국장)

PAGE 3

0008

61883

기안용지

분류기호 문서번호	국연 2031 -	(전화:)	시행상 특별취급	
보존기간	영구·준영구. 10. 5. 3. 1	장	관	
수신처 보존기간				
시행일자	1990. 12.17.			

보조기관			협조기관		문서통제
	국장	전결			1990.12.18
	과장				
기안책임자		송영완			발송인 1990.12.18 외무부

경유		발신명의	
수신	법무부장관		
참조	법무실장		

제목	제47차 유엔인권위 회의

91.1.28-3.8간 제네바에서 개최될 예정인 표제회의 잠정의제를 별첨 송부하오니 동 회의 참가대책 수립등에 참고하시기 바랍니다.

첨 부 : 표제회의 잠정의제 (E/CN.4/1991/1) 1부. 끝.

0009

주 제 네 바 대 표 부

재내(정) 2031-1287 1990.12. 7

수신 : 장관

참조 : 국제기구조약국장

제목 : 제 47차 유엔인권위 회의

91.1.28-3.8간 당지에서 개최되는 표재회의 잠정의제를 별첨 송부합니다.

첨부 : 동 잠정의제 (E/CN.4/1991/1) 2부. 끝.

주 제 네 바 대 사

68030

1990.

0010

UNITED
NATIONS

Economic and Social Council

Distr.
GENERAL

E/CN.4/1991/1
5 November 1990

Original: ENGLISH

COMMISSION ON HUMAN RIGHTS
Forty-seventh session
25 January to 8 March 1991

PROVISIONAL AGENDA

Note by the Secretary-General

Duration and venue of the session

1. The forty-seventh session of the Commission on Human Rights will be held at the United Nations Office at Geneva from 28 January to 8 March 1991. The first meeting will be convened at 11 a.m. Monday, 28 January 1991.

Provisional agenda

2. The provisional agenda, prepared in accordance with rule 5 of the rules of procedure of the functional commissions of the Economic and Social Council, is reproduced below.

Pre-sessional working groups

3. The forty-seventh session of the Commission is expected to be preceded by meetings of four groups in connection with the following items:

(a) Item 12 (b): Working Group on Situations, composed of five members of the Commission, to examine situations referred to the Commission by the Sub-Commission on Prevention of Discrimination and Protection of Minorities under Economic and Social Council resolution 1503 (XLVIII) of 27 May 1970 (Commission resolution 1990/55, Council resolution 1990/41) is scheduled to meet from 21 to 25 January 1991;

(b) Item 14: an open-ended working group established to examine, revise and simplify the draft body of principles and guarantees for the protection of mentally-ill persons and for the improvement of mental health care (Commission resolution 1990/38, Economic and Social Council resolution 1990/37) is scheduled to meet from 29 October to 9 November 1990;

GE.90-13725/8296A

(c) Item 15: the group of three members of the Commission appointed under article IX of the International Convention on Suppression and Punishment of the Crime of Apartheid to consider reports submitted by States parties in accordance with article VII of that Convention (Commission resolution 1990/12, Economic and Social Council decision 1990/223) is scheduled to meet from 21 to 25 January 1991;

(d) Item 23: an open-ended working group established to draft a declaration on the right and responsibility of individuals, groups and organs of society to promote and protect universally recognized human rights and fundamental freedoms (Commission resolution 1990/47, Economic and Social Council resolution 1990/40) is scheduled to meet from 16 to 25 January 1991.

In-session working groups

4. In connection with item 11, the Commission, by decision 1990/115, and the Economic and Social Council, by decision 1990/249, requested the working group established at the forty-sixth session pursuant to paragraph 3 of General Assembly resolution 44/167 of 15 December 1989 to continue its work as a sessional working group during the forty-seventh session with a view to presenting its recommendations to the Commission.

5. In connection with item 20, the Commission, by resolution 1990/45, and the Economic and Social Council, by resolution 1990/39, decided to establish at its forty-seventh session an open-ended working group to continue consideration of the revised draft declaration on the rights of persons belonging to national, ethnic, religious and linguistic minorities.

6. Any decisions and resolutions affecting the provisional agenda of the forty-seventh session of the Commission, which may be taken by the General Assembly at its forty-fifth session or by the Economic and Social Council at its organizational session in 1991, will be brought to the attention of the Commission in an addendum to the present document. The annotations to the items listed in the provisional agenda will also be issued in an addendum.

0012

Provisional agenda

1. Election of officers.

2. Adoption of the agenda.

3. Organization of the work of the session.

4. Question of the violation of human rights in the occupied Arab territories, including Palestine.

5. Violations of human rights in southern Africa: report of the *Ad hoc* Working Group of Experts.

6. The adverse consequences for the enjoyment of human rights of political, military, economic and other forms of assistance given to the colonial and racist régime in southern Africa.

7. Question of the realization in all countries of the economic, social and cultural rights contained in the Universal Declaration of Human Rights and in the International Covenant on Economic, Social and Cultural Rights, and study of special problems which the developing countries face in their efforts to achieve these human rights, including:

   (a) Problems related to the right to enjoy an adequate standard of living; foreign debt, economic adjustment policies and their effects on the full enjoyment of human rights and, in particular, on the implementation of the Declaration on the Right to Development;

   (b) Popular participation in its various forms as an important factor in development and in the full realization of all human rights.

8. Question of the realization of the right to development.

9. The right of peoples to self-determination and its application to peoples under colonial or alien domination or foreign occupation.

10. Question of the human rights of all persons subjected to any form of detention or imprisonment, in particular:

    (a) Torture and other cruel, inhuman or degrading treatment or punishment;

    (b) Status of the Convention against Torture and Other Cruel, Inhuman or Degrading Treatment or Punishment;

    (c) Question of enforced or involuntary disappearances.

11. Further promotion and encouragement of human rights and fundamental freedoms, including the question of the programme and methods of work of the Commission:

    (a) Alternative approaches and ways and means within the United Nations system for improving the effective enjoyment of human rights and fundamental freedoms;

(b) National institutions for the promotion and protection of human rights;

(c) Co-ordinating role of the Centre for Human Rights within the United Nations bodies and machinery dealing with the promotion and protection of human rights.

12. Question of the violation of human rights and fundamental freedoms in any part of the world, with particular reference to colonial and other dependent countries and territories, including:

(a) Question of human rights in Cyprus;

(b) Study of situations which appear to reveal a consistent pattern of gross violations of human rights as provided in Commission resolution 8 (XXIII) and Economic and Social Council resolutions 1235 (XLII) and 1503 (XLVIII): report of the Working Group on Situations established by the Commission at its forty-seventh session.

13. Measures to improve the situation and ensure the human rights and dignity of all migrant workers.

14. Human rights and scientific and technological developments.

15. Implementation of the International Convention on the Suppression and Punishment of the Crime of Apartheid.

16. Implementation of the Programme of Action for the Second Decade to Combat Racism and Racial Discrimination.

17. Status of the International Covenants on Human Rights.

18. Effective functioning of bodies established pursuant to United Nations human rights instruments.

19. Report of the Sub-Commission on Prevention of Discrimination and Protection of Minorities at its forty-second session.

20. Rights of persons belonging to national, ethnic, religious and linguistic minorities.

21. Advisory services in the field of human rights.

22. Implementation of the Declaration on the Elimination of All Forms of Intolerance and of Discrimination Based on Religion or Belief.

23. Drafting of a declaration on the right and responsibility of individuals, groups and organs of society to promote and protect universally recognized human rights and fundamental freedoms.

24. Status of the Convention on the Rights of the Child.

25. Draft provisional agenda for the forty-eighth session of the Commission.

26. Report to the Economic and Social Council on the forty-seventh session of the Commission.

0014

OFFICE DES NATIONS UNIES A GENÈVE

CENTRE POUR LES DROITS DE L'HOMME

UNITED NATIONS OFFICE AT GENEVA

CENTRE FOR HUMAN RIGHTS

Téléfax: (022) 733 98 79
Télégrammes: UNATIONS, GENÈVE
Télex: 28 96 96
Téléphone: 734 60 11 731 02 11

G/SO 214 (25-2)

RÉF. Nº:
(à rappeler dans la réponse)

Palais des Nations
CH-1211 GENÈVE 10

The Secretary-General of the United Nations presents his compliments to the Minister for Foreign Affairs of the Republic of Korea and has the honour to refer to Commission on Human Rights resolution 1990/14 of 23 February 1990 entitled "Popular participation in its various forms as an important factor in development and in the full realization of all human rights". A copy of the resolution is attached.

In operative paragraph 2 of that resolution, the Commission requested the Secretary-General, in preparing a study regarding the question of the extent to which the right to participation has been established and has evolved at the national level, to be submitted to the Commission on Human Rights at its forty-seventh session, to use once again all channels at his disposal to collect the relevant information and substantive views and comments on the study on popular participation contained in document E/CN.4/1990/8 and attached to this note.

The Secretary-General would be most grateful if the views and comments which His Excellency's Government may wish to submit for the preparation of that study could be forwarded to the Centre for Human Rights, United Nations Office at Geneva, CH-1211 Geneva 10, if possible by 18 January 1991.

4 December 1990

0015

1990/14. Popular participation in its various forms as an important factor in development and in the full realization of all human rights

The Commission on Human Rights,

Recalling the resolutions and decisions of the General Assembly and the Economic and Social Council relating to the question of popular participation in its various forms as an important factor in development and in the full realization of all human rights,

Recalling also its resolutions on popular participation, including resolution 1989/14 of 2 March 1989 by which it requested the Secretary-General to submit a report containing comments on the study on popular participation in its various forms as an important factor in development and in the full realization of all human rights (E/CN.4/1985/10 and Add.1 and 2) made by Governments, United Nations organs, specialized agencies and non-governmental organizations for consideration at its forty-sixth session,

1. Takes note with appreciation of the report of the Secretary-General (E/CN.4/1990/8) containing, inter alia, information on the substantive replies received so far;

2. Requests the Secretary-General, in preparing a study regarding the question of the extent to which the right to participation has been established and has evolved at the national level, to be submitted to the Commission on Human Rights at its forty-seventh session, to use once again all channels at his disposal to collect the relevant information and substantive views and comments on the study on popular participation;

3. Decides to consider the question of popular participation at its forty-seventh session under the agenda sub-item "Popular participation in its various forms as an important factor in development and in the full realization of all human rights".

38th meeting
23 February 1990

RES/HR/90/31
GE.90-18543

0016

UNITED
NATIONS

Economic and Social Council

Distr.
GENERAL

E/CN.4/1990/8
10 November 1989

ENGLISH
Original: ENGLISH

COMMISSION ON HUMAN RIGHTS
Forty-sixth session
Item 8 (c) of the provisional agenda

QUESTION OF THE REALIZATION IN ALL COUNTRIES OF THE ECONOMIC, SOCIAL AND CULTURAL RIGHTS CONTAINED IN THE UNIVERSAL DECLARATION OF HUMAN RIGHTS AND THE INTERNATIONAL COVENANT ON ECONOMIC, SOCIAL AND CULTURAL RIGHTS, AND STUDY OF SPECIAL PROBLEMS WHICH THE DEVELOPING COUNTRIES FACE IN THEIR EFFORTS TO ACHIEVE THESE HUMAN RIGHTS

POPULAR PARTICIPATION IN ITS VARIOUS FORMS AS AN IMPORTANT FACTOR IN DEVELOPMENT AND IN THE FULL REALIZATION OF ALL HUMAN RIGHTS

Report of the Secretary-General

1. By paragraphs 2 and 3 of its resolution 1989/14 of 2 March 1989, the Commission on Human Rights requested the Secretary-General to submit a report containing comments on the study on popular participation in its various forms as an important factor in development and in the full realization of all human rights (E/CN.4/1985/10 and Add.1 and 2) made by Governments, United Nations organs, specialized agencies and non-governmental organizations which had not yet commented thereon, for consideration by the Commission at its forty-sixth session.

2. In addition, in paragraph 5 of the above-mentioned resolution, the Commission requested the Secretary-General to use all channels at his disposal to collect the relevant information and to prepare on this basis a study regarding the question of the extent to which the right to participation has been established and has evolved at the national level, and to submit that study to the Commission at its forty-seventh session.

GE.89-13810/2105a

0017

3. Accordingly, in a note verbale of 23 June 1989, the Secretary-General invited Governments which had not yet done so to make comments on the above-mentioned study, if possible by 8 September 1989. Similarly, the Under-Secretary-General for Human Rights, by a letter of the same date, invited United Nations organs, specialized agencies and non-governmental organizations in consultative status to do the same for submission to the Commission on Human Rights at its forty-sixth session. It may be noted that similar requests were made by the Secretary-General in 1985, 1986, 1987 and 1988, pursuant to resolutions of the Commissiom on Human Rights. The replies received are contained in documents E/CN.4/1986/11 and Add.1, E/CN.4/1987/11, E/CN.4/1988/11 and Add.1, and E/CN.4/1989/11.

4. Pursuant to paragraph 5 of resolution 1989/14, and with a view to the report to be submitted to the forty-seventh session of the Commission on Human Rights in 1991, the Secretary-General invited Governments, in a note verbale of 30 June 1989, to forward any information they may wish to submit on the extent to which the right to participation has been established and has evolved at national level. By a letter of the same date, the Under-Secretary-General for Human Rights also invited United Nations organs, specialized agencies and non-governmental organizations in consultative status to forward similar information.

5. At 1 November 1989, two substantive replies had been received containing comments on the study on popular participation in its various forms as an important factor in development and in the full realization of all human rights (E/CN.4/1985/10 and Add.1 and 2) pursuant to paragraphs 2 and 3 of Commission resolution 1989/14. The United Nations Economic and Social Commission for Asia and the Pacific, in a communication dated 31 July 1989 stated that the relevance of document E/CN.4/1985/10 and Add.1 and 2 to ESCAP activities regarding a regional social development strategy and a regional survey of the quality of life was noted. ESCAP will keep the document in mind in its further work on these topics. The International Sociological Association (ISA), in a letter dated 27 July 1989, indicated that the aforementioned study was presented to the ISA Executive Committee at its recent annual meeting and that the Executive Committee offered its full support for the study and its conclusions. These comments should be read together with those contained in the above-mentioned prior reports.

6. In addition, replies have been received relating to paragraph 5 of Commission resolution 1989/14 which will be taken into consideration in preparing the report for the Commission's forty-seventh session. These replies came from: Canada, Dominican Republic, United Nations Economic Commission for Latin America and the Caribbean, United Nations Economic and Social Commission for Western Asia, Baptist Theological Seminary, International Institute of Higher Studies in Criminal Sciences, International Planned Parenthood Federation, Survival International, The World Education Fellowship, Trickle Up Program, Inc., World Futures Studies Federation. They are available for consultation at the Secretariat.

0018

UNITED
NATIONS

Economic and Social Council

Distr.
LIMITED

E/1990/L.26
23 May 1990

ORIGINAL: ENGLISH

First regular session of 1990
Agenda item 3

HUMAN RIGHTS QUESTIONS

Bolivia*+: draft resolution

Enlargement of the Commission on Human Rights and the further promotion of human rights and fundamental freedoms

The Economic and Social Council,

Recalling General Assembly resolution 44/167 of 15 December 1989,

Recognizing the responsibilities of the Commission on Human Rights under the Charter of the United Nations,

Appreciating the contribution made by the Commission on Human Rights to the cause of human rights and recognizing the need to reinforce it,

Reaffirming that the Commission on Human Rights shall be guided by the standards in the field of human rights laid down in the various international instruments concerned with the protection and the promotion of human rights,

Aware of the fact that the promotion, protection and full realization of all human rights and fundamental freedoms, as legitimate concerns of the world community should be guided by the principles of non-selectivity, impartiality and objectivity, and should not be used for political ends,

---

* In accordance with rule 72 of the rules of procedure of the Economic and Social Council.

\+ On behalf of the Member States of the United Nations that are members of the Group of 77.

90-13139 2324Z (E) /...

0013

Emphasizing the importance of further improving the effective functioning of the Commission in the field of of human rights,

Convinced that in order to achieve universally recognized objectives, improvements in the functioning of the Commission and measures of rationalization should be a matter for continuous consideration,

Taking note of the relevant section of the final document of the Ninth Conference of Heads of State or Government of Non-Aligned Countries adopted at Belgrade on 7 September 1989 stating the need to strengthen the role and efficiency of the United Nations and to reinforce United Nations mechanisms,

Stressing that the Special Rapporteurs and working groups established by the Commission on Human Rights are some of the key elements in analysing, reporting and monitoring human rights, which are essential for the promotion and protection of human rights and fundamental freedoms in all countries,

Noting decision 1990/115 of 9 March 1990 of the Commission on Human Rights,

1. *Decides* that the membership of the Commission on Human Rights shall be increased to fifty-three and that the ten additional seats should be allocated among the regional groups of Africa, Asia and Latin America and the Caribbean on the basis of the principle of equitable geographical distribution;

2. *Further decides* that the enlarged membership of the Commission on Human Rights shall be elected in 1991 and that the provisions contained in paragraphs 3, 4 and 5 below shall take effect at the forty-eighth session of the Commission;

3. *Authorizes* the Commission on Human Rights to meet exceptionally between its regular sessions, provided a majority of State members of the Commission so agrees;

4. *Recommends* that the mandates of the Thematic Rapporteurs and working groups established or to be established by the Commission shall, unless otherwise decided, be of three years' duration, requests the Secretary-General to provide the Rapporteurs and working groups with all necessary assistance to carry out their mandates in the best possible conditions, and calls on all Governments to co-operate fully with them and to support and promote their activities by ensuring unhampered access to all relevant sources of information;

5. *Decides* that, in the week following the session of the Commission on Human Rights, the Bureau shall meet to make suggestions as to the organization of work of the Commission, including the effective use of conference time and facilities;

6. *Requests* the Secretary-General to prepare a report on the organizational implications of the present resolution for consideration by the Commission on Human Rights at its forty-seventh session and subsequent submission of the Commission's observations to the first regular session of the Economic and Social Council in 1991.

0020

관리 번호	91 -36

	분류번호	보존기간

발 신 전 보

번 호 : WGV-0050 910110 1603 DP 종별 :

수 신 : 주 제네바 대사 . 총영사

발 신 : 장 관 (국연)

제 목 : 제 47차 유엔인권위

표제회의 관련, 대책수립에 참고코자 하니 하기관련 보고바람.

1. 아국대표단 구성에 관한 귀견
2. 아국관련사항 토의 예상시기
3. 아국 인권관련문제 거론 예상사안
4. 기타 참고사항. 끝.

(국제기구조약국장 문동석)

1991. 6. 30. 에 예고문에 의거 인반문서로 재분류됨

앙 고 재	91 년 1 월 10 일	UN 과	기안자		과 장		국 장		차 관	장 관
			송영완				전결			

보안통제	외신과통제

0021

제 47차 유엔인권위

91. 1. 14.
국제연합과

1. 개최시기 : 91.1.28-3.8. (6주간)

2. 아국 인권문제거론 가능의제

   ○ 의제 10항 (피구금자 인권문제) : 임수경 등 불법방북과 관련한 범법자 처리경과 및 고문사건등 거론 가능
   ○ 의제 12항 (각국의 인권위반사례) : 보안법 개폐문제, 전노협, 전교조 문제등 거론가능

3. 제 46차 유엔인권위 아국 인권문제거론 사례

   ○ 90.2.16. 북한대표는 의제 10(피구금자 인권문제)관련, 임수경등 관련하여 아국인권 탄압 비난
   ○ 2.20-28간 World Council of Churches등 일부 NGO가 타국과 더불어 아국의 인권상황을 거론함.
   ○ 한편 2.28. 미대표의 북한인권 비난발언에 대한 북측의 답변권 행사중 아국의 인권상황 비난 발언

4. 금차 인권위에서의 아국 인권문제 토의 전망

   ○ 예년과 같이 의제 10.12.하에서 아국 인권문제가 거론될 가능성 큼. 동 의제는 2월중순-3월초에 다루어질 것임. (회의일정은 1월말 확정됨)

0022

관리번호 91-51

원 본

외 무 부

종 별 :

번 호 : GVW-0077 일 시 : 91 0114 1900

수 신 : 장관(국연)

발 신 : 주 제네바 대사대리

제 목 : 제 47차 유엔인권위

대:WGV-0050

대호, 표제회의 관련 사항을 아래 보고함.

1. 옵서버 대표단 구성

- 예년의 예에 따라 본직, 이량참사관, 김종훈서기관 및 본부 담당관과, 가능하면 법무부 관계관으로 구성하는 것이 좋은 것으로 사료됨.

2. 아국 관련사항 토의 예상시기

- 금차 회의 의제중 아국관련 사항이 거론될 수 있는 의제는 의제 10 항(고문등 피구금자 인권) 및 의제 12 항(세계인권상황)으로 의제별 토의 일정은 회의개회직후 확정 예정임. 제 46 차 인권위 경우 의제 10 항은 제 3 주 중반부터 3일간, 의제 12 항은 제 4 주 부터 6 일간 토의한바 있음.

3. 아국관련 거론 예상 사안

가. 임수경 사건등 불법 방북사건, 베를린 3 자회담 대표 구속등 남북한 접촉과 관련된 사건

나. 국가 보안법 개정문제

다. 간첩죄등으로 복역중인 장기복역수 문제

라. 전노협 및 교원 노조활동등 노동문제 관련 구속사건.끝.

(대사대리 박영우-국장)

예고:91.6.30 까지

1991.6.30. 에 예고문에 의거 일반문서로 재분류됨

국기국 차관 1차보 2차보 안기부

PAGE 1

91.01.15 08:48

외신 2과 통제관 BW

0023

관리 번호	91 -74

기 안 용 지

분류기호 문서번호	국연 2031-112	(전화 :)	시 행 상 특별취급	
보존기간	영구·준영구. 10. 5. 3. 1.	장 관		
수 신 처 보존기간				
시행일자	1991. 1. 15.			
보조기관 국 장	전 결	협조기관		문 서 통 제
과 장				검열 1991. 1. 16 통 제 관
기안책임자	송영완			발 송 인
경 유 수 신 참 조	법무부장관 법무실장	발신명의		1991. 1. 16 외무부
제 목	제 47차 인권위원회			

연 : 국연 2031-61863 (90.12.17)

1. 1991.1.28-3.8.간 스위스 제네바에서 개최 예정인 제47차 유엔인권위원회(Commission on Human Rights)회의에 당부는 정부 옵서버 대표단을 구성, 파견할 예정입니다.

2. 금차 인권위원회에서는 연호로 송부한 잠정의제 10항 (피구금자의 인권문제) 및 의제 12항(세계인권 위반사례) 토의시 아국 인권문제가 거론될 가능성이 있으며 주제네바대사는 금번 회의에서

/ 계속 /

0024

1505-25(2-1) 일(1)갑
85. 9. 9. 승인 "내가아낀 종이 한장 늘어나는 나라살림"

190㎜×268㎜ 인쇄용지 2급 60g/㎡
가 40-41 1990. 5. 28

아국 인권상황 설명등을 위하여 귀부직원 참석이 바람직 할 것으로

건의하여 왔는 바, 귀부 인권업무담당 직원의 참석이 가능할시 동

직원 성명을 당부로 조속 통보하여 주시기 바랍니다.

3. 한편, 금번 유엔인권위원회에서는 최근 A.I.등 국제민간

인권단체가 90년중 아국인권상황 악화를 우려하는 내용의 인권보고서를

발간함에 따라, 아국관련 문제들이 거론될 가능성이 어느때 보다 높아

동 회의에 앞서 충분한 사전 준비가 필요할 것으로 사료되는 바, 하기

사항에 대한 귀부의견을 가능한 한 상세하고 포괄적으로 작성, 91.1.25.

까지 회보하여 주시기 바랍니다.

- 아 래 -

가. 아국의 전반적 인권상황 관련 정부입장

나. 문익환, 임수경, 서경원 불법 방북사건의 사법처리 경과

및 정부입장

다. 베를린 3자회담 대표 구속등의 사법처리 경과 및 정부입장

라. 국가보안법등 개폐에 관한 금후 처리 전망 및 방침

마. 전노협 및 교원노조 활동에 관한 정부입장

/ 계속 /

0025

1505-25(2-2) 일(1)을 85. 9. 9. 승인 "내가아낀 종이 한장 늘어나는 나라살림" 190mm×268mm 인쇄용지 2급 60g/m² 가 40-41 1990. 5. 28

바. 간첩죄등으로 복역중인 장기복역수 문제

사. 고문방지등 피구금자 인권보호를 위한 조치

아. 기타 참고자료. 끝.

검 토 필(1991. 6. 30.)

일반문서로 재분류 (1991.12. 31.)

0026

1505-25(2-2) 일(1)을 85. 9. 9. 승인 "내가아낀 종이 한장 늘어나는 나라살림" 190㎜×268㎜ 인쇄용지 2급 60g/㎡ 가 40-41 1990. 5. 28

관리번호	91-77

기 안 용 지

분류기호 문서번호	국연 2031 - 152	(전화:)	시 행 상 특별취급	
보존기간	영구·준영구. 10. 5. 3. 1	장	관	
수 신 처 보존기간				
시행일자	1991. 1. 21.			

보조기관	국 장	전 결	협조기관		문서통제
	과 장				1991. 1. 22
기안책임자		송영완			발 송 인

경 유 수 신 참 조	국가안전기획부장	발신명의		발송 1991. 1. 22 외무부
제 목	제 47차 인권위원회			

1. 당부는 1991. 1.28-3.8간 스위스 제네바에서 개최예정인 제 47차 유엔인권위원회(Commission on Human Rights)회의시 우방국대표 또는 민간인권단체등에 의한 북한의 인권문제 거론 방안을 검토중입니다.

2. 금차 인권위원회에서는 별첨 잠정의제 10항(피구금자의 인권문제) 및 의제 12항(세계 인권 위반사례) 토의시 북한의 인권문제를 거론할 수 있을 것인 바, 북한의

0027 //계속...

(2)

인권침해 거론문제에 관한 귀부의견 및 하기 자료를 91.1.31.한 당부로 송부하여 주시기 바랍니다.

- 아 래 -

가. 북한 형법상 인권침해의 소지가 있어 거론함이 바람직한 조항 및 동 설명자료

나. 북한의 인권침해사례 (구체적인 자료)

다. 기타 참고자료. 끝.

첨부: 1. 인권위원회 개요 1부.

2. 제47차 인권위원회 잠정의제 1부. 끝.

일반문서로 재분류 (1991.12.31.

검 토 필(1991.6.30.)

0028

관리번호 91-76

기 안 용 지

분류기호 문서번호	국연 2031 - 151	(전화:)	시 행 상 특별취급	
보존기간	영구 · 준영구. 10. 5. 3. 1	장		관
수 신 처 보존기간				
시행일자	1991. 1. 21.			

보조기관	국 장	전 결	협조기관		문서통제
	과 장				검열 1991. 1. 22 통제관
기안책임자		송영완			발 송 인

경 유		발신명의	발송 1991. 1. 22 외무부
수 신	법무부장관		
참 조	법무실장		
제 목	제 47차 인권위원회		

연 : 국연 2031-112 (91.1.15)

1. 연호, 당부는 제 47차 유엔인권위원회(91.1.28-3.8)에서 우방국대표 또는 민간인권단체등에 의한 북한의 인권문제 거론 방안을 검토중인 바, 동 거론대상사안으로서 자의적이고 포괄적인 인권제한을 규정하고 있는 북한 형법의 제문제점을 지적할 것을 고려하고 있습니다.

0029 //계속...

(2)

2. 상기 인권위원회시 북한 형법의 제문제점 거론에 대한 귀부의견 및 북한 형법상 인권침해의 소지가 있어 지적할 필요가 있는 조항에 대한 설명자료를 91.1.31.한 당부로 송부하여 주시기 바랍니다.

3. 당부는 인권관련 국제회의시 북한 형법과 더불어 북한의 구체적 인권유린사례도 거론할 것을 검토중인 바, 동 자료는 국가안전기획부에 요청중임을 참고하시기 바라며 북한인권문제 거론과 관련한 의견이 있을시 당부로 회보하여 주시기 바랍니다. 끝.

일반문서로 재분류 (1991.12.31.)

검 토 필(1991. 6.30.)

0030

관리번호	91-80

	분류번호	보존기간

발 신 전 보

번 호 : WGV-0105 910121 1929 DA 종별 :

수 신 : 주 제네바 대사 . 총영사 대리

발 신 : 장 관 (국연)

제 목 : 제 47차 인권위원회

대 : GVW-0016

1. 본부는 표제회의시 북한 인권상황 거론 가능성을 검토하기 위하여 관계 부처에 북한의 구체적 인권침해 사례 및 북한 형법의 인권적 차원에서의 문제점을 통보해 줄 것을 요청중임.

2. 본부는 유엔인권위등 인권관련 국제회의에서 북한인권문제를 지속적으로 제기하는 것이 북한의 개방을 유도하는 데에도 기여할 것으로 보고있음. 그러나 남북한 관계의 현실에 비추어 현단계에서는 가급적 우방국 대표 또는 NGO에 의해 거론되도록 유도함이 바람직하며 부득이 아측이 직접 제기하는 경우, 적절한 의제하에 구체적 인권침해 사례를 지적, 제 3자에게 매우 적절한 인권 문제 제기라는 인식을 갖도록 자연스럽게 단계적으로 이를 추진해 나가는 것이 좋을 것으로 봄. 이러한 견지에서 금번 인권위대책 관련, 대호 귀관 검토 의견에 추가하여 건의할 사항이 있으면 지급 보고바람. 끝.

일반문서로 재분류 (1991.12.31.)

(국제기구조약국장 문동석)

검 토 필(1991. 6. 30.)

앙고재	91년 1월 21일	과	기안자	과 장	국 장	차 관	장 관
			(서명)	(서명)	(서명)		(서명)

보안통제	외신과통제
(서명)	

0031

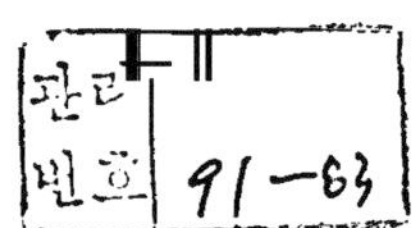

기 안 용 지

분류기호 문서번호	국연 2031- 156	(전화 :)	시 행 상 특별취급	
보존기간	영구·준영구. 10. 5. 3. 1.	장 관		
수 신 처 보존기간				
시행일자	1991. 1. 22.			
보조기관 국 장	전 결	협조기관		문 서 통 제
과 장				1991. 1. 23
기안책임자	송영완			발 송 인
경 유 수 신 참 조	통일원장관	발신명의		1991. 1. 23
제 목	제 47차 인권위원회			

대 : 이고 02201-4487 (90.12.19)

1. 당부는 91.1.28-3.8간 스위스 제네바에서 개최 예정인 제 47차 유엔인권위원회(Commission on Human Rights) 회의시 우방국 대표 또는 민간인권단체등에 의한 북한의 인권상황 거론 방안을 검토 중인 바, 동 거론대상 사안으로서 자의적이고 포괄적인 인권제한을 규정하고 있는 북한 형법의 제문제점 및 북한의 구체적 인권침해 사례 제기를 고려하고 있습니다. 동 회의 대책수립에 참고코자 하오니

/ 계속 /

0032

1505-25(2-1) 일(1)갑 190㎜×268㎜ 인쇄용지 2급 60g/㎡
85. 9. 9. 승인 "내가아낀 종이 한장 늘어나는 나라살림" 가 40-41 1990. 5. 28

인권위원회에서의 북한인권문제 거론과 관련한 의견이 있으실시 1.31.한

당부로 송부하여 주시기 바랍니다.

2. 또한, 표제회의에서 북측이 우리의 인권상황에 대해 비난

발언을 할 가능성도 매우 높은 바, 이에 대비코자 하니 90.1.1-12.31.

(1년)간 신청자에 대한 허가비율 및 불허자에 대한 불허사유를 함께

송부하여 주시기 바랍니다.

첨 부 : 인권위원회 개요 1부. 끝.

일반문서로 재분류 (1991.12.31.)

검토필 (1991.6.30.)

0033

1505-25(2-2) 일(1)을
85. 9. 9. 승인
"내가아낀 종이 한장 늘어나는 나라살림"
190mm×268mm 인쇄용지 2급 60g/m²
가 40-41 1990. 5. 28

관리번호 91-86

원 본

외 무 부

종 별 :

번 호 : GVW-0129 일 시 : 91 0122 1630

수 신 : 장관(국연)

발 신 : 주 제네바 대사대리

제 목 : 제 47차 유엔인권위

대:WGV-0105

연:GVW-0016

대호 금차 유엔인권위 대책 수립관련, 연호 당관 검토사항 이외에 아래 사항을 참고 바람.

1. 북한 인권문제 거론에 따른 아국인권 상황제기

0 북한 인권문제가 거론될 경우, 북한은 아국 인권상황 특히 불법방북 및 접촉 사건을 제기할 가능성이 많음. 현재 불법 방북인사 문제에 대해서는 91.12.13. 구주의회 결의와 같이 아국 정부 입장을 비판적으로 보는 시각이 일부국가 정부 및 의회 차원에서 뿐만 아니라 일부 NGO 에도 상존하고 있음.

따라서 인권위시 불법 방북 문제를 위요한 남. 북한 대결 상황을 가능한한 피하고 북한 인권부재 상황을 부각시키기 위해서는, 동 문제에 대한 제 3 자의 이해 제고를 위한 설명자료 준비가 필요함.

2. 금차 인권위 전망

0 금차 인권위에서는 걸프전쟁에 따라 이라크의 국내 및 쿠웨이트 침공에 따른 인권 위반문제가 크게 대두될 것이며, 예년과 같이 팔레스타인, 쿠바, 중국,미얀마, 라이베리아, 중남미, 최근 소련 및 동구 문제등이 부각될 것으로 예상됨.

3. 정책 및 고려사항

0 북한인권문제를 제기하기로 결정한 경우에는 사전에 주요우방국 및 NGO 소재 아국 공관을 통해 관련 자료 수교 및 발언 교섭을 행하는 것이 필수적임.끝.

(대사대리 박영우-국장)

예고:91.6.30 까지

1991.6.30 에 예고문에 의거 일반문서로 재분류됨

국기국 장관 차관 1차보 2차보 청와대 안기부

PAGE 1

91.01.23 08:28

외신 2과 통제관 BW

0034

관리 번호 91-152

외 무 부

종 별 :

번 호 : GVW-0156　　　　일 시 : 91 0124 1830

수 신 : 장관(국연)

발 신 : 주 제네바 대사대리

제 목 : 제 47차 유엔인권위 전망

금 1.23. 및 24 일 당관 이량참사관은 유엔인권사무국의 MOLLER 진정서 담당관 및 PACE 표제 회의 담당관을 각각 오찬에 초청, 표제회의 전망등에 대해 협의한바 동 담당관들의 주요 언급내용 아래 보고함.(김종훈서기관 동석)

1. 금차 회 의 전망

- 금차 회의 최대 관심사안은 걸프사태 특히 피점령 쿠웨이트내 인권상황이 될것이며, 쿠웨이트측은 회의 개회직후 동 문제를 별도의 소의제하에서 다루기 위하여 의제 추가를 제의할 가능성이 있음.

- 최근 소련문제도 대두될 것이나, 크게 이슈화 되기는 어려울 것으로 보이며, 쿠바 문제도 걸프사태에 따라 예년에 비해 비교적 조용히 토의될 것으로 전망됨.

- 금차회의 의장단 구성은 아래와 같음.

0 의장: 페루

0 부의장: 가나, 독일, 우쿠라이나

0 라포터: 일본

2. 유엔인권회의에서 북한 인권문제 거론 가능성

- 유엔인권 회의에서 북한 인권문제가 거의 거론되지 않는 것은 기본적으로 각국 정부 및 NGO 가 북한에 대하여 정치적으로 관심을 가지고 있지 않기 때문이며, 또한 현실적으로 북한 인권상황에 대한 구체적 자료를 구하기 어렵기 때문임.

국기국 1차보 안기부

PAGE 1　　　　91.01.25 06:02

외신 2과 통제관 DO

0035

3. 기타

- 1503 절차에 따라 진정서 실무위에서 이미 기각된 사건에 대해 다시 진정서가 제출될 경우에도 업무절차상 인권사무국은 관계국에 동 진정서를 송부하고 있으며, 이경우에 당사국은 관련자료를 이미 제출한 바있다는 내용의 답신 공한을 사무국에 제출하면 될것임.끝.

(대사대리 박영우-국장)

예고:91.12.31. 일반

검토필(1991.6.30.)

19 91.12.31. 에 예고문에 의거 일반문서로 재분류됨

PAGE 2

0036

주 제 네 바 대 표 부

제내(정) 2031-103　　　　　　　　　　　　　　　　1991. 1.25

수신 : 장관

참조 : 국제기구조약국장

제목 : 제 47차 유엔인권위 잠정의제 주석 자료 송부

91. 1.28-3.8간 당지에서 개최되는 제 47차 유엔인권위 잠정의제 주석 자료를 별첨 송부합니다.

첨부 : 동 자료(E/CN.4/1991/1/Add. 1) 1부.　끝.

주 제 네 바 대 사

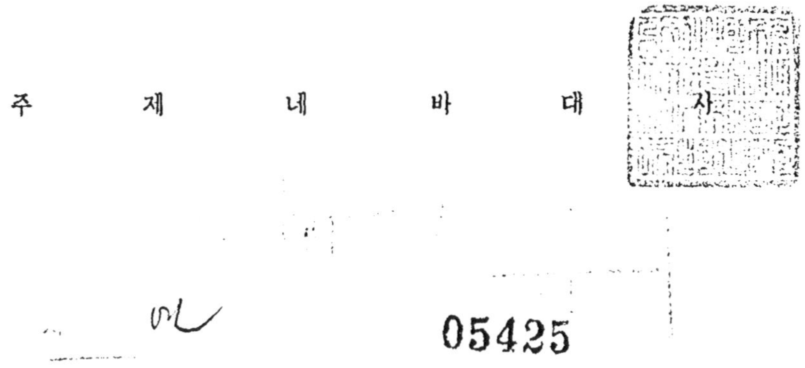

05425

0037

관리 번호	91 -155

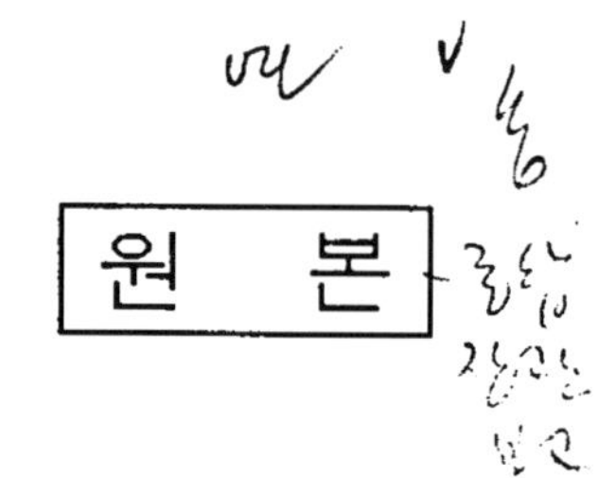

원 본

외 무 부

종 별 :

번 호 : GVW-0156 일 시 : 91 0124 1830

수 신 : 장관(국연)

발 신 : 주 제네바 대사대리

제 목 : 제 47차 유엔인권위 전망

금 1.23. 및 24 일 당관 이량참사관은 유엔인권사무국의 MOLLER 진정서 담당관 및 PACE 표제 회의 담당관을 각각 오찬에 초청, 표제회의 전망등에 대해 협의한바 동 담당관들의 주요 언급내용 아래 보고함.(김종훈서기관 동석)

1. 금차 회 의 전망

- 금차 회의 최대 관심사안은 걸프사태 특히 피점령 쿠웨이트내 인권상황이 될것이며, 쿠웨이트측은 회의 개회직후 동 문제를 별도의 소의제하에서 다루기 위하여 의제 추가를 제의할 가능성이 있음.

- 최근 소련문제도 대두될 것이나, 크게 이슈화 되기는 어려울 것으로 보이며, 쿠바 문제도 걸프사태에 따라 예년에 비해 비교적 조용히 토의될 것으로 전망됨.

- 금차회의 의장단 구성은 아래와 같음.

0 의장: 페루

0 부의장: 가나, 독일, 우쿠라이나

0 라포터: 일본

2. 유엔인권회의에서 북한 인권문제 거론 가능성

- 유엔인권 회의에서 북한 인권문제가 거의 거론되지 않는 것은 기본적으로 각국 정부 및 NGO 가 북한에 대하여 정치적으로 관심을 가지고 있지 않기 때문이며, 또한 현실적으로 북한 인권상황에 대한 구체적 자료를 구하기 어렵기 때문임.

국기국 1차보 안기부

PAGE 1

91.01.25 06:02

외신 2과 통제관 DO

0038

3. 기타

- 1503 절차에 따라 진정서 실무위에서 이미 기각된 사건에 대해 다시 진정서가 제출될 경우에도 업무절차상 인권사무국은 관계국에 동 진정서를 송부하고 있으며, 이경우에 당사국은 관련자료를 이미 제출한 바있다는 내용의 답신 공한을 사무국에 제출하면 될것임.끝.

(대사대리 박영우-국장)

예고:91.12.31. 일반

검 토 필(1991. 6. 30.)

일반문서로재분류(1991 .12 .31.)

PAGE 2

0039

법 무 부

인권 2031-22 503-7045 1991. 1. 26.

수신 외무부장관

제목 제47차 유엔 인권위원회

1. 국연 2031-112 ('91.1.15)와 관련입니다.

2. 당부에서는 제47차 유엔 인권위원회에 참가할 대상자로 당부소속 검사 권영석 (Kwon Young-Suk)을 추천합니다.

끝.

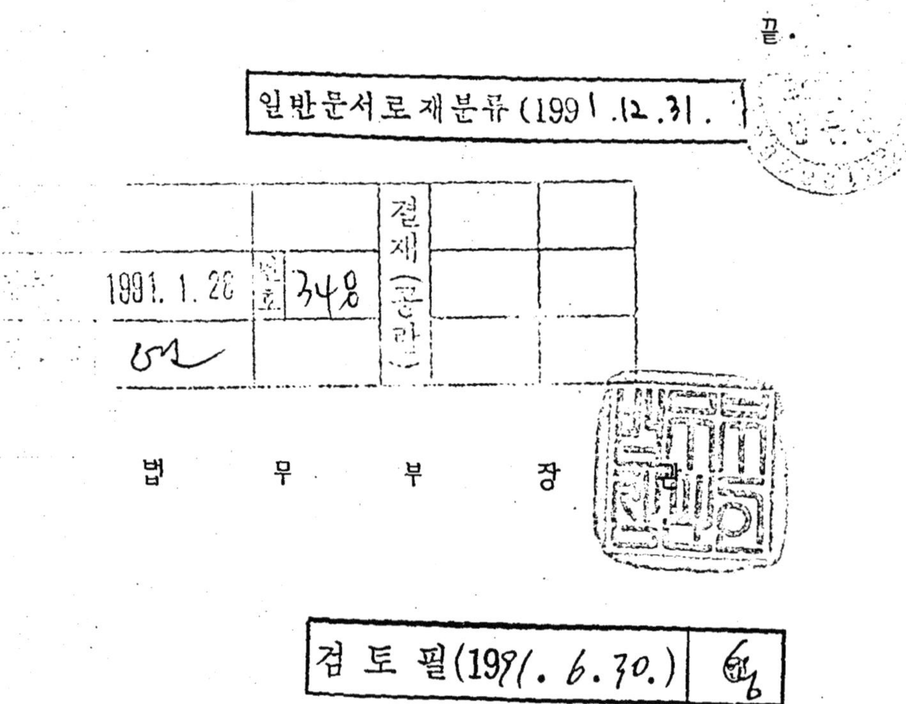
일반문서로 재분류 (1991.12.31.)

1991. 1. 28 번호 348 결재 (공람)

법 무 부 장

검 토 필(1991. 6. 30.)

0040

(첨부 6)

'90년도 남북교류신청자 허가비율 및 불허사유

(통일원 작성)

구분 목적	신 청	처리결과		승인비율 (%)	불 허 사 유
		승 인	불 허		
북한방문	199명	187명	12명	94	국민적 합의에 기초하지 않은 대북 통일협상
남한방문	306명	306명	.	100	
접 촉	235건	206건	29건	88	해당분야의 전문성 미비, 실현가능성 희박, 북한의 대남선전 이용가능성

0041

원 본

암호수신

외 무 부

종 별 :

번 호 : GVW-0182 일 시 : 91 0128 1730

수 신 : 장관(국연,법무부,기정)

발 신 : 주 제네바 대사대리

제 목 : 제 47차 유엔 인권위 회의(1)

1. 표제회의가 금 1.28 오전 당지 PALAIS DES NATIONS 에서 QUISUMBING 제 46 차 회의 의장의 사회로 개최되어, 동 의장의 개회사, MARTENSON 유엔 인권 담당 사무차장의 연설에 이어 의장단 선출 및 의제 채택이 있었음.

2. 금일 선출된 의장단은 아래와 같음.

의장: BERNALES BALLESTEROS 페루 상원부의장(유엔 인권위 용병문제 특별 보고관)

부의장: MARTIUS 주 제네바 독일 대표부 공사

VASSILENKO 우크라이나 키에프 대학 교수

AMOO-GOTTFRIED 주 제네바 가나 대표부 대사

라포터: TAUCHI 주 제네바 일본대표부 1 등 서기관

3. 회의의제 (E/CN.4/1991/1) 채택후 이라크 대표는 금차 인권위가 걸프사태를 포함한 인권문제를 토의하는데있어 이중적인 기준을 적용하지 않기를 요청하면서 이라크 민간인에 대한 폭격은 유엔 헌장에 위배되며, 금번 회의시 문제문제가 토의되어야 할것이라고 주장하였음. 한편 쿠웨이트 대표는 제 45 차 유엔 총회에서 채택된 이라크의 쿠웨이트 점령관련 결의안(45/170)에서 인권위가 점령쿠웨이트의 인권 상황을 검토토록 요청한바 있으므로, 의제 12 항(세계 인권 위반 사례)에 동 문제를 소의제로 추가하여 토의할것을 제의함. 의장은 상기 제안을 오후 의장단 회의시 검토키로 함.

4. 한편 금차 회의에 북한측은 당지 대표부의 이철 대사, 박덕훈 참사관, 김철수 및 저용영 서기관으로 대표단을 구성, 사무국에 통보한 것으로 파악됨.

끝

(대사대리 박영우-국장)

국기국 차관 1차보 2차보 청와대 안기부 법무부

PAGE 1

91.01.29 06:06

외신 2과 통제관 FE

0042

기 안 용 지

분류기호 문서번호	국연 2031 -	(전화 :)	시 행 상 특별취급	
보존기간	영구 · 준영구. 10. 5. 3. 1	차 관	장 관	
수 신 처 보존기간				
시행일자	1991. 1. 29.			

보조기관		협조기관		문서통제
국 장		제 1차관보		
과 장				
기안책임자	송영완			발 송 인

경 유 수 신 참 조	건 의	발신명의		
제 목	제 47차 유엔인권위원회 대표단 파견			

1. 1991.1.28-3.8간 스위스 제네바에서 개최예정인 제 47차 유엔인권위원회에 아래와 같이 정부 옵서버 대표단을 정부대표 및 특별사절의 임명과 권한에 관한 법률 제 3758호에 의거 임명, 파견코자 하오니 재가하여 주시기 바랍니다.

2. 특히 금번 인권위원회기간중 북한의 인권상황 거론방안을 검토중이며 또한 북측에 의한 아국 인권문제 거론 가능성도 높다고 사료되는 바, 동 대표단으로 하여금 이에 적극 대처토록 할 예정입니다.

0043

//계속...

(2)

- 아 래 -

가. 회 의 명 : 제 47차 유엔인권위원회

(Commission on Human Rights,

Forty-Seventh Session)

나. 참가목적

o 인권보장 문제에 대한 각국 입장과 국제적 동향파악

o 아국의 인권상황에 대한 정부입장 설명

o 우방국대표 또는 민간인권단체를 통한 북한의 인권침해 사례 및 북한 형법의 제문제점 지적 (검토중)

o 일부 반한인권단체의 아국인권상황 거론시 이에 대한 적극 대처

다. 대 표 단

o 수석대표 : 주제네바 대사대리 박영우

o 대 표 : 주제네바 참사관 이 량

법무부 인권과장 유국현

(91.2.25-3.2간 참석)

주제네바 2등서기관 김종훈

0044 //계속...

(3)

국제연합과 사무관 송영완

(91.2.10-2.20간 참석)

법무부 인권과 검사 권영석

(91.2.18-2.28간 참석)

(당부 및 법무부 출장직원의 파견기간을

달리하여 가급적 회의 주요부분을 모두

참석토록 배려함)

첨 부 : 유엔 인권위원회 개요. 끝.

0045

(첨 부)

인권 위원회(Commission on Human Rights) 개요

1. 설립근거

   o 1946년 ECOSOC 결의에 의하여 설치

2. 구 성

   o ECOSOC에서 선출하는 임기 3년의 43개 위원국으로 구성

   o 91.5월 경사리 1차 회의에서 10개국을 추가 선출하여 위원국이 53개국으로 증가될 예정

   o 유엔인권위 옵서버국 : 남.북한등 74개국

3. 기능 및 권한

   o 인권위원회의 활동은 다음 제사항에 관한 제안, 권고 및 보고서를 ECOSOC에 제출하는 것을 목적으로 함.

     - 국제인권장전

     - 시민적 자유, 여성의 지위, 정보의 자유 및 유의사항에 관한 국제적 선언 또는 규약

     - 인종, 성, 언어 또는 종고에 의한 차별금지

     - 기타 인권에 관한 일체의 사항

4. 회 기

   o 매년 2월이 시작하는 주부터 6주간

5. 주요의제

   o 피구금자 인권문제

   o 세계 각국의 인권위반 사례

   o 아랍 피점령지, 남아공 인권위반 문제

   o 기타 인권위의 조직, 행정문제등

0046

6. 유엔 인권위원회 위원국(43개국) 명단

지 역	국 명
아 시 아 (10개국)	방글라데시, 사이프러스, 인도 (이상 1991) 이락, 파키스탄, 필리핀 (이상 1992) 인니, 일본, 중국, 호주 (이상 1993)
서구 및 기타 (9개국)	벨지움, 카나다, 스웨덴 (이상 1991) 프랑스, 이태리, 미국 (이상 1992) 독일, 오지리, 폴투갈 (이상 1993)
중 남 미 (8개국)	콜롬비아, 쿠바, 파나마 (1991) 브라질, 멕시코 (이상 1992) 알젠틴, 페루, 베네주엘라 (이상 1993)
아프리카 (11개국)	이디오피아, 모로코, 스와질랜드 (이상 1991) 가나, 마다가스카르, 세네갈, 소말리아 (이상 1992) 브룬디, 감비아, 모리타니아, 잠비아 (이상 1993)
동 구 (5개국)	소련, 우크라이나 (이상 1991) 헝가리, 유고 (이상 1992) 체코 (이상 1993)

* ( ) 은 임기 만료 년도

0047

관리 번호	91 -107

	분류번호	보존기간

발 신 전 보

번 호 : WGV-0149 910130 1112 DA 종별 :

수 신 : 주 제네바 대사 대리 ~~/ 총영사~~

발 신 : 장 관 (국연)

제 목 : ~~제 47차 유엔인권위 (대표단 통보)~~

대 : GVW-0077

연 : WGV-0050

1. 표제회의 아국 옵서버 대표단은 귀직을 수석대표로 하고 이량참사관, 법무부 유국현(Yoo, Kook Hyun) 인권과장, 김종훈서기관, 국제연합과 송영완(Song Young Wan) 사무관, 법무부 인권과 권영석 (Kwon, Young-Suk) 검사로 구성하였으니 사무국에 통보바람.

2. 대표단 훈령, 회의자료 및 출장직원 회의참석기간은 추보 예정임. 끝.

일반문서로 재분류 (1991. 12. 31.)

(국제기구조약국장 문동석)

검 토 필(1991. 6.30.)

앙 고 재	91년 1월 30일	과	기안자		과 장		국 장		차 관	장 관
			송영완				전결			

보안통제	외신과통제

0048

원 본

외 무 부

종 별 :

번 호 : GVW-0196 일 시 : 91 0129 1700

수 신 : 장 관(국연,법무부,기정)

발 신 : 주 제네바 대사대리

제 목 : 제 47차 유엔인권위 회의(2)

1. 금 1.29(화) 오전 표제회의는 별첨 의제별 토의일정을 채택하고 의제 4항 (피점령 아랍지역에서의 인권위반) 토의를 시작함.

2. 금차회의 주요의제 토의 일정은 아래와 같음.

- 피점령 아랍지역 인권문제 (의제 4,9):1.29(화)-2.4(월)
- 남아공 인권문제 (의제 5,6,15,16) :2.4(월)-2.7(목)
- 고문등 피구금자 인권 (의제 10): 2.13(수)-2.14(목)
- 세계인권상황 (의제 12): 2.19(화)-2.27(수)

3. 이날 회의에서 의장은 쿠웨이트 대표가 점령쿠웨이트내 인권상황을 의제 12항 (B) 의별도 소제목하에 토의할 것을 제의한 것과관련, 인권위가 동 제의를 수락할것을 요청하였는바, 이라크대표가 이에 반대 의사를 표명하였을뿐 별도의 제안이 없어, 쿠웨이트 제의가 채택됨.

4. 의제 4항 토의에서 팔레스타인, 쿠웨이트, 수단, 모로코 및 AI, ICJ 대표는 팔레스타인 지역등에서 이스라엘인인에 대한 무차별 총격, 불법구금 및 고문, 강제추방, 주거지파괴 및 가족재결합 불허등 인권위반 사례를 비난함.

특히 쿠웨이트 대표는 이라크의 쿠웨이트 침공으로 팔레스타인 문제에 대한 관심이 줄어들고 있으며, 쿠웨이트에서 취업중이던 팔레스타인인의 철수로 경제적 타격을 받고 있다고 말하고 이라크의 침공을 강력히 비난함. 동 발언도중 이라크 대표는 3차례의 의사진행 발언을 통해 쿠웨이트 대표발언이 의제와 관련없다고 주장하였으나, 의장은 쿠웨이트 발언을 계속토록 하였음.

5. 금차회의중 특별연설 예정인 주요고위 인사는 아래와 같음.

- 국가원수급: 우크라이나 대통령
- 외무장관: 콜롬비아, 룩셈브르크, 스웨덴, 인니, 루안다, 우루과이, 유고,

국기국 1차보 안기부 법무부

PAGE 1

91.01.30 08:59 WG

외신 1과 통제관

0049

파라과이

첨부: 금차 회의 일정.

(GVW(F)-0043). 끝.

(대사대리 박영우-국장)

COMMISSION ON HUMAN RIGHTS FORTY-SEVENTH SESSION

PROVISIONAL TIME-TABLE FOR THE CONSIDERATION OF AGENDA ITEMS RECOMMENDED BY THE BUREAU

DAY		1ST WEEK	2ND WEEK	3RD WEEK	4TH WEEK	5TH WEEK	6TH WEEK
MONDAY	AM	28 Jan 1 2	4 Feb 4 9	11 Feb 7 8 17 18	18 Feb 22	25 Feb 12	4 Mar 23 24 25
	PM		5 6 15 16	7 8 17 18	22	12	voting 12 14
TUESDAY	AM	29 Jan 4	5 Feb 5 6 15 16	12 Feb 11	19 Feb 12(b)	26 Feb 12	5 Mar voting 19 21
	PM	4	5 6 15 16	11	12(b)	12	voting 13 20
WEDNESDAY	AM	30 Jan 4	6 Feb 5 6 15 16	13 Feb 10	20 Feb 12(b)	27 Feb 12(b) 12 14	6 Mar voting 23 24 25
	PM	4 9	5 6 15 16	10	12	14	voting on any remaining drafts
THURSDAY	AM	31 Jan 4 9	7 Feb 5 6 15 16	14 Feb 10	21 Feb 12	28 Feb 21	7 Mar
	PM	4 9	7 8 17 18	10	12	19	
FRIDAY	AM	1 Feb 4 9	8 Feb 7 8 17 18	15 Feb voting 4 9 5 6 15 16	22 Feb voting 5 6 15 16 7 8 17 18 11	1 Mar 13 20	8 Mar 26 27
	PM	4 9	7 8 17 18	voting 4 9 5 6 15 16	voting 5 6 15 16 7 8 17 18 11	voting 10 22 12	26 27

0051

1991-01-29 15:49 KOREAN MISSION GENEVA 2 022 791 0525 P.01

공 란

관리번호	91-122

법　　무　　부

인권 2031-28　　503-7045　　1991. 1. 31.

수신 외무부장관

참조 국제기구조약국장

제목 제47차 유엔 인권위원회

1. 귀부 국연 2031-112 ('91.1.15) 및 당부 인권 2031-22 ('91.1.26)와 관련입니다.

2. 당부에서는 제47차 유엔 인권위원회에 참가할 대상자로 인권과장 고등검찰관 류 국 현 (Yoo Kook-Hyun)을 추가로 추천합니다. 끝.

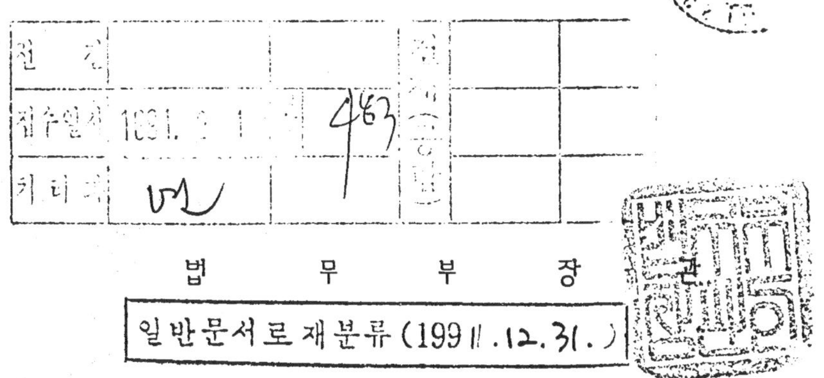

법　무　부　장　관

일반문서로 재분류 (1991.12.31.)

검토필(1991.6.30.)

0053

COMMISSION ON HUMAN RIGHTS FORTY-SEVENTH SESSION

PROVISIONAL TIME-TABLE FOR THE CONSIDERATION OF AGENDA ITEMS RECOMMENDED BY THE BUREAU

DAY	1ST WEEK	2ND WEEK	3RD WEEK	4TH WEEK	5TH WEEK	6TH WEEK
MONDAY AM	28 Jan 1 2	4 Feb 4 9	11 Feb 7 8 17 18	18 Feb 22	25 Feb 12	4 Mar 23 24 25
MONDAY PM		5 6 15 16	7 8 17 18	22	12	voting 12 14
TUESDAY AM	29 Jan 4	5 Feb 5 6 15 16	12 Feb 11	19 Feb 12(b)	26 Feb 12	5 Mar voting 19 21
TUESDAY PM	4	5 6 15 16	11	12(b)	12	voting 13 20
WEDNESDAY AM	30 Jan 4	6 Feb 5 6 15 16	13 Feb 10	20 Feb 12(b)	27 Feb 12(b) 12 14	6 Mar voting 23 24 25
WEDNESDAY PM	4 9	5 6 15 16	10	12	14	voting on any remaining drafts
THURSDAY AM	31 Jan 4 9	7 Feb 5 6 15 16	14 Feb 10	21 Feb 12	28 Feb 21	7 Mar
THURSDAY PM	4 9	7 8 17 18	10	12	19	
FRIDAY AM	1 Feb 4 9	8 Feb 7 8 17 18	15 Feb voting 4 9 5 6 15 16	22 Feb voting 5 6 15 16 7 8 17 18 11	1 Mar 13 20	8 Mar 26 27
FRIDAY PM	4 9	7 8 17 18	voting 4 9 5 6 15 16	voting 5 6 15 16 7 8 17 18 11	voting 10 22 12	26 27

0054

1991-01-29 18:49 KOREAN MISSION GENEVA 2 022 791 0525 P.01

법 무 부

인권 2031-**1549** 503-7045 1991. 2. 1.

수신 외무부장관

참조 국제기구조약국장

제목 업무협조 의뢰

제47차 유엔 인권위원회 회의에 정부대표단의 일원으로 참석할 당부소속 류국현 인권과장이 동 회의 참석기간중 유엔 인권사무국을 방문하여 국제인권규약보고서 제출을 위하여 필요한 제반절차를 협의코자 하오니 관계자와의 면담, 관련자료 수집 등이 이루어 질 수 있도록 협조하여 주시기 바랍니다. 끝.

법 무 부 장 관

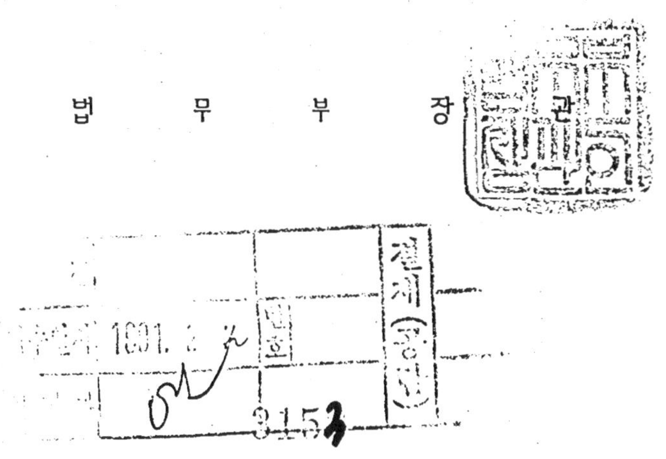

0055

공 란

공 란

공　　　　란

공　　　란

공 란

공 란

공 란

공 란

원 본

외 무 부

종 별 :

번 호 : GVW-0221 일 시 : 91 0201 1630

수 신 : 장 관 (국연,법무부,기정)

발 신 : 주 제네바 대사대리

제 목 : 제 47차 유엔인권회의(3)

1. 표제회의는 1.30-1.31간 의제 4항(피점령 아랍지역 인권문제) 및 의제 9항(자결권) 토의를 계속한바 주요 토의내용 아래 보고함.

가. 의제 4항

0 정부 및 NGO 대표들은 이스라엘 정부가 팔레스타인등 아랍점령지역에서 지속적이고조직적인 인권위반 행위를 하고 있다고비난하고, 점령지역으로부터의 철수 및 모든 이해당사자 참가하의 국제회의 개최를 통한 문제해결을 촉구함.

0 동 대표들은 특히 민간 시위자에 대한 총격, 불법구금 및 고문, 장기간의 통금실시에 따른 팔레스타인의 일상생활의 어려움, 강제추방, 계속되는 유태인의 유입,학교 폐쇄등을 비난하고 골란고원 및 남부 레바논에서의 인권상황에도 관심을 기울일 것을 촉구함.

0 오지리, 사우디, UAE 대표등은 이라크의 쿠웨이트침공으로 팔레스타인 문제에대한 국제적관심이 약화되었다고 말하면서 이라크의 침공을 비난함.

나. 의제 9항

0 BALLESTEROS 용병문제 특별 보고관은 금차회의 보고서(E/CN.4/1991/14)설명을통해 말디브, 코모로, 모잠비크등 아프리카 지역에서 용병의 활동으로 자결권이 위협을 받는 사례를 비난하고, 특히 남아공 정부의 용병지원 사례를 언급함.

0 NGO 인 PAX CHRISTI 대표는 티벳, 동티몰, 사이프러스, 팔레스타인, 발틱 및 KURD 족문제등에서 자결권이 보장되어야 하며, 이를 위해 인권위등 UN 관련기관이 새로운 관심을 기울여야 할 것이라고 강조함.

0 또한 INT'L FED.OF HUMAN RIGHT 는 KURD 족문제, 미주법률가 협회의는 미국의파나마 공격, LIBERATION 은 스리랑카에서의 타밀족에 대한 각종 인권위반

국기국 안기부 법무부

PAGE 1 91.02.02 08:51 FC

외신 1과 통제관

0064

문제를 집중 언급함.

2. 한편 1.31. JACQES POOS 룩셈브르크 외무장관은 EC 를 대표한 특별연설을 통해 이라크의 쿠웨이트 침공, 소련정부의 발틱제국에 대한 강압통치를 비난함.

동 장관은 최근의 사례는 지속적이고 조지적인 인권침해가 궁극적으로는 지역분쟁을 야기한다는 것을 입증하고 있다고 말하고, 국제사회가 인권보장을 위한 활동을 통해 세계평화 보장을 위해 노력하는 것이 필요하다고 강조함.

3. 또한 1.30 JARAMILLO 콜롬비아 외무장관은 특별연설을 통해 걸프전쟁 발발에유감을 표명하고, 동 전쟁이 국가간 빈부격차를 확대하게 될 것이며, 자연환경 악화, 대량 난민발생 및 마약거래 증가등의 문제를 야기할 것이라고 말함.

동 장관은 개도국 고급인력 유출, 남북간 기술이전의 저조, 개도국의 무역환경의 악화등에 우려를 표명하고, 자국의 민주화 정책을 설명함.끝.

(대사대리 박영우-국장)

원 본

암호수신

외 무 부

종 별 :

번 호 : GVW-0224 일 시 : 91 0201 1900

수 신 : 장관(국연,법무부,기정)

발 신 : 주 제네바 대사대리

제 목 : 제 47차 유엔인권위 회의(4)

1. 금 2.1. 표제회의는 의제 4 항 및 9 항으로 토의를 계속한바, 오후 회의시 미국대표는 의제 9 항(자결권) 관련 발언을 통해 자결권의 요체는 국민이 자신의 정부구성을 결정하는 것이라고 말하고 국민의 뜻에 따라 정기적인 자유민주선거가 실시되어야 하며, 세계각지에서의 자유선거의 실시를 위해 UN 이 노력해야 할것이라고 강조함.

동 대표는 동구, 중남미, 몽고, 나미비아에서의 자유선거 및 민주화 추진, 남아공 집권당의 1 인 1 투표시 실시 약속을 평가하고 알바니아에서도 일당통치에 대한 강한 도전이 있음을 언급함.

2. 한편 동 대표는 자결권이 존재하지 않는 국가를 거론하면서 쿠바, 북한, 베트남 및 아프간에서는 아직 자유선거가 실시되지 않고 있다고 말하고, 미얀마 군사정권의 선거결과에 불이행을 비난함.

또한 미국은 소련의 발틱제국에 대한 강제 합병을 인정한 적이 없으며 동국민들이 자신의 장래를 결정하려는 열망을 계속 지지할 것이라고 말하고 소련정부의 무력 사용은 페레스트로이카 및 글라스노스트 기본원칙에도 위배되는바, CSCE파리헌장을 준수, 무력이 아닌 평화적 대화를 추구할 것을 촉구함.

3. 미국측은 90 년도 제 46 차 회의에서도 자결권 보장을 위한 자유선거의 중요성을 강조하고 북한의 자유선거제도 부재를 언급한바 있었음. 끝.

(대사대리 박영우-국장)

국기국 청와대 안기부 법무부

PAGE 1

91.02.02 07:26

외신 2과 통제관 BT

0066

5240

기 안 용 지

분류기호 문서번호	국연 2031 -	(전화:)	시 행 상 특별취급	FAX 송부.
보존기간	영구·준영구. 10. 5. 3. 1	장		관
수 신 처 보존기간				
시행일자	1991. 2. 5.			

보조기관	국 장	전 결	협조기관		문서통제 1991. 2. 6 외무부
	과 장				
기안책임자		송영완			

경 유		발신명의		검열 1991. 2. 6
수 신	법무부장관			
참 조	법무실장			

제 목	제 47차 유엔인권위원회

대 : 인권 2031-22(91.1.26) 및 2031-28(91.1.31)

대호, 정부대표 및 특별사절의 임명과 권한에 관한 법률 제3758호에 의거, 귀부 인권과장 류국현 고등검찰관과 권영석검사가 표제회의 정부대표단 일원으로 발령되었음을 알려드리오니 회의참석에 필요한 조치를 취하여 주시기 바랍니다. 끝.

0067

기 안 용 지

분류기호 문서번호	국연 2031- 5241	(전화 :)	시 행 상 특별취급	
보존기간	영구·준영구. 10. 5. 3. 1	장 관		
수 신 처 보존기간				
시행일자	1991. 2. 5.			

보조기관	국 장	전 결	협조기관		문서통제
	과 장				1991. 2 외무부
기안책임자		송영완			발 송 인

경 유 수 신 참 조	법무부장관 법무실장	발신명의		국연 1991. 2. 6
제 목	제 47차 유엔인권위원회			

연 : 국연 2031-112 (91.1.15)

연호, 표제회의 자료(가의제 주석)를 별첨 송부하오니 동 회의 대책수립에 참고하시기 바랍니다.

첨 부 : 상기자료 1부. 끝.

0068

공 란

공　　란

공　　　란

공 란

공　　란

원 본

외 무 부

종 별 :

번 호 : GVW-0243 일 시 : 91 0205 1630

수 신 : 장관(국연,법무부,기정)

발 신 : 주제네바대사대리

제 목 : 제 47차 유엔인권위 회의(5)

1. 표제회의는 금 2.5. 오전 의제 4,9항 토의를 마치고 오후부터 5,6,15,16항 (남아공 인권) 토의를 시작함.

2. 의제 4항관련, 대부분의 정부 및 NGO 대표들은 이스라엘 정부가 팔레스타인 지역등 피점령 아랍지역에서 과잉 폭력행사등 각종 인권위반 행위를 하고 있다고 비난하고, 동지역에서 전시민간인 보호에 관한 제 4차 제네바 협약을 준수할 것과 동 지역문제 토의를 위해 모든 이행 당사자가 참가하는 국제회의를 개최할 것을 촉구함.미국대교는 모든 당사자의 자제를 요청하고 이스라엘 보안군의 과잉조치, 이스라엘민간인에 대한 로케트 공격, 팔레스타인인 간의 폭력행위등에 우려를 표명함.

3. 이스라엘 대표는 자국의 생존권에 대한 위협이 상존하고 있음을 설명하고 중동 지역문제의 해결은 국제회의가 아닌 이해당사자간의 직접 교섭을 통해서 이뤄져야하며, 동 교섭에는 PLO 가 아닌 팔레스타인인의 진정한 대표기관이 참여해야 할 것이라고 말함. 또한 동 대표는 금년초부터 실시되고 있는 팔레스타인 지역에대한 봉금은 주민생활에 위협을 주고 있지 않으며, 식량 및 의약품도 원활히 공급되고있다고 밝힘.

4. 한편 2.1 오후 의장은 특별성명을 통해 91.1.16.부터 팔레스타인 점령지역에대한 봉금실시로 식량보급등 점령지역 민간인생활에 심각한 영향을 미치고 있다고 말하고 인도적 견지에서 이스라엘 정부가 필요한 조치를 취하여 줄것을 요청함. 또한 2.4 회의시 동의장은 상기 성명 발표에 대해 일부 대표가 절차상의 문제점을 제기하였다고 밝히면서, 동성명은 개인자격으로 발표한 것이라고 말함.

5. 의제 9항 토의에서 서방국가 뿐만 아니라 소련, 중국, 쿠바등 정부대표등은 이라크의 쿠웨이트 점령을 비난하면서 유엔안보리 결의에 따른 즉각 철수를 촉구함. 서방 대표들은 발틱문제에 대한 소련정부의 무력사용을 비난함.

국기국	장관	차관	1차보	2차보	중아국	정문국	안기부	법무부
					V			

PAGE 1 91.02.06 03:11 CG

외신 1과 통제관

0074

또한 많은 정부 및 NGO 대표등은 캄보디아문제와 관련하여 협상 진전을 평가하였으며, 미얀마, 아프간, 스리랑카, 동티몰, 서사하라, 에리트리아, 유고의 코소보 지역 및 KURD 측에 대한 자결권 보장 문제를 제기하였으며 파키스탄 대표는 카시미르지역문제를 언급함.

6. 한편 2.4 오전 STEN ANDERSSON 스웨덴 외무장관, 2.5 오전 LENNOX BOYD 영국외무성 정무차관은 각각 특별 연설을 통해 이라크의 쿠웨이트 침공 및 각종 인권유린 행위를 강력히 비난하면서 인권존중이 정치적 안정 및 국제적 안전보장과 밀접한 관련이 있다고 강조함. 또한 발틱문제에 대한 소련정부의 무력사용에 우려를 표명하고평화적인 교섭을 통한 문제해결을 촉구함.

7. 이라크 대표는 답변권 행사를 통해 미국등 연합군의 이라크 폭격, 영국정부의 이라크 유학생에 대한 구금 및 원폭 피해국인 일본정부의 연합군 지원을 비난하고,쿠웨이트가 역사적으로 이라크의 일부분임을 주장함. 이에대해 영국대표는 이라크 유학생은 이라크군 소속으로 유학중이므로 전쟁포로로 취급되며 동인들의 구금은 강제추방을 위한 사전조치라고 설명함.

또한 일본대표는 자국이 겪은 패전의 경험을 상기시키면서 이라크에 대해 안보리 결의 준수를 통해 금번 사태를 평화롭게 해결토록 촉구한바있다고 밝힘.끝.

(대사대리 박영우-국장)

PAGE 2

0075

공 란

공　　　란

공 란

공 란

대 한 민 국
외 무 부

국연 2031- 5240　　　　1991. 2. 6.

수신 법무부장관

참조 법무실장

제목 제 47차 유엔인권이사회

대 : 인권 2031-22(91.1.26) 및 2031-28(91.1.31)

대호, 정부대표 및 특별사절의 임명과 권한에 관한 법률 제3758호에 의거, 귀부 인권과장 류국현 고등검찰관과 권영석검사가 표제회의 정부대표단 일원으로 발령되었음을 알려드리오니 회의참석에 필요한 조치를 취하여 주시기 바랍니다. 끝.

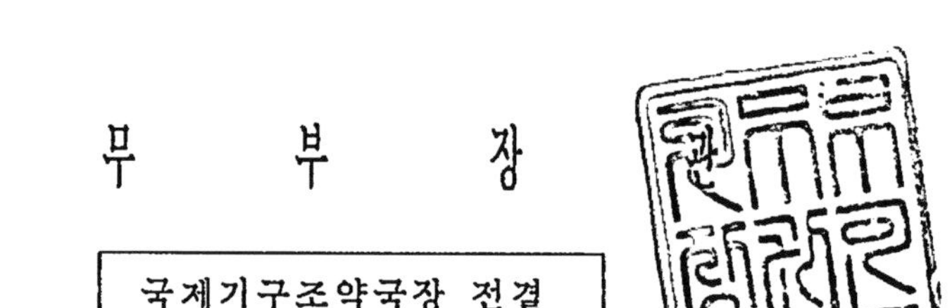

외 무 부 장

국제기구조약국장 전결

0080

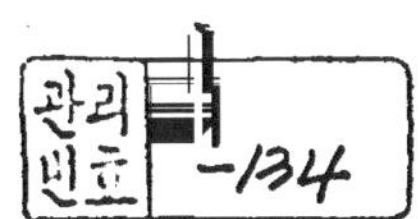

관리번호 -134

법 무 부

인권 2031-32 503-7045 1991. 2. 6

수신 외무부장관

참조 국제기구조약국장

제목 제47차 유엔 인권위원회 회의 대비자료 송부

1. 국연 2031-112 ('91.1.15)와 관련입니다.

2. 귀부에서 요청한 회의 대비자료를 별첨과 같이 송부합니다.

3. 기타 자료는 "법과 질서 그리고 인권" 책자 및 기히 송부한 대응자료 등을 참고하시기 바랍니다.

첨부 : 관련자료 1부. 끝.

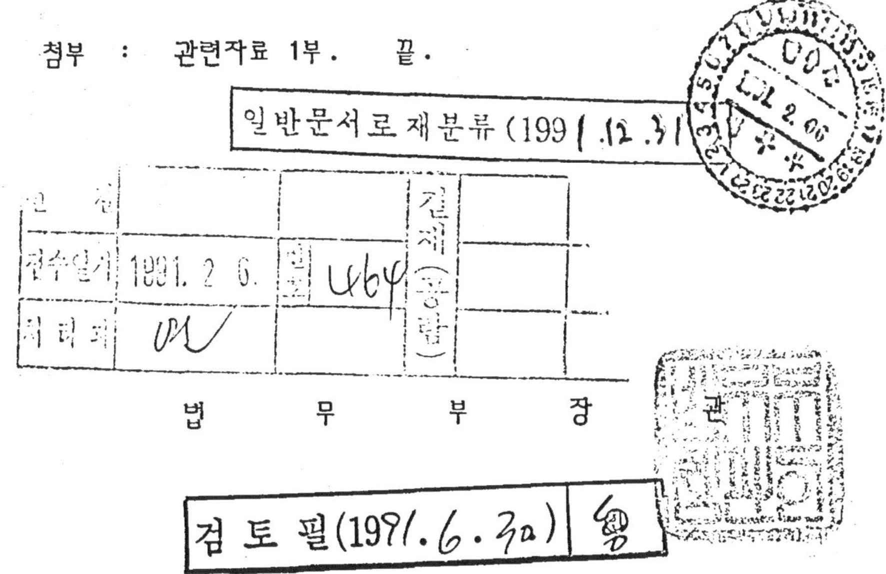

일반문서로 재분류 (1991.12.31)

접수일시	1991. 2. 6.		464	결재(공람)
처리과				

법 무 부 장 관

검토필 (1991.6.30)

0081

공　　란

공 란

베를린 3자회담 대표 등 구속에 관한 정부입장

o 범민족대회 추진본부 대표 3명은 공동선언문에서 우리 정부를 반통일 세력으로 매도하면서 통일반대, 외세 및 분열주의 세력에 쐐기를 박겠다고 선언하고

o 유엔 사무총장에게 보내는 편지에서 1995년을 "통일의 해"로 선정하고, 한반도 주둔 외국군 및 핵무기 철수, 유엔 분리가입 반대, 평화협정 체결, 국가보안법 철폐 등을 주장하여 북한의 구성원과 회합. 통신하면서 그들의 주장, 활동에 동조하고 있음

o 북이 주장하는 조국통일 5대 방침에 따르면, 조국통일을 위해서는 남과 북의 각계각층 인민들과 각 정당 사회단체 대표들로 구성되는 대민족회의를 소집하여 여기에서 통일문제를 협의하자고 되어 있어

o 위와 같은 범민족대회 개최나 공동선언문의 발표 등은 북한이 대남 적화통일을 위한 이른바 통일전선전술의 일환으로 우리 정부를 배제하고, 우리 사회내에 반국가 세력을 부식, 혼란을 조성하여 남한 체제를 전복시키려 하는 폭력적화혁명전략에 동조하는 것이 될 뿐 아니라 체육인. 문화인들의 법절차에 따른 비정치적이고 순수한 교류와는 달리 남북관계 개선에도 악영향을 끼칠 뿐임

0084

o 이처럼 이들의 행위는 "남북교류와 협력을 목적"으로 하는 차원에서가 아니라, 북의 대남 적화통일전략을 이롭게 한다는 인식하에 이에 동조한 것으로서, 우리 국가의 안전과 자유민주적 기본질서를 위해하는 행위이기 때문에 남북교류협력에관한법률의 적용요건인 "정당하다고 인정되는 범위"를 객관적으로 벗어나고, 오히려 북의 불순목적에 이용당함으로써 우리의 자유민주적 기본질서에 위해를 줄 위험성이 크므로 구속하기에 이른 것임

o 비록 민족통일이 우리 온 국민의 염원이긴 하나, 국민적 합의없는 자의적인 행위는 통일에 도움이 되기는 커녕 남북관계 개선노력에 지장을 줄 뿐 아니라 우리 국민의 생존, 자유에 중대한 위협이 된다고 할 것임

o 따라서 정부로서는 법원의 판결과 통상적인 형집행절차에 따라 처리되어야 할 것으로 생각하여 다른 고려에 의한 석방은 검토하고 있지 않음

0085

전노협 및 전교조 활동에 관한 정부입장

1. 전 노 협

o 전노협의 결성탄압주장에 대하여

- 우리 정부는 전노협의 결성을 방해하거나 탄압한 사실이 없음

- 전노협의장인 단병호는 물론, 지금까지 어느 누구도 전노협을 조직했다거나 전노협에 가입했다는 이유로 처벌받은 적이 없음

- 결사의 자유는 우리 헌법이 보장하는 바이며, 현행법상으로는 반국가 단체나 이적단체, 그리고 범죄를 목적으로 하는 범죄단체를 제외하고는 단체를 구성하거나 가입했다는 이유로 처벌할 수 없음

- 전노협은 반국가단체나 이적단체, 그리고 범죄단체로 아직까지 인정된 적이 없음

- 90.1.22. 전노협의 결성대회를 원천 봉쇄한 것은 당시의 집회가 사전신고되지 않았고 폭력집회화할 가능성이 컸기 때문임

- 단병호는 90.1.22 결성대회 전에도 수차의 집회를 통해 노동해방, 농산물 수입개방 반대, 노태우 정권타도를 주장하였고, 그 집회들은 결국 수천개의 화염병과 돌을 던져 경찰관들을 부상케 하는 집회가 되었음

- 우리 정부는 어떤 집회를 봉쇄하여 단체결성을 저지할 수 있다고 생각하고 있지 않으며, 단지 집회의 적법성과 폭력성 여부만을 고려한 것 뿐임

0086

o 전노협의 활동탄압주장에 대하여

- 먼저 전노협의장 단병호등의 주장을 요약하면 다음과 같음

  . 현 정권은 군부독재정권이며, 가진자들을 비호하고, 노동자들을 탄압하고 있음

  . 노동법도 노동운동을 보호하는 것이 아니라 가진 자들의 노동력 착취와 노동자들에 대한 탄압을 보장해 주는 악법임

  . 노총은 노동자들을 위한 단체가 아니라, 사용자의 이익만을 위하여 활동하는 어용 단체임

  . 이러한 현실을 타개하기 위해서는 전노협과 같은 새로운 노동자 단체를 조직하여 노동악법 개정에 적극 투쟁하여야 함

- 그러나 현행 노동법은 노동자는 노조를 조직하여 임금등 근로조건의 개선을 위해 사용자와 협의 할수 있고, 노동자의 주장이 받아들여지지 않을 경우 쟁의발생을 신고하고, 10일내지 15일의 냉각기간이 경과된후 과반수의 찬성이 있으면 파업, 태업등의 쟁의행위를 할 수 있도록 되어 있음

0087

- 이러한 노동법의 내용중에 개정할 조항이 있다면, 그 의견을 수렴하여 평화적 시위나 청원등을 통해 정당이나 국회, 정부가 이를 반영하도록 해야 할 것임

- 만약 이와같은 과정을 통해서도 그 주장이 받아들여지지 않는다면 결국 선거에서 그 의사를 표시하거나, 정당을 조직하여 선거에 참가하는 것이 민주주의 국가의 시민적 행동이라 할 것임

- 폭력시위를 통해 법률개정을 요구하고, 나아가 선거에 의하여 출범한 정권의 타도를 외친다면 세계의 어떠한 정부도 이를 방관하지 않을 것이라고 생각함

- 우리 정부는 노동운동가들이 전노협이라는 단체를 조직하여 노동법의 개정을 추진하고, 정부의 노동정책이나 사용자들의 태도를 비판하는 것을 문제삼고 있는 것이 아님

- 단지, 불법폭력집회를 주최하고, 노동조합법상 적법한 제3자가 아님에도 개별회사의 노사협의나 노동쟁의에 개입하는 행위를 문제삼고 있을 뿐임.

0088

2. 전교조

ㅇ 우리 헌법은 근로자의 단결권, 단체교섭권 및 단체행동권을 보장하고 있지만, 공무원에 대해서는 이를 제한하고 있음

ㅇ 공무원에 대해 노동권을 제한한 것은 공무원이 국민전체에 대한 봉사자라는 지위의 특수성을 갖고 있고, 담당 직무가 직접으로 공익에 연관되기 때문일 것임

ㅇ 교원들중 국공립학교의 교원들은 그 신분이 공무원이므로 헌법과 국가공무원법에 따라 노동권이 제한되고 있고, 사립학교의 교원들은 공무원의 신분은 아니지만 사립학교법에서 국공립학교의 교원들에 준하여 노동권이 제한되고 있음

ㅇ 우리 헌법과 법률이 공무원이나 교원에 대하여 노동권을 보장하지 않고 있다는 이유로 우리 법체계를 '후진적'이라거나 '인권경시'라고 비난 한다면 이는 단순한 생각임

ㅇ 오히려 국민전체에 대한 봉사자로서의 충실을 요구하며 근로자로서의 욕구는 상대적으로 절제하겠다는 우리 국민 특유의 헌법적 결단이요 가치질서의 선택이라 할 것임

0089

o 물론 이러한 선택은 영구불변의 것이 아니라 새로운 국민적 합의와 지지에 의하여 헌법과 법률의 개정절차에 따라 개정될 수 있는 것임

o 그러나 개정전에 있어서는 민주시민으로서 헌법과 법률을 지켜야 한다는 것은 당연하다 할 것임

o 전교조에 관련된 사람들은 일반적 결사로서 이러한 개정주장을 한 것이 아니라, 현행 헌법과 법률을 무시하고 먼저 노동조합을 결성한 것임

o 즉, 먼저 범법행위를 하고 합법성 쟁취 투쟁을 벌이고 있는 것임

o 우리 정부는 전교조에 관련된 사람들이 법률의 개정을 촉구하고, 헌법재판소에 사립학교법의 위헌제청신청을 하였다는 이유로 문제삼고 있는 것이 아님

o 단지 단결권이 금지되어 있음에도 노동조합을 결성하고, 신고하지 않고 개최한 불법집회들을 문제삼고 있는 것일 뿐임

0090

정치범 . 장기수 문제

o 정치범이 무엇인가에 대해서는 말하는 사람마다 그 개념규정을 달리 하고 있음

o 그러나 정치범을 어떻게 규정하던 간에 정치범으로 지칭되고 있는 사람들은 모두 간첩행위 또는 정부의 전복을 기도하는 등 우리의 실정법을 위반하여 재판을 받고 재판과정에서 충분한 증거가 드러나 유죄판결이 선고된 사람들임

o 북한과 좌익세력의 위협에 대처하여 우리 국가의 안전과 국민의 생존 및 자유를 확보하기 위하여 국가보안법이 있는 것이며, 따라서 우리의 체제를 전복하기 위한 반국가활동이나 북한의 대남적화통일 전략.전술에 동조하는 반국가사범등을 정치범이라는 이름아래 석방해야 한다는 것은 더 나아가 우리나라가 공산화되어도 좋다는 뜻이 되는 것임

0091

o 대한민국의 헌법이념을 파괴하고 국가주권을 무시하는 실정법위반 행위를 한 사람들에 대하여는 엄중처벌할 수 밖에 없으며, 이러한 국가보안법 위반사범들을 정치범이라는 이유로 특별한 취급을 하여야 한다는 주장은 그 국가의 안전과 국민의 생존권을 신중히 고려하지 못한 독단적 견해임

o 그리고 소위 인권단체에서 장기수의 석방을 요구하고 있으나 제6공화국에 들어와 1988.12.21. 까지 수회에 걸친 사면조치로 인해 현재 구금중인 장기수는 대부분 사안이 중한 간첩사범이므로 더욱 실정법을 무시하고 이들을 석방할 이유는 없음.

0092

고문방지 등 피구금자 인권보호를 위한 조치

o 우리 정부로서는 제6공화국 출범 이후 사회전반의 민주화 추세에 따라 신장된 국민의 인권의식에 부응하기 위하여 인권침해방지를 위한 나름대로의 노력을 경주하여 왔고, 특히 부당한 구속과 수사 과정에서의 고문행위를 근절하겠다는 강력한 의지를 수차 천명하여 왔음

o 이에 따라 검사의 구속장소 감찰을 강화하여 월 1회에 한하지 않고 필요할 때마다 수시로 감찰하고, 자체 구속장소가 없는 수사관서에 대하여도 불법사례 유무를 조사하여 수사과정상 적법절차가 준수 되도록 하고 있음

o 한편 수시로 각 검찰청 단위별로 사법경찰관에 대한 지도교양을 통하여 수사과정에서의 적법절차를 철저히 준수하도록 독려하고 있음. 현재 검찰에서 하고 있는 사법경찰관에 대한 지도교양방법은 구체적인 송치사건과 관련하여 교양책자를 발간하여 수사상의

0093

과오를 지적, 시정케 하고 있는 외에도 수시로 수사실무교육 등을 통해 지도하고 있으며, 특히 수사요원의 인권의식 함양에도 많은 노력을 기울이고 있음

o 앞으로도 정부는 일선 수사기관에 대한 지휘감독을 보다 철저히 하고 수사요원에 대한 지속적인 인권의식 함양을 통하여 수사과정에서의 인권침해방지에 만전을 기하도록 하며, 아울러 과학적 수사장비와 수사기술을 도입하여 수사를 과학화 하도록 계속 노력할 것임

o 또한 고문방지협약에의 가입을 전향적으로 추진중에 있음

0094

원 본

암호수신

외 무 부

종 별 :

번 호 : GVW-0248 일 시 : 91 0206 1430

수 신 : 장관(국연)

발 신 : 주 제네바 대사대리

제 목 : 제 47차 유엔인권위 관련자료 요청

표제회의 관련 참고코저 하니 "남. 북 교류 협력에 관한 법률" 영문 번역문또는 영문요록을 지급 송부 바람. 끝.

(대사대리 박영우-국장)

국기국

PAGE 1

91.02.07 07:25

외신 2과 통제관 BT

0095

관리 번호	91 -137

	분류번호	보존기간

발 신 전 보

번 호 : WGV-0191 910207 1845 BX 종별 :

수 신 : 주 제네바 대사. 총영사

발 신 : 장 관 (국연)

제 목 : 제 47차 인권위

연 : WGV-0149

1. 연호, 인권위대표단 출장기간은 아래와 같은 바, 적절한 호텔에 예약 조치바람. (도착 항공편은 추후 통보 예정)

- 유국현 : 2.27-3.5.
- 송영완 : 2.19-2.28.
- 권영석 : 2.18-2.26.

2. 법무부 유과장은 귀지 출장기간중 인권규약 가입에 따른 인권보고서 작성과 관련한 재반문제 협의를 위하여 사무국 직원을 면담코자 하니 적절한 인사와 가급적 2.28. 또는 3.1. 오찬토록 주선후 결과 보고바람. 끝.

(불가시 면담)

(국제기구조약국장 문동석)

1991.6.30 에 예고문에 의거 인반문서로 재분류됨

앙고재	91년 2월 7일	국연과	기안자		과 장		국 장		차 관	장 관
			송영완		(서명)		전결			(서명)

보안통제	외신과통제
(서명)	

0096

주 제 네 바 대 표 부

재네(정) 2031-149　　　　　　　　　　　　　　　1991. 2. 8

수신 : 장관

참조 : 국제기구조약국장

제목 : 제 47차 유엔인권위 자료 송부

연 : GVW-0224

연호, 2.1 의제 9항(자결권) 토의시 미국수석대표가 행한 연설문을 별첨 송부합니다.

첨부 : 상기연설문 1부. 끝.

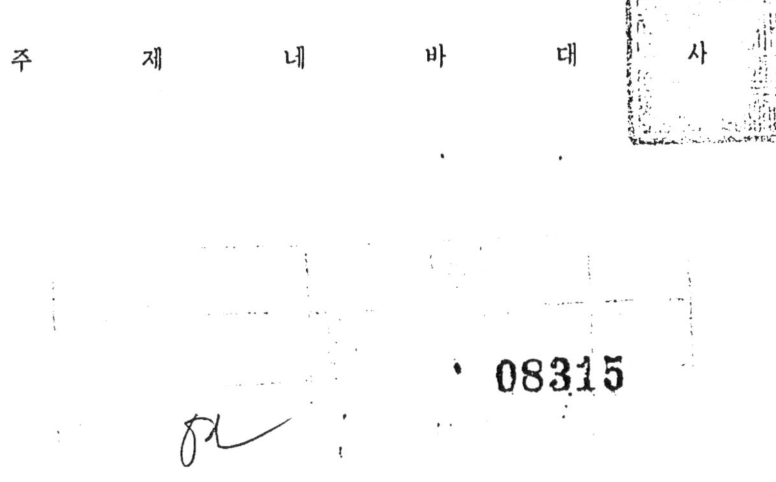

주 제 네 바 대 사

08315

0097

UNITED STATES MISSION TO INTERNATIONAL ORGANIZATIONS
GENEVA, SWITZERLAND

(EMBARGOED UNTIL DELIVERY)

47TH SESSION OF THE U.N. COMMISSION ON HUMAN RIGHTS

S T A T E M E N T

BY

J. KENNETH BLACKWELL

UNITED STATES REPRESENTATIVE TO THE
UNITED NATIONS COMMISSION ON HUMAN RIGHTS

ON

ITEM 9

SELF-DETERMINATION

February 1, 1991

(Check against Delivery)

0098

UNITED NATIONS HUMAN RIGHTS COMMISSION

FORTY-SEVENTH SESSION

ITEM 9

THE RIGHT OF PEOPLES TO SELF-DETERMINATION

AND ITS APPLICATION TO PEOPLES UNDER COLONIAL OR

ALIEN DOMINATION OR FOREIGN OCCUPATION

Mr. Chairman, we speak today under the shadow of a grim and terrible denial of the right to self-determination. The great challenge facing the United Nations today is whether it possesses the civil courage to erase that shadow. A broad range of countries, with full authority of the United Nations, are embarked on this course. And they will succeed.

There is no more blatant denial of self-determination than hostile, unprovoked imposition of foreign rule. But removing that army of occupation does not, by itself, guarantee self-determination.

Self-determination is a complex idea, and the ways and means of attaining it will vary from nation to nation. At its core, self-determination means that people have the right to choose their form of government. There are different formulas for achieving this, but all of them have one thing in common: the existence of institutions and political processes that allow individuals to shape their political futures, peacefully, and in accord with their wishes and priorities.

The sole way to ensure this outcome is government based on the consent of the governed. That, we believe, is the only legal and moral form of governance: based on popular will, tested by periodic elections, protected by secret ballot, and validated by a free press. In a democracy, the government is the servant of the people. One-party states, dictatorships, and totalitarian regimes tend toward the opposite. They make people the servants of the government.

Self-determination is not a "Western" institution, or a luxury that only wealthy nations can afford. It is part of the common culture of humanity. In Botswana, self-determination is

0093

the mix of indigenous governance and multiparty democracy. In Western Samoa, it is the distribution of power between the Matai, who are heads of extended families, and the people, who now elect Matai to Parliament through universal suffrage. In The Gambia, tribal chiefs and members of Parliament, all popularly elected, share in the division of power.

Self-determination, Mr. Chairman, is the political expression of human autonomy. It is as essential to men's spirit as food and drink is to their bodies. That is why Namibians stood in line for hours, not for bread or water, but for the ballot. Nicaraguans and Haitians risked life and limb to vote in the freest elections in their histories -- not to rubber-stamp the status quo, but to vindicate their right of self-determination. That is why thousands marched, and some died, in Vilnius and Port-au-Prince.

The world is a freer place today than it was last year. We rejoice in these changes. The last decade's revolution of self-determination is consolidating its gains. Democratic transitions were made in Bulgaria, Chile, Czechoslovakia, Haiti, Hungary, Namibia, Nicaragua, Panama, and Poland. Last week, Sao Tome and Principe joined the trend with democratic elections that ended fifteen years of single-party leftist rule. In Africa, numerous countries are adopting multiparty systems. South Africa's ruling national party has publicly committed itself to majority rule and the principle of one man, one vote. This extraordinary progress, along with the other welcome signs from South Africa, should be encouraged by the Commission. Further democratic movements emerged in Romania and Mongolia as those two nations held their first free elections. Even in Albania we are witnessing brave challenges to one-party rule.

As these emerging democracies are learning, free elections are necessary, though not sufficient, to ensure self-determination. It also requires the protection of rights that check runaway majoritarianism. These guarantees -- freedom of the press, assembly, and association; the secret ballot and the right of political participation; and the right to leave any country, including one's own -- are the core of universally declared human rights. They channel human expression, and thus are essential in distinguishing men from other beings. But they are also the building blocks of self-determination. Without them, tyranny of the majority prevails, or the society is rent by ethnic, racial, and religious differences. Under those conditions, self-determination withers on the vine.

0100

The framers of the American Constitution understood that these guarantees were necessary to ensure that a multiplicity of parties, sects, and institutions would flourish and check each other. In all democracies, competing interests -- whether a free press, political parties, labor unions, churches, or other interest groups -- tug and pull at one another, define public issues, facilitate the flow of information, allow individuals to express their preferences and prevent one group or sect from gaining the upper hand and oppressing others. As James Madison wrote in The Federalist Papers, with society "broken into so many parts, interests, and classes of citizens, the rights of individuals, or of the minority, will be in little danger from interested combinations of the majority."

My government is engaged in helping emerging democracies learn the practical aspects of free elections and the protection of minority rights. The Citizens' Democracy Corps and the National Endowment for Democracy are at work to speed the process of democratization. In Copenhagen, we and the other CSCE states agreed that the will of the people, freely and fairly expressed through periodic and genuine elections, is the basis of the authority and legitimacy of all government. The Charter of Paris reinforced that declaration. At the 1990 session of the United Nations General Assembly, President Bush called on the UN to formalize its efforts in promoting free elections by establishing a special coordinator for electoral assistance. The Secretary General, acting under the mandate of the General Assembly, will soon seek the views of Member States on how the UN can support the principle of free elections. We hope those responses are positive and constructive.

Now, along with the good news comes some bad: In many parts of the world, self-determination exists only in the dreams of oppressed people.

Cuba, North Korea, and Vietnam have yet to hold free elections. We are still waiting for the Soviet-installed government in Afghanistan to commit itself to free elections. The military regime in Myanmar, rather than yield to the outcome of free and fair elections, disregarded those results and embarked on a brutal campaign of repression. With respect to Cambodia, we are awaiting agreement on a comprehensive settlement which will allow free and fair elections organized and conducted by the United Nations. We hope that this special and tragic situation can be resolved soon.

Despite the emergence of political parties, greater freedom of expression, independent trade unions, and some competitive elections, the USSR's forcible and unlawful incorporation of Estonia, Latvia, and Lithuania continues. We have never recognized this forcible incorporation, and will continue to support the aspirations of the Baltic peoples to determine their future.

We believe that the use of force by the Soviet government in the Baltics fundamentally and tragically contradicts the basic principles of perestroika, glasnost, and democratization. We continue to believe that these reforms have offered the best prospect of continued improvement in U.S.-Soviet relations.

Above all, Soviet interests themselves require that the reform process go forward. Enduring U.S.-Soviet cooperation, indeed partnership, depends on it. That partnership is impossible in the absence of shared values.

It is difficult for our delegation to understand how force can be used, especially now, to suppress newly emerging democratic institutions. We continue to encourage the Soviet Union to become a full participant in shared values expressed in the Charter of Paris, as adopted by CSCE countries on November 21, 1990. For that to happen, we believe that peaceful dialogue, not force, is the only legitimate option.

0102

관리번호	91-141

원 본

외 무 부

종 별 :

번 호 : GVW-0259 일 시 : 91 0208 1100

수 신 : 장관(국연)

발 신 : 주 제네바 대사대리

제 목 : 제 47차 인권위

대: WGV-0191

대호관련, 이량참사관은 당지 유엔인권센타의 KLEIN 인권규약 담당관(여)을 법무부 유과장과의 협의인사로 2.28(목) 오찬 주선하였음. 끝

(대사대리 박영우-장관)

예고: 91.6.30 까지

1991.6.30 에 예고문에 의거 일반문서로 재분류됨

국기국 장관 차관 1차보 2차보 청와대 안기부

PAGE 1 91.02.09 06:13

외신 2과 통제관 CF

0103

원 본

외 무 부

종 별 :

번 호 : GVW-0264 일 시 : 91 0208 1620

수 신 : 장관(국연,법무부,기정)

발 신 : 주 제네바대사대리

제 목 : 제 47차 유엔인권위 회의(6)

1. 표제회의는 2.8.오전 의제 5,6,15,16 (남아인공) 토의를 마치고 의제 7,8 (경제 사회적 권리보장) 및 의제 17,18 (국제 인권협약 현황) 토의를 시작함.

2. 의제 5,6,15,16항 토의에서 정부 및 NGO 대표들은 2.1. DE KLERK 남아공 대통령이 발표한 LAND ACT, GROUP AREA ACT 및 DEVELOPMENT OFBLACK COMMUNITIES ACT 의 조기폐지 약소, POPULATIONREGISTRATION ACT 의 폐지의사 표명등 그간의 아파타이트 철폐를 위한 조치를 평가함.

또한 최근의 MANDELA ANC 부의장과 INKHATA 지도자 BUTHELEZI 간의 종족분쟁 종식 합의를 평가하면서 ANC 가 제안한 남아공내 모든 정당이 참여하는 회의개최를촉구함.

3. 회의 대표들은 상기 발전에도 불구, 남아공내 아파타이트 관련 입법 및 인권위반 행위가 상존하고 있으며, 남아공 정부가 인권위 산하 남아공 문제 실무위원회 위원의 방문을 불허하는등 문제점을 지적하고, 아파타이트 철폐를 위한 완전하고 돌이킬수 없는 조치가 있을때까지 남아공 제재는 계속되어야 할것이라고 강조함.

4. 이번 회의에서 언급된 남아공내 주요 인권위반 사례 등은 아래와 같음

- 재판없이 무기한 구금을 할수 있는 INTERNALSECURITY ACT 의 계속적인 적용
- 정치범의 미석방 및 망명인사의 귀국에 대한각종 정치적 행정적 장애 상존
- 구금자에 대한 각종 고문 및 시위자에 대한 발포
- 종족간 분쟁에 대한 경찰의 방조
- 이스라엘과 남아공간의 핵을 포함한군사적.경제적 유착

2. 한편 2.5 오후 LEONID KRAVCHNK 우크라이나 최고회의 의장은 특별 연설을 통해 인권문제가 현 세계의 발전에 있어 중요한 요소이며, 인간가치의 무시 및 국제법위반이 무력 분쟁을 야기하며 생명의 권리를 위협하고 있음을 걸프전쟁이 보여주고 있다고

국기국 안기부 법무부

PAGE 1

91.02.09 06:40 DA

외신 1과 통제관

0104

말함. 또한 동의장은 민주화 염원 및 인권보장에 대한 욕구가 자국내 모든 국민의 공통 관심사이나, 과거 정부 조치에 기인한 문제등이 있어 민주화 과정이용이하지 만은 않다고 말하고 크리미아 타타르족에 대한 지위 회복 문제를 언급함.

6. 금 2.9. STOLTENBERG 놀웨이 외무장관은 특별연설을 통해 리투아니아와 리트비아에 대한 무력행사는 민주주의 및 인권이 보장된 새로운 유럽건설의 희망을 위협하였으며, CSCE 정신및 유엔 인권관련 협약에 위배된다고 말하고 소련내 소수민족 문제 및 경제난등 어려움을 이해하나 모든 문제는 평화적으로 해결되어야 할것이라고 강조함. 동 장관은 이라크의 쿠웨이트 철수를 촉구하고 포로등에 대한 불법대우, 화학무기 위협 및 환경 파괴등을 비난함. 또한 동장관은 외국과의 정치적, 경제적 관계에서의 인권 관련 문제에 관심을 기울여야 하며, 민주화 과정의 국가중경제적 어려움을 겪고있는 국가에 대한 지원이 필요하다고 말하고, UN이 인권관련 자문 활동을 적극 추진할 것 을요청함.

끝.

(대사대리 박영우-국장)

PAGE 2

0105

분류기호 문서번호	국연 2031- 32	협 조 문 용 지 ( )	결재	담당	과장	국장
시행일자	1991. 2. 9.			(서명)	(서명)	(서명)
수 신	영사교민국장 (사본: 총무과장, 비상계획관)	발 신	국제기구조약국장 (서명)			
제 목	출장통보					

제 47차 유엔인권위원회 대표단으로 스위스 제네바에 출장 예정인 하기인에 대하여 출국 확인등 조치를 취하여 주시기 바랍니다.

o 법무부 유국현 인권과장 : 2.27-3.5. 파견

o 법무부 권영석 인권과 검사 : 2.18-2.26. 파견

o 외무부 송영완 국제연합과 사무관 : 2.19-2.28. 파견.

끝.

0106

1505-8일(1) 190㎜×268㎜(인쇄용지 2급 60g/㎡)
85. 9. 9 승인 "내가아낀 종이 한장 늘어나는 나라살림" 가 40-41 1989. 11. 14

관리 번호	91 -148

	분류번호	보존기간

발 신 전 보

번 호 : WGV-0203 910211 1748 DP 종별 :

수 신 : 주 제네바 대사 총영사

발 신 : 장 관 (국연)

제 목 : 제 47차 인권위원회

연 : WGV-0191

대 : GVW-0248

1. 연호, 법무부 유과장은 2.27(수) 21:45시 SR-729편으로, 유엔과 송사무관은 2.19(화) 21:25시 BA-740편으로 각각 귀지 도착예정임.(권검사는 별도 통보)

2. 표제회의 관련자료는 금파편 송부함.

~~3. 대호, 남북교류 협력에 관한 법률 영문 또는 영문요록은 없다함.~~

끝.

(국제기구조약국장 문동석)

1991.6.30. 에 예고문에 의거 인반문서로 재분류됨

앙고재	91년 2월 11일	유엔과	기안자		과 장		국 장		차 관	장 관
			송영완		(서명)		전결			(서명)

보안통제	외신과통제
(서명)	

0107

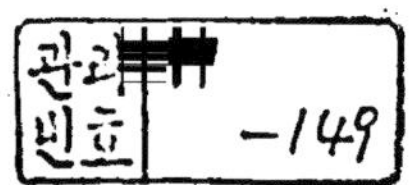
관리번호 -149

기 안 용 지

분류기호 문서번호	국연 2031-310	(전화 :)	시 행 상 특별취급	
보존기간	영구·준영구. 10. 5. 3. 1.	장	관	
수 신 처 보존기간				
시행일자	1991. 2. 11.			
보조기관 국 장	전 결	협조기관		문 서 통 제
과 장				검인 1991. 2. 11
기안책임자	송영완			발 송 인
경 유 수 신 참 조	주제네바대사	발신명의		1991. 2. 11 외무부
제 목	제 47차 인권위원회 관련자료			

대 : GVW-0248

1. 표제회의와 관련, 회의참가 대책 및 참고자료를 별첨 송부합니다.

2. 대호, "남북교류 협력에 관한 법률" 영문 번역문 또는 영문요록은 작성된 것이 없다함을 참고바랍니다.

/ 계속 /

0108

1505-25(2-1) 일(1)갑
85. 9. 9. 승인 "내가아낀 종이 한장 늘어나는 나라살림" 190㎜×268㎜ 인쇄용지 2급 60g/㎡
가 40-41 1990. 5. 28

첨 부 : 1. 제 47차 인권위원회 대책

2. 회의대비자료 (법무부)

- 조용술 관련자료

- 베를린 3자회담 대표등 구속에 관한 정부입장

- 전노협 및 전고조 활동에 관한 정부입장

- 정치법.장기수 문제

- 고문방지등 피구금자 인권보호를 위한 조치

3. 유엔인권위 회의관련 의견 및 북한형법 (안기부)

4. 북한의 반민주 반인권 실상 (안기부)

5. 북한형법 개요(영문) (해외공보관)

6. '90년도 남북교류 신청자 허가비율 및 불허사유(통일원)

끝.

0109

관리 번호	91-154

분류번호	보존기간

발 신 전 보

번 호 : WGV-0211 910212 1848 CG 종별 :

수 신 : 주 제네바 대사, 총영사 (사본 : 주호주, 카나다, 일본대사) WAU-0084 WCN-0142 WJA-0620

발 신 : 장 관 (국연)

제 목 : 일본에 대한 배상 청구

1. 캔버라발 AFP 보도(2.5자)에 따르면, 호주, 카나다의 재향군인회가 일본정부에 대하여 제2차 세계대전 당시 일본이 자행한 전쟁포로의 살해 및 학대등에 대한 손해배상 청구문제를 제47차 인권위에서 제기하였고 이를 ICRC 가 지지하고 있다고 함. 동 배상청구는 1인당 2만불로 계산하여 배상청구 총액이 수십억불에 달할 것으로 보도됨.

2. 또한, 동보도에 의하면, 이에 대하여 일본정부는 1952년 일본-연합국간의 평화협정에 따라 일체의 배상책임이 없다는 입장이며 배상청구인측은 일본과의 평화협정체결 당사자(정부)가 국민개개인의 기본권 침해에 대한 손해배상 청구권을 포기케 할 처리는 없다는 입장이라고 함.

3. 상기관련, 업무에 참고코자 하니 제47차 인권위에서 제기된 일본정부에 대한 배상청구 단체명, 배상청구내역, 토의 내용등 상세 적의 파악, 보고바람. 끝.

(국제기구조약국장 문동석)

1991. 6. 30 에 예고문에 의거 일반문서로 재분류됨

아주국장 :

앙 고 재	91년 2월 12일	과	기안자		과 장		국 장		차 관	장 관
							전결			

보안통제	외신과통제

0110

00247 ASI/AFP-ANOB-----
u 1 Australia-Japan 02-05 0389

Japanese POWs lodge claim for billions in compensation

CANBERRA, Feb 5 (AFP) - Almost 10,000 Australian prisoners of the Japanese during World War II -- or their widows -- are part of an international claim lodged in Geneva for compensation from the Japanese government.

The International Commission of the Red Cross has backed the claim, lodged on Monday by a Canadian veterans' group, before the United Nations International Human Rights Commission.

Apart from Canadians and Australians, the claim also covers POWs from the United States, the Netherlands and New Zealand.

The claim is for several billion dollars in compensation, with individual payments of 20,000 U.S. dollars to an estimated 200,000 claimants being sought.

Gordon Jamieson, an official with the specially-formed Australian Ex-POWs Committee, said Tuesday his group had already submitted a list of 6,057 Australia POWs or their widows to the International Human Rights Commission.

Another list of 3,500 Australian claimants is being prepared.

About 22,000 Australians were POWs of the Japanese of which about 8,000 died while in captivity.

The statement notes that Japan maintains it is not liable as any compensation to be paid was provided for in the 1952 Peace Treaty entered into between Japan and the allied powers.

7

0111

..r the Treaty, individual compensation payments were to be made from ..zed Japanese assets in respective allied nations, but in Australia's case this only resulted in payments of between 30 and 100 Australian pounds.

The POW submission argues that the individual human rights of allied prisoners of war and civilian internees were not affected by the Peace Treaty.

The basis of the argument is that allied governments, as Treaty signatories, had no legal authority under international law to remove the basic legal rights of their citizens.

An opinion from the International Committee of the Red Cross was incorporated in the material presented to the International Human Rights Commission.

It stated that a country remained responsible for breaches of the Geneva conventions "and may not absolve itself from responsibility on the grounds that those who committed the breaches have been punished.

"For example it remains liable to pay compensation," the opinion said.

jt/mjc/mb

AFP 051209 GMT FEB 91

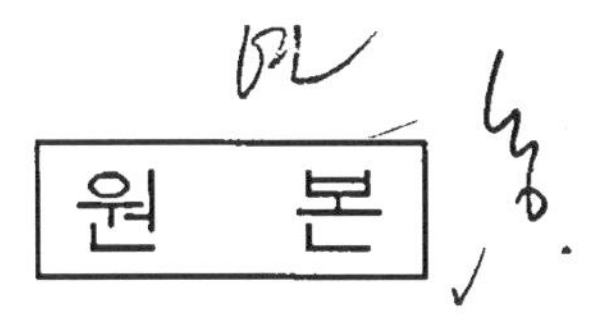

외 무 부

종 별 :

번 호 : GVW-0284 일 시 : 91 0212 1200

수 신 : 장관(국연,법무부,기정)

발 신 : 주 제네바대사대리

제 목 : 제 47차 유엔인권위 회의(7)

1. 표제회의는 2.11. 야간까지 회의를 연장, 의제 7,8,17,18 토의를 계속 하였으며, 2.12. 오전 동토의를 마치고 오후 부터는 의제 11항 (인권위 활동등 인권증진 방안) 토의를 시작할 예정임.

2. 의제 8항 (발전의 권리)관련, 2.11. 미국대표 (ABRAM 주제네바 대사)는 발전은 권리가 아닌 경제적 목표이며, 개인적 권리 및시민적 자유가 보장 되어야 성취될수 있다고 전제하고 2차 대전후 40년간의 대조적인 사례로서 남.북한 및 동.서독이 있다고 언급 하였는바 동 발언 요지는 아래와 같음

- 동일한 국민, 같은역사, 균등한 지원하에서 남한의 경제는 번성하고 있으며,오염되고 가난에 찌든 전체주의 체제하의 북한보다 남한의 생활수준은 몇배나 높음

- 상기 각 경우에 있어 인권이 보장된 곳에서 경제가 융성 하였으며, 인권이 조직적으로 부인되는 곳에서는 경제는 실패하고, 시장은 침체되고, 국민들은 가능하기만 하면 동 지역을 떠나려 했음.

- 자유만으로 경제적 성공이 보장 되지는 않으나 압제는 경제적 실패를 확실히보장함.

- 정치적, 시민적 권리와는 달리 발전의 권리는 명확한 개념 및 실현성이 결여되어 있어 동권리가 보장 되기전에 기본적 자유는 실현될수 없다는 의미를 함축하고 있어 위험성이 있음.

- 각국 정부는 국내 개혁을 통해서만 궁극적으로 국민을 부양할수 있으며, 보츠오나가 하나의 사례임.

- 1993년 세계 인권 회의에서 발전과 인권규약상 기본적 권리와의 관계 문제가 토의 되어야 할것임.

국기국 1차보 정문국 안기부 법무부

PAGE 1 91.02.13 05:43 DA

외신 1과 통제관

0113

3. 한편 2.11. ANATOLY DENISSAV 소련연방 최고회의 위원은 특별연설을 통해 발틱 사태에 대한 정부입장을 자세히 설명하면서 금번 사태는 동지역내 극단주의 반대파 그룹간에 비합헌적 군대결성등 권리투쟁의 결과이며, 라트비아에서의 유혈사태는 동 내무성 산하 보안권 조직간의 충돌 결과라고 말하고 개별적이고 우발적인 사건으로 중앙정부를 비난하는 것은 바람직하지 않으며 동 사태는 대화, 자제, 협상을 통해 해결되어야 할것이라고 언급함. 또한 동 위원은 자국이 독재로 회귀하고 있다는 우려는 근거가 없으며 앞으로도 CSCE 파리 헌장을 준수할 것이라고 말함.

4. 의제 7,8항 토의에서 대부분의 서구 및 동구 대표들은 시민적, 정치적 권리와 경제적, 사회적, 문화적 권리의 불가분 성 및연계성을 언급하면서 경제발전을이유로 기본적 인권이 제한 되어서는 안된다고 강조 하였으며, 이태리 대표는냉전체제 종식등 국제환경 변화를 감안, 경제적 권리등의 보장에도 관심을 기울일것을 제의함. 한편 대부분의 개도국 대표들은 지난 10년간 대부분 개도국의 경제실정이 악화되고 있는바, 외채문제 조기해결 및 신국제 경제질서 확립을 통해 개도국내 경제적 권리등이 보장되어야 할것이라고 말하고, 발전의 권리의 중요성을 강조함. 바이로러시아 대표는 체르노빌 사건의 피해를 언급 하면서 환경 문제의 중요성을 강조함.

5. 의제 17,18 토의에서 대표들은 인권협약 산하 위원회간의 협력체제 강화, 동위원회에 대한 정규 유엔예산의 지원 필요성, 동 위원회의 인권침해 방지 역할 재고를 위한 특별보고관 및 NGO 참여 방안을 언급함. 호주 대표는 미국 및 중국의인권규약 가입을 촉구 하였으며, 스웨덴 대표는 사형 금지에 관한 제 2 의정서의 조기발효 필요성을 강조함.

끝.

(대사대리 박영우-국장)

PAGE 2

0114

외 무 부

종 별 :

번 호 : GVW-0287 일 시 : 91 0212 1630

수 신 : 장관(국연,법무부,기정)

발 신 : 주 제네바 대사대리

제 목 : 제 47차 유엔 인권위 회의(8)

1. 금 2.12 오전 표제회의는 의제 7,8,17,18 토의를 마쳤음.

2. 이날 회의 종료 직전 북한 대표 (박덕훈 참사관)는 전일 미국대표의 발언에대한 답변권 행사를 통해 아래와 같이 발언함.

- 한반도 분단에 책임이 있는 미국대표가 한반도 현실을 모르고 있음.

- 북한국민은 정치, 경제, 사회적 권리를 향유하며, 복지의 혜택을 받고 있음.

- 북한은 독자적 경제를 유지하며 발전하고 있고, 미국의 경제 봉쇄에도 불구 45-87 년간 경제규모가 450 배 증가함.

- 전세계적인 화해 무두와 함께 작년부터 한반도 에서도 최고위급 회담이 개최되고 있으며, 2.11 에는 남.북한 당국이 국제 체육대회에 단일팀을 보내기로 합의한바 있음.

- 미국이 국제적 심판관으로서 행동하는 것은 중지 되어야 함.

끝

(대사대리 박영우-국장)

국기국 1차보 정문국 안기부 법무부

PAGE 1 91.02.13 06:28 DA

외신 1과 통제관

0115

원 본

외 무 부

종 별 :

번 호 : GVW-0310　　　　일 시 : 91 0215 2030

수 신 : 장관(국연,법무부,기정)

발 신 : 주 제네바 대사대리

제 목 : 제 47차 유엔 인권회의(9)

1. 표제회의는 2.14 오전 의제 11 항 토의를 마치고 의제 10항 (고문등 피구금자 인권) 토의를시작하였음.

2. 의제 11항 토의에서 정부 및 NGO 대표들은 유엔 주관으로 93년 개최 예정인세계 인권회의가 68년 테헤란 회의이후 25년만에 개최되는 회의로서 세계적인 인권 보장의 현황 및 향후방향을 검토하는 중요한 계기임을 강조함.

3. 미국, 덴마크 등 서방측 대표들은 지난 수십년동안 유엔에서의 인권 활동이 인권 관련각종 국제 규범의 제정에 집중 되었었다고말하고, 이제는 동 규범의 광범위한 시행 및 규범위반 사례에 대한 시정에 관심을 가져야 할것이라고 강조하고 세계인권 회의에서 동 방안이 토의되어야 할 것이라고 말함. 덴마크 대표는인권보장의강화를 위해서 국가간의 대화가 필요하며, 인권문제에서의 국제적 협력을위해서는인권 상황에 대한 TRANSPARANCY 확보가 최선책이라고 말함. 또한 미국 대표는유엔인권회의 의제의 정치화 및 선별화경향에 우려를 표명하고 세계 인권 회의가 유엔인권 활동을 재검토하는 계기가 되어야 할것이라고 강조함.

4. 중국대표는 유엔에서의 인권문제 토의시 이중적 기준, 선별성, 실리주의가 팽배하고 있다고 말하고 세계 인권회의에서는 정치체제등 국내여건이 다른 국가의 견해도 고려되어야 할 것이라고 언급함.

인도대표는 동 회의시 특정국가의 인권문제가 토의되어서는 안될것이며, 타인 또는 타국의 권리를 존중하지 않으므로써 발생하는 인권위반문제에도 관심을 가져야할 것이라고 말함.

5. 독일 및 벨지움 대표는 90년도 경사리결의(90/48)에 따라 인권위가 과반수 위원국 제의가 있는 경우 특별회의를 개최할수있게 된것을 평가함.

6. 의제 10항 토의에서 KOOIJAMANS 고문문제 특별보고관은 자신의 제 6차 보고서(

국기국　안기부　법무부

PAGE 1

91.02.16 10:17 FA

외신 1과 통제관

0116

E/CN.4/1991/7)설명을 통해, 고문사건은 진상을 파악하기가 어려운 특성 때문에정부를 비판하기 위한 도구로 사용될 가능성이 있다고 말하고 자신은 사건의진위를판단할 지위가 아니므로 해당정부가 정확한 정보를 제공하여 줄것을 요청함. 또한동 보고관은 쿠웨이트 정부가 제출한 점령쿠웨이트내 인권 상황 보고서가 곧 발표될예정이라고 말하고, 90년 필리핀 방문 및 금년도 인니 정부의 방문 초청을 평가하였으며, 코스타리카 정부가 제안한 구금시설 정기 방문에 관한 선택의정서(고문방지협약관련)의 채택 필요성을 강조함. 한편 상기 보고서에는 52개국관련 고문사건이포함되어 있는바, 아국과 관련하여서는 홍성담사건등에 대한 아국정부의 답변내용이 포함됨.

7. 또한 TOSEVSKI 강제 실종 실무위 의장은 동실무위 보고서(E/CN.4/1990/20) 설명을 통해 83년에 총 4070 건의 강제 실종이 동 실무위에 접수된 이래로 매년 동숫자가 감소되는 추세이며,90년도에는 44개국 관련 434 건이 접수되었다고 밝힘. 동 의장은 민주화과정 국가에서 인권위반자에 대한 불처벌(IMPUNITY) 사례가 빈번하다고 지적하고 인권 보장의 차원에서 동문제에 관심을 가져야 하며, 강제 실종 문제와관련한 국제 규범이 조속히 채택되어야 할것이라고 강조함.

8. 미국대표는 고문의 존재는 도덕성과 인권의 개념을 부인하는 것이며, 동 정부가 금명간 고문방지 협약을 비준할 것이라고 언급하고, 현재이라크 관련 3420 건의강제 실종 사건이 미결상태에 있다고 지적함. 또한 쿠웨이트 대표는 점령 쿠웨이트 지역에 서의 이라크의 각종 고문행위 및 강제구금등 인권 유린 상황을 비난하였음.

9. AI 대표는 강제 실종이 군사정권하에서만존재하는 것이 아니며, 보안군등 인권 위반자에 대한 비처벌이 강제 실종 사건을 유발하는 주요요인이 되고 있다고 말하고 페루, 필리핀.스리랑카, 과테말라, 콜롬비아, 모리타니아에서의 사례를 언급함. 또한 INT'L FEDERATION OF HUMAN RIGHT는 베트남, 중국, 서부사하라지역에서의 불법 체포 및 실종문제를 언급함. 끝

(대사대리 박영우-국장))

관리 번호 91-157

원 본

외 무 부

종 별 :

번 호 : GVW-0311 일 시 : 91 0215 2100

수 신 : 장관(국연,법무부,기정)

발 신 : 주 제네바 대사대리

제 목 : 제 47차 유엔 인권위 회의(10)

1. 금 2.15. 표제회의는 의제 10 항(고문등 피구금자 인권) 토의를 계속하였으며, 오후에는 의제 4 항 및 9 항 관련 8 개 결의안 및 결정안을 채택함.

또한 이날 회의어서는 NASTES 루마니아 외무장관 및 NSANZIMANA 루안다 법무장관의 특별 연설이 있었음.

2. 오후 회의에서 WCC 산하 국제 교회 위원회 대표는 페루 및 필리핀에서의불법구금 및 강제 실종 사건을 상세히 거론함. 또한 동 대표는 아국과 관련하여 KNCC 의 발표를 인용, 90 년도 11 개월간 1,746 명의 양심수가 체포되었는바,이는 전년도에 비해 50 퍼센트 증가된 것이며 이중 40 퍼센트가 국가보안법에따라 SPY 로서 체포되었다고 말하고 평화 및 통일을 위한 활동이 전복활동으로서 간주되고 있다고 주장함. 아국 대표단은 2.18(월) 회의시 답변권 행사를 통해 상기 발언을 반박할 예정임.

3. 이날 회의에서 NGO 대표들은 고문 및 강제 실종문제와 관련하여 알젠틴,쿠바, 모로코(서부사하라) 엘살바돌, 이란, 인니, 필리핀, 중국, 케냐, 자이레를 비난하였으며, MINORITY RIGHTS GROUP 대표는 유럽국가에서의 망명자에 대한 구금사례를 언급함.

4. 한편 의제 4 항 (피점령 아랍지역 인권) 및 의제 9 항 ((134)결권) 관련아래 결의안이 채택됨.

가. L. 2(피점령 아랍지역 인권)

- 호명 부표결과 L.2(A) 는 찬성 28, 반대 1(미국), 기권 0, L.2(B) 는 28:1:11 로 각각 채택됨.

나. L.3(피점령 시리아지역 인권)

- 호명부표결과 32:1(미국):8 로 채택됨.

국기국 장관 차관 1차보 2차보 청와대 안기부 법무부

PAGE 1

91.02.16 11:06

외신 2과 통제관 BW

0118

다. L.7 (피점령 아랍지역내의 이스라엘인 이주 반대)

- 38:0:1(미국) 로 채택

라. L.5 (피 점령 팔레스타인 지역 인권)

- 호명 부표결과 29:1(미국):12 로 채택

마. 의장이 제안한 L.4 (캄보디아 사태), L.6(아프간사태), L.8/REV. 1 (서사하라문제)는 부표없이 채택됨.

5. 상기 피점령 아랍지역 인권 결의안과 관련 서방대표들은 금년도 결의안 내용이 예년에 비해 일방적인 입장이 강조되었으며, 표현이 너무 강경하다고 비판함.

6. 표제회의는 토의 순서를 변경, 의제 10 항 토의를 마치고 2.19(화) 부터는 의제 12 항(세계인권 상황) 토의에 들어갈 예정임. 끝

(대사대리 박영우-국장)

예고 91.6.30 까지

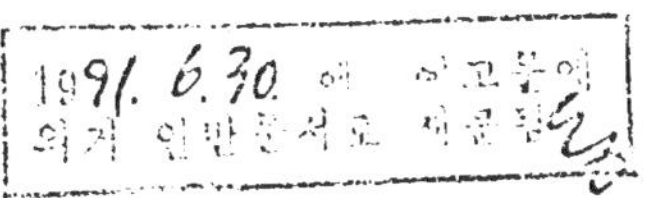
1991. 6.30 에 예고문에 의거 일반문서로 재분류됨

PAGE 2

0119

관리번호 91-167

법 무 부

인권 2031-38 503-7045 1991. 2. 19.

수신 외무부장관

참조 국제기구조약국장

제목 제47차 유엔 인권위원회 회의 대비자료 송부

1. 국연 2031-151 ('91.1.22)와 관련입니다.

2. 귀부에서 요청한 회의 대비자료를 별첨과 같이 송부하오며,

3. 인권관련 국제회의시 북한형법, 기타 북한 인권유린사례의 거론방안에 대하여는 당부에서는 이견이 없습니다.

첨부 : 관련자료 1부. 끝.

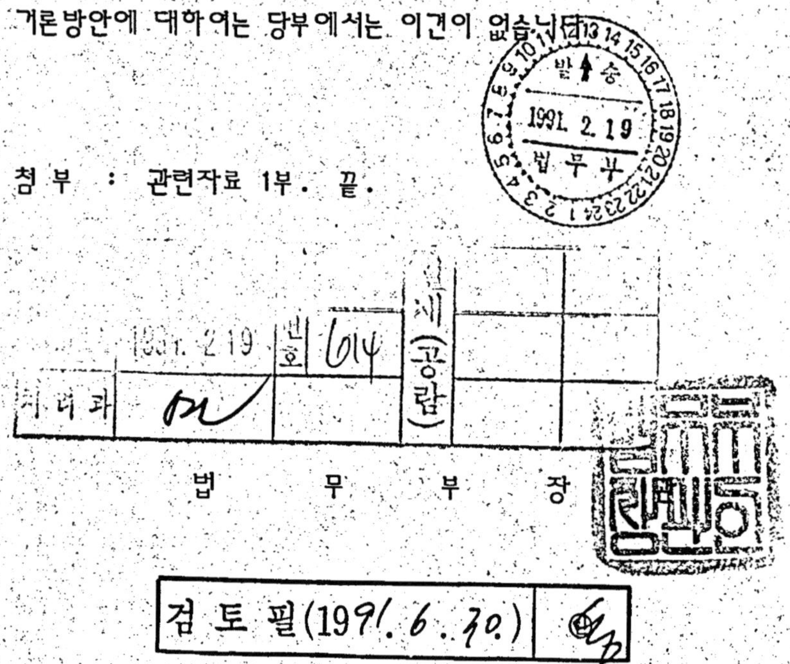

법 무 부 장

검토필(1991. 6. 30.)

0120

북한형법의 반인권성 기타 문제점에 대한 설명자료

1. 목적과 기능상의 특징

o 대부분의 나라가 자기나라의 체제수호를 위한 법률적 장치를 갖고 있지만 이는 외부의 침략세력으로부터 국가와 국민을 지키고자 하는 방어적 안보형사법인데 비하여, 북한형법은 한반도 전역의 공산혁명을 달성하는데 장애가 되는 모든 세력들을 적발 처단하기 위한 공격적인 형벌법임

o 그리고 자유민주주의국가의 형사법이 법제정서부터 법해석.적용, 법집행에 이르기까지 기본권보장을 최우선 과제로 하는데 비하여 북한형법은 오로지 계급투쟁과 프롤레타리아 독재의 위력한 무기이고 그들의 정치노선을 실현시키고 그들이 원하는 공산주의적 인간으로 개조시켜 이를 장악키 위한 가장 강력한 수단으로 구실함

o 북한형법은 이러한 목적과 기능을 수행하기 위하여 대부분 비민주적, 반인권적, 반통일적 조항으로 구성되어 있음

0121

2. 비민주성과 반인권성

o 우신, 이떤 범죄적 행위에 대한 해당규정이 없으면 그 행위와 가장 비슷한 죄에 관한 조항을 적용함으로써 유추해석을 정면으로 허용하고, 또한 민족반역행위에 대하여는 과거 일제시대의 행위까지 소급하여 처벌함으로써 형법의 기본원리인 죄형법정주의를 완전히 무시하고 있음

o 그리고 소위 반혁명범죄와 살인죄에 대하여는 형사소추의 시효제도를 인정하지 않고 있으며 이는 소급 처벌규정과 함께 반혁명범죄자에 대하여 그가 살아있는 한 영원히 처벌을 면하지 못하도록 하고 있음

o 또한 반혁명범죄에 대하여는 형의 감경이나 집행유예를 할 수 없도록 할 뿐만 아니라 예외없이 불신고죄를 두고 있음

o 또한 특이한 것으로, 판사가 오판을 하거나 형량을 그릇되게 한 경우 담당판사를 부당재판죄로 처벌하고, 재판소는 자기사업에 대하여 주석과 당앞에 책임을 지도록 함으로써 사법권의 독립을 완전히 부정하고 있음

o 그외 당과 국가정책을 비방하거나 반동적인 사상을 조작, 전파하거나 반동적인 낙서나 투서를 한 자를 반동선전선동죄로 처벌하고, 사회주의. 공산주의운동, 노동운동을 반대하기만 하여도 사회주의국가 반대죄로

0122

처벌하며, 또 북한은 노동자의 천국이라고 하면서도 태업행위를 금지 함으로써 노동자의 기본권을 완전 박탈하고 있음

3. 반통일성

o 대한민국을 "원쑤" 또는 "적" 이라고 표현하면서 북한주민이 다른나라 또는 원쑤의 편으로 도주하면 조국반역죄로 처벌하고 외국대사관에 정치적 망명을 요구하는 행위도 이에 해당됨

o 또한 대한민국을 "미제국주의의 식민지" 라고 하면서 미제국주의의 식민통치를 도와주는 행위를 한 자는 민족반역죄로 처벌하는 바, 이는 그들에게 협조하지 않거나 정적 관계에 있는 자들을 숙청하거나 남한의 지도급인사들을 처단할 수 있는 근거조항으로 구실함

o 그리고 위의 조국반역죄나 민족반역죄, 반동선전선동죄, 사회주의국가 반대죄 뿐만 아니라 모든 반혁명범죄자들은 교육이나 교양에 의한 개조가 불가능하기 때문에 대부분 사형에 처하고 전재산을 몰수함

o 또 특이한 것은 부르죠아 문화를 반영한 문예작품, 물건들을 반입하거나 유포한 자들을 부르죠아문화 반입.유포죄로 처벌하고 있음

0123

관리 번호	91 -162

원 본

외 무 부

종 별 :

번 호 : GVW-0317 일 시 : 91 0219 1000

수 신 : 장관(국연)

발 신 : 주 제네바 대사대리

제 목 : 일본에 대한 배상청구

대: WGV-0211

1. 대호 인권위에 참석중인 호주, 카나다 및 ICRC 대표와 접촉, 확인한 사항을 아래 보고함.

가. 호주 대표가 확인한바에 의하면 호주 QUEENSLAND 주 재향군인회가 대호손해 배상 청구문제를 금차 인권위에 COMMUNICATION 으로 제기하였다고 하며, 그밖의 사항은 당지에서는 파악이 어렵다고 함.

나. ICRC 대표에 따르면 대호 청구문제가 2-3 년전에 인권위 또는 인권소위에 제기될 예정이라고 들은바 있을 뿐이며, ICRC 측에서 동건에 대해 간여한적은없다고 함. 또한 카나다 대표는 대호 내용에 대해 아는바 없다고 함.

2. 대호 문제가 유엔 인권위에 제기될 경우 의제 10 항 및 12 항 토의시 동재향군인회를 대신하여 다른 NGO 대표가 발언하거나, 동 NGO 요청에 따라 상기내용이 인권위 문서로서 배포되는 방법이 예상되는바, 현재까지 동건 관련 발언 또는 문서 배포는 없었음. 그밖에 동 재향군인회가 진정서(COMMUNICATION)를 1503 절차에 따라 유엔 인권 사무국에 제출할 가능성도 있는바, 그 경우에는 동절차가 비밀 사항이므로 파악이 어려움. 끝

(대사대리 박영우-국장)

예고 : 91.6.30. 까지

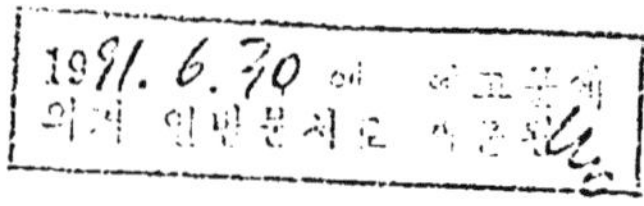

국기국 차관 1차보 2차보 아주국 구주국

PAGE 1

91.02.19 21:24

외신 2과 통제관 CH

0124

관리 번호 91-163

원 본

외 무 부

종 별 :

번 호 : GVW-0318　　　　일 시 : 91 0219 1000

수 신 : 장관(국연,법무부,기정)

발 신 : 주 제네바 대사대리

제 목 : 제 47차 유엔인권위 회의(11)

1. 금 2.18 표제회의는 의제 10 항 토의를 계속하였으며, 오전에는 GEZA JESZENSZKY 헝가리 외무장관, 오후에는 ABED AL SAMIE OMER 수단 인권담당장관의 특별연설이 있었음.

2. 오후회의에서 당관 이량참사관은 2.15. WCC 산하 국제교회 위원회 대표의 아국관련 발언에 대한 답변권 행사를 통해 아래와 같이 발언함.

- 상기 NGO 가 양심수라는 광범위하고 아직 정의가 확립되지 않은 용어를 사용하므로써 아국에 대한 그릇된 인식을 주려한것은 유감임.

- 88 년 이래 아국 정부는 인권보장 및 민주발전을 위해 광범위하고 획기적인 조치를 취해왔으며 90 년도 아국의 2 개 인권규약 및 선택의정서 가입은 상기조치를 대변하고 있음.

- 상기 NGO 발언에서 언급된 숫자는 국내실정법 위반자에 관한 것이며, 동 NGO 가 염두에 두고 있는 것으로 보이는 양심수의 범주에는 포함되지 않음

3. 이날 회의에서 이태리, 스위스, 벨지움, 폴투갈 대표들은 일부 국가에서인권 위반 행위를 한 군인 및 정부관리들을 화합이라는 명목하에 처벌하지 않음으로써 고문 행위 및 강제실종이 묵인되는 현상에 우려를 표명하고, 동 IMPUNITY 문제를 인권위에서 토의할 것을 제의함. 또한 금차회의시 코스타리카가 제안한 구금 시설 정기 방문에 관한 고문방지 형식 선택의정서의 채택 필요성을강조하였으며, 고문 문제 특별보고관 및 강제실종 실무위 위원의 특정국가 방문에따른 후속 조치가 이행되지 않고 있다고 말하고 페루, 과테말라등을 지적함.

4. 또한 중국대표는 고문, 불법구금 및 강제실종등에 대한 NGO 의 비판에 대해 자국 정부가 천안문사건 관련자에 대해 공정한 재판의 권리를 부여하고 있으며, 티벳주민의 인권보장등을 위해 노력하고 있다고 주장함. 페루대표는 작년도 신정부

국기국　장관　차관　1차보　2차보　중아국　안기부　법무부

PAGE 1　　　　91.02.19 23:00

외신 2과 통제관 CH

0125

출범위후 국내상황 및 정부의 민주화 조치를 설명함.

5. 고문 및 강제실종 사례와 관련 NGO 대표들이 언급한 국가는 아래와 같음.

- 중국, 스리랑카, 인니(동티몰)필리핀, 자이레, 페루, 과테말라, 혼루라스,칠레, 모로코(서사하라)

또한 놀웨이 대표는 케냐에서의 고문사례의 우려를 표명하였으며, 폴부갈대표는 동티몰 인권상황과 관련 인니정부를 비난함.

6. JESZENSZKY 헝가리 외무장관은 특별연설을 통해 인권위반은 국내문제로서 간주될 수 없다고 전제하고 현재 아프간, 이란, 엘살바돌, 미얀마, 쿠바, 루마니아, 이락, 피점령 쿠웨이트에서의 인권위반에 대한 유엔기관이 토의하는 것은정당하다고 말함. 동 장관은 특히 이라크의 쿠웨이트 침공을 강력히 비난하였으며, 발틱에서의 소련군의 무력사용, 루마니아에서의 소수민족에 대한 인권침해등에 우려를 표명함. 또한 자국정부가 93 년도 세계인권 회의를 부다페스트에 유치할 용의가 있음을 공식적으로 밝힘. 한편 이라크 및 쿠바대표는 답변권 행사를통해 동 장관의 자국발언을 반박함. 끝

(대사대리 박영우-국장)

예고:91.6.30 까지

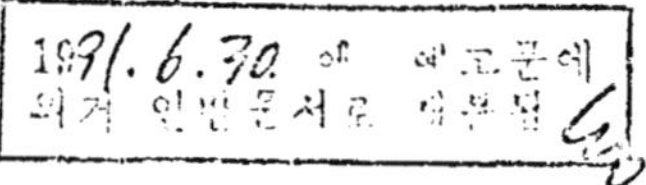

PAGE 2

0126

관리번호	91-166

원 본

외 무 부

종 별 :

번 호 : GVW-0325 일 시 : 91 0220 1000

수 신 : 장관(국연,법무부,기정)

발 신 : 주 제네바 대사대리

제 목 : 제 47차 유엔 인권위 회의(12)

연: 제네(정) 2031-10

1. 금 2.19 표제회의는 의제 10 항 토의를 마치고, 야간에는 의제 12 항(세계 인권상황) 토의를 시작하여 1503 절차에 따른 진정서 심의를 비공개로 하였음.

2. 이날 오후 회의에서 NGO 인 INT'L ASSOCIATION OF DEMOCRATIC LAWYERS 대표는 모로코 및 아국의 인권상황을 거론한바, 아국 관련 발언 내용은 아래와 같음.

- 남한에서는 내년 1 천 2 백여명이 정치적 이유로 투옥되며, 서울 및 목포교도소에 수용되어 있는 정치범들은 자의적이고 조직적인 폭력의 대상이 되고 있음. "한민련"이 발간하는 "한국소식"에 의하면 수감자들은 각종 불법처우 및 고문을 당하고 있음.

- 90.7 월 법무분 정치적 성향의 인사들이 정치범을 방문하는 것을 금지하였음.

- 90.9 월 6 명의 외래의사가 교도소내 검진을 한 결과, 36 건의 응급처리 사례가 확인됨.

3. 상기 NGO 는 평양집회에 참가한바 있는 친북성향의 단체로서 89. 8 월 제 41 차 인권 소위시에도 아국관련 상황에 대해 언급한바 있으며, 상기 발언내용은 연호 "남한의 민주 및 인권을 위한 국제법률가 위원회" 명의의 1503 절차 관련 진정서 내용과 동일함.

4. 상기 발언에 대해 당관 이량 참사관은 답변권을 행사하여 아래와 같이 반박함.

- 상기 NGO 가 아국정부에 대해 왜곡된 입장을 가지고 있는 것은 잘 알려진바와 같으며, 금번 발언 내용은 허위로 일관됨.

- 언급된 사건들이 진실로 존재한다면 피해자 또는 가족들이 고문 관련 조사 및 배상에 관한 법적 절차에 따라 동 문제를 법원에 제기하지 않았는지 의심스러움. 지난 1 월 서울 형사지법에서 고문 경찰관에 대해 최고 5 년의 징역형을선고한 것은 상기

국기국 장관 차관 1차보 2차보 청와대 안기부 법무부

PAGE 1 91.02.20 21:33

외신 2과 통제관 CA

0127

절차의 실효성을 입증하고 있음.

-또한 정부 비판언론을 포함한 국내 언론매체에 동 사건들이 보도된 사실이없다는 것도 동 발언의 허구성을 입증함.

5. 한편 오전회의에서 화란대표는 강제 실종 실무위 보고서 및 고문 문제 특별 보고관 보고서의 내용을 인용하면서 이락, 스리랑카, 필리핀, 터키, 수단, 버마, 인도, 중국 및 아국의 사례를 비판함. 동 대표는 몇건의 고문 사건에 대해한국정부가 동 고문사실을 부인하였으며, 조사과정에서의 피의자들의 발언이 사실로 밝혀진 점을 언급한바, 진실을 강요하는 것은 고문 금지 의무에서 면제된다는 한국정부의 견해는 받아들이기 어렵다고 언급함.

6. 동 화란대표는 상기 발언에 앞서 동 연설문을 아국 대표단에 전달한바 있음. 이와 관련, 아국 대표단은 동 대표와 사전 접촉, 금번 연설에서 아국 사례가 언급되는 것 자체가 여타 51 개국의 사례에 비추어 볼때 균형을 잃고 공정치 못한 처사이며, 또한 동 보고서내에서 아국정부의여타 설명 내용은 생략한채 부수적인 내용만을 추출, 아국정부의주된 논거라고 비판하는 것은 사실을 오도하고, 고문 문제 특별 보고관 활용에 협조적인 아국정부의 이미지를 손상할 우려가 있다는 요지의 아측 입장을 통보한바 있음.

7. 이날 회의에서 케냐, 폴투갈, 이란, 인니 대표는 답변권을 행사, NGO 및타정부 대표의 자국 인권문제 비판내용을 반박함.

8. 본부 송영완 사무관은 예정대로 당지 도착함. 끝

(대사대리 박영우-국장)

예고 : 91.6.30 까지

원 본

외 무 부

종 별 :

번 호 : GVW-0336 일 시 : 91 0221 1100

수 신 : 장관(국연,법무부,기정)

발 신 : 주 제네바 대사대리

제 목 : 제 47차 유엔 인권위 회의(13)

1. 금 2.20 표제회의는 의제 12항 토의를 계속하여 오전에는 비공개로 1503 절차 진정서 심의를 하였으며, 오후에는 야간까지 회의를 연장, 정부및 NGO 대표 발언을 청취함 또한 이날 회의에서는 NIMY NGIMBI 자이레 부수상 및 GROSESPIELL 우루과이 외무장관이 특별 연설을 하였음.

2. 미국 수석대표 (BLACKWELL 인권담당 대사)는 이라크가 국내에서 뿐만 아니라 점령 쿠웨이트에서 민간인 학살 행위등을 자행하고 있다고 구체적 인권 위반 사례를 열거, 비난 하였으며, 독재 체재로서 쿠바, 이란, 중국, 미얀마의 인권상황을 비난함. 또한 국내 내전등 징정불안에 따라 인권 위반 행위가 빈번한 국가로서 엘살바돌, 과테말라, 모리타니아, 스리랑카를 지적하고 발틱 사태 관련 소련 정부의무력 사용을 비난하면서, 유고 및 사이프러스 문제는 당사자간 대화와 협상을 통해 해결 되어야 할것이 라고 말함. 동 대표는 인권 상황이 개선된 국가로서 동구, 소련, 네팔, 베넹, 칠레, 하이티를 열거함.

3. 상기 미국대표 발언시 언급되지는 않았으나, 발언직후 회의장에서 배포된 연설문에는 아래와 같이 북한에 대한 비난 내용이 포함되어 있음.

- 북한은 가장 기본적인 인권 마저 보장 하기를 거부하면서, 주민을 국가와 당의 전권에 철저히 예속시키고 있음.

- 가혹한 형법은 망령, 당 또는 국가에 대한 비판, '반혁명' 인쇄물 소지등 광범위한 정치적 위반 행위에 대해 사형을 규정하고 있음.

- 각종 보고서에 따르면 10만명 이상의 정치범 및 가족이 여러곳의 수용소에 수용되어 있음.

4. 파키스탄 대표는 카시미르 문제와 관련 인도정부를 비난 하였으며, 에디오피아 및 브룬디 대표는 사이프러스 문제를 언급함.

국기국 안기부 법무부

PAGE 1

91.02.21 22:40 DA

외신 1과 통제관

0129

5. AI 대표는 과테말라, 이라크, 중국, 미안마, 스리랑카, 수단, 시리아에서 심각한 인권 위반행위가 계속 되고 있다고 말하고 특히 최근 인권위가 이라크 및 중국의 인권 상황이 악화 되었음에도 불구, 아무런 조치를 취하지 않았음을 지적하였으며, 인권위가 객관적이고 지속적으로 이라크의 인권 상황을 감시할 것을 촉구함. ICJ 대표도 이라크의 쿠르드족 학살등 심각한 인권상황에 인권위가 침묵을 지켰다고 비난 하였으며, 알젠틴 정부의 인권위반 행위자 사면 및 과테말라 인권상황 악화를 언급함.

6. 국제교회 위원회는 과테말라, 수단, 엘살바돌, 스리랑카 문제를, INT'L ASSOCIATION OFDEMOCRATIC LAWYERS 는 터키 및 과테말라 문제를, PAX ROMANA 는 과테말라 문제를, WORLD MOVEMENTOF MOTHERS 는 아동 인신매매 문제를 언급함. 그밖에 NGO대표들이 비난한 국가는 아래와 같음.

- 이라크, 이란, 터키, 필리핀, 미얀마, 소련, 혼두라스, 콜롬비아, 자이레, 니제, 에디오피아, 파키스탄.

7. 법무부 권영석 검사는 예정대로 당지 도착회의 참석중임.

끝

(대사대리 박영우-국장)

주 제 네 바 대 표 부

제네(정) 2031-196 1991. 2.21

수신 : 장관

참조 : 국제기구조약국장

제목 : 제 47차 유엔인권위 회의 관련 문서 송부

표제회의 의제 10항 관련, Kooijmans 고문문제 특별보고관 보고서 및 강제실종위 보고서를 별첨 송부합니다.

첨부 : 1. 고문문제 특별보고관 보고서(E/CN.4/1991/17) 1부.

2. 강제실종위 보고서(E/CN.4/1991/20, Add. 1) 각 1부. 끝.

주 제 네 바 대 사

선 결		결		
접수	1991.2.5	11718		
처리과				

0131

주 제 네 바 대 표 부

제네(정) 2031-5 1991. 2.21

수신 : 장관

참조 : 국제기구조약국장

제목 : 제 47차 유엔인권위 회의 관련 발언문 송부

연 : GVW-0284, 0311, 0325, 0336

1. 연호, 표제회의 관련 미국, 화란 및 NGO인 국제교회위원회대표 발언문과 아국 대표의 발언문을 별첨 송부합니다.

2. 또한 Jeszenszky 헝가리 외무장관등 주요정부 및 NGO대표의 연설문을 별첨 송부합니다.

첨부 : 1. 미국대표 발언문(의제 8항) 1부.
2. 미국대표 발언문(의제 12항) 1부.
3. 화란대표 발언문(의제 10항) 1부.
4. 국제교회위원회 대표 발언문(의제 10항) 1부.
5. 아국대표 발언문 2부.
6. 기타 연설문 각 1부. 끝.

1991. 6. 30 에 예고문에 의거 인반문서로 재분류됨

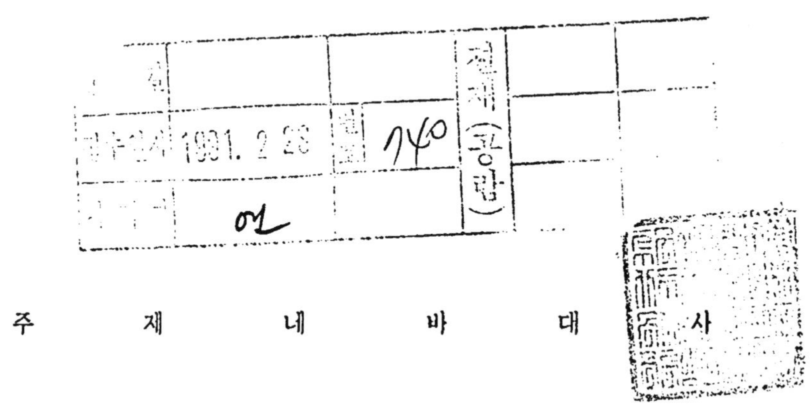

주 제 네 바 대 사

0132

1. 미국대표 연설문(의제8)

UNITED STATES MISSION TO INTERNATIONAL ORGANIZATIONS
GENEVA, SWITZERLAND

EMBARGOED UNTIL DELIVERY

47TH SESSION OF THE UN COMMISSION ON HUMAN RIGHTS

STATEMENT

BY

AMBASSADOR MORRIS B. ABRAM

AGENDA ITEM 8: THE RIGHT TO DEVELOPMENT

FEBRUARY 11, 1991

Check Against Delivery

Highlights:

-- Development is not a right but an economic goal whose achievement depends on respect for individual rights and civil liberties.

-- After forty years of competition between statist governments and market democracies, we now know that economies prosper where human rights are respected and stagnate where human rights are systematically denied.

-- "Freedom alone may not guarantee economic success; but repression most certainly guarantees economic failure."

-- Unlike political and civil rights, the right to development defies not only precise definition but immediate or ultimate realization. It is little more than a dangerous incitement because it implies that fundamental freedoms can not be fully realized until all people enjoy the right to development.

0133

The government of the United States remains deeply committed to development wherever people yearn for a better life. We know that today more than one third of the world is ill-clothed, ill-housed, and ill-fed; we know that the plight of the less of the least grows more extreme. We care about development and will continue to expend our treasure and energies to help advance it throughout the world. We will continue to examine new concepts for encouraging economic growth. And we will participate in future discussions in all U.N. fora where development and human rights are raised.

How can development be best achieved? Some argue that development is not a goal but a right that requires the moral and coercive authority of law for its enforcement. We believe in another vision: that development is a goal that depends on respect for individual rights and civil liberties.

How have these competing visions fared in the laboratory of human affairs? The post-war period has produced, unintentionally, a forty-year controlled experiment in development. North Korea and South Korea. West Germany and East Germany. The same people, the same history. Essentially equal resources bases. But South Korea's economy is thriving, and its standard of living is many times higher than in North Korea's polluted, poverty-stricken totalitarian regime. In each case economies prospered where human rights were respected; where they were systematically denied, economies failed, markets stagnated, and the people left -- if they could leave -- taking with them society's most precious resource: their talent and ingenuity.

Freedom alone may not guarantee economic success; but repression most certainly guarantees economic failure.

Why? Because the protection of human rights is a <u>sine qua non</u> for sustainable development. Where these rights are respected, the rule of law prevails. Businesses take risks and invest capital. That attracts foreign investment, which infuses developing economies with capital, skilled labor, know-how, and greater markets.

Development requires protection of the human right to own property, so that investors and inventors will know that the fruits of their labors will not be seized by the state. Otherwise, the wells of ingenuity and entrepreneurship dry up and economies stagnate.

0134

Development requires equality of opportunity, without consideration of race, religion, caste or color, so that individuals may go as far as their abilities can carry them. And development requires the chance for full political participation of all citizens to assure from governments an honest accounting. A centrally-planned economy, unchecked by the ballot and the press, invites graft, corruption, and favoritism. These are the self-inflicted obstacles to development.

These rights promise liberty to pursue economic goals, not equality in their achievement. But those nations which have put liberty ahead of equality have ended up doing better by equality than those with the reverse priority.

The civil and political rights in the Universal Declaration are more or less pristine. They can be defined and enforced because they mandate a specific, precise relationship between the individual and the state. When we speak of freedom from imprisonment without a fair trial, we know what liberty is at stake. Like other fundamental freedoms, it protects the citizen from the state. Like other fundamental freedoms, it is achieved the moment governments stop abridging individual liberties.

We still have a long way to go before international respect for these principles is complete. The world is a still a dangerous place for individuals who fear their governments. The star chamber, the third degree, the knock at the door are not historical curiosities but, in some places part of the statecraft of repression. Much of our original mandate has not yet been met.

Given these undone labors, why are we dealing with a right to development? Unlike political and civil rights, it defies not only precise definition but immediate or ultimate realization. According to the Report on the Global Consultations on the Right to Development, "[t]he right to development is the right of individuals, groups, and peoples to participate in, contribute to, and enjoy continuous economic, social, cultural and political development, in which all human rights and fundamental freedoms can be fully realized."

What exactly does this mean? If it is a national right why is it on the agenda of the Human Rights Commission? Development issues properly belong in U.N.

forums that have a mandate to deal with development, such as UNDP, UNICEF, WIPO, WHO, or UNCTAD. But if development is a national right, then musn't it, as with all other rights, oblige someone, something, or some state to protect and respect it? Would it oblige the World Bank or a commercial bank to forgive a loan or to give money to build a tunnel, a railroad, or a school house? It seems preposterous. Yet that is precisely what the Report implies by stating that "[f]ailure to take into account the principles of the right to development in agreements between States and the World Bank, the IMF, and commercial banks with regard to external debt repayment and structural adjustment, frustrates the right to development and all human rights."

If it's not a national right, then is it an individual right? To whom is it owed and from where does it come? It's nowhere in the Universal Declaration, the document that should guide the work of this Commission. If it is a right, then who owes the duty to protect it? If it is a human or national right, is everyone or every state entitled to the same amount? By what measure do we calculate its realization? We know how to measure compliance with civil and political rights, since they tell governments what not to do. The right to freedom of thought, conscience, and religion under Article 18 of the Universal Declaration is realized the moment the state stops infringing it, and assures that others will do the same. But how do we quantify the right to development? How does the state "realize" the human right to development? How do we know when the right has been "realized"?

A great deal of time, money, and resources have been expended on trying to explain and "realize" this right. But the explanations do not explain, and the effort only distracts from solving the desperate want of human needs. It hasn't fed one child or created one job. It neither enlightens this Commission nor the outside world because it cannot stand up to even rudimentary legal analysis.

The right to development, I believe, is little more than an empty vessel into which vague hopes and inchoate expectations can be poured. But ideas have consequences. And this idea is a dangerous incitement because it implies that the fundamental freedoms cannot be fully realized until all people enjoy the right to development.

0136

Even the poorest societies can protect their citizens from torture and imprisonment. It doesn't cost one penny to integrate a lunch counter. It doesn't cost one penny to give people the right to vote. It doesn't cost one penny to allow them to bow their heads in prayer or to speak their minds. All governments can respect these things without draining their treasury. Those freedoms need not await the millennium or depend on the achievement of some economic goal. To say that is to empower and excuse those regimes that would suppress the rights of their citizens in the name of "development."

Development is be a worthy goal; we don't doubt that. But not every worthy goal is a right. And development neither replaces nor predicates fundamental freedoms. To place it side by side with those ancient rights that have illuminated the world and bettered the lives and livelihoods of men, debases the meaning of human rights. To call everything a human right does not to increase respect for fundamental liberties; it threatens to bring the whole concept into disrepute.

I sound this tocsin because we now know, after forty years of a hard and bitter cold peace, that men can be ruled by force or can rule by law. Men will ultimately choose the latter. We now know that the tensions of caste, creed, or color can either be suppressed by an iron fist or tempered by a common devotion to human rights. Men ultimately will choose the latter. These rights knit society together because they are the root, branch, and bole of being human. But if we dilute those human rights, or lump them together on a wish list of what we would like to make of our world, then they mean nothing, and the rule of law will fail.

The world can generate wealth sufficient to assuage famine, ignorance, and disease. For that to happen, governments must make the internal reforms that will enable them to eventually feed their people. This Commission, and future human rights assemblies leading to the 1993 World Conference on Human Rights, should be mindful of the fundamental links between human rights and development. The focus of this Commission and that Conference should be, as the General Assembly stated, "[t]o examine the relation between development and [those rights] . . . set out in the International Covenants on Human Rights." We are mindful of this mandate, and hope it will be the focus of that Conference.

0137

1. 미국대표 연설문 (의제 12)

UNITED STATES MISSION TO INTERNATIONAL ORGANIZATIONS
GENEVA, SWITZERLAND

(EMBARGOED UNTIL DELIVERY)

47TH SESSION OF THE U.N. COMMISSION ON HUMAN RIGHTS

S T A T E M E N T

BY

J. KENNETH BLACKWELL

HEAD OF THE UNITED STATES DELEGATION TO
THE UNITED NATIONS COMMISSION ON HUMAN RIGHTS

ON

ITEM 12
VIOLATIONS OF HUMAN RIGHTS AND FUNDAMENTAL FREEDOMS
IN ANY PART OF THE WORLD

February 20, 1991

(Check against Delivery)

0138

UNITED NATIONS HUMAN RIGHTS COMMISSION

FORTY-SEVENTH SESSION

ITEM 12

VIOLATIONS OF HUMAN RIGHTS AND FUNDAMENTAL FREEDOMS

IN ANY PART OF THE WORLD

Mr. Chairman, the history of humanity features an incessant struggle between aggressive violence and respect for the rights and interests of others. Civil rights are inherent in civilization; that is obvious from the word itself. On a larger scale, it is clear that nations which respect the human rights and fundamental freedoms of their own citizens do not assault neighboring countries or seek to seize their lands and livelihood.

Promoting respect for human rights and fundamental freedoms in all countries everywhere makes a vital contribution to our mutual search for a new world order based on the peaceful settlement of disputes and respect for international law. We can see this in Article 55 of the United Nations Charter, which begins with the words, "With a view to the creation of conditions of stability and well-being which are necessary for peaceful and friendly relations among nations." Then, after a few intervening lines, the same article of the Charter states that the United Nations shall promote "universal respect for, and observance of, human rights and fundamental freedoms for all without distinction as to race, sex, language, or religion."

The United Nations Commission on Human Rights is thus the world's preeminent international body which seeks to promote the effective enjoyment of human rights and fundamental freedoms. Regional institutions have their place, but the activities and appraisals of regional bodies are not and cannot be a substitute for resolute action by the United Nations Human Rights Commission. We cannot close our eyes to injustices here, asserting that we intend to deal with them elsewhere. The Commission on Human Rights operates under the United Nations Charter, the cornerstone of our worldwide organization, and

0139

pursuant to the Universal Declaration of Human Rights, a momentous document whose very name establishes its universal standing and role.

In that same spirit of universality and balance, the United States Department of State prepares an annual report on human rights practices around the world, for submission to the Congress. The annual report contains an objective description of the human rights situation in all other countries -- those friendly to the United States and those that are not.

The United States does not attempt to appraise ourselves; that is the prerogative of others. Nor do we claim to have attained perfection in implementing human rights and fundamental freedoms; that is our goal. We well understand that the struggle to promote human rights is a lengthy and difficult process.

The history of the United States attests to that. On July 4, 1776, our Declaration of Independence proclaimed that "all men are created equal." But it took the United States Government almost one hundred years to put that principle into effect, after a bloody civil war in which one side fought to save the Union and the other fought to save slavery. I have a strong reason to remember that, for I am the great great grandson of a former slave. Thus, from my personal heritage, I have a special obligation to speak out about human rights.

In the forty-five years since the United Nations Charter was signed -- and in the six months since Iraq assaulted its neighbor Kuwait -- the relationship between world peace and respect for human rights has become so obvious that to note it here may even seem boring. But this relationship is not boring, Mr. Chairman, for dictatorial regimes often succumb to blood lust or avarice. That certainly occurred on August 2, 1990, when Iraqi troops initiated their brutal terror against the Kuwaiti people and other innocent civilians who happened to be present. Torture, kidnaping, imprisonment, summary execution, and wholesale looting of private property became common practices in a land that had been peaceful and prosperous.

Eyewitnesses have told of Iraqi soldiers engaging in random reprisal killings of innocent civilians, and of assembling groups of boys, some of them as young as 12 years old, and then executing them in front of their families. In one particularly harrowing episode that occurred in September, a Kuwaiti physician responded to a distress call from the staff of the Kuwait maternity hospital, only to find upon his arrival there the bodies of 72 premature infants whom Iraqi troops had removed from their incubators and dumped callously on the ground. That obscenity permitted the soldiers to cart off the equipment, part of Iraq's systematic campaign to strip Kuwait of its medical facilities. In other incidents reported by eyewitnesses, Iraqi forces disconnected patients from life-support systems, turned patients out of beds, expelled the mentally ill from institutions so that they wandered along the roads and died of exposure, and denied civilians medical care or access to hospitals.

The atrocities perpetrated in Kuwait will rank as one of the cruelest episodes in the long saga of human rights abuses carried out by the regime of Saddam Hussein. Within Iraq, the regime's human rights record remains abysmal. As in previous years, there continues to be a persistent pattern of torture, summary executions, disappearances, arbitrary detentions, and the use of excessive force. We hope that the forthcoming liberation of Kuwait from Iraqi invaders will also help create a new situation of greatly increased respect for the human rights of the people of Iraq.

Other Fundamentally Repressive Societies

As in Iraq and occupied Kuwait, dictatorial regimes can persist only by resorting to systematic repression and the use of excessive force. Although the rhetorical excuses and cultural overtones tend to be unique, each repressive regime turns its back on the Universal Declaration of Human Rights and other accepted standards of the international community. Instead, self-appointed "guardians" or "guides" or "vanguards of the people" permit the individual to exercise only certain rights -- in small doses, and only as long as the ruling class happens to find that convenient.

Cuba is another country whose officials claim to act on behalf of the people and decide what rights they may enjoy. Last year, the Commission adopted resolution 1990/48, which called for the Cuban Government to cease its reprisals against human rights activists and respond to the many unanswered questions posed by the 1988 working group which visited Cuba. In addition, it asked the Secretary General to report on the results of his continuing contacts.

When the Human Rights Commission adopted resolution 1990/48, Cuban President Fidel Castro told the press not to imagine "that we will obey one word." At the time, Gustavo Arcos and other human rights monitors were besieged in their family home in Havana by what the Cuban Government referred to as a "spontaneous" demonstration -- even though the participants traveled there in buses, by prearrangement.

0141

This disdain for the Commission is not new. When the 1988 working group asked to visit Quivican Prison, Cuban authorities replied that the prison was closed. In fact, however, Quivican Prison was operating then and is operating now. Many human rights activists are imprisoned within it.

The United States Government welcomes the recent report of the Secretary General and the efforts he has made to carry out the reponsibilities that the Commission assigned to him. Yet it is clear that Cuba has not responded to questions asked by the working group, and has not ended its repressive measures directed against human rights activists.

Americas Watch, a respected non-governmental organization, has recently published a report which gives the following description of the current situation in Cuba:

> Cuba's human rights practices are sharply at odds with international standards. Cuban laws that curtail basic rights enumerated in the Universal Declaration of Human Rights -- freedom of expression, association, assembly and movement, and the rights of privacy and due process -- remain in force. There are no legal institutions independent of the Government and the governing Communist Party that could ensure respect for such rights. There are no free press, no opposition political parties, no independent judiciary, no independent labor unions, and no legally recognized human rights organizations.

Amnesty International and Freedom House, two other respected non-governmental organizations, have also published recent reports that document continuing human rights violations in Cuba. Given world trends involving greater democracy and increased respect for human rights, Cuba is more and more isolated in its refusal to adhere to internationally accepted standards.

Serious human rights abuses continue to afflict the people of Iran. In his November 1990 report to the General Assembly, the special rapporteur cited instances of torture, execution after summary proceedings, and detention or imprisonment on political grounds. He concluded that "the enormous quantity and variety of allegations and complaints received from very diverse sources . . . provide a credible factual basis for the belief that human rights violations occur frequently in the country and that government action to prevent and remedy such violations has not been sufficient to put an end to them."

0142

Iran's human rights record also involves harassment of and discrimination against religious minorities, including the Baha'i community. There remains reason for deep concern about repression of peaceful political dissent, exemplified by the arrest and detention last summer of more than twenty people who had signed an open letter to the President of Iran that demanded greater political freedom.

Iranian exiles, too, have raised their voices in urging greater respect for human rights within Iran. But on April 24, 1990, there occurred a deplorable incident: the assassination of Professor Kazem Rajavi, a former Iranian diplomat who was living in exile in Coppet, Switzerland. In its resolution 1990/8, adopted without a vote, the Sub-Commission on Prevention of Discrimination and Protection of Minorities paid tribute to Prefessor Rajavi's memory, praised his dedication and struggle for the promotion and protection of human rights, and strongly condemned the assassination.

There are some positive developments, for the Government of Iran has expressed its desire to cooperate with the United Nations. Within the past year, Iran has permitted the special rapporteur to make two visits. We hope that the Government of Iran will give full cooperation to the special rapporteur in seeking to promote the effective enjoyment of human rights and fundamental freedoms, and will intensify its efforts to investigate and rectify allegations of abuses.

In China, martial law has been lifted, and some reform programs have been resumed. In addition, the Chinese Government has shown a new willingness to conduct serious discussions on human rights issues, as evidenced by the December 1990 visit to China of the Assistant Secretary of State for Human Rights and Humanitarian Affairs. But the regime still seeks to dominate all aspects of Chinese society, and there continue to be serious abuses of human rights. Chinese authorities have maintained their practice of employing overwhelming force against ethnic unrest, as occurred in the suppression of several small pro-independence demonstrations in Tibet and of a violent uprising among Muslims in southwest Xinjiang province. Hundreds still languish in detention for their part in the pro-democracy demonstrations of 1989, even though no charges have been filed. Prison sentences have recently been imposed on about two dozen others, but in many cases the underlying "crime" appears to have been the peaceful expression of political opinions. In addition, hundreds if not thousands of participants in the 1989 demonstrations have been assigned, without trial, to camps for reeducation through labor.

On a structural level, the United States remains deeply concerned about persistent reports of repressive Government control over religious, scholarly, and trade union activity. New laws have been adopted codifying restrictions on assembly, expression, and the press; these and other freedoms remain tightly restricted.

North Korea is another country that continues to deny its people the most fundamental human rights, completely subordinating the individual to the prerogatives of the ruling party and the state. A draconian penal code prescribes capital punishment for a wide range of political offenses, including defection, slander of party or state, and possession of "reactionary" printed matter. Reports indicate that there are more than 100,000 political prisoners and family members in a network of prison camps located in isolated areas.

In May 1990, Myanmar's military regime raised the expectations of the people of Myanmar and the world by holding national elections which it had promised would lead to a transfer of power to a civilian government. In those elections, the National League for Democracy (NLD) won over 80 percent of the seats in the new national assembly.

Rarely, though, has any government moved so suddenly to deflate expectations it aroused. The results of the elections were entirely negated, and nine months afterwards nothing has changed in Burma. NLD leader Aung San Suu Kyi remains under house arrest. NLD chairman Tin Oo remains in jail. Acting NLD leader Kyi Maung has been jailed as well. Political detentions continue on a large scale, and about 50 elected members of the new national assembly are currently being held. There continue to be frequent and credible reports of torture in Myanmar prisons, and even the country's Buddhist monks have suffered repression and intimidation. We believe that the international community should resolutely urge that the Myanmar regime release all political prisoners and carry out the results of the elections held last May. In addition, we are convinced that the Human Rights Commission should act to appoint a special rapporteur who will investigate human rights abuses.

Insurgencies and Other Forms of Civil Unrest

Mr. Chairman, civil unrest takes many forms. In some cases, legitimate efforts to express political views or promote the interests of certain groups are met by arbitrary violence conducted by government officials, whether civilian or military. Here we enter the lexicon of disappearances, detentions, torture, killings, and summary or arbitrary executions.

0144

In other cases, social or political tensions -- or, alternately, criminal or separatist tendencies -- inspire some individuals or groups to take up arms against the government of their country. Here we witness insurgencies or even civil war.

National order, let alone the new world order of which we all dream, cannot be built on random or indiscriminate violence. Assigning responsibility or blame is often a daunting task, but respect for human rights is almost always the first casualty of civil unrest. We regret to take note of many situations in which this has occurred.

El Salvador is a nation struggling to strengthen its democratic institutions and traditions in the midst of a violent insurgency. In November 1990, the FMLN launched -- for the second time in twelve months -- a nationwide offensive that claimed at least 600 casualties and employed civilians and their homes as shields in combat. For the first time in this conflict, the FMLN introduced the use of surface-to-air missiles. Most recently, FMLN guerrillas murdered two U.S. crewmen after shooting down their helicopter, and the FMLN now adamantly refuses to turn the murderers over for prosecution by competent judicial authorities.

The continuing hostility between the FMLN and the legitimately elected Government is the root cause of human rights abuses that occur on both sides in El Salvador. We equally deplore the murder of Jesuit priests and of non-combatant personnel of the United States. In both cases, we insist that justice be done. Further, we urge the FMLN to make a true commitment to peace and respect for human rights by agreeing to a ceasefire before the March elections. That would permit the people of El Salvador to express their political preferences with dignity and security.

In 1990, very serious human rights abuses were committed by the security forces of the Guatemalan Government as well as by Guatemalan insurgents. The human rights situation in Guatemala thus deteriorated to its worst point since 1986, when civilian rule resumed.

With almost total impunity, Guatemalan security forces and civil patrols committed most of the major violations of human rights, including extrajudicial killings, torture, and disappearances of human rights activists, unionists, indigenous inhabitants, and street children. The independent office of the Guatemalan human rights ombudsman repeatedly denounced the previous government for its lack of political will to protect human rights.

Guatemalan guerrilla forces also committed major violations, including extrajudicial killings, indiscriminate use of land mines, kidnaping, forced labor and recruitment, and the use of children in combat.

On November 11, 1990 and January 6, 1991, the Guatemalan people participated in two rounds of peaceful, free, and fair elections. A new government was inaugurated on January 14, and the United States has already initiated a new human rights dialogue. We commend the new government's dedication to improving the human rights situation, and we note that President Serrano has already taken some important first steps to assert greater control over the military.

Mauritania's poor human rights record continues to deteriorate. Government security forces are responsible for widespread abuses, including torture, summary executions, and extrajudicial killings. These human rights violations have mainly been committed against Halpulaars, blacks who are culturally and ethnically distinct from the ruling group, which mainly consists of Hassaniya-speaking Maurs. It is impossible to determine how many black Mauritanians have been summarily executed, but large number of victims have been reported in almost every town and village along the river border with Senegal.

The United States is pleased that Indonesia and Portugal are seeking to resolve their differences concerning East Timor, in part through the good offices of the Secretary General. We encourage Indonesia and Portugal to pursue these discussions.

Sri Lanka has been beset by brutal insurgencies. Although the JVP -- which some observers have compared to Pol Pot's Khmer Rouge -- was crushed by early 1990, violent Tamil separatists continue to wage a bloody guerrilla war against the Sri Lankan Government. Still, it is important to note that there have been human rights abuses by all parties to the conflict, including violations committed by government forces.

The United States applauds the decision of the Sri Lankan Government to establish a human rights task force, and we commend its efforts to maintain communal harmony and promote military discipline while fighting a violent insurgency. Sri Lanka, a practicing democracy, must conduct vigorous investigations of extrajudicial killings and disappearances, and must bring those responsible to justice.

<u>Discriminatory Treatment and Tensions Among Groups</u>

Mr. Chairman, the Universal Declaration of Human Rights emphatically establishes that "all human beings are born free

0146

and equal in dignity and rights" (Article 1) and that everyone is entitled to enjoy human rights and fundamental freedoms "without distinction of any kind, such as race, color, sex, language, religion, political or other opinion, national or social origin, property, birth or other status" (Article 2).

In effect, those who discriminate against particular groups of people, or otherwise treat them improperly, are making the assertion that some individuals are more human than others. We reject that; we repudiate it; we condemn it as a lie. Civilization simply has no room for racist behavior, nor for any other treatment that differentiates among individuals based on the groups to which they belong. A new world order must be built on tolerance and mutual respect; there is no alternative.

Under a previous item on the Commission's agenda, my delegation reiterated the longstanding conviction of the United States that the racist system of apartheid in South Africa must be brought to an end. We welcomed President De Klerk's announcement that he plans to introduce legislation repealing the remaining "pillars of apartheid." This reaffirmed our conviction that change in South Africa is irreversible and that the unconscionable system of apartheid will be replaced by a new non-racial democracy.

In another statement given during this session, my delegation indicated its belief that the question of the violation of human rights in the occupied Arab territories is a complex one which must be understood in the context of the pressing need for an overall peace settlement. Further, we expressed our concern about the employment by Israeli security forces of excessive lethal force, and about violence directed at Israeli civilians and security personnel. We are convinced that civil violence does not contribute to the search for peace, and we hope that there will be full respect for the human rights of all inhabitants of the region.

The incorporation of the Baltic states into the Soviet Union has never been recognized by the United States. We believe that the people of Estonia, Latvia, and Lithuania are fully entitled to continue their struggle for peaceful negotiations with Soviet authorities leading toward self-determination. In the middle of January, the Soviet response was cold, bitter attacks on public installations in Lithuania and Latvia, resulting in the deaths of at least twenty citizens.

The United States is gravely concerned about these acts of violence, as well as other abuses by military and paramilitary forces involving violations of human rights and fundamental freedoms. We call on the Government of the USSR to carry out its announced determination to conduct a thorough investigation and bring to justice those found responsible. Further, we ask the Government of the USSR to honor its repeated pledges to refrain from the use of force and conduct discussions with each of the Baltic states, so as to permit them to take their own decisions concerning self-determination.

Yugoslavia is wrestling with vexing issues that relate to the constituent peoples and how they relate to each other. In our view, the solution lies not with intimidation, the use of force, or curbs on human rights, but in careful negotiations among the democratically elected leaders of the various parts of Yugoslavia.

With respect to Cyprus, the United States Government continues its strong support for the efforts of the UN Secretary General to bring about an end to the island's divisions. A comprehensive political settlement acceptable to both sides would be a major step toward enhancing and safeguarding the human rights of all the people of Cyprus.

Positive Trends

Up to this point, Mr. Chairman, most of my statement has been a description of difficult and regrettable situations. But within the past year, there have also been positive trends in all regions of the world, attesting to greater democracy and increased respect for human rights. Let me comment on and commend a number of these positive developments.

East Central Europe has been the site of the most sweeping improvements. Free elections have been held throughout the region. The people of Poland, Hungary, Czechoslovakia, and Bulgaria have taken strides in reforming their economies and also their legal structures and institutions, so as to enshrine the rule of law and protection for human rights. Romania has taken steps in these directions, but we remain concerned about the treatment of minorities, guarantees for independent media, and gaps in overall progress toward democratization. Albania has promised that free multi-party elections will be conducted at the end of March. That will be the first time in forty years, and the United States will carefully monitor Albania's progress toward greater respect for human rights.

The Government of the USSR has made considerable strides in bringing basic freedoms of speech, press, association, and conscience to the people of the Soviet Union. With regard to most of these rights, the Supreme Soviet has enacted legislation that calls for these freedoms to be respected. In relation to freedom of movement, Soviet authorities have produced the draft text of a new law. We would encourage the Supreme Soviet to move expeditiously toward enacting a law on entry and exit that will fully implement the USSR's international obligations.

In other respects, however, the USSR has discovered that the road to a society based on respect for law is long and arduous. There have been delays in establishing a legal and judicial system with sufficient power and independence to be effective in enforcing the human rights and fundamental freedoms prescribed in legislative enactments. Further, executive decrees have been used to achieve short-term ends, and that may undermine long-term reform of legal institutions and procedures.

In Nepal, sweeping changes in the political system led to a new constitution which guarantees fundamental human rights, multi-party parliamentary democracy, and constitutional monarchy with sovereignty vested in the people. Even before promulgation of the new constitution, public statements of the interim government demonstrated its firm commitment to human rights. Political and religious detainees have been released, and there has been an end to almost all limitations on the exercise of freedoms of religion, speech, press, and association. The Government of Nepal abolished the ban on political parties and trade unions, eliminated authoritarian statutes, and ceased to enforce almost all existing restrictive laws. Workers' rights are now entitled to much greater respect. This spring, for the first time in thirty years, Nepal will hold multi-party elections.

In Benin, 1990 was a year of dramatic improvements with regard to human rights. A transition government was formed, in order to move Benin from a military-dominated regime with a Marxist-Leninist ideology to a civilian, multi-party democracy. The transition government released all remaining political prisoners, encouraged freedom of expression, facilitated the return of exiles so that they could participate in the reform process, and oversaw the development of a new constitution that contains many human rights safeguards, including a prohibition on torture. In addition, the transition government invited several international monitoring organizations to visit Benin and welcomed the formation of a domestic monitoring group. Multi-party legislative and presidential elections are scheduled to be held in February and March 1991.

The United States is especially pleased with the peaceful manner in which Chile returned to democracy. In December 1989, the people of Chile participated in free and fair presidential and congressional elections. In March 1990, a democratically elected government and congress took office for the first time in many years. The new democratic government of Chile should be commended for its decision to establish a commission to investigate previous human rights violations, as well as for its strong support for human rights efforts in international forums.

In Haiti, the human rights situation took a major step forward by means of presidential elections in December and legislative elections in January. Both electoral processes were considered free and fair, and Haiti will at last have a government formed as the result of a freely contested election. To ensure the constitutional and human rights of all citizens, the newly elected government will need to carry out considerable reforms in relation to Haiti's law enforcement and judicial institutions. We hope and believe that the new democratic government will rise to the challenge.

Prospects and Horizons

Mr. Chairman, these accounts of victories and triumphs should make it clear that the world community's efforts to promote human rights are aligned with the forces of history and and the forces of destiny. Respect for individual rights is at the core of national and international progress. Patience, tolerance, and mutual respect are key factors in seeking to resolve situations of civil unrest. Repressive societies have a very limited future, and discrimination has no place in the new world order to which we aspire.

In the final analysis, Mr. Chairman, nations which respect human rights do not assault their neighbors, and nations which assault their neighbors do not respect human rights. The new world order requires respect for human rights as well as the peaceful settlement of disputes and respect for international law. Nothing less will meet the world's needs or bring about the harmony and justice that the world's people demand.

Twenty-six-year-old Jose Antonio Sanz Campo of Cuba cannot be here, for he was killed in police custody on May 31, 1990, after his arrest for illegally selling mangoes. Neither can Li Mingchi of China be here with us, for he was detained in June after making a speech at Beijing University. He was charged with "counterrevolutionary" conspiracy, and at the end of the year remained in custody. Neither will we benefit from meeting and talking with a particular sixteen-year-old Kuwaiti boy, a student at al-Farwaniyya Secondary School. He was arrested by Iraqi occupying forces on October 1, after violating the night curfew. Over a period of five days, he was repeatedly punched

0150

and beaten. Then his left arm was marked with the letter H, by means of a hot skewer. Nor can we speak with Jappie Andres Matabogo of South Africa, who was allegedly beaten to death on July 23 while in custody for supposedly having relieved himself in a public place. Neither will truck driver Roberts Murnieks of Latvia ever walk again on earth, for he is said to have been killed in January when Black Beret troops opened fire on a bridge, attempting to block traffic.

These victims of gross violations of human rights cannot speak for themselves. We must do justice to their memory and fulfill our solemn responsibility as guardians of the world's conscience. Thank you, Mr. Chairman.

2. 화란대표 연설문

PERMANENT MISSION OF
THE KINGDOM OF THE NETHERLANDS

56 Rue de Moillebeau, 1209 GENEVA

STATEMENT
BY
ELISABETH TEEKAMP
OF THE OBSERVER DELEGATION
OF THE KINGDOM OF THE NETHERLANDS
TO THE 47th SESSION OF THE COMMISSION ON HUMAN RIGHTS

GENEVA, MONDAY 18 FEBRUARY 1991

Agenda-item: 10
Question of the human rights of all persons subjected to any form of detention or imprisonment
- Question of enforced or involuntary disappearences
- Torture and other cruel, inhuman or degrading treatment or punishment

Check against delivery

0152

5237-5-90

Agpt 10

Mr. Chairman,

After about eleven years of bad news, the Working Group on Disappearances finally is bringing some good news to the Commission. My delegation has looked at the various graphs at the end of the Group's report and was struck in particular by the graph in Annex I. It represents the development of disappearances world-wide from 1973 to date, a special feature which the Group is showing to the Commission for the first time. The good news, then, is that the overall trend over the last eight years is downward: the annual number of disappearances is, on the whole, declining. The report - and the Chairman in his introductory statement - point out that one can lie with statistics and that therefore the graph should be looked at with a great deal of care. Fair enough, but the news remains good news just the same and should be welcomed as such. This delegation shares the working group's view that the overall decline may be attributed to a decrease in authoritarian rule in the world. It also shares the view that, nevertheless, the Commission should continue to give close attention to the question of disappearances. Particularly relevant is the Group's argument that the phenomenon of disappearances does not end "until the last of the outstanding cases has been clarified".

One particular feature in the middle of the world-wide graph, is the bulge in the year 1983. The report points to the fact that the hugh number for that year is due, for the most part, to the whole-sale disappearance of over 2,000 Barzani Kurds in Iraq, for which the Iraqi Government, to this day, has failed to give a satisfactory answer.

The report reserves quite a few pages for a situation that deservedly has preoccupied the Group for a number of years

0153

already. I am referring to the situation of disappearances in Sri Lanka. In fact, the whole of the human rights situation is of continuing concern to my Government. We appreciate that the Sri Lankan Government is co-operating with the Working Group and that a visit has been planned for the summer of this year. By contrast, in september last year, Sri Lankan authorities confiscated over 500 reports on disappearances as well as other documents and photographs which were supposed to be given to the Group. The Group rightly protested to this, while referring to resolution 1990/76, which as members are aware, not only deals with the question of access to human rights procedures but also with reprisals. Even though most of the documents were returned to the Group, the fact itself remains reprehensible. Hopefully, the Group's visit to the country will not be marred by any similar deficiencies.

Mr Chairman,

When looking at both the Working Group's report and at the report by professor Kooijmans on torture, one is struck by a feature that is without parallell in the history of the Commission. For never before have there been two separate reports from two different sources on the same country under the same item during the same session. Both the Group and Professor Kooijmans, within a month from one another, carried out a mission to the Philippines, at the invitation of the Government. Their respective reports are models of its kind. Strikingly, the recommendations in the reports are complementary, if not identical and provide a solid basis for a continuing the dialogue between Manilla and the pertinent procedures of the Commission. The reports give rise to concern, but are encouraging at the same time in asmuchas the Government of the Philippines must be counted among the most co-operative among the constituency of the Commission.

A valuable angle in the Working Group's concluding observations on the Philippines is the following. The

0154

report, in various places, points out that the situation of the Philippines is ~~not unique.~~ Various underlying features may be seen in other countries as well. This is particularly true where the Group states that persistence of poverty and social injustice sooner or later induces structured opposition. ''Sustained unequality breeds insurgence, says the Working Group, just as subversion leads to militarization and repression. (...) Soon an entire country is swept into a spiral of violence form which escape is invariably difficult." It would seem to this delegation that the Commission ought to keep these words in mind as it is studying other situations of human rights around the globe.

Mr. Chairman,

My delegation commends the Special Rapporteur on Torture and other cruel, inhuman or degrading treatment or punishment for his excellent report reflecting the horrifying picture of the use of torture in the world today.

Again, all regions are represented and, as compared to last year's report, the number of communications on alleged cases of torture or severe maltreatment as well as for urgent appeals has increased again. It is encouraging to note that more Governments provide information to and cooperate with the Special Rapporteur, although on the other hand we would welcome more invitations by Governments to the Special Rapporteur to visit their countries and to look at it from the angle of preventing practices of torture. To seek advice in combatting this most heinous form of human rights violations is a sign of strength instead of weakness. Fortunately awareness that the prohibition of torture belongs to the rules of <u>ius cogens</u> has become universal. As the Special Rapporteur rightly stated in his report much has been accomplished with regard to detailed standard setting but one cannot but speak of failure in day to day practice. Implementation is the keyword now. The recommendations by the Special Rapporteur need follow up by this Commission and by Governments. Only Governments can in the end make the

0155

choices they have to make to respect the physical integrity of their citizens. Violence breeds violence, the vicious circle must be broken. Governments are accountable to the world community for acts of torture committed by their officials. My delegation therefore expresses its concern with regard to several severe cases of torture which are reported by the Special Rapporteur.

One example of a country which has internationally committed itself to combat torture but seems to encounter difficulties in the implementation of its commitment is Turkey. The report of the Special Rapporteur contains 16 pages on urgent appeals and Government replies related to allegations of torture, especially in several Police Headquarters spread over the country. Information available to my government indicates that the occurence of torture in prisons has decreased. The report Turkey presented to the Committee against Torture at its last session gave also rise to the concern that torture continued in that country.

Sudan showed some form of cooperation with the special rapporteur. Reports on arrests and torture of about 80 people, including trade union activists, medical doctors, lawyers and human rights activists in Sudan at the end of 1989 and the beginning of 1990 and urgent appeals of the Special Rapporteur have apparently been answered by the Sudanese government by presenting lists to the Special Rapporteur containing 345 names of political detainees, their date ofarrest and date of release. However, no information was presented as to allegations of torture.

The Government of the Republic of Korea was informed by the Rapporteur about hundreds of cases involving trade union activists, students and political dissidents who were detained since April 1989, several of them had allegedly been tortured. The Government replied to the allegations and denied them. It furthermore argued that the complaints on alleged torture were absolutely unacceptable because the statements of detainees made under investigation turned out

0156

to be true. In this delegation's view such a clarification is of a doubtful nature. It would seem to indicate that in the view of the Government of Korea the extortion of truthful statements would be exempted from the prohibition of torture, an untenable position.

Urgent appeals were sent to the Government of Burma on several occasions, mostly with respect to activists, members of the National League for Democracy or leaders of the Democratic Party who were arrested. Fears had been expressed that torture was widespread. The ugly details of the methods used, including curry powder treatment cannot be left unanswered by the Government of Burma.

The Government of Iraq received an urgent appeal concerning the arrest and alleged torture of Kuwaiti citizens. It stated there was no truth to the specific allegations. From other sources it is well known that the Iraqi occupying forces perpetrated acts of torture.

In India several cases of ill-treatment were inquired and judged to be well-founded. So the judicial system did offer victims a remedy although the court left it "to them to move the appropriate civil or criminal courts for suitable action including compensation and criminal prosecution".

My delegation appreciates that the Government of China looked again into the case of Tseten Norgye which we referred to last year. We are not in a position to value the information provided in paragraph 40 of the report. A more recent urgent appeal concerning Sichoe Dorje from Lhasa was so far left unanswered.

Mr. Chairman

Impunity is perhaps the single most important factor contributing to the phenomenon of disappearances as well as torture. Both Mr. Kooijmans' report and the report of the

0157

Working Group Disapearances provide potent arguments that impunity is a factor to be reckoned with, also by this Commission. Impunity, although not a violation of human rights *per se* is a phenomenon, on a large scale, can accelerate the spriral of violence and exacerbate the decline of the human rights situation. At least two conclusions may be drawn from this: first, combating impunity should become even more of a priority item for individual Governments. Second, this Commission, or the Sub-Commission, should begin to pay attention to this particular matter in a structured and comprehensive manner.

Thank you, Mr. Chairman

0158

3. 국제교회선교회 연설문

United Nations Commission on Human Rights
47th Session 1991

Oral Intervention
Commission of the Churches on International Affairs

Item 10: Question of the Human Rights of All Persons subjected to any form of detention or imprisonment, in particular: torture, enforced and involuntary disappearances.

Mr. Chairperson,

The World Council of Churches continues to be extremely concerned about the human rights violations associated with detention, torture of prisoners and the anguishing experience of enforced disappearance. In this regard, we would like to express strong support for the work and reports of the Working Group on Enforced or Involuntary Disappearances, the Special Rapporteur on Summary or Arbitrary Executions and the Special Rapporteur on Torture. We recommend that the member countries of the Commission give their firm support to this work, establishing more efficient methods to ensure compliance with their recommendations. Similarly, we recommend that the Commission provide a substantial increase to the financial resources which they require. This would allow for an increased number of on-site visits and would enhance the quality of the work. The appointment of Special Experts or Rapporteurs for those countries which, according to the reports, reveal a consistent pattern of systematic human rights violations would further strengthen the work of these thematic mechanisms.

The World Council of Churches considers the draft Declaration on the Protection of All Persons from Enforced or Involuntary Disappearances to be extremely important. We urge members of the Commission to support the speedy adoption of this instrument.

Philippines

We would like briefly to draw the attention of the Commission to the issue of warrantless arrests in the Philippines. The July 9,1990 decision by the Supreme Court states that rebellion, subversion, and their related offences are continuing crimes and allows the police to arrest persons without a judicial warrant on the basis of suspicion of subversion or rebel activity. We fear that this may lead to abuses of basic rights governing arrest and detention because a) anyone can be suspected as a rebel; b) it has become easy to plant and manufacture evidence; c) warrantless arrests invite torture, solitary confinement, and un-counseled confession and d) there is little proof, since the Supreme Court ruling, that habeas corpus remains a potent remedy to reveal violations of a person's right to due process. Our member churches in the Philippines interpret warrantless arrests as a de facto return to martial law.

We welcome the report on the Philippines produced by the Working Group on Enforced Disappearances and urge the Commission to ensure adequate follow-up to the recommendations outlined in this report.

0159

South Korea

The World Council of Churches remains deeply concerned by the situation of prisoners of conscience in South Korea. As of Nov.30, 1990 the Human Rights Committee of the National Council of Churches in Korea reported 1,746 prisoners of conscience officially arrested in 1990, an average of more than 5 persons per day. This is three times the figure of 1.6 arrests per day under Chun Doo Hwan's 5th Republic. Furthermore, the 1990 arrests represent an increase of 50 percent over last year's figure of 900. Forty percent of these people were arrested as spies, under the National Security Law; as phenomenon of the long division of Korea, wherein work for peace and reunification is considered by the state to be subversive activity.

Peru

The state of human rights in Peru is a deep concern to the World Council of Churches. According to Peruvian government figures, more than 20,000 people, the majority of whom are civilians (indigenous peasants), have lost their lives in politically motivated violence since 1980. Peruvian church agencies and human rights organizations estimate that more than 3,000 people have disappeared in that country since 1983. We note with deep concern that, for the fourth consecutive year, Peru is the country with the highest number of new cases of disappearances in the world according to the most recent report of the Working Group on Enforced or Involuntary Disappearances. The drama of enforced disappearance, which affected 232 people in 1990, must end and those responsible for this crime must be sanctioned whatever their status or rank.

In October 1990 the World Council of Churches sent a delegation to Peru to observe first hand the state of human rights in that country. The mission was comprised of distinguished political, judicial and religious leaders from eight countries. It was able to travel extensively throughout the country, visiting the cities of Lima, Ayacucho, Pucallpa and Tarapoto. In these different regions, the delegation met with a wide spectrum of the civil, religious, professional, political and military sectors of society, including several Ministers of government and the President of the Republic.

With the inauguration of the new government of President Fujimori, and the promises of change and respect for human rights which were outlined in the election campaign, the World Council of Churches hoped that the illegal acts and abuses perpetrated by the security forces would cease and that Peru would respect the international covenants. While we recognize the extremely difficult situation of political violence existing in Peru, we believe that no government can justify violating the law and international covenants in the name of fighting armed insurgent groups. Unfortunately, until now, there does not appear to have been a change in the counterinsurgency strategy and the same methods which, during the past decade, produced extrajudicial executions, disappearances and torture continue to be used.

In October 1990, common graves were discovered in a place called Chilcahuaycco, in the province of Huamanga, Ayacucho. In these graves, the bodies of eighteen people were found, among them five minors. They had been detained and subsequently disappeared on September 21 and 22, 1990 during a

0160

joint operation conducted by soldiers from the Castropampa military barracks and a patrol of "Montoneros" (peasant civil defense groups organized by the military). The relatives of the victims denounced this incident to the Public Prosecutor and human rights organizations in September. Members of our delegation were, in fact, in Ayacucho when the graves were discovered and received testimony directly from the relatives. Similar occurrences have been reported in Iquicha, Ayacucho. The Bishop of Pucallpa, in the Peruvian Amazon, denounced the existence of "dumping grounds" of bodies in a swampy area near the city where at least five bodies were hurled down from helicopters.

Military barracks in the zones under a state of emergency are under the authority of the Political-Military Commands (affecting nearly 50% of the population) and serve as clandestine detention centres. Here, presumed terrorists or even people deemed to be suspicious are subjected to brutal interrogations which often lead to disappearance or summary execution.

Until now, the new government has not shown its will to punish those responsible for human rights violations and, to the contrary, recently promoted two generals accused of being responsible for the prison and Cayara massacres. Moreover, in December 1990, President Fujimori issued Supreme Decree 171-90 which established that all crimes committed by the military in the zones under a state of emergency would be dealt with through military courts and that the identity of those responsible would be kept anonymous. The World Council of Churches welcomes the news that a few days ago, the Peruvian Congress annulled this decree.

The international community can not continue to ignore the extremely grave situation of human rights violations, which since 1983 has been repeated year after year in Peru. The World Council of Churches calls upon the members of this Commission to ensure an adequate treatment of the situation in Peru and, in view of the urgency of the situation, appoint a Special Expert or Rapporteur to Peru.

0161

4. 아국대표의 답변권 행사

Right of Reply

18 February 1991

1. On behalf of the Republic of Korea, my delegation wishes to comment on the reference made by the Commission of Churches on International Affairs to my country under item 10 in its Statement of 15 February 1991.

First, my delegation wishes to point out with regret that the representative of the NGO, by taking advantage of broadly defined terminology like "prisoners of conscience", the definition of which is yet to be refined, has given a false impression of my country.

2. Since the current Government, hailed for its human rights policy, was inaugurated in 1988 wide-ranging reforms and innovative measures have been undertaken with a view to promoting fundamental freedom and human rights and laying the foundations for democratic development.

3. The accession by my Government to the two international human rights instruments last year, namely, the International Covenant on Economic, Social and Cultural Rights, and the International Covenant on Civil and Political Rights and its Optional Protocol represents the most significant steps taken towards the promotion of human rights and fundamental freedom.

4. Those figures referred to in the NGO's statement are violaters of our national laws and in no way come under the category of "prisoners of conscience" which the NGO has seemingly in mind.

Thank you, Mr. Chairman.

0162

Right of Reply

February 19, 1991

This afternoon, my delegation heard the references made to my country by a representative of the International Association of Democratic Lawyers, which we found full of distortion and slanders.

In view of the well-known bias and disposition of the NGO towards my Government, my delegation at first wished to dismiss them. However, lest our silence should be interpreted as acquiescence, my delegation has decided not to give it a free ride in this august forum.

First, even granted what the NGO insisted as what it was, we wonder why even a single case had not been referred to the court in accordance with the pertinant legal procedure regarding investigation and compensation on torture and ill treatment cases.

In our country, every citizen is entitled to fully enjoy rights guaranteed under such laws and procedures.

The sentence commuted by the Seoul district court last month for a maximum of 5 years to the police officials who committed torture and ill treatment, clearly demonstrates how effectively and respectfully our system of legal redress and compensation in the tortured case operates.

Second, if these cases referred to really happened, let me ask why not a single case of torture has been reported in our mass media including the ones critical to our Government which fully enjoy freedom of expression in our open society.

Thank you.

0163

Permanent Mission of the Republic of Hungary
to the United Nations Office
and Other International Organizations
Geneva

ADDRESS

by

H.E. Mr. Géza Jeszenszky
Minister for Foreign Affairs
of the Republic of Hungary

at the 47th Session of the
Commission on Human Rights

February 18, 1991

0164

Check against delivery!

It fills me with special emotion that I have the honour and privilege to address this distinguished Commission, representing the first freely and democratically elected Government of Hungary since 1947.

Two years ago it was here at this Commission that I started my political activities in the international scene, as a spokesman of tens of thousands of Hungarians who sent letters in defence of human rights in Ceaucescu's Romania. Then I had the pleasure of meeting informally with several members. At that time I could still only hope that the much desired political transformation of Central and Eastern Europe would come about quickly. Today we all have to be proud that democracy, freedom and respect for human rights have prevailed over the totalitarian systems. Since 1989 we have a very good chance to shape a world that would not suffer the burden of East-West tensions, and in which the immense potential of humankind could be devoted to forging a global community engaged in the pursuit of peace, justice and respect for human rights.

Meanwhile our dreams of a new world order have been shaken by the events in the Gulf region, but we believe that once the war is over, the solidarity, wisdom and strength of our global community will enable us to build a world that appeared to us as a possibility in 1989-90. We for our part continue to be committed to the commonly shared values of democracies based on the free will of the individuals and the rule of law, as well as to prosperity through economic liberty and social justice for the benefit of all without any distinction.

We certainly understand that the protection of human rights and fundamental freedoms must start in our own backyard. As a result, we are in the process of filling in any gaps that may exist in Hungary's adherence to international human rights instruments and in ensuring the translation of the principles contained therein into national legislation and practice.

It gives me great pleasure to report to you that Hungary is among the states that have ratified the largest number of human rights instruments. Our interest in and genuine contribution to the promotion of the protection and implementation of human rights are evidenced by Hungary's acceptance of the competence of all committees of the United Nations that deal with complaints with regards to violations of human rights. Our human rights policy today is open; criticism or complaints either submitted by other State Parties or by our own citizens against our country's course of action may be raised.

We are however aware of the fact that adherence to international standards and the appropriate adjustments of national legislation may not guarantee full enjoyment of human rights and fundamental freedoms. The Government of Hungary is therefore in the process of developing a series of measures which will facilitate the practical implementation of human rights principles.

International protection of human rights enjoys priority in the foreign policy of Hungary. Along with other democratic states we remain unreservedly committed to call upon states to respect their obligations voluntarily assumed under the Charter, as well as the human rights instruments adopted by the United Nations. In our view it is not only the right, but also the obligation of us all to keep control of compliance with universally recognized norms and standards and to be at the same time accountable to the United Nations and its competent organs, including the Commission of Human Rights. Therefore we will not hesitate to strive for the realization of the basic principles of protection of human rights, wherever and whenever need may be. It is our political, legal and moral right, responsibility and obligation to defend the individual victims of any violation of human rights.

We will at the same time come out resolutely against all those attempts, which - taking cover behind the principle of non-intervention in internal affairs - refuse listening to the call of the international community for respecting human rights. Violations of universally recognized human rights cannot be considered as internal affairs.

To put it into a historical context, if I may, I would like to call the attention of the Commission to the record of the United Nations regarding actions taken on cases of violations of human rights and fundamental freedoms in the past as well as its implications for the present.

It is indeed a lesson of history for us to recall the undeniable legitimacy of the United Nations in keeping the Hungarian question on its agenda following the suppression of the 1956 revolution and freedom fight. The list may continue with the violations of human rights by numerous military dictatorships all over the world in the 70's, the case of Poland in the early 80's and the human rights violations as reported in detail more recently to our Commission in Afghanistan, Iran, El Salvador, Myanmar, Cuba, Romania, Iraq or occupied Kuwait.

In this respect I would like to reiterate our condemnation of Iraq's aggression against Kuwait, the gross human rights violations against the people of Kuwait as well as against its own population. We find it unacceptable that Iraq does not respect the fundamental rules of humanitarian law regarding the treatment of prisoners of war in the context of the conflict in the Gulf and by joining others we call upon Iraq to comply fully with the relevant resolutions of the Security Council so that Kuwait's sovereignty and peace in the region can be restored.

The Hungarian Parliament as well as the Government have condemned the use of force, which resulted in irreplaceable losses of life in the Baltic Republics only some weeks ago. These actions of Soviet forces, which we understand were unauthorized, are at variance with the obligations undertaken in the Charter of Paris, constitute violations of human rights, therefore they are of legitimate concern for this Commission.

The new democratic Government of Hungary has given its support to the legitimate aspirations of the peoples of the Baltic Republics to determine their own future. We call upon the parties concerned to exercise utmost restraint and to seek an exclusively peaceful resolution of their dispute.

As it is well-known, two years ago Hungary was amongst the first to raise her voice in condemnation of the violations of human rights in Romania, a neighbouring country with a large Hungarian speaking minority. When the time comes we will be the first to acknowledge that there is no need to keep the situation under review

0166

in that country. This time has not yet come. While we recognize that during the past year there has been an improvement in Romania in respect of human rights, but the very objective report by the Special Rapporteur on Romania throws some light on the continuing violations of human rights. Among others it highlights unresolved problems of the minorities such as inadequate access to education in the mother tongue, especially at high-school and university levels. As long as incited violence claims human lives, demonstrators are suppressed by use of force, and discrimination against minorities continues to occur, the attention and help of the international community is still needed.

Hungary has consistently advocated at all multilateral fora that the community of nations should pay particular attention to the issue of the protection of national, ethnic, religious and linguistic minorities. Therefore we welcome the ever growing recognition of the importance of this question in our world of today. It was heartening for us that the Charter of Paris, signed only some months ago, specifically stated: the rights of minorities must be fully respected as part of universal human rights.

Being aware of our responsibility toward the effective exercise of all human rights and fundamental freedoms, we have initiated the elaboration of an international instrument within the framework of the United Nations on the universal protection of minorities. In our view such an instrument may be based on the following: the provisions of the International Covenant on Civil and Political Rights, the principles of the Draft Declaration on the rights of minorities currently under discussion in the Commission and the relevant documents of the CSCE process.

International monitoring, including on-the-spot inquiry and individual complaint mechanism, should form integral parts of such an instrument taking into account the already existing norms and procedures of a number of human rights conventions adopted by the United Nations.

Our proposal derives from our commitment to make better use of the rich contribution the minorities undoubtedly offer to the life of our contemporary societies as well as to provide international guarantees for the protection of their rights and identity. We are at the same time convinced that institutionalized protection of the rights of the minorities could give a new impetus to international cooperation and could indeed enhance confidence in inter-state relations.

We are conscious of the leading role of the United Nations and, in particular, its Commission on Human Rights, in promoting the safeguarding of human rights and fundamental freedoms. We believe that this key role has to be maintained and further strengthened, and consequently we appreciate all efforts which aim at improving the effectiveness of United Nations activities and mechanisms in the field of human rights. We noted with satisfaction resolution 45/155 adopted by the General Assembly, which decided to convene at a high level a World Conference on Human Rights in 1993. We see in this recommendation an important opportunity for member States to contribute to the rethinking and revising of a United Nations mechanism, the effectiveness of which is of interest to every nation.

0167

Hungary, for its part, is ready to make a significant contribution to the preparatory processes of the World Conference, and through that to further strengthening the role of the United Nations in the human rights field. We are convinced that the planned World Conference will greatly contribute reviving the commitment of all member States to promoting human rights and fundamental freedoms in all parts of the world.

Let me take this opportunity to officially announce to this distinguished Commission the readiness of the Hungarian Government to host the World Conference of 1993 in Budapest. We would feel greatly honoured if the United Nations chose our capital for the venue of that important world event. We are convinced that our efforts together with the invigorating atmosphere of the reborn democracy in Hungary would significantly contribute to ensuring the success of the Conference.

The idea of free individual in a free world is very close to our hearts and minds. The power of human rights and fundamental freedoms which transcends frontiers must continue to be a major driving force of our activity in supporting respect for these rights and freedoms. There cannot be one single individual victim of violations of human rights whose fate could avoid our attention. Behind every individual victim there is an individual tragedy. Our message to the victims must be solidarity. Our message to the violators must be accountability. To do otherwise we would be escaping from our responsibilities.

0168

UNITED STATES MISSION TO INTERNATIONAL ORGANIZATIONS
GENEVA, SWITZERLAND

47TH SESSION OF THE UN COMMISSION ON HUMAN RIGHTS

STATEMENT

BY

AMBASSADOR MORRIS B. ABRAM

AGENDA ITEM 11:

THE 1993 WORLD CONFERENCE ON HUMAN RIGHTS

FEBRUARY 12, 1991

Check Against Delivery

Highlights:

-- The standard-setting work of the U.N. human rights bodies is almost complete. Attention should now be shifted to the continuing violations of those standards, the inability of the Commission to enforce them, and the politicization and selectivity of the Commission's work.

-- If the 1993 World Human Rights Conference is to succeed, it must follow the mandate of the UN General Assembly to examine the relationship between development and respect for the International Covenants on Human Rights, to assess the progress and setbacks in human rights since the adoption of the Universal Declaration, and to evaluate effectiveness of existing human rights standards and enforcement mechanisms.

-- A thorough examination of the Commission and its Human Rights Center, its Subcommission, and the organization of the UN's human right work, is long overdue.

-- The 1993 Conference must not be an occasion for self-congratulation, but one of critical, balanced self-assessment of the shortcomings and obstacles to complete respect for human rights.

0169

- Agenda Item 11 -
- "1993 World Conference on Human Rights" -

If we are going to honor the 45th anniversary of the Universal Declaration of Human Rights -- and that ought to be one reason for holding the 1993 World Conference on Human Rights -- we might begin by recognizing that the world is not divided between those countries that say they believe in human rights, and those who say they do not. It is divided between countries that protect human rights, and those that do not.

Today, most governments have signed, or signified assent, to the many international declarations, covenants, proclamations, and protocols that define human rights. The major standard-setting work of this Commission has been done. Now comes the hard work of shining the light where abuses still occur. That work won't be finished in the next hundred days, or even a thousand days; perhaps not even in the life of this Commission. But let us begin.

In these meetings we focus on the busy present or the near future. We rarely look to the past. We sometimes forget that the United States entered the multilateral center stage less than seventy-five years ago. We entered, here in Geneva, in the name of self-determination and democracy. We remained, irretrievably, for four reasons -- the preservation of democracy, respect for human rights, the peaceable settlement of disputes, and the elimination of war.

The articulation and defense of human rights is part of our political culture and national character. The Declaration of Independence, which set forth those rights -- of life, liberty, and the pursuit of happiness -- severed our ties with England, sparked a revolution in France, and antedated another seminal declaration of human rights -- the Declaration of the Rights of Man. Throughout our history, we have believed, as Abraham Lincoln believed, that we had a vocation to assist others in securing these rights. "While man exists," he once said, "it is his duty to improve not only his condition, but to assist in ameliorating that of mankind."

When Winston Churchill and Franklin Roosevelt met at Argentia Bay in August 1941, it wasn't to sign a secret protocol or to divide territorial spoils. They met to renounce publicly those intentions and to pledge their governments to defend freedom from want and freedom from fear.

0170

Four months later we entered a war, as President Roosevelt said, "looking forward to a world founded upon four essential human freedoms" -- freedom of speech and expression; freedom of every person to worship God in his own way; freedom from want; and freedom from fear.

This pledge to the international protection of the rights of man undergirded our determination to make human rights a keystone of the United Nations. I was a young Army officer in San Francisco when the Charter was signed. It was a time of great hope and expectation for a new world order based on collective security and human rights.

Most of us expected these things to be the keystones of the Charter. Yet few people at that time knew that the proposal for this Commission was inserted into the Charter deliberations only after intensive, eleventh-hour lobbying by consultants to the U.S. Delegation to the Conference, including Judge Joseph Proskauer, James T. Shotwell, and Frederick Nolde. Judge Proskauer bluntly told Secretary of State Stettinius that the American people would never support a Charter that did not give human rights a central place. Stettinius was persuaded. He changed the U.S. position and in turn persuaded the other Charter signatories of the wisdom of this view. According to one eyewitness at the Proskauer/Stettinius meeting: "It was that afternoon that the Commission on Human Rights was born."

I also attended the 1968 Teheran Conference on Human Rights. That, too, was a time of hope and expectation. The two international Covenants had come into existence just two years before. Some hoped that the Covenants would accomplish what the Charter had failed to do: To oblige nations to honor, not just to acknowledge, the rights set out in the Universal Declaration.

What have we accomplished since Teheran? The record is mixed. The Commission, though now willing to focus on country-specific abuses, concentrates its energies, year after year, on a select few, leaving little time to discuss problems elsewhere. Torture, which should be at the core of this Commission's work, gets two days -- two days! -- of discussion. Israel, the Occupied Territories, and South Africa get two weeks. Whole regions are exempt from scrutiny. The drafting and standard-setting exercises continue, often on projects of narrow significance. Development is discussed as a right, not a goal, distracting us from continuing violations of core human rights abuses.

0171

Mr. Chairman, we're not content with the status quo. Not in our own nation; not here in this Commission, or in its Subcommission, or in the many parts of this planet where pledges to respect human rights have not been kept.

We read in these international covenants about freedom of speech. We read about freedom of the press, and conscience, and assembly, and about the right to protest for other rights. We all have read these things. Ninety governments have read them, too. They must have, because they signed the Covenant on Civil and Political Rights and undertook its solemn obligations. But how many of them can say they respect the letter and the spirit of their promises?

Mr. Chairman, the vocabulary of rights has been exhausted. The world does not want for another proclamation of human rights. Such grand documents cannot protect individuals who still must fear their rulers. Nor does the world want for the proliferation of things some would call rights.

Maybe here and at the 1993 conference, we ought to talk less about rights, and more about their continued violation. Instead of self-congratulation, maybe we should begin the hard task of honest self-assessment. Instead of coining new rights, maybe we should begin to examine the enforcement of those that already exist in plenitude. Instead of praising this Commission, maybe we should begin to ask why its work is so selective, and its enforcement so minimal. These things are hard to do, I know. But let us begin.

We already have a blueprint for a successful conference. It was drawn in General Assembly Resolution 45/155. First, it calls for a review and assessment of progress and setbacks in human rights since the adoption of the Universal Declaration of Human Rights. Second, it calls for the Conference "[t]o examine the relation between development and the enjoyment of [those rights] as set out in the International Covenants on Human Rights." This properly recognizes that human rights are the key to development, not the "right to development." Third, it calls for evaluations of how to improve implementation of existing human rights standards and the effectiveness of methods and mechanisms.

UNGA Resolution 45/155 places the focus -- the sole focus -- where it ought to be: on the Universal

0172

Declaration of Human Rights and the two accompanying Covenants, on compliance with those two instruments, and on improving the work of existing UN human rights bodies.

Given these instructions, the Conference should discuss compliance with the two International Covenants -- Political and Civil on the one hand, Social, Cultural, and Economic on the other -- on their own merits and in two separate committees. The Conference should concentrate on the full realization of political and civil rights. It should emphasize methods of implementation throughout the UN system. It should look for more effective measures to encourage coordination and information-sharing among UN agencies. It should consider how to achieve more effective interplay between UN and regional human rights bodies.

It should be an occasion to assess the work of this Commission, which does not reflect today's human rights priorities. It should be an occasion to consider reorganizing the work of the UN's human rights bodies, so that duplication and wasteful redundancies are eliminated. It should be an occasion to examine the role of the Subcommission, which does not reflect the wishes of this Commission. If that situation does not improve by 1993, the World Conference should take a hard look at the need for a Subcommission.

It can be an occasion to strengthen those functions of the Human Rights Center that bring a small measure of relief to those whose human rights are daily abused: advisory services, technical assistance, 1503 procedures, and the special rapporteurs. I was recently reminded of this when visited by an ambassador whose government is under Special Rapporteur scrutiny. He told me that his government, its judiciary and its police, lacked not the will to respect human rights, but the knowledge of how to do it. There was no tradition of due process, no training of their police or of their magistrates, and no means to teach these things. But there was the will to learn. That is what advisory services are for.

We want to see this Conference yield some important results. For this to happen, its participants must acknowledge that last year's revolution in human rights, like the one two centuries before it, holds some inescapable truths about mankind. We should apply those lessons, instead of contenting ourselves with yet another sterile proclamation.

0173

This Conference can be part of the search for a better life for those still without life's bare necessities. It can do this by emphasizing the crucial, causal, central link between respect for fundamental freedoms and the development of men and nations.

It can be a stock-taking time, if we let it: to assess where we are, and what we must do, to bring about real respect for human rights. It should not be a forum to obfuscate rights by focusing attention on distracting, chimerical goals. Nor should we be afraid to ask why this Commission is so limited, and so selective, in its scrutiny and censure. What obstacles exist, for example, to the production of an annual, balanced, comprehensive assessment of human rights practices throughout the world, either by this or some other regional human rights body?

These are some of the questions we would like addressed in 1993. Self-criticism and honest assessment is not always easy. But they are inevitably good things. So let us begin.

END

0174

PERMANENT MISSION OF DENMARK
TO THE
UNITED NATIONS OFFICE
AT GENEVA

47th SESSION OF

THE UNITED NATIONS COMMISSION ON HUMAN RIGHTS

ITEM 11. THE WORLD CONFERENCE ON HUMAN RIGHTS

Statement by

Jakob Esper Larsen

Ambassador

Permanent Representative

of

Denmark

on behalf of

the Nordic Countries

on February 12, 1991.

<u>Check against delivery</u>

0175

Mr. Chairman,

I have the honour to speak on behalf of the five Nordic Countries, Finland, Iceland, Norway, Sweden and my own country Denmark, on agenda item 11, the preparation of the World Conference on Human Rights.

The Nordic Countries share a number of important ideas on the organization of society and the relations between the state and the individual citizens living on its territory. The peoples and governments of the Nordic Countries are deeply committed to pluralistic democracy, the rule of law and respect for human rights.

It is therefore only natural that we have common views on the goals and prospects for the international cooperation on human rights in the coming years.

The Nordic Countries welcome the adoption by consensus at the 45th session of the General Assembly of resolution 45/155 by which it was decided to convene, at a high level, a World Conference on Human Rights in 1993. The conference should serve as a forceful tool for promotion and protection of respect for human rights, an issue of growing importance in international affairs. The Conference requires careful and extensive preparations in spirit of cooperation.

The resolution by the General Assembly has in a balanced way set the major objectives for the Conference.

One of the main objectives for the Conference is to examine ways and means to improve implementation of already existing human rights standards and instruments. The conference will evaluate the methods and mechanisms applied by the United Nations in the field of human rights and formulate recommendations for further improvements of the effectiveness of the United Nations activities and mechanisms in this field.

For several decades normsetting was the most urgent task for the cooperation on human rights in the United Nations.

Building on the foundation layed by the universal declaration the United Nations have established an impressive and comprehensive framework of international legal obligations in the field of human rights through the International Covenant on Civil and Political Rights and its optional protocols and the International Covenant on Economic, Social and Cultural Rights, the International Convention on the Elimination of all Forms of Racial Discrimination and the Convention against Torture, as well as other instruments.

The adoption by the General Assembly at its 44th Session in 1989 of the Convention on the Rights of the Child and the second optional protocol to the International Covenant on Civil and Political Rights aiming at abolition of death penalty constitute important extensions of this framework. On the basis of the conventions important work is being undertaken in order to further clarify the precise implications of the civil and political rights, and the economic, social and cultural rights.

Now we have a solid foundation in international law for the common efforts of the international community to promote human rights and ensure that they are realized in practice.

0177

A major objective for the coming years is to cooperate on implementation of obligations already undertaken to respect human rights.

In the development of international instruments on human rights and in the subsequent monitoring of implementation it has been a fundamental assumption that human rights are by nature universal. The Nordic Countries hold the view - shared by many other countries - that the universality of human rights is part of their very essence and that it is of paramount importance to preserve the universality also in the future. This concept should be recognized in all its aspects by the World Conference.

It is only when states abide by their international obligations and effectively implement the instruments to which they by their own free will have subscribed that the potential of these instruments can be fully realized. This is why the Nordic Countries believe that the World Conference should devote particular attention to securing universal adherence to and effective monitoring of compliance with existing instruments.

The Nordic Countries would like to mention two keywords for the further progress of international cooperation in the field of human rights.

One keyword is dialogue. It is imperative that all states are willing to engage themselves in sincere dialogue on all human rights issues in order to promote further realization of human rights. It is difficult to develop formal norms to ensure genuine dialogue. But maybe the conference could state our common political commitment to participate sincerely in dialogue on all aspects of implementation of human rights as recognized by the international community.

0178

Another keyword is transparency. To day the world is much more transparent than it was when human rights was taken up as a main theme for the United Nations. Modern communication technology, the evolution of the mass media and the extensive development of international cooperation has made is possible to establish information on the human rights situation all over the world much more accurately than just a few decades ago. Yesterday it was relatively easy to hide or camouflage human rights violations. Today it is much more difficult. Transparency is the best way to ensure an adequate basis for our cooperation on human rights.

Mr. Chairman,

A prime objective for the World Conference will be to examine the relations between development and the enjoyment by everyone of economic, social and cultural rights as well as civil and political rights. The Nordic Countries are of the opinion that this very important objective deserves our most careful consideration. The Nordic Countries are convinced that there is a close relation between development and the conditions for realization of human rights. We share the view that there can be no sustainable development without democracy, rule of law and respect for human rights. Allow me, Mr. Chairman, to quote from the Communique of the Nordic Ministers of development cooperation meeting in Norway in September 1990:

"The connection between democracy, human rights and sustainable development has become more and more evident. In the context of international development cooperation it has now been recognized that open democratic systems and respect for human rights give impetus to efforts to achieve development, economic

0179

efficiency and equitable distribution."

The Ministers of development cooperation expressed their determination to continue to work towards ensuring that the question of human rights and democracy are integrated into the efforts for the multilateral aid organizations. They declared that the Nordic Countries are prepared to provide active and concrete support for bilateral and multilateral efforts aiming at promoting human rights and development of democracy.

The Nordic Countries see the World Conference as a welcome opportunity to develop these ideas further and to explore ways and means to transform them into reality.

Over the last years the activities of the United Nations in the field of human rights have increased significantly. As a consequence the Center for Human Rights has been burdened with increased demands for supportive action. It goes without saying that in these circumstances the Center for Human Rights requires more resources in order to be able to carry out its tasks in an efficient manner. This necessity for more resources should be recognized by the competent bodies of the United Nations even in periods with zero-growth of the United Nations budget as a whole.

The Nordic Countries would like to take this opportunity to stress the important role which the NGO's have in the global efforts to promote and defend human rights. They provide a crucial contribution to the proper formulation of relevant principles and programmes in the United Nations and represent a vital channel for promoting international awareness of human rights issues. The Nordic Countries suggest that it would be appropriate for the World Conference to recognize the importance of NGO's in the international interaction in the field of human rights.

Mr. Chairman,

The Nordic Countries attach great importance to the coming World Conference. Therefore we intend to participate actively and constructively in the preparations which are needed for the success of the Conference.

Thank you, Mr. Chairman.

INTERNATIONAL SECRETARIAT
1 Easton Street London WC1X 8DJ
United Kingdom

Our reference:

Direct line:

United Nations Commission on Human Rights
47th Session
Agenda Item 10

Delivered: 14 February 1991

ENFORCED OR INVOLUNTARY DISAPPEARANCES

ORAL INTERVENTION BY AMNESTY INTERNATIONAL

Mr Chairman,

The draft Declaration on the Protection of All Persons from Enforced or Involuntary Disappearances has long been awaited by the victims and relatives of this horrendous phenomenon as well as by the international community. "Disappearances" violate some of the most fundamental human rights protected under international law and an instrument which specifically prohibits this practice and which sets out the steps that should be taken by states to clarify, punish and prevent its occurrence is urgently needed.

Enforced disappearance continues to be widely used or tolerated by some governments as a means of eliminating dissent and of terrorizing the community. In 1990 alone the Working Group on Enforced or Involuntary Disappearances transmitted 962 new cases to 20 different governments. [Since the Working Group was set up in 1980 it has transmitted approximately 20,000 cases of enforced or involuntary disappearance to some 45 different governments.]

The practice of "disappearances" is no longer associated primarily with military dictatorships characterized by a total disregard for the rule of law. On the contrary, in Amnesty International's experience, "disappearances" are increasingly prevalent in countries with elected civilian governments where a wide range of legal remedies are theoretically available to victims and relatives. Yet, as a result of the clandestine nature of this method of repression, legal mechanisms intended to protect the individual have rarely proved to be effective against a practice specifically designed to flout the rule of law and to ensure the impunity of the perpetrators.

The impunity enjoyed by security forces and other perpetrators constitutes a typical feature of "disappearances" and has been described by the Working Group as "perhaps the single most important factor contributing to the phenomenon of disappearance...". When governments turn a blind eye, when investigations are not pursued, when state institutions do not function effectively and when those responsible for such violations are not brought to justice it is inevitable that "disappearances" will continue to occur in ever-increasing numbers. When "disappearances" occur in the context of counter-insurgency operations, impunity becomes, in the words of the Working Group, "almost endemic". Amnesty International knows of almost no case of perpetrators being brought to justice in these circumstances. The response of governments to the violent action of armed opposition groups can never constitute a pretext for a State to evade its responsibility of preventing human rights violations and of bringing the violators to account.

Amnesty International wishes to draw the Commission's attention today to the continuing practice of "disappearances" in six countries. Of these, five have held national elections in the last five years and have legal remedies in place that should offer protection against "disappearance". Five

☎ 01-833 1771 Telegrams: Amnesty London WC1 Telex: 28502 0182

of the six countries have in recent years established institutions specifically mandated to deal with human rights issues. [such as special commissions, presidential advisers or ombudsmen.] In addition, all of these states are a party to one or several of the main international or regional human rights instruments.

One of the most important guarantees for the protection of those unlawfully deprived of their liberty is that of habeas corpus. Yet all too often in cases of "disappearance" this important safeguard is undermined or ignored. The Working Group has recommended that affected governments "engage in a systematic revision of habeas corpus procedures, repairing their deficiencies".

In PERU Amnesty International has received reports of more than 3,500 cases of "disappearance" since 1983. Such reports have continued to reach the organization since the new government took office in July 1990. Last October Ernesto Rafael CASTILLO PAEZ, a 22-year-old student, was arrested in Lima by the police. [There were numerous witnesses to his "disappearance".] Following fruitless visits to police stations, his relatives presented a habeas corpus petition. In an exceptional move a judge took steps to secure the release of Castillo Paez, but important evidence was concealed or tampered with by the police authorities who did not comply with the order for his release. A higher court then also ordered his release and initiated proceedings to determine the responsibility of senior police officials. Most recently, however, in a controversial decision, the Supreme Court reportedly annulled these decisions and the fate of Ernesto Rafael Castillo Paez has not been clarified.

In the PHILIPPINES, the victims of "disappearance" have often been members of lawful non-governmental organizations. Maria Nonna SANTA CLARA and Angelina LLENARESAS, both social workers at the Ecumenical Center for Research and Development, "disappeared" in Camarines Sur in April 1989. There is considerable evidence that they were detained by the military. Habeas corpus hearings on their behalf took place before the Regional Trial Court in Manila, which made a ruling in favour of the petitioners. Yet in January 1990 the Supreme Court, without giving reasons, referred the case to the government's Human Rights Commission. If the Supreme Court had confirmed the first court's ruling, the military authorities would have been called to account for the fate of the two "disappeared" women. Nothing is known about their current whereabouts but their relatives and lawyers, as well as witnesses to the "disappearance", are reported to have received death threats.

Those committed to the cause of justice in their respective communities [are frequently viewed as threats to the security of the state and] often become targets of "disappearance". In SRI LANKA, where several thousand people have "disappeared" in the context of the current conflict, Kumaraguru KUGAMOORTHY, a member of the Tamil minority who was active in the defence of civil rights, was detained by a group of armed men, one in camouflage uniform, and "disappeared" in September 1990. The search undertaken by his relatives has included letters to the President of Sri Lanka and to the Minister of State for Defence. His whereabouts remain unknown.

It is not only those perceived as a threat to the security of the state who become victims of "disappearance". In GUATEMALA, where "disappearances" occur in endemic proportions, Maria Josefa TIU TOJIN, a 30-day-old baby, "disappeared" in August 1990. She was arrested with her mother, Maria TIU TOJIN, by the military in the Quiché region during a counter-insurgency operation. Dozens of peasants who were also detained are witnesses to the fact that both mother and child were held by the Guatemalan military. Both remain "disappeared".

In some countries those who are actively working on behalf of victims of human rights violations often become targets of the abuses they are trying to prevent. In COLOMBIA, where at least 200 people have "disappeared" in the last year, Alirio de Jesús PEDRAZA BECERRA, a lawyer acting on behalf of a number of trade unionists who had been detained and tortured, "disappeared" in Bogotá in July 1990. Eight men who identified themselves as members of the security forces abducted him in front of two police officers who did nothing to prevent the abduction.

Neither the police nor the armed forces have admitted holding him, and they have reportedly obstructed investigations by refusing to identify the police witnesses.

In a prevailing climate of fear and a deteriorating human rights situation relatives may feel at such great risk themselves that they dare not even report a "disappearance". In MAURITANIA since mid-1989 government operations particularly directed against black African villagers of the "Hal-pulaar" ethno-linguistic group, [mainly in the south of the country], have resulted in the arrest of hundreds of villagers. Amnesty International has received reports that many of them have since effectively "disappeared" and their fate remains unknown. Friends and relatives of those arrested fear arrest themselves if they attempt to draw attention to these cases.

Mr Chairman,

The international community has an urgent responsibility to take all possible measures to ensure that the practice of "disappearances" does not persist. Despite the efforts of the Working Group [on Enforced or Involuntary Disappearances], the vast majority of cases transmitted by it to governments have still not been clarified, while numerous other cases do not even come to the attention of the international community - the most disadvantaged, the poor, the inhabitants of remote rural areas, the illiterate and those without access to any form of assistance remain the unknown victims of "disappearance".

The adoption of the draft Declaration would represent universal recognition of the pressing need for the greater protection of all potential victims of "disappearance" and would reaffirm in a concrete form the often stated commitment of the international community that this abhorrent phenomenon must not be allowed to continue.

Amnesty International urges this Commission to give serious consideration to the draft Declaration with a view to its early adoption and transmission through to the General Assembly.

Thank you, Mr Chairman.

0184

INTERNATIONAL SECRETARIAT
1 Easton Street London WC1X 8DJ
United Kingdom

Our reference:

Direct line:

UN Commission on Human Rights
47th Session
Agenda Item 12

Delivered: 20 February 1991

ORAL STATEMENT BY AMNESTY INTERNATIONAL

Mr Chairman,

Situations of grave human rights violations, wherever they occur, are the legitimate concern of the world community and the Commission on Human Rights has the responsibility to examine them and to take timely and adequate measures to bring them to an end. In this task, the Commission should take due note of well-attested information from a variety of sources, including the reports of its own monitoring mechanisms. Whenever a government is blatantly ignoring universally-accepted human rights standards, the failure of the Commission to take up the situation may encourage that government to believe that it can continue to act with impunity. For countless victims it is simply too late to delay action until a deteriorating human rights situation has developed into one of crisis proportions.

Amnesty International has often urged the Commission to maintain adequate scrutiny of situations under examination until a demonstrable and sustained improvement is clearly established. In this regard Amnesty International welcomed the decision at the last session of the Commission to transfer consideration of the human rights situation in HAITI to agenda item 12. We hope that the accession by the interim government to the International Covenant on Civil and Political Rights on 6 February will lay a foundation for the new government to find solutions to serious and long-standing human rights violations in that country. However, Amnesty International believes the Commission's recent consideration of GUATEMALA has not corresponded to the gravity of that situation which has, if anything, deteriorated since Guatemala was removed from scrutiny under agenda item 12. The report of the Commission's Expert is further evidence that perpetrators of past human rights violations on a gross scale remain immune from prosecution and that widespread "disappearances" and extrajudicial executions have continued. The Commission must now take urgent steps to address this situation.

☎ 01-833 1771 Telegrams: Amnesty London WC1 Telex: 28502

0185

In recent years the Commission has failed to take action on flagrant violations of human rights in IRAQ, which were brought to its attention repeatedly. The international community has shown considerably more interest in the Iraqi Government's abuse of human rights since the invasion of Kuwait last August. Yet it is imperative that the Commission takes action, as requested by the Sub-Commission, also to address the long-standing pattern of human rights violations by the Government of Iraq. It must do so in a way that will ensure objective and sustained scrutiny of the situation that is not influenced by other considerations.

A year ago, the Commission also elected to take no action on the situation in CHINA despite convincing evidence of the killing, detention and ill-treatment of pro-democracy activists in 1989 described in a report by the UN Secretary-General, as well as information from other sources which also detailed the long-term pattern of human rights violations in China, including Tibet. Of immediate concern is the situation of some 26 pro-democracy activists who were arbitrarily held without charge for periods of 12 to 17 months in contravention of China's Constitution and law. Since November 1990 they have faced charges of "counter-revolutionary" activity leading to prison terms after trials that fall far short of international standards of fairness. Amnesty International considers most of them to be prisoners of conscience.

The Commission has examined the situation in MYANMAR since its decision on that country in 1989. Here, too, continuing human rights violations remain a matter of grave concern. Frequent mass arrests of suspected government opponents, including prisoners of conscience, occurred throughout 1990. Most recently, on 16 January, five more people, four of them elected to parliament for the National League for Democracy, were detained and joined the thousands already imprisoned. Many of them are detained without charge or trial while others have been charged with breaking martial law orders and sentenced to long terms of imprisonment by military tribunals established in July 1989. These tribunals, whose procedures do not conform to international standards for a fair trial, can also impose death sentences against which there is no appeal to a higher judicial authority. Reports also persist of routine and widespread torture and ill-treatment of political prisoners by the Military Intelligence Service and other security agencies.

There are still other situations where the Commission's expressions of concern have not been followed by sustained scrutiny. In 1987 the Commission adopted a resolution on SRI LANKA. Although the government has, since 1989, granted access to the International Committee of the Red Cross and has taken some other steps aimed at containing abuses, grave and widespread human rights violations have persisted for more than seven years and continue in 1991. These have occurred in the context of government measures to suppress armed opposition movements in the northeast and the south. Abuses, by opposition groups, including the torture and killing of prisoners, have

0186

been extensive but Amnesty International believes that this cannot absolve the government of its responsibility to curb violations committed by the security forces. During 1990, thousands of people, including young children, "disappeared" or were extrajudicially executed by government forces in the northeast after the Liberation Tigers of Tamil Eelam had renewed its offensive against the government in June. In the south, "disappearances" and extrajudicial executions continued to be carried out by government forces and "death squads" linked to them, although to a lesser degree than in 1989. However, last year evidence of the scale of violations committed in the south in 1988 and 1989 mounted, indicating that tens of thousands of people had "disappeared" or had been extrajudicially executed. The government has taken no effective steps to clarify the fate of these or the thousands of other people who have "disappeared" or been killed in recent years.

Other situations of persistent and serious violations of human rights need and deserve the attention of the international community if established patterns of abuse are to be halted. In the time that remains, Amnesty International wishes to mention two of these.

A pattern of serious human rights violations has emerged in SUDAN since the military coup of June 1989. New arrests of people who non-violently oppose the government are still being reported every month. Although many are later released, at least 300 such prisoners remain in detention. They include human rights activists, lawyers, doctors and trade unionists many of whom have been subjected to torture and ill-treatment, usually while they were held incommunicado in secret detention centres. Most are detained without trial, although a small number have been sentenced after trials that fall far short of international standards of fairness. Those sentenced to death are not allowed to appeal to a higher court or allowed proper legal representation at their trials.

In SYRIA, thousands of suspected opponents of the government continue to be detained under state of emergency legislation in force since 1963. Many are prisoners of conscience. Most are detained without charge or trial, some for more than 20 years, while others remain in prison after the expiry of their sentences. Some are held in place of relatives who are sought by the authorities. Two women arrested in March 1986 are still detained, although their wanted relatives were themselves arrested in March and April 1987. Untried political detainees have reportedly been ill-treated and tortured. In four cases during 1990 this allegedly resulted in the death of the detainee. No official investigation into these deaths is known to have been carried out.

Mr Chairman,

In all of these situations the government concerned has persistently failed to respect internationally-recognized human rights standards. More than 40 years ago the Universal

0187

Declaration of Human Rights was adopted precisely because, as the Preamble states, "disregard and contempt for human rights have resulted in barbarous acts which have outraged the conscience of mankind". If the international community, as represented by this Commission, is to uphold fundamental human rights standards it must confront with objectivity and impartiality all situations where these are systematically abused. Situations of grave human rights will persist, some will worsen, and some may even contribute to future conflicts, unless this Commission is seen to have the will to take decisive action.

Thank you, Mr Chairman.

원 본

외 무 부

종 별 :

번 호 : GVW-0346　　　　일 시 : 91 0222 1810

수 신 : 장 관(국연,법무부,기정)

발 신 : 주 제네바 대사대리

제 목 : 제 47차 유엔인권위 회의(14)

1. 표제 회의는 2.21. 야간회의에 이어 2.22.오전까지 의제 12항 토의를 계속하였으며, 오후에는 남아공인권, 경제적 권리 및 국제인권협약등에 관한 결의안을 심의할예정 임. 한편 2.21.오전에는 SULAIMAN AL-MUTAWA 쿠웨이트 기획장관, 오후에는 EWIGE AVICE 불란서 외무차관의 특별연설이 있었음

2. AL-MUTAWA 쿠웨이트 장관은 이라크군이 10만여명의 쿠웨이트 민간인을 불법체포하였으며 고문 및 학살행위가 계속 자행되고 있다고 말하고 현재 30만명이 쿠웨이트내에 거주하며 45만명이 망명중에 있다고 밝힘. 동 장관은 이라크가 ICRC 등민간단체의 쿠웨이트 입국을허가 할것을 촉구함. 또한 폴란드, 호주, 카타르, 사우디, 바레인, UAE 대표등도 이라크를 강력히 비난함.

3. 알젠틴, 유고, 쿠바등 9개국 대표는 사이프러스 사태와 관련, 터어키정부의점령 영구화 기도를 비난하고, 유엔 결의에 따른 동문제 해결을 촉구함.

4. 리비아 대표는 챠드에 수용중이던 6백여명의 리비아인 전쟁포로를 미국 정부가 나이제리아 및 자이레를 경유, 납치하였다고 비난하였는바, 나이제리아 및 자이레대표는 답변권을 행사, 자국정부가 국제관련에 따라 동 리비아 포로들이 통과하도록 편의를 제공하였을 뿐 이라고 반박함. 또한 호주대표는 이라크, 미얀마, 중국,스리랑카, 동티몰, 휘지, 이란, 피점령아랍지역, 과테말라의 인권상황과 발틱사태에 대한 소련의 무력 사용을 비난함.

5.JOSEPH VOYAME 루마니아 관련 특별보고관은 보고서 (E/CN.4/1991/30) 설명을 통해 동국의 상황이 계속 호전되고는 있으나 일부 심각한 인권위반 사례가 상존하고 있으며, 전화도청, 불법체포 및 비밀감금이 계속되고 있다고 말하고 동 정부가 헝가리 소수족을 비롯 일반국민에 대한 인권보장을 위해 계속 노력할 것을 촉구함.

6. 세계노조연맹 대표는 콜롬비아, 과테말라, 수단, 이란, 자이레에서의 노조

국기국　1차보　정문국　안기부　법무부

PAGE 1　　　　91.02.23　09:41 WG

외신 1과 통제관

0183

관련자 탄압 및 인권위반 행위, 이라크의 쿠웨이트내 이주노동자에 대한 탄압행위를 비난하고 통독후 동독출신 노동자에 대한 차별 문제를 제기함.

또한 ANDEAN COMMISSION OF JURIST 대표는 콜롬비아및 칠레문제, WORLD FEDERATION OF DEMOCRATIC YOUTH대표는 엘살바놀 문제, FOUR DIRECTIONS COUNCIL대표는 과테말라 문제, LIBERATION 대표는 인니인권상황을 집중 비난함. 그밖에 MOVEMENTAGAINST RACISM 등 많은 NGO 대표들이 쿠르드족의 인권침해 상황을 제기하면서 터키, 이라크 및 시리아 정부를 비난함.끝.

(대사대리 박영우-국장)

0l (3) 7 ✓

원 본

외 무 부

암호수신

종 별 :

번 호 : GVW-0359 일 시 : 91 0225 1930

수 신 : 장관(국연)

발 신 : 주 제네바 대사

제 목 : 제 47차 유엔인권위(15)

1. 2.25 표제회의 모로코 대표단은 아측에게 1993 년 개최 예정인 세계 인권회의(WORLD CONFERENCE ON HUMAN RIGHTS)에 관한 별첨 결의안을 제출키로 했다고 알려면서 아국이 동 결의안의 공동 제안국이 되어 줄것을 요청하였음.

2. 동 결의안은 세계 인권회의 제 1 차 준비회의를 제네바에서 91.9.9-13 간 개최할 것과 LDC 의 회의 참석 지원을 위한 각국의 자발적 회의 분담금 납부 요청 및 제 48 차 인권위에서 세계 인권회의를 의제로서 다룰것을 그 주요 내용으로 하고 있음.

3. 모로코 대표단은 인권위가 동 결의안을 콘센서스로 채택할 수 있도록 각국과 협의중이라 하며 남. 북한을 비롯하여 약 50 개국에게 공동제안국이 되어 줄것을 요청중이라함.

4. 상기 결의안은 모로코 공동제안국이 되어줄것을 요청중인 국가중 상당수가 공동제안국 제안을 수락할 것으로 보이며, 인권위가 동 결의안을 채택하는데 특별한 문제가 없을 것으로 보이는바, 모로코측 요청을 수락코자 하니 별도 지침있을시 2.26 한 회시 바람.

5. 옵서버 국가도 ECOSOC 기능 위원회 의사 규칙 69 조 3 항에 따라 결의안공동제안이 될수 있음을 첨언함.

첨부: FAX(상기결의안) 1 부. 끝

(GVW(F)-80)

(대사 박수길-국장)

국기국 장관 차관 1차보 2차보 청와대 안기부

PAGE 1 91.02.26 06:12

외신 2과 통제관 FE

0191

25 - 2 - 1991

GVW(T)-0080 /02251/00 첨부.

M O R O C C O

DRAFT RESOLUTION ON THE WORLD CONFERNCE ON HUMAN RIGHTS

Bearing in mind the objectives of the Charter of the United Nations and the Universal Declaration of Human Rights to promote and encourage respect for human rights and fundamental freedoms for all, without distinction as to race, sex or religion ;

Guided by the principles governing its mandate as the body responsible inter alia, for considering all aspects of human rights calling for the active participation of all members of the international community ;

Considering that, under the Charter of the United Nations and other international human rights instruments all States have an obligation to promote international co-operation for the promotion, effective implementation and protection of all human rights and fundamental freedoms and to create the best possible conditions to that everyone may enjoy these rights and freedoms, which are and remain indivisible and inter-related ;

Recalling the historic developments which have taken place in international relations since the International Conference on Human Rights held at Teheran in 1968 and, in particular, the increasingly greater importance that is universally being attached to the question of promotion, protection and effective realization of all human rights ;

Aware that respect for human rights throughout the world calls for the further intensification of the efforts of the world community and international bodies and for appropriate initiatives at the international, regional and national levels ;

Recalling General Assembly resolution 45/155 of 11 december 1990, which relates to convening in 1993 of a World Conference on Human Rights and in which the General Assembly requested the Commission on Human Rights to make recommendations to the Preparatory Committee for the Conference on issues of concern to it ;

.../...

0192

7-7-1

The Commission on Human Rights :

1 - Welcomes the decision of the United Nations General Assembly to convene a World Conference on Human Rights at a high level in 1993 ;

2 - Recognizes the importance of the holding of a World Conference on Human Rights for the effectiveness of joint action by the United Nations and Member States to guarantee the promotion, the effective implementation, the protection and the defence of all human rights ;

3 - Welcomes the nomination of Mr Jan MARTENSON, Under-Secretary-General for Human Rights as Secretary-General of the World Conference on Human Rights ;

4 - Appeals to all Member States of the United Nations, the Members of the specialized agencies and to observers to take part in accordance with the practice of the General Assembly, in the Preparatory Committee for the World Conference on Human Rights in order to help to create the necessary conditions for the success of the World Conference ;

5 - Recommends that its chairperson, the chairpersons or other designated members of human rights experts bodies, including the chairpersons of bodies established under international treaties or their designated representatives, as well as special and thematic rapporteurs, and chairpersons or designated members of working groups to take part in the work of the Preparatory Committee and to contribute to the preparations for the World Conference ;

6 - Invites its chairman to inform the Preparatory Committee of the debate on the World Conference that took place at the 47th session of the Commission, and in particular of the contents of this resolution and its annex ;

7 - Recommends to the Secretary-General of the World Conference on Human Rights to convene the first meeting of the Preparatory Committee in Geneva from 9 to 13 september 1991 ;

.../...

8 - Requests the Secretary-General of the World Conference to organize informal consultations among all UN member States to be held for a working-day in advance of the first meeting of the Preparatory Committee in order to prepare in particular the election of the five-member Bureau with due regard for equitable geographical representation, in accordance with General Assembly resolution 45/155 ;

9 - Also recommends that the rules of procedure for the work of the sessions of the Preparatory Committee shall be those of the functional commissions of the Economic and Social Council, in so far as applicable ;

10 - Recommends to the Secretary-General of the Conference to prepare suggestions, to be considered by the Preparatory Committee, on background documentation, including reference material on sources of information in the field of human rights ;

11 - Requests the Secretary-General to invite contributions of extra-budgetary resources to meet, inter alia, the cost of participation of representatives of least developed countries in the preparatory meetings and the Conference itself, in conformity with operative paragraph 7 of General Assembly resolution 45/155 ;

12 - Requests the Secretary-General of the United Nations to report to Commission at its forty-eight session on the progress of the work toward the World Conference on Human Rights ;

13 - Decides to consider this question at its forty-eight session under a new item titled " World Conference on Human Rights ".

0194

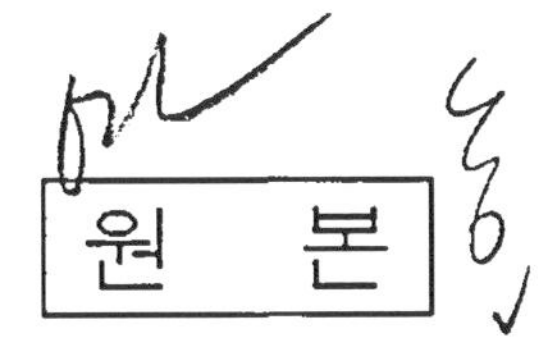

원 본

외 무 부

종 별 :

번 호 : GVW-0361 일 시 : 91 0226 1100

수 신 : 장관(국연,법무부,기정)

발 신 : 주 제네바 대사

제 목 : 제 47차 유엔인권위 회의(16)

1. 표제 회의는 2.25. 야간까지 회의를 연장, 의제 12항 토의를 계속하였음.

2. 영국대표 (MICHAEL WESTON 주 쿠웨이트 대사)는 이라크의 쿠웨이트 침공이후 이라크군의 조직적인 약탈행위, 서방 외국인에 대한 가혹행위, 쿠웨이트시 파괴등자신이 직접 목격한 사례와 민간인 학살등에 대해 목격자로부터 전해들은 바를 언급하고, 이라크군의 만행이 계속되고 있다고 비난함. 에집트대표는 이라크의 쿠웨이트침공은 위험한 전례라고 말하고 이라크의 국내 및 쿠웨이트에서의 인권 유린행위를비난함. 한편 쿠바 및 파레스타인 대표는 연합군의 이라크 폭격을 비난함.

3. 소련대표는 이라크를 비난하고, 아프간내 상황이 개선되고 있지 않으며, 엘살바돌 인권 상황이 계속 악화되고 있다고 우려를 표명한 반면 칠레의 민주화를 평가함. 중국 대표는 자국의 티벳 통치 정당성을 강조하였으며, 이라크를 비난하면서 연합군의 지상공격에 유감을 표명함. 인도대표는 의제 12항 토의시 선별적인 토의가 지양되어야 한다고 말하고 휘지에서의 인종 차별 헌법제정등 인권 위반 상황을 집중 거론함.

4. 그밖에 정부 대표들이 인권문제와 관련, 거명한 국가들은 아래와 같음.

- 사이프러스, 과테말라, 엘살바돌, 미얀마, 알바니아, 허가리 및 루마니아내 유고 소수민족 문제

5. 한편 NGO 인 AMERICAN ASSOCIATION OF JURISTS대표는 한국전 당시와 금번 걸프사태 관련 안보리 결의등 유엔의 조치를 평가하고 보다 효율적이고 실질적인 국제평화 및 안전 보장을 위한 유엔 기능 강화의 필요성을 강조함. 또한 INT'L LEAGUE FORHUMAN RIGHTS 대표는 스리랑카, 이라크및 중국등 심각한 인권 침해국에 대해 인권위가 인권 침해 방지를 위한 구체적 조치를 취하지 않고 있음을 비판함.

6. 기타 NGO 대표들은 아래 국가의 인권상황은 집중 거론, 비판함.

국기국 1차보 정문국 안기부 법무부

PAGE 1

91.02.26 22:06 DN

외신 1과 통제관

0195

- INT'L UNION OF STUDENTS: 과테말라

- 세계개혁 교회 연맹: 필리핀

- INT'L ASSOCIATION OF EDUCATORS FOR WORLD PEACE:중국, 리비아, 쿠바

- FRIENDS OF THE EARTH: 과테말라, 미얀마, 멕시코및 환경파괴에 따른 원주민 인권문제

- INT'L ASSOCIATION FOR THE DEFENCES OF RELIGIOUS LIBERTY:에집트-CHRISTIANDEMOCRATIC INT'L : 터키, 자이레, 칠레, 니카라과, 쿠바, 발틱제국

- ROMANI UNION: 동구권내 집시들의 인권 상황

- WORLD UNIRERSITY SERVICE: 엘살바돌, 과테말라,콜롬비아, 스리랑카

7. 한편 이날 회의에서 과테말라 인권 상황을의제 21항(인권자문 활동)에서 토의하자는 베네주엘라등 중남미안과 의제 12항에서 토의하자는 불란서등 서구안이 표결에 붙여진바, 중남미안이 21:18:5 로 채택됨. 끝

(대사 박수길-국장)

PAGE 2

0196

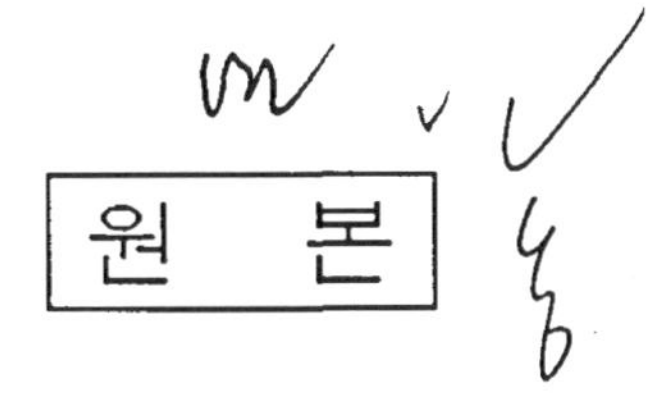

외 무 부

종 별 :

번 호 : GVW-0373 일 시 : 91 0227 1200

수 신 : 장관(국연,법무부,기정)

발 신 : 주 제네바 대사

제 목 : 제 47차 유엔 인권위 회의(17)

1. 표제회의는 2.26 자정까지 회의를 연장, 의제 12항 관련 공개토의 및 1503 절차 관련 비공개 심의를 계속 하였음. 또한 이날 오전에는 EDMUNDO VARGAS CARRENO 칠레 외무차관의 특별연설이 있었음.

2. 카나다, 놀웨이, 일본, 오지리, 스웨덴 대표는 아래 국가들의 인권 침해 사례를 열거하면서 세계인권 상황을 언급함.

- 이락 (국내 및 피점령 쿠웨이트), 이란, 시리아, 미얀마, 중국, 캄보디아, 아프간, 스리랑카, 인니, 수단, 이디오피아, 소말리아, 모리타니아, 엘살바돌, 과테말라, 쿠바, 페루, 하이티, 소련 (발트제국 문제), 알바니아, 사이프러스

상기 거론된 국가외에 카나다 대표는 인도 카시미르 지역 등에서의 인권 침해문제, 놀웨이 대표는 케냐 반체제 지도자 문제, 오지리 대표는 유고코스보 에서의소수민족 박해문제를 언급하였음. 한편 여타 대표들의 중국 비판 발언과는 달리,일본 대표는 중국인권 상황 호전 되었으며, 앞으로 동 정부의 개선 노력을 기대한다고 언급함.

3. 교황청 대표는 동구권의 변혁을 환영하고 걸프전쟁의 조속한 종결을 희망하면서 최근 발트제국의 유혈사태에 심각한 우려를 표명하고, 동국 국민의 인권 보장을 위한 관계 정부간의 대화 및 평화적 문제 해결 노력을 촉구함. 또한 체코 대표는 이라크의 쿠웨이트 침공 및 소련의 발트제국 무력행사, 쿠바에서 불법체포등 인권위반 사례를 비난하고 소수민족 보호문제를 언급함.

4. 이날 회의에서는 GALINDO POHL 이란문제 특별대표 보고서 (E/CN.4/1991/35) AMOS WAKO 불법처형 문제 특별 보고관 보고서 (E/CN.4/1991/36) 에대한 설명이 있었음. 이란문제와 관련, 서방정부 대표들은 이란정부가 POHL 특별 대표 의제 2차 이란 방문을 허가하는등 인권위 활동에 협조적임을 평가한 반면, 동국내에서 불법 처형, 고문 및 바하이등 소수 종교신자에 대한 인권 유린사례가 상존함을 비판함.

국기국 안기부 법무부

PAGE 1

91.02.28 06:56 DA

외신 1과 통제관

0197

또한 WAKO 특별 보고관은 불법처형 사례가 매년 증가하고 있다고 말하고 국내 소요및 분쟁에 대해 인권위 등이 효과적인 대응방안을 강구, 무고한 인명의 희생을 방지하도록 노력할것을 촉구함. 상기 보고서에 의하면 WAKO 보고관은 지난 1년간 45개국 정부에 불법 처형 관련 질의 서한을 발송하여 17개국이 답변자료를 제공하였으며, 64건의 긴급사안에 대해 25개국 정부에 긴급전문을 발송, 15개 정부로부터회신이 있었음.

5. NGO 대표들이 언급한 인권침해 사례발생 국가는 아래와 같음.

- INT'L LEAGUE FOR THE RIGHTS AND LIBERATION OF PEOPLES: 중남미 국가 에서의 IMPUNITY 남용문제

- GREEK ORTHODOX ARCHDIOCESAN: 알바니아, 사이프러스

- WOMEN'S INT'L LEAGUE FOR PEACE AND FREEDOM: 내전 상황에서의 여성의 인권침해문제 (엘살바돌, 과테말라, 필리핀, 스리랑카)

- CARITAS INTERNATIONALIS: 세계 각지역에서의 내전에 따른 총 15-20 백만명의국내 난민 보호문제.

끝

(대사 박수길-국장)

PAGE 2

0198

원 본

외 무 부

종 별 :

번 호 : GVW-0380 일 시 : 91 0228 1100

수 신 : 장 관(국연,법무부,기정)

발 신 : 주 제네바 대사

제 목 : 제 47차 유엔인권위 회의(18)

1. 표제 회의는 2.27.자정까지 회의를 연장, 의제12항 및 14항 (과학기술 발전과 인권) 토의를 마치고 의제 24항 (아동의 권리) 토의를 시작함.

2. NGO 인 INT'L ORGANIZATION FOR THE ELIMINATION OF ALL FORMS OF RACIAL DISCRIMINATION 대표는 중국, 에디오피아, 혼두라스, 쿠바, 사우디 및 북한의 인권상황을 비판함.

동 대표는 북한내 전주민이 구금상태하에 있으며, 고문, 실종, 권력남용이 만연되어 있고, 장애자는 차별 매문에 평양 거주가 금지되어있다고 말함.

3. 상기 발언에 대해 북한 대표 (박덕훈참사관)는 답변권 행사를 통해, 아래와 같이 반박함.

- 동 단체가 3년 계속 정치적 의도하에 북한에 대한 비방발언을 하고 있음.

- 북한에서는 사회주의 헌법에 따라 정치적, 시민적 자유가 보장되어 있으며, 고문 및 불법구금은 철저히 금지되어 있음.

- 장애자에 대해서는 평양등지에 특별 COMPOUND를 설립, 보호하고 있음.

4. 룩셈브르크 (EC 의장국)대표는 이라크등 28개국의 인권문제를 언급한바, 2.26 서방 주요국대표 발언시 언급된 국가외에 베트남내 인권위반사례, 카시미르 사태와 관련, 인도정부가 NGO대표의 동 지역 방문을 허가할 것을 요청하는 내용이 추가되어 있음. 스위스 대표는 특별 보고관제도 운영등 인권위 활동이 한시적이고 객관성이 결여되어 있는 경우가 있다고 지적하고보다 효율적인 인권조사 방법을 강구할 것을 촉구함.

5. 이란대표는 국제여론 및 정치적 고려매문에 인권위 회의등에서 동국 인권 상황이 악용되었다고 말하고 자국정부의 인권 보장노력을 고려, 인권위 산하 동국관련 특별대표의 활동이 종료되어야 할것이라고 강조함. 또한 이라크대표는 미국등

국기국 1차보 정문국 안기부 법무부

91.03.01 10:33 WG

외신 1과 통제관

0193

연합국의 걸프전쟁 계속 추진을, 파나마 대표는 쿠바 인권 상황을 비난함.터키대표는 그리스내 터키계 회교도 주민에 대한 차별및 인권위반 행위를 거론하면서 그리스정부를 비난한바, 동건과 관련, 양국대표는 2차례씩의 답변권을 행사함.

6. NGO 인 WORLD CONFERNCE ON RELIGION AND PEACE 및 INT'L WORK GROUP FOR INDIGENOUS AFFAIRS 대표로서 발언한 미얀마 야당인사 및 승려는 동정부의 90.5월 선거결과 불이행, 야당 및 종교계 인사에 대한 탄압을 비난하고 인권위가 동국인권상황을 공개리에 토의할 것을 촉구함.

7. 이날 회의에서 의제 12항 관련, 17개국 대표가 답변권을 행사함.

8. 한편 의제 14항 토의에서 정부 및 NGO대표들은 정신질환자의 인권 보장 방안강구, 환경 보호를 통한 지역주민 인권보장의 필요성을 강조함.

NGO 인 INT'L FEDERATION OF HUMAN RIGHTS 대표는 미얀마 정부가 한국, 일본, 태국회사에 대해 삼림벌목을 허가하여 동국의 환경 파괴가 가속되고 있다고 언급함.

9. 법무부 유국현 과장은 예정대로 당지도착하였음. 끝

(대사 박수길-국장)

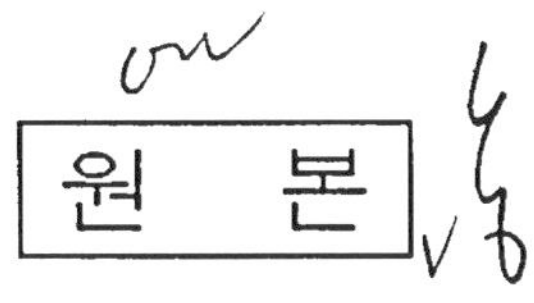

외 무 부

종 별 :

번 호 : GVW-0399 일 시 : 91 0304 1740

수 신 : 장 관(국연,기정,법무부)

발 신 : 주 제네바 대사

제 목 : 제 47차 유엔인권위 회의(19)

1. 표제 회의는 2.28, 3.1. 및 3.4 오전 회의시 의제 24 (아동의 권리) 의제 22 (신앙에 따른 차별철폐문제) 토의를 마치고 의제 21 (인권자문 활동)토의를 시작함.

또한 2.28 오후에는 RODAS MEGAR 과테말라 외무차관, 3.4 오전에는 VAN-DUNEM 앙골라 외무장관의 특별 연설이 있었음. 동 회의는 3.5(화) 오전까지 의제 19, 13, 20, 23, 25 을 토의, 전의제에 대한 토의를 마치고, 동일 오후부터 결의안을 심의할 예정임.

2. 의제 24항 토의내용

가. VITIT MUNTARBHORN 아동 인신매매 문제특별 보고관은 동인의 보고서 (E/CN.4/1991/51)설명을 통해 상기 문제가 전세계적 현상으로 상업주의, 통신 및 기술의 급속한 발전에 따라 악화되고 있으며, 국제적 범죄조직이 관여되어있다고 말하고, 아동 노동력 착취, 향락관광의 폐해를 언급함.

나. 대부분 정부 및 NGO 대표들은 아동권리협약의 조기 발효를 높이 평가하고 동협약의 국내적용을 위한 각국정부의 계획수립, 시행및 NGO 의 적극적인 협력을 촉구함.

다. NGO INT'L ABOLITIONIST FEDERATION 대표는 대만에 10만명의 아동이 강제로 매춘행위에 종사하고 있으며, 이들이 주로 원주민 및 중국본토 출신이라고 밝힘. INT'L ASSOCIATION OF DEMOCRATICLAWYERS 대표는 콜롬비아, 하이티, 브라질등 중남미국가 및 인도등에서 신장등 장기밀매가 성행하며, 동 목적을 위한 아동납치등의 행위가 늘어 나고있다고 말함.

또한 기타 NGO 대표들은 중남미지역에서 독재정권하에서 부모의 실종으로 많은 고아로자라고 있는 문제, 터키내 쿠르드족 아동에 대한 인권위반 문제등을 언급함.

3. 의제 22항 토의내용

국기국 1차보 안기부 법무부

PAGE 1

91.03.05 08:40 WG

외신 1과 통제관

0201

가. VIDAL D'ALMEIDA RIBEIRO 신앙문제 특별보고관은 보고서 (E/CN.4/1991/51) 설명을 통해 종교에 따른 차별 및 박해문제가 최근 동구지역등에서 급격히 개선되고 있다고 평가함.

나. 미국대표 는디벳에서의 불교승려 및 중국에서의 기독교 관계자에 대한 공식적인차별 및 박해사례, 쿠바에서의 여호아증인 교도처형, 이란에서의 바하이 교도 및 기독교도에 대한 박해를 비난하고, 이란정부의 신앙문제 특별 보관 방문초청 조치를 평가 함.

다. 중국, 인도, 소련대표등은 종교의 자유등을 보장하기 위한 자국의 입법 및 정책을 밝혔으며, 시리아 대표는 이스라엘의 팔레스타인에 대한 차별 및 인권침해를 비난함.

라. NGO 대표들은 아래 국가에서의 종교에 따른 차별 및 박해사례를 언급함.

- 중국, 싱가폴, 사우디, 모리타니아, 시리아, 폴란드, 프랑스, 루마니아, 쿠바, 멕시코, 미국, 중동회교국가

마. 한편 세계노조연맹 대표는 체코 정부가 프라하소재 동단체 사무소를 91.7월 폐쇄키로 결정하였다고 비난한바, 체코대표는 상기 결정이 확정된 것은 아니라고 답변함.

4. 의제 21항 토의

가. 대부분 정부대표들은 인권사무국의 인권자문활동의 중요성을 높이 평가하고 동 활동의 효율성 제고를 위해 국내 및 지역별 인권관련기관의 활동 확대, 유엔자문 활동 기금에대한 각국정부의 기여금 확대 확대 필요성을 강조함. 또한 서방국대표들은 심각하고 조직적인 인권위반 사례가 상존하고 있는 과테말라 및 적도기니 인권상황을 동 의제에서 토의하는 것이 적절치 못하다고 언급함.

나. 많은 NGO 대표들도 과테말라의 인권상황이 심각하게 악화되고 있다고 말하고 동 문제는 의제 12항에서 토의되어야 할 것이라고 강조함.

5. 한편 3.1. 의제 5항 남아프리카 인권 상황에관한 결의안 (L.22) 이 이례적으로 부표없이 채택된바, 동 결의안은 아파타이트 철폐시까지는 남아공 제재가 계속 되어야 하며, 인권위산하 남아공에 관한 전문가 그룹의 활동시한을 2년간 연기하면서 남아공 정부에 대해 동그룹활동에 대한 협조 제공을 촉구하는 내용임.끝.

(대사 박수길-국장)

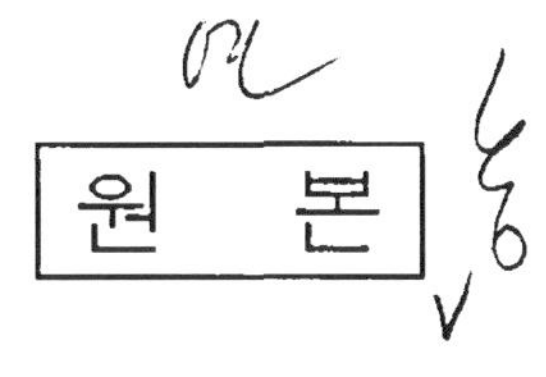

외 무 부

종 별 :

번 호 : GVW-0413 일 시 : 91 0306 1200

수 신 : 장관(국연,법무부,기정)

발 신 : 주제네바대사

제 목 : 제 47차 유엔인권위 회의(20)

1. 표제회의는 3.5.오전 전의제에 대한 토의를 마치고, 결의안 심의를 시작하였음.

이날 오전에는 ALEXIS FRUTOS VAESKAN 파라과이 외무장관, MARIE-DENIS FABIEN JEAN-LOUIS 하이티 외무장관 특별연설이 있었음.

2. 의제 19(인권소위 활동) 토의에서 대부분대표들은 인권소위에서 추진중인 토착민 권리에 관한 선언 초안 작성 작업을 평가하고 93년' 세계 토착민의 해'까지 국제규범의 제정을촉구함. 또한 인권소위가 본연의 임무 범위를 벗어나 인권위에서 심의중인 특정국가에 대한 인권상황 결의를 채택하는등 인권위와 중첩되는 활동을 하고있으며, 연구활동이 과도히 확대되고 있다고 비판하고 인권소위위원의 독립성 보장필요성을 강조함. 특히 미국대표는 정부관리가 소위위원이 되거나, 동위원이 인권위정부대표단에 포함되어서는 안될 것이라고 말하고 위원 활동에 대한 정부압력 제거를 위한 조치로 인권소위 특정의제 표결시 비밀부표제를 도입하는 것이 바람직하다고말함. 쿠바,중국,에디오피아 대표등은 소위 활동이 정치화 성향을 보이고 있다고 주장하고 특정의제에 대한 비밀 투표제 도입을 반대함.

3. 의제 13(이주 노동자 인권보장) 토의에서 대표들은 제 45차 유엔총회에서 이주 노동자 및가족의 권리 보호에 관한 협약이 채택된 것을 평가함.

NGO 대표들은 이씨내에서의 비유럽계 노동자에대한 인종차별 문제, 체코 및 불가리아내의 베트남 노동자 처리문제, 걸프사태와 관련한 외국노동자 권리 보장 문제등을 언급함.

4. 의제 20(소수민 권리) 토의에서 소수민 권리에 관한 선언초안 작성 비공식 실무위 의장(유고)은동 회의시 주요 쟁점으로서 소수민 권리가 개인적 권리인지 또는집단적 권리인지의 문제, 동권리를 향유할 수 있는 사람의 정의 문제가 대두되었다고 설명함. 미국대표는 애매하고 부정확한 집단적 권리로서 소수민의

국기국 1차보 정문국 안기부 법무부

PAGE 1

91.03.06 22:02 DN

외신 1과 통제관

0203

권리를 주장하는것보다는 모든 정부가 시민적,정치적 기본권을 철저히 준수함을써 소수민 보호가 가능할 것이라고 말함.

5. 이날 오후에 의제 10,11,14,21,22항 관련채택된 29개의 결의안 중 환경관계 2개 결의안을 제외한 여타 결의안은 투표없이 채택되었는바, 주요결의안 아래와 같음.

가. L.51(세계인권 회의)

- 모로코등 90개국이 공동제안한바, 93년세계인권회의 관련 준비회의를 91.9.9-9.13간 개최토록 제한하며 동 준비회의 지침을 포함하고있음. 아국 및 북한도 동 결의 공동제안국으로참여함.

나. 77(불법구금)

- 3년 임기의 5명의 독립전문가로 구성된 실무위를 구성, 각국의 불법구금 사례에 대한 조사 활동을 수행함.

다. L.28(인권 및 환경), L.70(유해폐기물문제)

- 아프리카등 개도국들이 제안하였으며, 미국등 서방대표는 인권위에서 동 문제를 토의하는 것이 적합치 않다고 비판한바, 투표결과 채택됨.끝.

(대사 박수길-국장)

PAGE 2

0204

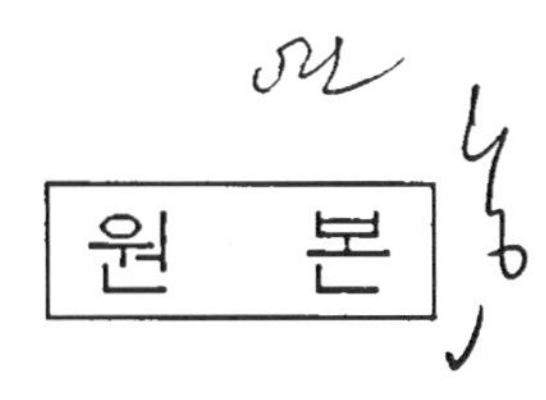

외 무 부

종 별 :

번 호 : GVW-0419　　　　일 시 : 91 0307 1530

수 신 : 장 관(국연,법무부,기정)

발 신 : 주 제네바 대사

제 목 : 제 47차 유엔인권위 회의(21)

1. 표제회의는 3.6자정까지 회의를 연장, 결의안심의를 계속하여 총 31개 결의안을 채택한바, 이중 25개 결의안이 표결없이 채택됨. 이날 채택된 주요 결의안은 아래와 같음.

가. 이라크 점령하의 쿠웨이트 인권상황 (L.40/REV.1)

- 찬성 41: 반대 1(이라크): 기권 0 으로 채택됨

- 동 인권상황을 조사하기 위하여 특별보고관을 임명하고, 동 보고관의 조사 보고서를 유엔총회 및 인권위에 보고토록함

나. 이라크 인권상황(L.68)

- 30:1 (이라크): 10 (중국, 쿠바, 인도등)으로 채택됨

- 동국의 인권문제, 특히 불법 처형, 고문 및 강제실종, 쿠르드족에 대한 인권유린 행위를 비난하고 이를 조사하기 위해 특별보고관을 임명하며, 동 보고관의 보고서를 총회 및 인권위에 보고토록 함.

- 지난 5년간 서방국가들은 동국관련 결의안 채택을 추진하였으나 실패한 바 있어 이번결의안 채택은 의미가 있음.

다. 쿠바인권 상황(L.88)

- 22:6 (중국, 에디오피아, 이락, 소련등): 15

- 유엔사무총장이 특별대표를 지명, 동 대표가 쿠반인권문제에 관해 동 정부 및 주민과 접촉하고, 그결과를 명년도 인권위에 보고토록함.

- 88년도 인권위 결의에 따라 인권위 조사단이 88년 동국을 방문한바 있으며, 금번 결의로 사무총장 대표가 주민등과 접촉하는등 실제적으로 동국인권 상황을 조사할 수 있게됨.

라. 기타 국가 인권상황

국기국　1차보　정문국　안기부　법무부

PAGE 1　　　　91.03.08 11:36 WG

외신 1과 통제관

0205

- 루마니아, 엘살바돌, 하이티, 아프간 인권상황을 조사하기 위해 임명된 특별보고관 및 대표등의 임기가 1년 연장됨.

- 알바니아 인권상황 관련 정치범 석방, 기본권 보장등 민주화 조치를 촉구함.

- 이스라엘의 남부 레바논 점령 및 인권위반행위를 비난함.

마. 인권 소위 위원의 독립성 강화(L.71)

- 23:4(쿠바,중국등): 15로 채택됨

- 인권 소위위원들의 독립성 강화 방안으로 특정국가 인권상황 결의안 표결시 비밀투표가 가능하도록 경사리 산하위원회 의사규칙 제 59조에 주석을 첨가토록 경사리에 권고

바. 인권위반의 책임문제(L.60)

- 우쿠라이나등이 제안한바, 국세법위원회가 국가책임에 관한 협약 초안 작업시인권 위반행위에 대한 국가책임 문제를 검토할 것을 요청하는 내용임.

2. 동 회의는 3.7.1503 절차 관련 토의를 종결하고, 이란 인권상황 결의안을 심의할 예정인바, 이로써 금차회의 토의 및 결의안 채택은 종결됨. 3.8 에는 차기회의 의제 및 금차회의 보고서를 채택하고 폐회할 예정임.끝.

(대사 박수길-국장)

0206

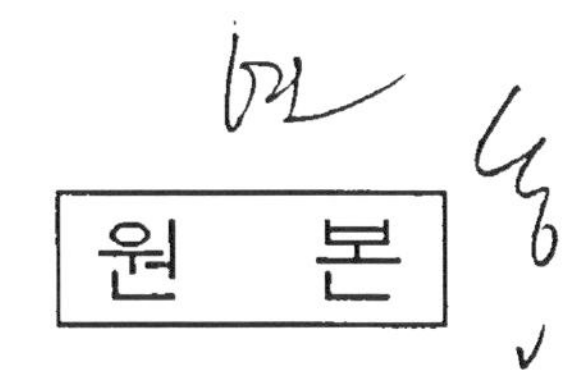

외 무 부

종 별 :

번 호 : GVW-0437 일 시 : 91 0308 2100

수 신 : 장 관(국연,법무부,기정)

발 신 : 주 제네바 대사

제 목 : 제 47차 유엔 인권위 회의(22)

1. 표제회의는 금 3.8 오후 금차 회의보고서를 채택하고 폐회함.

2. 한편 3.7 오전 회의에서는 이란 인권 상황결의안 (L.91) 이 관계국간 막후 협의를 거쳐의장 제안으로 상정되어 표결없이 채택됨. 동결의안은 주요 쟁점이었던 이란문제 특별대표의 임무 종료 문제를 이번회의에서 확정하지않고, 명년도 인권위에 제출될 동 대표의 보고서를 심의한 후에 동국 인권상황에 진전이있을 경우 임무를 종료키로 하였음.

3. 금차 인권위 회의 종합 평가등은 별전 보고하겠음. 끝

(대사 박수길-국장)

국기국 1차보 정문국 안기부 법무부

PAGE 1

91.03.09 09:38 WG

외신 1과 통제관

0207

주 제 네 바 대 표 부

제네(정) 2031-235 1991. 3. 8

수신 : 장관

참조 : 국제기구조약국장

제목 : 제 47차 유엔인권위 회의 관련 자료 송부

표제회의 관련 자료를 별첨 송부합니다.

첨부 : 1. Int'l Organization for the Elimination of All Forms of Racial Discrimination 대표 발언문(2.27일자) 1부.

2. 불법처형 특별보고관 보고서(E/CN.4/1991/36) 1부.

3. 아동인신매매 문제 특별보고관 보고서(E/CN.4/1991/51) 1부.

4. 신앙문제 특별보고관 보고서(E/CN.4/1991/56) 1부.

5. 제 42차 인권소위 의장 보고서(E/CN.4/1991/48) 1부.

6. 이란인권 상황 보고서(E/CN.4/1991/35) 1부. 끝.

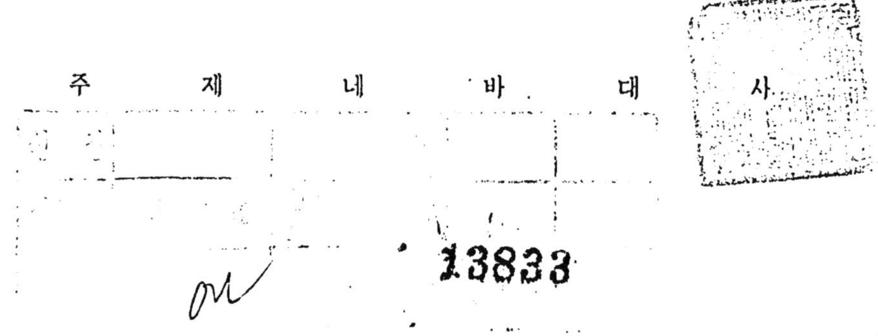

주 제 네 바 대 사

13833

0208

관리번호 91-237

기 안 용 지

분류기호 문서번호	국연 2031 - 586	(전화 :)	시행상 특별취급	
보존기간	영구 · 준영구. 10. 5. 3. 1	장 관		
수신처 보존기간				
시행일자	1991. 3. 12.			

보조기관			협조기관		문서통제
	국 장	전 결			1991. 3. 14
	과 장				
기안책임자		송영완			발송인 1991. 3. 14 외무부

경 유		발신명의	
수 신	법무부장관		
참 조	법무실장		
제 목	제47차 유엔인권위 주요 발언문 송부		

연 : GVW-0284, 0311, 0325, 0336

주제네바대사의 연호 보고관련, 제47차 유엔 인권위원회에서의 미국, 화란, 국제교회위원회 대표의 연설문 및 아국대표의 답변권행사 발언문을 별첨 송부하오니 업무에 참고하시기 바랍니다.

첨 부 : 1. 미국대표 연설문(의제 8항 및 12항) 각 1부

0203 /계속..

(2)

2. 화란대표 연설문 (의제 10항) 1부

3. 국제교회위원회 대표연설문 (의제 10항) 1부

4. 아국대표의 답변권행사 발언문 2부.　끝.

검 토 필(1991.6.30.)

일반문서로재분류(1991.12.31.)

0210

관리 번호	91 —700

원 본

외 무 부

종 별 :

번 호 : GVW-0447 일 시 : 91 0312 1800

수 신 : 장관(국연,법무부,기정)

발 신 : 주 제네바 대사

제 목 : 제 47차 유엔 인권위 회의 (23-최종)

(자료응신 11 호)

91.1.28-3.8 간 개최된 표제회의 종합관찰 및 평가를 아래 보고함.

1. 회의 참가

가. 43 개 위원국, 78 개 옵서버국, 13 개 정부간 기구 2 개 민족해방 운동기구 및 140 개 민간 인권단체(GNO) 대표가 참가함.

나. 북한측에서는 당지 대표부 박덕운 참사관이 참가함.

2. 아국 및 북한관련 사항

가. 아국 관련사항

- 친북성향의 NGO 인 INT'L ASSOCIATION OF DEMOCRATIC LAWYERS 가 교도 행정과 관련 아국을 집중 거론하였음. 또한 WCC 산하 국제 교회 위원회가 페루 및 필리핀 인권 상황을 거론하면서 국가 보안법 위반 사건에 대한 KNCC 발표를 인용, 아국문제를 언급함.

상기 발언들에 대해 아국 대표는 답변권을 행사, 동 주장을 반박함.

- 화란대표는 고문문제 특별 보고관 보고서의 내용을 분석 9 개국 사례를 거론하면서 아국의 일부 답변내용을 비판함.

나. 북한관련 사항

- 미국대표는 의제 8 항(발전의 권리) 토의시 인권 및 경제분야에 있어 남. 북한 발전을 비교하면서 북한의 전체주의 체제를 비판하였으며, 이에대해 북한측은 답변권 행사를 통해 반박함.

또한 미국대표는 의제 9 항(자결권) 토의시 자유선거제도 부재국가로서 쿠바등과 함께 북한을 언급하였으며, 의제 12 항 관련 연설문에서는 북한의 형법 내용 및 강제수용소 문제등을 비판함.

국기국 장관 차관 1차보 2차보 청문국 청와대 안기부 법무부

PAGE 1 91.03.13 07:18

외신 2과 통제관 BW

0211

- NGO 인 INT'L ORGANIZATION FOR THE ELIMINATION OF ALL FORMS OF RACIALDISCRIMINATION 은 북한의 강압체제 및 장애자 박해문제를 언급한바 북한측은 동 단체가 정치적 의도하에 비방발언을 하고 있다고 반박함.

3. 일반토의 사항

가. 걸프전과 관련, 이라크 국내 및 점령 쿠웨이트에서의 인권위반 상황에 대한 정부 및 NGO 비판이 부각되었으며, 남아공, 피점령아랍지역, 미얀마, 중국,동티몰, 스리랑카, 필리핀, 시리아, 이란, 과테말라, 페루, 콜롬비아, 쿠바, 알바니아, 소련내 발트제국, 수단, 자이레 인권문제가 집중거론됨.

나. 상기 관련 이라크, 피점령 쿠웨이트, 이란, 쿠바, 엘살바돌, 하이티, 아프간, 루마니아 인권상황을 조사하기 위한 특별보고관 및 특별대표에 대한 임명 또는 동 임기 연장이 결의되었음. 특히 서방측 제안대로 이라크 특별보고관 임명이 최초로 결정되었으며, 쿠바 문제관련 특별대표 임명이 결의된것은 특기할만한 사항임. 또한 이란문제 특별대표의 임기 종료 문제를 금차 회의시 결정치않고 차기 회의시 확정키로 한것은 동 결의안을 위요한 대결을 피하고자 한 서방측과 이란측의 교섭의 결과인바, 많은 참가 대표로부터 평가를 받은바 있음.

다. 금번 회의 결의에 따라 5 명의 독립전문가로 구성된 불법구금 문제 실무위가 구성되므로써 동 활동이 주목되고 있음. 또한 많은 정부 및 NGO 대표들은중남미 국가에서 정부가 고문행위자를 처벌치 않는 현상(IMPUNITY)을 집중 비판하였으며, 93 년도 세계인권회의에 대한 많은 관심을 표명하였음.

그밖에 인권소위 위원 독립문제등 인권위 개선방안, 아동, 소수민 및 토착민의 권리문제에 대한 토의가 대두되었음.

라. 금차회의에서는 1 개국 국가원수급 인사, 10 개국 외무장관, 5 개국 장관 및 4 개국 외무차관이 특별연설을 통해 세계인권 상황 및 자국 특수 상황에 대해 입장을 표명함으로써 인권위에 대한 높은 관심을 보였음.

마. 92 년 회의부터는 인권위원국이 현재 43 개국에서 53 개국으로 증가됨에 따라 인권위 회기 연장 문제가 금년도 경사리에서 토의될 예정임.

4. 평가 및 건의

가. 90.2 월 제 42 차 인권위 임수경 사건을 직접 거론한바 있는 북한은 90.8 월 인권소위에 이어 금차 회의에서도 직접발언을 하지 않았으며 2 차례의 답변권 발언에서도 종전과 달리 아측에 비난 내용이 전혀 없이 남. 북대화 진전을 평가하는등

아측을 직접 자극하지 않으려는 태도를 보여주었음.

이것은 인권위 회의시 전체주의 국가에 대한 비판분위기가 팽배되어 있음에비추어 아측에 의해 북한 인권문제가 대두될 경우 동파급 효과를 우려하였기 때문인 것으로 보임.

나. 아측으로서는 금년에 구성될 불법 구금문제 실무위를 비롯, 기존의 고문 문제 특별보고관 활동에 지속적으로 관심을 기울여야 할것으로서 판단되며, 아동 및 소수민 보호문제 토의, 세계인권회의 준비과정에도 적극 참여하는 것이 바람직할 것임.끝.

(대사 박수길-국장)

예고:91.12.31. 일반

일반문서로 재분류 (1991 .12 .31 .

검 토 필(1991.6.30.)

PAGE 3

0213

報告畢

長官報告事項

1991. 3. 13.

國際機構條約局
國際聯合課 (12)

題目 : 第 47次 유엔人權委員會 結果 報告

第 47次 유엔人權委員會가 91.1.18-3.8間 제네바에서 開催되었는 바, 同 會議結果를 아래 要約 報告드립니다.

1. 會議參加 現況

- 121個國 (43個 人權委員國 및 78個 옵서버國)
- 13個 政府間 機構 및 140個 民間人權團體(NGO)
- 我國代表團 : ______ ←

2. 유엔人權委員會 重點 討議事項

- 被拘禁者 人權問題
- 世界各國의 人權違反事例 : 이락 점령하의 쿠웨이트, 쿠바, 중국, 발트지역, 루마니아, 엘살바돌, 과테말라등
- 아랍 被占領地, 남아공 人權違反 問題
- 其他 人權委의 組織, 行政問題等

공람	담 당	과 장	국 장	차관보	차 관	장 관
	(서명)	(서명)	(서명)	(서명)	(서명)	

0214

3. 我國關聯 事項

가. 我國 人權問題 擧論 (3회)

- ㅇ 國際敎會委員會 : KNCC의 報告書 인용, 90年度 11개월간 1,746名의 良心囚가 逮捕되었다고 言及
- ㅇ 國際法律家協會 : 政治的 目的의 拘束者 現況 및 拘禁者 人權狀況 擧論
- ㅇ 和 蘭 : 拷問이 행해지는 나라의 하나로서 我國擧論

나. 我國代表의 答辯權 行使

- ㅇ 人權團體의 言及內容에 대해서는 答辯權 行使, 不當性 指摘
- ㅇ 和蘭代表의 發言은 拷問이 행해지는 9個國中 하나로 我國을 言及하여 答辯權을 行使하기에는 不適切함을 감안, 同 代表를 個別 接觸, 我國 人權狀況 改善을 위한 政府의 措置 說明

4. 北韓關聯 事項

가. 北韓 人權問題 擧論 (3회)

- ㅇ 美 國
  - 議題 8項(發展의 權利) 討議時 人權 및 經濟分野에 있어 南.北韓 發展을 比較하면서 北韓의 全體主義 體制 批判
  - 또한 議題 9項(自決權) 討議時 自由選擧制度 不在國家로서 쿠바 등과 함께 北韓을 言及하였으며, 議題 12項 關聯 演說文에서는 北韓의 刑法 內容 및 強制收容所 批判

0215

º 人種差別 撤廢를 위한 國際機構

- 北韓의 獨裁體制 및 障碍者 迫害等 批判 (我側 이랑 參事官은 上記 NGO 代表를 事前 接觸, 北韓의 人權關聯 資料를 傳達하고 北韓 實相에 대하여 詳細히 說明)

나. 北韓代表의 答辯權 行使

º 美側 發言에 대하여 1回 答辯權 行使, NGO 發言에 대해서는 同 團體가 政治的 意圖下에 誹謗發言을 하고 있다고 反駁

다. 北側 態度 評價

º 北韓은 90.2月 第 46次 人權委에서 임수경 事件을 直接 擧論한 바 있으나 90.8.月 人權小委에 이어 今次 會議에서도 直接 我國非難 發言을 하지 않음. 또한 2회의 答辯權 行使時에도 從前과 달리 我側 非難內容이 전혀 없이 南.北韓對話 進展을 評價하는등 我側을 直接 자극하지 않으려는 態度 견지

5. 向後 人權會議 對策 (建議)

가. 北韓 人權狀況 擧論對策

º 國際人權團體를 통한 北韓 人權問題 擧論

- A.I., Asia Watch 等에 대한 北側 人權現況 說明 積極 展開
- 北韓 人權實態 調査를 위한 同 團體들의 訪北活動 積極 勸誘
- 北韓 實相에 관한 資料의 持續的, 體系的 送付 및 同 團體의 北韓 人權問題 提起 督勵

º 國內人權團體 育成

- 長期的으로, 國內 人權團體를 유엔 ECOSOC 登錄團體(NGO)로 育成, 同 團體가 北韓의 人權實相을 擧論하고 陳情書를 提出하는등 北韓의 開放 誘導 活動을 展開토록 推進

0216

나. 我國 人權狀況 弘報

ㅇ 人權規約 加入에 따른 人權報告書 (최초) 作成時 我國의 人權狀況 詳細 記述

- 91.7.9.한 作成, 提出豫定

ㅇ 不法 拘禁問題 實務委 및 拷問問題 特別報告官 活動 對策 樹立

- 最近 接受된 被拘禁者 人權問題(고문, 비인도적 대우등)에 관한 陳情書에 대한 政府 答辯書 作成 提出等 愼重 對處 豫定

ㅇ 其　　他

- 兒童 및 小數民 保護問題 討議, 世界人權會議(1993) 準備過程에 積極 參與

- 끝 -

0217

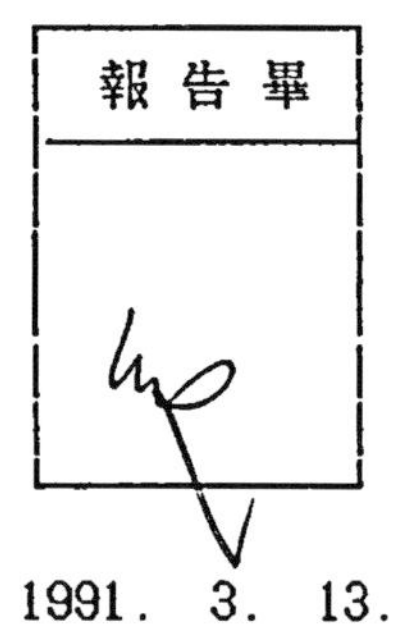

長 官 報 告 事 項

1991. 3. 13.

國際機構條約局
國際聯合課 (12)

題目 : 第 47次 유엔人權委員會 結果 報告

第 47次 유엔人權委員會가 91.1.18-3.8間 제네바에서 開催되었는 바, 同 會議結果를 아래 要約 報告드립니다.

1. 會議參加 現況

- 121個國 (43個 人權委員國 및 78個 옵서버國)
- 13個 政府間 機構 및 140個 民間人權團體(NGO)

2. 유엔人權委員會 重點 討議事項

- 被拘禁者 人權問題
- 世界各國의 人權違反事例 : 이락 점령하의 쿠웨이트, 쿠바, 중국, 발트지역, 루마니아, 엘살바돌, 과테말라등
- 아랍 被占領地, 남아공 人權違反 問題
- 其他 人權委의 組織, 行政問題等

0218

3. 我國關聯 事項

가. 我國 人權問題 擧論 (3회)

- o 國際敎會委員會 : KNCC의 報告書 인용, 90年度 11개월간 1,746名의 良心囚가 逮捕되었다고 言及
- o 國際法律家協會 : 政治的 目的의 拘束者 現況 및 拘禁者 人權狀況 擧論
- o 和　　　蘭 : 拷問이 행해지는 나라의 하나로서 我國擧論

나. 我國代表의 答辯權 行使

- o 人權團體의 言及內容에 대해서는 答辯權 行使, 不當性 指摘
- o 和蘭代表의 發言은 拷問이 행해지는 9個國中 하나로 我國을 言及하여 答辯權을 行使하기에는 不適切함을 감안, 同 代表를 個別 接觸, 我國 人權狀況 改善을 위한 政府의 措置 說明

4. 北韓關聯 事項

가. 北韓 人權問題 擧論 (3회)

- o 美　國
  - 議題 8項(發展의 權利) 討議時 人權 및 經濟分野에 있어 南.北韓 發展을 比較하면서 北韓의 全體主義 體制 批判
  - 또한 議題 9項(自決權) 討議時 自由選擧制度 不在國家로서 쿠바 등과 함께 北韓을 言及하였으며, 議題 12項 關聯 演說文에서는 北韓의 刑法 內容 및 强制收容所 批判

0219

ㅇ 人種差別 撤廢를 위한 國際機構

- 北韓의 獨裁體制 및 障碍者 迫害等 批判 (我側 이랑 參事官은 上記 NGO 代表를 事前 接觸, 北韓의 人權關聯 資料를 傳達하고 北韓 實相에 대하여 詳細히 說明)

나. 北韓代表의 答辯權 行使

ㅇ 美側 發言에 대하여 1回 答辯權 行使, NGO 發言에 대해서는 同 團體가 政治的 意圖下에 誹謗發言을 하고 있다고 反駁

다. 北側 態度 評價

ㅇ 北韓은 90.2月 第 46次 人權委에서 임수경 事件을 直接 擧論한 바 있으나 90.8.月 人權小委에 이어 今次 會議에서도 直接 我國非難 發言을 하지 않음. 또한 2회의 答辯權 行使時에도 從前과 달리 我側 非難內容이 전혀 없이 南.北韓對話 進展을 評價하는등 我側을 直接 자극하지 않으려는 態度 견지

5. 向後 人權會議 對策 (建議)

가. 北韓 人權狀況 擧論對策

ㅇ 國際人權團體를 통한 北韓 人權問題 擧論

- A.I., Asia Watch 等에 대한 北側 人權現況 說明 積極 展開
- 北韓 人權實態 調査를 위한 同 團體들의 訪北活動 積極 勸誘
- 北韓 實相에 관한 資料의 持續的, 體系的 送付 및 同 團體의 北韓 人權問題 提起 督勵

ㅇ 國內人權團體 育成

- 長期的으로, 國內 人權團體를 유엔 ECOSOC 登錄團體(NGO)로 育成, 同 團體가 北韓의 人權實相을 擧論하고 陳情書를 提出하는등 北韓의 開放 誘導 活動을 展開토록 推進

0220

나. 我國 人權狀況 弘報

o 人權規約 加入에 따른 人權報告書 (최초) 作成時 我國의 人權狀況 詳細 記述

- 91.7.9.한 作成, 提出豫定

o 不法 拘禁問題 實務委 및 拷問問題 特別報告官 活動 對策 樹立

- 最近 接受된 被拘禁者 人權問題(고문, 비인도적 대우등)에 관한 陳情書에 대한 政府 答辯書 作成 提出等 愼重 對處 豫定

o 其　他

- 兒童 및 小數民 保護問題 討議, 世界人權會議(1993) 準備過程에 積極 參與

- 끝 -

0221

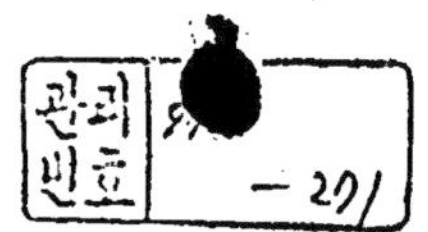

기 안 용 지

분류기호 문서번호	국연 2031-6517	(전화 :)	시행상 특별취급	
보존기간	영구·준영구. 10. 5. 3. 1.	장	관	
수신처 보존기간				
시행일자	1991. 3. 21.			

보조기관			협조기관		문서통제
	국 장	전 결			1991. 3. 22
	과 장				
기안책임자	송 영 완				발 송 인

경 유 수 신 참 조	법무부장관 법무실장	발신명의	
제 목	제 47차 유엔인권위원회 개최 결과		

91.1.18-3.8.간 스위스 제네바에서 개최된 제 47차 유엔인권위원회 결과(개요)를 별첨 송부하오니 업무에 참고하시기 바랍니다.

첨 부 : 제 47차 유엔 인권위원회 개요 1부. 끝.

검 토 필(1991. 6. 30.)

0222

1505-25(2-1) 일(1)갑
85. 9. 9. 승인 "내가아낀 종이 한장 늘어나는 나라살림"
190㎜×268㎜ 인쇄용지 2급 60g/㎡
가 40-41 1989. 6. 8

주 제 네 바 대 표 부

제네(정) 2031-661　　　　　　　　　　1991. 7.29

수신 : 장관

참조 : 국제기구조약국장

제목 : 제 47차 유엔인권위 보고서

91. 1.28-3.8간 당지에서 개최된 표제회의 보고서를 별첨 송부합니다.

첨부 : 동 보고서(E/1991/22) 1부. 끝.

주 제 네 바 대 사

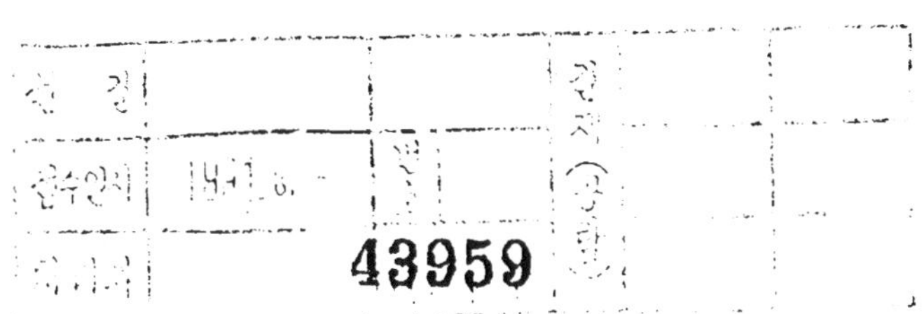

0223

OFFICE DES NATIONS UNIES À GENÈVE

CENTRE POUR LES DROITS DE L'HOMME

UNITED NATIONS OFFICE AT GENEVA

CENTRE FOR HUMAN RIGHTS

Téléfax: (022) 733 98 79
Télégrammes: UNATIONS, GENÈVE
Télex: 412 962 UNO CH
Téléphone: 734 60 11 731 02 11

RÉF. N°: G/SO 224/1 (1-2)
(à rappeler dans la réponse)

Palais des Nations
CH-1211 GENÈVE 10

The Secretary-General of the United Nations presents his compliments to the Minister for Foreign Affairs of the Republic of Korea and has the honour to refer to Economic and Social Council resolution 1991/30 of 31 May 1991, entitled "Right of persons belonging to national, ethnic, religious and linguistic minorities". A copy of the resolution is attached.

By this resolution, the Economic and Social Council authorized an open-ended Working Group of the Commission on Human Rights to meet for 20 fully-serviced meetings to complete its second reading of the draft declaration on the rights of persons belonging to national, ethnic, religious and linguistic minorities.

The Secretary-General has the honour to inform His Excellency's Government that the Working Group will meet from 2 to 13 December 1991 at Geneva.

30 September 1991

0224

ECONOMIC AND SOCIAL COUNCIL

Res. 1991/30. Rights of persons belonging to national, ethnic, religious and linguistic minorities

The Economic and Social Council,

Recalling Commission on Human Rights resolution 1991/61 of 6 March 1991,

1. Authorizes an open-ended working group of the Commission on Human Rights to meet for 20 fully-serviced meetings in an inter-sessional session at the beginning of December 1991 to complete its second reading of the draft declaration on the rights of persons belonging to national, ethnic, religious and linguistic minorities, and with a view to submitting the text to the Commission on Human Rights at its forty-eighth session;

2. Requests the Secretary-General to provide the working group with all the assistance it may require for the continuation of its drafting work.

0225

주 제 네 바 대 표 부

제네(정) 2031-997　　　　　　　　　　　　　　　　1991. 11. 20.

수신 : 장관

참조 : 국제기구국장

제목 : 유엔인권위 강제실종실무위 회의

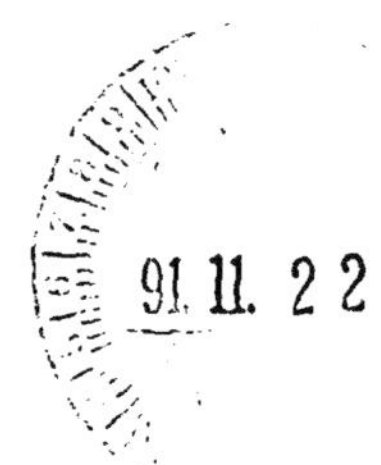

대 : 연이 2031-36141

1. 연호 표제관련 강제실종으로 부터의 보호에 관한 선언 초안(90.8)과 금번회의시 토의 결과로 나온 초안을 별첨 송부합니다.

2. 금번 회의시 작성된 초안은 불어원본으로부터 비공식 번역된 것으로서 문구상 다소의 수정 여지가 있음을 첨언합니다.

첨부 : 상기 초안 각 1부.　끝.

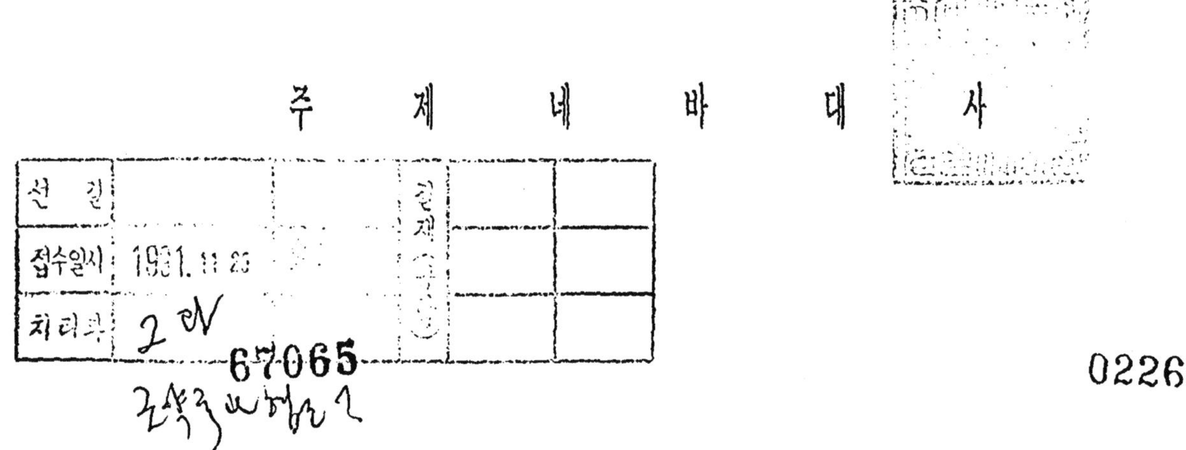

0226

Mi Ormouk

ANNEX

ENGLISH*
Original: FRENCH

91. 11 회의결의

DRAFT DECLARATION ON THE PROTECTION OF ALL PERSONS FROM ENFORCED DISAPPEARANCE

The General Assembly,

Considering that, in accordance with the principles proclaimed in the Charter of the United Nations and other international instruments, recognition of the inherent dignity and of the equal and inalienable rights of all members of the human family is the foundation of freedom, justice and peace in the world,

Bearing in mind the obligation of States under the Charter of the United Nations, in particular, Article 55, to promote universal respect for, and observance of, human rights and fundamental freedoms,

Deeply concerned that in many countries often in a persistent manner enforced disappearances occur, in the sense that persons are arrested, detained or abducted against their will or otherwise deprived of their liberty by officials of different branches or levels of Government, or by organized groups or private individuals acting on behalf of, or with the support, direct or indirect, consent or acquiescence of the Government, followed by a refusal to disclose the fate or whereabouts of the persons concerned or a refusal to acknowledge the deprivation of their liberty, thereby placing such persons outside the protection of the law,

Considering that enforced disappearance undermines the deepest values of any society committed to respect for the rule of law, human rights and fundamental freedoms, and that the systematic practice of such acts is of the nature of a crime against humanity,

---

* An unofficial translation.

7810a

0227

Recalling resolution 33/173 of 20 December 1978, by which the General Assembly expressed concern about the reports from various parts of the world relating to enforced or involuntary disappearances, as well as about the anguish and sorrow caused by these disappearances, and called upon Governments to hold law enforcement and security forces legally responsible for unjustifiable excesses which might lead to enforced or involuntary disappearances of persons,

Recalling also the protection afforded to victims of armed conflicts by the Geneva Conventions of 12 August 1949 and the Additional Protocols of 1977,

Having regard in particular to the relevant articles of the Universal Declaration of Human Rights and the International Covenant on Civil and Political Rights which protect the right to life, the right to liberty and security of the person, the right not to be subjected to torture and the right to recognition as a person before the law,

Having regard further to the Convention Against Torture and Other Cruel, Inhuman or Degrading Treatment or Punishment, which provides that States Parties shall take effective measures to prevent and punish acts of torture,

Bearing in mind the Code of Conduct for Law Enforcement Officials, the Basic Principles on the Use of Force and Firearms by Law Enforcement Officials, the Declaration of Basic Principles of Justice for Victims of Crime and Abuse of Power and the Standard Minimum Rules for the Treatment of Prisoners,

Affirming that, in order to prevent enforced disappearances, it is necessary to ensure strict compliance with the Body of Principles for the Protection of All Persons under Any Form of Detention or Imprisonment, contained in its resolution 43/173 of 9 December 1988, and with the Principles on the Effective Prevention and Investigation of Extra-legal, Arbitrary and Summary Executions, contained in Economic and Social Council resolution 1989/65 of 24 May 1989 and endorsed by General Assembly resolution 44/162 of 15 December 1989.

0228

Bearing in mind that, while the acts which comprise enforced disappearance constitute a violation of the prohibitions found in the aforementioned international instruments, it is none the less important to devise an instrument which characterizes all acts of enforced disappearance of persons as a very serious offence, setting forth standards designed to punish and prevent its commission,

Proclaims the present Declaration on the Protection of All Persons from Enforced Disappearance, as a body of principles for all States,

Urges that all efforts be made so that this Declaration becomes generally known and respected.

Article 1

1. All acts of enforced disappearance is an offence to human dignity. It is condemned as a denial of the purposes of the Charter of the United Nations and as a grave and flagrant violation of the human rights and fundamental freedoms proclaimed in the Universal Declaration of Human Rights and reaffirmed and developed in international instruments in this field.

2. Such act of enforced disappearance places the persons subjected thereto outside the protection of the law and inflicts severe suffering on them and their families. It constitutes a violation of the rules of international law guaranteeing, *inter alia*, the right to recognition as a person before the law, the right to liberty and security of the person and the right not to be subjected to torture and other cruel, inhuman or degrading treatment or punishment. It also violates or constitutes a grave threat to the right of life.

Article 2

1. No State shall practise, permit or tolerate enforced disappearances.

2. States shall act at the national and regional levels and in cooperation with the United Nations to contribute by all means to prevent and eradicate enforced disappearance.

0229

Article 3

Each State shall take effective legislative, administrative, judicial or other measures to prevent and terminate acts of enforced disappearance in any territory under its jurisdiction.

Article 4

1. All acts of enforced disappearance shall be offences under the criminal law punishable by appropriate penalties which shall take into account their extreme seriousness.

2. Mitigating circumstances may be established in national legislation for individuals who, having participated in enforced disappearances, are instrumental in bringing the victims forward alive or in providing voluntarily information which would contribute to clarify cases of enforced disappearance.

Article 5

In addition to such criminal penalties as are applicable, enforced disappearances render their perpetrators and the State or State authorities which organize, acquiesce in or tolerate such disappearances liable at civil law, without prejudice to the international responsibility of the State concerned in accordance with the principles of international law.

Article 6

1. No order or instruction of any public authority, civilian, military or other, may be invoked to justify an enforced disappearance. Any person receiving such an order or instruction shall have the right and duty not to obey it.

2. Each State shall ensure that orders or instructions directing, authorizing or encouraging any enforced disappearance are prohibited.

3. Training of law enforcement officials shall emphasize the above provisions.

0230

Article 7

No circumstances whatsoever, whether a threat of war, a state of war, internal political instability or any other public emergency, may be invoked to justify enforced disappearances.

Article 8

1. No State shall expel, return ("refouler") or extradite a person to another State where there are substantial grounds to believe that he would be in danger of enforced disappearance.

2. For the purpose of determining whether there are such grounds, the competent authorities shall take into acount all relevant considerations including, where applicable, the existence in the State concerned of a consistent pattern of gross, flagrant or mass violations of human rights.

Article 9

1. The right to a prompt and effective judicial remedy as a means of determining the whereabouts or state of health of persons deprived of their liberty and/or identifying the authority ordering or carrying out the deprivation of liberty, is required to prevent enforced disappearance under all circumstances, including those referred to in article 7.

2. In such proceedings, competent national authorities shall have access to all places holding persons deprived of their liberty and to each part thereof, as well as to any place in which there are grounds to believe that such persons may be found.

3. Any other competent authority entitled under law of the State or any other international legal instruments to which a State is a party may also have access to such places.

0231

Article 10

1. Any person deprived of liberty shall be held in an officially recognized place of detention and, in conformity with national law, be brought before a judicial authority promptly after detention.

2. Accurate information on the detention of such persons and their place or places of detention, including transfers, shall be made promptly available to their family members, counsel or to any other persons having a legitimate interest in the information unless a wish to the contrary has been expressed by the persons concerned.

3. An official up-to-date register of all persons deprived of their liberty shall be maintained in every place of detention. Additionally, each State shall take steps to maintain similar centralized registers. The information contained in these registers shall be made available to the persons mentioned in paragraph 2 above, to any judicial or other competent and independent national authority as well as to any other competent authority entitled under law of the State concerned or any other international legal instrument to which a State concerned is a party seeking to trace the whereabouts of a detained person.

Article 11

All persons deprived of liberty must be released in a manner permitting reliable verification that they have actually been released and, further, have been released in conditions in which their physical integrity and ability to exercise their rights are assured.

Article 12

1. Each State shall establish rules under its national law indicating those officials authorized to order deprivation of liberty, establishing the conditions under which such orders may be given, and stipulating penalties for officials, who without legal justification refuse to provide information on any detention.

0232

2. Each State shall likewise ensure strict supervision, including a clear chain of command, of all law enforcement officials responsible for apprehensions, arrests, detentions, custody, transfers and imprisonment, and of other officials authorized by law to use force and firearms.

Article 13

1. Each State shall ensure that any person having knowledge or a legitimate interest who alleges that a person has been subjected to enforced disappearance has the right to complain to a competent and independent State authority and to have that complaint promptly, thoroughly and impartially investigated by that authority. Whenever there are reasonable grounds to believe that an enforced disappearance has been committed, the State shall promptly refer the matter to that authority for such an investigation, even if there has been no formal complaint. No measure shall be taken to curtail or impede the investigation.

2. Each State shall ensure that the competent authority shall have the necessary powers and resources to conduct the investigation effectively, including powers to compel attendance of witnesses and production of relevant documents and to make immediate on-site visits.

3. Steps shall be taken to ensure that all involved in the investigation, including the complainant, counsel, witnesses and those conducting the investigation, are protected against ill-treatment, intimidation or reprisal.

4. The findings of such an investigation shall be made available upon request to all persons concerned, unless doing so would jeopardize an ongoing criminal investigation.

5. Steps shall be taken to ensure that any ill-treatment, intimidation or reprisal or any other form of interference on the occasion of the lodging of a complaint or the investigation procedure is appropriately punished.

6. An investigation, in accordance with the procedures described above, should be able to be conducted for as long as the fate of the victim of enforced disappearance remains unclarified.

0233

Article 14

Any person alleged to have perpetrated an act of enforced disappearance in a particular State shall, when the facts disclosed by an official investigation so warrant, be brought before the competent civil authorities of that State for the purpose of prosecution and trial unless he has been extradited to another State wishing to exercise jurisdiction in accordance with the relevant international agreements in force. All States should take any lawful and appropriate action available to them to bring all persons presumed responsible for an act of enforced disappearance within their jurisdiction or under their control to justice.

Article 15

The fact that there are grounds to believe that a person has participated in acts of an extremely serious nature such as those referred to in article 4.1, regardless of the motives, shall be taken into account when the competent authorities of the State decide whether or not to grant asylum.

Article 16

1. Persons alleged to have committed any of the acts referred to in article 4 shall be suspended from any official duties during the investigation referred to in article 13.

2. They may be tried only by the competent courts of ordinary law in each State, to the exclusion of any other special court, in particular military courts.

3. No privileges, immunities or special exemptions shall be admitted in such trials, without prejudice to the provisions contained in the Vienna Convention on Diplomatic Relations.

4. Such persons presumed responsible for such acts shall be guaranteed fair treatment in accordance with the relevant provisions of the Universal Declaration of Human Rights and other relevant international agreements in force at all stages of the investigation and eventual prosecution and trial.

0234

Article 17

1. Acts constituting enforced disappearance shall be considered a continuing offence as long as the perpetrators continue to conceal the fate and the whereabouts of persons who have disappeared and these facts remain unclarified.

2. When the remedies provided for in article 2 of the International Covenant on Civil and Political Rights are no longer effective, the statute of limitations for criminal cases shall be suspended until these remedies are re-established.

3. Statutes of limitations where they exist, relating to acts of enforced disappearance shall be substantial and commensurate with the extreme seriousness of the offence.

Article 18

1. Persons who have, or are alleged to have, committed offences referred to in article 4.1 shall not benefit from any special amnesty law or similar measures that might have the effect of exempting them from any criminal proceedings or sanction.

2. In the exercise of the right of pardon, the extreme seriousness of acts of enforced disappearance shall be taken into account.

Article 19

The victims of acts of enforced disappearance and their dependants shall obtain redress and shall have the right to adequate compensation, including the means for as complete a rehabilitation as possible. In the event of the death of the victim as a result of an act of enforced disappearance, the dependants shall also be entitled to compensation.

0235

Article 20

1. States shall prevent and suppress the abduction of children born of parents subjected to enforced disappearance and of children who were born during their mother's enforced disappearance, and shall devote their efforts to the search for, and identification of, the children and to the restitution of the children to their families of origin.

2. Considering the need to protect the best interests of children referred to in the preceding paragraph, there shall be an opportunity, in States which recognize a system of adoption, for a review of the adoption of such children and, in particular, for annulment of any adoption which originated in enforced disappearance. Such adoption should, however, continue to be in force, if consent is given, at the time of the review mentioned above, by the child's closest relatives.

3. The abduction of children of parents subjected to enforced disappearance or of children born during their mother's enforced disappearance, and the act of altering or suppressing documents attesting to their true identity shall constitute an extremely serious offence, which shall be punished as such.

4. For these purposes, States shall, where appropriate, conclude bilateral or multilateral agreements.

Article 21

The provisions of the present Declaration are without prejudice to the provisions enunciated in the Universal Declaration of Human Rights or in any other international instrument, and shall not be construed as restricting or derogating from any of the provisions contained therein.

외 무 부

110-760 서울 종로구 세종로 77번지 / (02) 723-8934 / (02) 723-3505

문서번호 연이 20314-58935
시행일자 1991.11.26.
(경유)
수신 법무부장관
참조

취급		장 관
보존		
국 장	전결	
심의관		
과 장		
기안	여승배	협조

제목 인권위원회 보고서 송부

금차 유엔총회에 제출된 47차 인권위원회 보고서를 별첨 송부하니 업무에 참고바랍니다.

첨부 : 인권위원회 보고서 1부. 끝.

0237

정 리 보 존 문 서 목 록					
기록물종류	일반공문서철	등록번호	2019040009	등록일자	2019-04-04
분류번호	734.21	국가코드		보존기간	영구
명 칭	유엔 인권위원회 사무국 공한, 1991				
생 산 과	국제연합과	생산년도	1991~1991	담당그룹	
내용목차					

0001

OFFICE DES NATIONS UNIES À GENÈVE

CENTRE POUR LES DROITS DE L'HOMME

UNITED NATIONS OFFICE AT GENEVA

CENTRE FOR HUMAN RIGHTS

Téléfax: (022) 733 98 79
Télégrammes: UNATIONS, GENÈVE
Télex: 28 96 96
Téléphone: 734 60 11 731 02 11

Palais des Nations
CH-1211 GENÈVE 10

RÉF. N°: G/SO 214 (3-3-7)
(à rappeler dans la réponse)

The Secretary-General of the United Nations presents his compliments to the Minister for Foreign Affairs of the Republic of Korea and has the honour to refer to resolution 1990/23 entitled "Independence and impartiality of the judiciary, jurors and assessors and the independence of lawyers" adopted by the Sub-Commission on Prevention of Discrimination and Protection of Minorities on 30 August 1990. A copy of the resolution is attached.

In paragraph 4 of the resolution, the Sub-Commision decided to entrust the Special Rapporteur, Mr. Louis Joinet, with the preparation of a report:

(a) to make a system-wide analysis of the advisory services and technical assistance programmes of the United Nations as regards the independence of the judiciary and the protection of practising lawyers, propose means by which the co-operation between the programmes could be enhanced, and set forth guidelines and criteria to be taken into account in the provision of these services;

(b) to bring to the attention of the Sub-Commission information on legislative or judicial measures or other practices which have served to strengthen or to undermine the independence of the judiciary and the protection of practising lawyers in accordance with United Nations standards.

In paragraph 5, the Sub-Commission requested the Secretary-General to provide the Special Rapporteur with all the assistance necessary for the completion of his task.

In paragraph 6 of the resolution, the Sub-Commission requested the Secretary-General to transmit this resolution *inter alia* to Governments, requesting specific information on measures taken to strengthen the independence of the judiciary and lawyers or on practices which have undermined this independence.

./...

0002

In paragraph 7 of the resolution, the Sub-Commission decided to consider the above-mentioned report at its forty-third session under the agenda item entitled "Independence and impartiality of the judiciary and the independence of lawyers".

In order to enable the Special Rapporteur to carry out his task, the Secretary-General would be grateful to His Excellency's Government if, should it so desire, it could provide the information requested in paragraph 6 of Sub-Commission resolution 1990/23 and forward it to the Centre for Human Rights, United Nations Office at Geneva, CH-1211 Geneva 10, by 1 March 1991.

In submitting information, His Excellency's Government may wish to take into consideration the violations of international norms listed in the Special Rapporteur's preliminary working paper contained in paragraphs 34-36 of document E/CN.4/Sub.2/1990/35. A copy of this document is attached.

9 January 1991

0003

SUB-COMMISSION ON PREVENTION OF DISCRIMINATION

AND PROTECTION OF MINORITIES

Resolution

1990/23. Independence and impartiality of the judiciary, jurors and assessors and the independence of lawyers

The Sub-Commission on Prevention of Discrimination and Protection of Minorities,

Convinced that an independent and impartial judiciary and an independent legal profession are essential prerequisites for the protection of human rights and for ensuring that there shall be no discrimination in the administration of justice,

Recalling Commission on Human Rights resolution 1989/32 of 6 March 1989, by which the Commission requested that the Sub-Commission consider effective means to monitor the implementation of the Basic Principles on the Independence of the Judiciary and the protection of practising lawyers,

Recalling also its own resolution 1989/22 of 31 August 1989, by which it invited Mr. Louis Joinet to prepare a working paper on means by which the Sub-Commission could monitor the implementation of the Basic Principles on the Independence of the Judiciary and the protection of practising lawyers as requested in Commission on Human Rights resolution 1989/32,

Recalling further Commission on Human Rights resolution 1990/33 of 2 March 1990, by which the Commission endorsed Sub-Commission resolution 1989/22 and requested the Sub-Commission to study the working paper with a view to recommending initiatives which could be taken to effectuate the implementation of the Basic Principles on the Independence of the Judiciary and the protection of practising lawyers,

1. *Calls* on Governments to strengthen the independence of the judiciary and the protection of practising lawyers;

2. *Takes note with appreciation* of the working paper (E/CN.4/Sub.2/1990/35) prepared by Mr. Joinet in accordance with Sub-Commission resolution 1989/22 and Commission on Human Rights resolution 1990/33;

3. *Endorses* the recommendations made in that working paper (*ibid*., para. 76);

4. *Decides* to entrust Mr. Joinet with the preparation of a report:

(a) To make a system-wide analysis of the advisory service and technical assistance programmes of the United Nations as regards the independence of the judiciary and the protection of practising lawyers, propose means by which the co-operation between the programmes could be enhanced, and set forth guidelines and criteria to be taken into account in the provision of these services;

(b) To bring to the attention of the Sub-Commission information on legislative or judicial measures or other practices which have served to strengthen or to undermine the independence of the judiciary and the protection of practising lawyers in accordance with United Nations standards;

RES/HR/90/38
GE.90-18729

0004

5. *Requests* the Secretary-General to provide the Rapporteur with all the assistance necessary for the completion of his task;

6. *Requests* the Secretary-General to transmit this resolution to Governments, intergovernmental and non-governmental organizations, including professional associations of judges and lawyers, requesting specific information on measures taken to strengthen the independence of the judiciary and lawyers or on practices which have undermined this independence;

7. *Decides* to consider the above-mentioned report at its forty-third session under the agenda item entitled "Independence and impartiality of the judiciary and the independence of lawyers";

8. *Recommends* the following draft resolution to the Commission on Human Rights for adoption:

VI. *Independence and impartiality of the judiciary, jurors and assessors and the independence of lawyers*

The Commission on Human Rights,

Convinced that an independent and impartial judiciary and an independent legal profession are essential prerequisites for the protection of human rights and for ensuring that there shall be no discrimination in the administration of justice,

Recalling its resolution 1989/32 of 6 March 1989, by which it requested that the Sub-Commission on Prevention of Discrimination and Protection of Minorities consider effective means of monitoring the implementation of the Basic Principles on the Independence of the Judiciary and the protection of practising lawyers, and 1990/33 of 2 March 1990, in which it endorsed Sub-Commission resolution 1989/22 of 31 August 1989 inviting Mr. Joinet to prepare a working paper on means by which the Sub-Commission could monitor the implementation of the Basic Principles on the Independence of the Judiciary and the protection of practising lawyers, as requested in Commission on Human Rights resolution 1989/32,

Having examined the work done by the Sub-Commission relating to the independence and impartiality of the judiciary and the independence of lawyers,

Having examined also the working paper (E/CN.4/Sub.2/1990/35) prepared by Mr. Joinet in accordance with Sub-Commission resolution 1989/22,

1. *Welcomes* the recommendations made in that working paper (*ibid*., para. 76) and endorsed by the Sub-Commission in its resolution 1990/23 of 30 August 1990;

2. *Endorses* the decision of the Sub-Commission to entrust Mr. Joinet with the preparation of a report on strengthening the independence of the judiciary and the protection of practising lawyers as described in Sub-Commission resolution 1990/23;

3. *Requests* the Secretary-General to provide the Rapporteur with all the assistance necessary for the completion of his task;

0005

4. Recommends the following draft decision to the Economic and Social Council for adoption:

"The Economic and Social Council, taking note of Commission on Human Rights resolution ... of ..., endorses the decision of the Commission to welcome the decision of the Sub-Commission on Prevention of Discrimination and Protection of Minorities to entrust Mr. Joinet with the preparation of a report on strengthening the independence of the judiciary and the protection of practising lawyers as described in Sub-Commission resolution 1990/23, and approves the request of the Commission to the Secretary-General to give Mr. Joinet the assistance necessary for the completion of his task."

0006

UNITED
NATIONS

Economic and Social Council

Distr.
GENERAL

E/CN.4/Sub.2/1990/35
17 July 1990

ENGLISH
Original: ENGLISH/FRENCH

COMMISSION ON HUMAN RIGHTS
Sub-Commission on Prevention of
Discrimination and Protection
of Minorities
Forty-second session
Item 11 of the provisional agenda

THE INDEPENDENCE AND IMPARTIALITY OF THE JUDICIARY, JURORS AND ASSESSORS AND THE INDEPENDENCE OF LAWYERS

Working paper prepared by Mr. Louis Joinet on means in the area of monitoring by which the Sub-Commission could assist in ensuring respect for the independence of the judiciary and the protection of practising lawyers in accordance with resolution 1989/32 of the Commission on Human Rights

GE.90-12443/2192B

0007

CONTENTS

0008

Introduction

1. It is now universally recognized that fundamental rights and liberties can best be preserved in a society where the legal profession and the judiciary enjoy freedom from interference and pressure. Justice requires that everyone should be entitled to a fair and public hearing by a competent, independent and impartial tribunal, in accordance with the principles proclaimed in the Universal Declaration of Human Rights (art. 10), the International Covenant on Civil and Political Rights (art. 14), and other United Nations instruments.

2. By its decision 1980/124, the Economic and Social Council authorized the Sub-Commission to entrust Dr. L.M. Singhvi with the preparation of a report on the independence and impartiality of the judiciary, jurors and assessors, and the independence of lawyers.

3. The Special Rapporteur accordingly submitted preliminary and progress reports on the subject in 1980, 1981 and 1982 (E/CN.4/Sub.2/L.731, E/CN.4/Sub.2/481 and Add.1, and E/CN.4/Sub.2/1982/23). At the thirty-eighth session of the Sub-Commission, he introduced his final report on the subject (E/CN.4/Sub.2/1985/18 and Add.1-6) and drew attention, in particular, to his draft declaration on the Independence and Impartiality of the Judiciary, Jurors and Assessors and the Independence of Lawyers ("the Singhvi draft declaration") (E/CN.4/Sub.2/18/Add.5/Rev.1).

4. Pursuant to Sub-Commission decision 1985/107, the above study was circulated to the members of the Sub-Commission for comments. These comments are contained in document E/CN.4/Sub.2/1987/17, which was submitted to the Sub-Commission at its thirty-ninth session.

5. At the fortieth session of the Sub-Commission, the Special Rapporteur submitted a report containing comments and suggestions on the draft declaration (E/CN.4/Sub.2/1988/20) and a revised version of the draft declaration (E/CN.4/Sub.2/1988/20/Add.1 and Add.1/Corr.1).

6. At its fortieth session, the Sub-Commission, in resolution 1988/25, expressed "its appreciation and thanks to the Special Rapporteur, for the enduring and valuable contribution he made to the legal doctrine relating to the independence of justice, which is one of the primary prerequisites for the promotion and protection of human rights" and referred the Singhvi draft declaration to the Commission on Human Rights for further consideration. It also decided to consider the question of the Independence and Impartiality of the Judiciary, Jurors and Assessors and the Independence of Lawyers as a separate agenda item at its forty-first session.

7. At its forty-fifth session, the Commission, by resolution 1989/32, invited Governments to take into account the principles set forth in the Singhvi draft declaration in implementing the Basic Principles on the Independence of the Judiciary which had been adopted by the General Assembly in its resolutions 40/32 of 29 November 1985 and 40/146 of 13 December 1985. The Commission further recommended that Governments should provide for the protection of practising lawyers against undue restrictions and pressures in the exercise of their functions.

8. Finally, the Commission welcomed the creation by the Sub-Commission of a separate agenda item on the independence of judges and lawyers, and requested that the Sub-Commission use the agenda item to consider effective means of monitoring the implementation of the Basic Principles on the Independence of the Judiciary and the protection of practising lawyers.

9. At its forty-first session, in 1989, the Sub-Commission, in resolution 1989/22, responded to the Commission's request by inviting: "Mr. Louis Joinet to prepare, without financial implications, a working paper on means in the area of monitoring by which the Sub-Commission could assist in ensuring respect for the independence of the judiciary and the protection of practising lawyers as requested in Commission resolution 1989/32". Significantly, the words "in the area of monitoring" were proposed and added on the floor of the Sub-Commission "to make the mandate clearer" (see E/CN.4/Sub.2/1989/SR.38, para. 78).

10. At its forty-sixth session, the Commission, in resolution 1990/33, "endorsed the Sub-Commission resolution and requested the Sub-Commission to study the working paper with a view to recommending to the Commission any initiatives which could be taken to effectuate the implementation of the Basic Principles on the Independence of the Judiciary and the protection of practising lawyers".

11. Before determining what means the Sub-Commission might use to assist in ensuring respect for the independence of the judiciary and the protection of practising lawyers, it would be useful to review the steps which have already been taken by the United Nations in these domains and to examine the kinds of deviation from international norms which occur, as well as what steps are already being taken to prevent these deviations.

I. CURRENT UNITED NATIONS STANDARD-SETTING AND REPORTING ACTIVITIES

A. The independence of the judiciary

12. The first part of the mandate given to the writer of this paper is to study means by which the Sub-Commission can assist in ensuring respect for the independence of the judiciary.

1. Basic Principles on the Independence of the Judiciary

13. The Seventh United Nations Congress on the Prevention of Crime and the Treatment of Offenders, held at Milan (Italy) from 26 August to 6 September 1985, adopted by consensus "Basic Principles on the Independence of the Judiciary". The Congress documents were endorsed by the General Assembly in its resolutions 40/32 of 29 November 1985 and 40/146 of 13 December 1985; the latter which specifically welcomed the Basic Principles and invited Governments "to respect them and to take them into account within the framework of their national legislation and practice" (para. 2).

14. The Basic Principles set forth are principles concerning the independence of the judiciary, freedom of expression and association of judges as well as rules regarding the qualification, selection, training, conditions of service,

0010

tenure, immunity, discipline, suspension and removal of judges. The Basic Principles emphasize that the independence of the judiciary should be guaranteed by the State and enshrined in the Constitution or law of the country.

15. The Basic Principles, general though they are, represent the first intergovernmental standards spelling out the minimum standards of judicial independence and are the acknowledged yardstick by which the international community measures that independence.

16. The Commission on Human Rights called on Governments, when implementing the Basic Principles, to take into account the principles set forth in the draft declaration prepared by Dr. Singhvi.

2. Procedures for the effective implementation of the Basic Principles on the Independence of the Judiciary

17. Procedures have already been adopted to promote implementation of the Basic Principles on the Independence of the Judiciary.

18. An international expert meeting on the United Nations and law enforcement, held under the auspices of the United Nations in Baden (Austria) in November 1987, formulated draft procedures for the effective implementation of the Basic Principles on the basis of previous work carried out by the United Nations Social Defence Research Institute, in co-operation with the United Nations Crime Prevention Branch. These Procedures, approved by the Committee on Crime Prevention and Control at its tenth session, in Vienna, from 22 to 31 August 1988, were adopted by the Economic and Social Council on 24 May 1989 in its resolution 1989/60.

19. The Procedures call upon States to "adopt and implement ... the Basic Principles ... in accordance with their constitutional process and domestic practice". They also call on them to widely publicize the Basic Principles, in at least the main or official language or languages of the country and make the text available to all members of the judiciary. The Procedures recommend national and regional seminars and courses on the judiciary and its independence.

20. United Nations reporting procedures for monitoring implementation of the Basic Principles are established. States are asked to inform the Secretary-General every five years of the progress achieved in the implementation of the Basic Principles, including their dissemination, their incorporation into national legislation, the problems faced in their implementation at the national level and assistance that might be needed from the international community.

21. The Secretary-General is requested to prepare independent quinquennial reports to the Committee on Crime Prevention and Control on progress made with respect to the implementation of the Basic Principles, on the basis of the information received from Governments, as well as other information available within the United Nations system. The Procedures provide that in preparing these reports "the Secretary-General shall also enlist the co-operation of specialized agencies and the relevant intergovernmental organizations and

non-governmental organizations, in particular professional associations of judges and lawyers, in consultative status with the Economic and Social Council, and take into account the information provided by such agencies and organizations". The Secretary-General is requested to widely disseminate the Basic Principles, implementing procedures and the periodic reports on their implementation.

22. The Procedures call on the United Nations to provide technical co-operation to governments requesting assistance in improving their judicial systems and call on all entities within the United Nations system to "become actively involved in the implementation process".

3. Report prepared by the Secretary-General on the implementation of the Basic Principles on the Independence of the Judiciary

23. On the recommendation of the Committee on Crime Prevention and Control, the Economic and Social Council, by its resolution 1986/10 of 21 May 1986 (section V), invited States to inform the Secretary-General every five years, beginning in 1988, of the progress achieved in the implementation of the Basic Principles, including their dissemination, their incorporation into national legislation, the problems faced in their implementation at the national level and assistance that might be needed from the international community, and requested the Secretary-General to report thereon to the Committee on Crime Prevention and Control and the Eighth United Nations Congress on the Prevention of Crime and the Treatment of Offenders. The General Assembly welcomed this recommendation of the Council by its resolution 41/149 of 4 December 1986 on human rights in the administration of justice.

24. Pursuant to these resolutions, on 31 December 1987 the Secretary-General sent States a note verbale and a questionnaire on the implementation of the Basic Principles. Information was also requested from United Nations institutes on crime prevention and criminal justice as well as from non-governmental organizations in consultative status with the Economic and Social Council.

25. As of September 1989, according to the United Nations Crime Prevention Branch, the following States had replied to the note verbale: Algeria, Argentina, Australia, Austria, the Bahamas, Belgium, Bolivia, Brazil, Burundi, the Byelorussian Soviet Socialist Republic, Cameroon, Canada, Chad, China, German Democratic Republic, Germany, Federal Republic of, Holy See, Honduras, Iraq, Israel, Italy, Jamaica, Japan, Kuwait, Lesotho, Luxembourg, Madagascar, Malta, Mauritius, Mexico, Morocco, New Zealand, Nicaragua, Niger, Nigeria, Norway, Oman, Pakistan, Paraguay, Peru, Philippines, Poland, Portugal, Republic of Korea, Saint Lucia, Singapore, Spain, Sweden, Switzerland, the United Republic of Tanzania, Thailand, Tunisia, Turkey, Tuvalu, the Ukrainian Soviet Socialist Republic, the Union of Soviet Socialist Republics, the United Kingdom, Uruguay and Yugoslavia.

26. On the basis of the responses of these States, as well as of those of intergovernmental and non-governmental organizations, the Secretary-General will submit a report to the Eighth United Nations Congress.

0012

B. The protection of practising lawyers

27. The second area of concern of this report is the protection of practising lawyers.

28. The Seventh United Nations Congress on the Prevention of Crime and the Treatment of Offenders in 1985 recognized in its resolution on the role of lawyers that "adequate protection of the rights of citizens requires that all persons have effective access to legal services provided by lawyers who are able to perform effectively their proper role in the defence of those rights, and to counsel and represent their clients in accordance with the law and their established professional standards and judgement without any undue interference from any quarter". It therefore recommended to States that they "provide for protection of practising lawyers against undue restrictions and pressures in the exercise of their functions". This recommendation was repeated verbatim in Commission resolution 1989/32 and Sub-Commission resolution 1989/22.

29. Given the primordial role of lawyers in the defence of the rights of all citizens, it has come to be recognized that governments have a positive duty to protect their security. Thus, Dr. Singhvi noted in his final report that violence and harassment against lawyers "constitute a form of organized intimidation and put fundamental freedoms and human rights in double jeopardy". He therefore concluded that "A lawyer's safety and security must be ensured by the society and neither the State, nor any other authority, nor any individual litigant should be allowed to take any revenge in any form upon the lawyer or members of his family".

C. Basic Principles on the Role of Lawyers

30. The Seventh United Nations Congress on the Prevention of Crime and the Treatment of Offenders requested that the Eighth Congress and its preparatory meetings further consider the issue of the role of lawyers. On the basis of this request, the Committee on Crime Prevention and Control prepared draft basic principles on the role of lawyers. These draft principles were endorsed by the Economic and Social Council for submission to the Eighth United Nations Congress on the Prevention of Crime and the Treatment of Offenders which will meet in Havana (Cuba) from August to September 1990.

31. The draft basic principles on the role of lawyers focus special attention on the following issues: provision for effective access to legal assistance for all groups within society; the right of the accused to counsel and legal assistance of their own choosing; the education of the public on the role of lawyers in protecting fundamental rights and liberties; training and qualifications of lawyers, and the prevention of discrimination with respect to entry into the legal profession; the role of Governments, bar associations and other professional associations of lawyers; the right of lawyers to undertake the representation of clients or causes without fear of repression or persecution; and the obligation of lawyers to keep communications with their clients confidential, including the right to refuse to give testimony on such matters.

0013

32. Of particular importance with regard to the protection of practising lawyers are principles 16 and 17, which provide that:

"16. Governments shall ensure that lawyers ... (c) shall not suffer, or be threatened with, prosecution or administrative, economic or other sanctions for any action taken in accordance with recognized professional duties, standards and ethics.

17. Where the security of lawyers is threatened as a result of discharging their functions, they shall be adequately safeguarded by the authorities."

33. At its forty-sixth session, the Commission in resolution 1990/33 recommended that the Eighth Congress "consider as a matter of priority the draft basic principles on the role of lawyers elaborated by the Committee on Crime Prevention and Control, with a view to their adoption".

II. VIOLATIONS OF INTERNATIONAL NORMS

34. In his study, Dr. Singhvi correctly noted that the violation of the principle of the independence of justice "is by no means a stray occurrence" (para. 372). Indeed, he listed what he described as 26 "types of deviance" relating to judges and yet another 26 relating to lawyers. Because these occurrences are at the heart of the present study, it is perhaps worth repeating them.

35. Those which affect judges were categorized as follows:

(a) Dismissal, which sometimes involves removal or dismissal of an individual judge for refusal to decide a particular case in a particular manner, and sometimes involves collective removals and dismissals of judges or the abolition of entire courts when they are perceived as obstructing the projects, ambitions or objectives of the executive power. Amendment of laws affecting the tenure of judges so as to permit their dismissal or removal at the discretion of the executive is a related menace to the independence of judges;

(b) Transfer is known to be used either to punish a judge or remove him from a jurisdiction where his independence is considered a problem by the executive. Examples of the latter include the transfer from a criminal to a civil court of a judge who displayed sympathy for an accused belonging to a racial minority, or transfer of a courageous civil libertarian from a court of general jurisdiction to a tax court;

(c) Appointment of judges for a limited term or on an acting or officiating basis, and confirmation of judges in permanent posts and tenures on political considerations;

(d) In countries where promotion or confirmation of judges proceeds by established rules or conventions rather than by exercise of executive discretion, abrogation of rules or conventions for promotion may be considered as a variant of the punitive use of transfers;

0014

(e) Assassination and "disappearance" of judges, although less common than assassination and "disappearance" of lawyers, occurs with sufficient frequency and must be considered as a problem affecting the independence of the judiciary;

(f) Emergency measures occurring during states of exception which deprive the judiciary of its power to consider certain questions of constitutional law, to enforce its decisions or to try certain categories of cases and to curb and curtail the judicial function seriously impinge on the independence of judges. In some cases these aspects of their jurisdiction simply cease to exist, while in other cases they are transferred to military courts or other specially constituted courts whose partiality and whose lack of independence, juridical knowledge and experience is alarming. Sometimes these measures are taken without any formal promulgation of emergency;

(g) Adverse publicity, embarrassing accusations in public, and populist pressures to deflect the judiciary from its appointed role and to discredit it;

(h) Indirect and/or selective executive patronage;

(i) Inducement of extrajudicial assignments or important judicial assignments in the gift of the executive;

(j) Systematic denial of adequate budgets and support staff, denial of autonomy in internal administration, and inadequate pay, pension and other benefits and perquisites in the context of other comparable positions;

(k) Appointment of judges without reference to their integrity and ability or on a discriminatory basis or by denial of equal access to certain sections of the people;

(l) Exclusion of the judiciary from the process of making judicial appointments and lack of consultation with the judiciary or studied inattention to judicial advice in matters concerning the judiciary;

(m) Promotion of judges on the basis of extraneous considerations and neglect of ability and integrity in matters of judicial promotions;

(n) Use of temporary, ad hoc, part-time tenures by the executive to subject the judiciary to a psychosis of fear;

(o) Promise or expectation of post-retirement employment by the executive or by individuals, business firms and large corporations;

(p) Fear of vexatious, criminal, civil or disciplinary proceedings, particularly if the power to initiate or authorize such proceedings is not vested in the judiciary;

(q) Suspension or abrogation of the rights of the citizens, ouster of jurisdiction by reorganization of judicial functions, and vesting essentially judicial functions in non-judicial bodies;

0015

(r) Denial of social status by according lower precedence and generally adopting a less than respectful and courteous attitude towards the judiciary;

(s) Intemperate and ill-informed attacks by influential members of the executive or the legislature or by other official persons against the judiciary in parliamentary and other official fora and in mass media; electoral invective and retribution; partisan attacks by political parties;

(t) Questionable life styles of judges which provide grist for the gossip mill bringing the judiciary into disrepute;

(u) Private disputes of judges or excessive zeal of judges in prosecuting their own cases;

(v) Lack of restraint in making public pronouncements or the failure to observe the obligation of reserve; or overbearing behaviour; rudeness in court or outside;

(w) Unwillingness of a judge to withdraw from a borderline case involving incompatibility or possible conflict of interest;

(x) Membership of judges in organizations or movements which may go beyond good taste or accepted public morals or which may be committed to questionable aims or involved in objectionable activities or their association with such organizations;

(y) Senility and other forms of incipient or advanced incapacity;

(z) Judicial misbehaviour in the form of corruption, bribery, gross and palpable denial of justice.

36. Those affecting lawyers were said to be:

(a) Suspension or abolition of the Bar association or an official ban on the Bar association or curtailment of their functions;

(b) Denial of the right of freedom of association, assembly, thought, speech, expression and movement to lawyers and organizations of the legal profession;

(c) Punitive action against the leaders of the Bar and making examples of them in order to subdue the legal profession as a whole;

(d) Undermining the organization and leadership of the Bar from within and from outside, officially and otherwise;

(e) Disciplinary proceedings, disbarment, suspension from practice or prosecution of lawyers for acts within the proper scope of their professional duties, such as filing complaints about police mistreatment of a client, challenging the impartiality of a judge, challenging the legality of a law or administrative action, or defending the legality of a client's behaviour or statements;

(f) Threats, intimidation, disbarment, suspension from practice, contempt or breach of privilege proceedings, or prosecution of lawyers for statements made in legal proceedings or outside the context of a legal proceeding for criticizing individuals or régimes or proposing changes in the administration of justice;

(g) Selective and motivated prosecution, including raids, searches, seizures and other kinds of harassment, application of administrative sanctions against lawyers known for their defence of civil liberties, political defendants or social groups such as peasants, trade unions, or racial or religious minorities and for offences purportedly and ostensibly unrelated to these activities;

(h) Detention without charge or trial. Although security authorities normally do not offer reasons for such detention, it is often the case that a number of lawyers are detained at the same time and the lawyers selected are known for their activities as defence attorneys or advocates and advisers to opposition groups or disadvantaged of the society. The effect, and presumably the purpose, of such detention is to punish and intimidate lawyers who have demonstrated their willingness to provide such services, and to subdue and suppress the Bar as a whole;

(i) Torture and physical liquidation or "disappearance" of lawyers has been a serious problem in recent years in certain countries. In some cases the reasons for assassination are not known, but in others death threats or subsequent communiqués confirm that legal activities on behalf of certain individuals or groups was the reason. In some countries this has led to the result that no political defendant is able to find an independent and experienced criminal lawyer willing to defend him. Systematic assassination or "disappearance" of lawyers must therefore be considered not only a violation of the individual's right to life and liberty, but also a threat to the independence of the profession and a threat to human rights and fundamental freedoms;

(j) Lawyers are expressly barred from practice for political reasons in a small number of countries. For example, in one country, membership in certain political or professional organizations is considered as proof that the applicant does not support the "basic constitutional order", while in another country lawyers may be barred from practice despite commendable and notable professional records because they have not demonstrated sufficient support for the current political leadership of the country;

(k) Political patronage and preferment by the State and hostile discrimination by the State on political grounds;

(l) Politicization of the profession;

(m) Loss of professional identity;

(n) Decline in professional values and disregard of professional competence.

0017

37. These "types of deviance" are unfortunately widespread today. The Special Rapporteur on Summary or Arbitrary Executions of the Commission on Human Rights, Mr. S. Amos Wako, took note of "a particularly alarming trend, which is rapidly spreading, namely, the practice of death threats deliberately directed, in particular, against persons who play key roles in defending human rights and achieving social and criminal justice in a society (E/CN.4/1990/22, para. 472). He found that death threats are made against persons of various backgrounds and professions, in particular judges, lawyers, magistrates and prosecutors, etc., involved in trials, investigations or other legal proceedings (para. 449).

38. In the report on his visit to Colombia at the invitation of that Government (E/CN.4/1990/22/Add.1), the Special Rapporteur noted that "in recent years, the victims [of extra-judicial executions] have included a Minister of Justice, an Attorney-General of the nation, various justices of the Supreme Court and High Courts and many judges and judicial officials. A number of Ministers of Justice are reported to have been compelled to resign because of the death threats that hung over them and/or their relatives and some seven or eight judges have had to leave the country for the same reasons. In some cases, as in that of Judge Marta Gonzáles who was investigating the Urabá massacres, the reprisals by the so-called paramilitary groups against the judges even include the killing of some of their relatives. According to Asonal Judicial, the union representing judicial officials, one fifth of the 4,379 judges in Colombia today are under threat of death. In addition, not all the judges who have been threatened can benefit from police protection. However, it is said that when protection is provided it is inadequate, as the case of Judge Diaz Pérez demonstrates. The killing of judges and the lack of police protection led in 1989 to a number of strikes by judges and judicial officials throughout the country".

39. Similarly, in its 1987 report, the Commission's Working Group on Enforced or Involuntary Disappearances noted that "the enforced disappearance of defence lawyers and human rights advocates at the hands of government agents also appears to be on the increase" (E/CN.4/1987/15, para. 122).

40. In August 1989, the Centre for the Independence of Judges and Lawyers presented the Sub-Commission with a report entitled "The Harassment and Persecution of Judges and Lawyers", describing the cases of 145 judges and lawyers who had been harassed, detained or killed between January 1988 and June 1989. The list included 34 judges and lawyers killed, 37 detained and 38 who had been attacked or threatened with violence (E/CN.4/Sub.2/1989/SR.12, para. 46). The Sub-Commission responded in resolution 1989/22 by declaring itself "Disturbed at the continued harassment and persecution of judges and lawyers in many countries".

41. The violations, as Dr. Singhvi's list indicates, are not confined to violence against judges and lawyers, however. In 1989, the Sub-Commission heard from non-governmental organizations alleging that, in Malaysia, the Lord President of the Supreme Court and two of his colleagues were improperly dismissed by closed tribunals in conflict with the Basic Principles on the Independence of the Judiciary (E/CN.4/Sub.2/1989/SR.12, para. 56). It was also alleged that, in Chile, numerous cases which normally would be tried by

civilian courts had been transferred to military courts lacking the requisite impartiality (para. 61). In Liberia, it was asserted, three successive sets of Supreme Court justices had been removed from office at the request of the President in three years. (para. 62).

III. POSITIVE EXPERIENCES

42. In the face of these violations, numerous measures are being taken at different levels all around the world. As Dr. Singhvi said, "The battle of independence has to be fought on many fronts, not once and for all, but every day" (para. 377). The most important fronts, as Dr. Singhvi noted, are the fight to expurge arbitrary authoritarianism and the destruction of the judiciary during states of exception. But deviance, as he recalled, "is not always open and turbulent. It comes creeping in many insidious and subtle ways" (para. 380).

43. Parallel to Dr. Singhvi's reference to a "typology of deviance", it may be appropriate here to refer to a "typology of strengthening measures", some of which are described below.

A. Legislative protections

44. The Basic Principles on the Independence of the Judiciary set forth a series of measures which States can take to provide the legal and practical framework for the independence of the judiciary. These include: a constitutional guarantee of judicial independence; assuring that the judiciary has jurisdiction over all issues of a judicial nature and the authority to decide which issues are within its competence; trials by ordinary courts using established legal procedures; the provision of adequate resources to the judiciary; freedom of association and expression of judges; methods of appointment and promotion which ensure integrity and safeguard independence; guaranteeing adequate conditions of service; assuring a guaranteed tenure for judges; providing that judges may only be disciplined or removed for incapacity or misbehaviour in accordance with established standards of judicial conduct and only after a fair hearing, etc.

45. Many States have gone further than these basic steps in protecting judicial independence. Some countries, for instance, such as Costa Rica, Guatemala, Honduras, Panama and Peru, guarantee in their Constitution that the judiciary receive a fixed percentage of the Government's budget. This is said to reduce financial independence on the executive. Others attempt to protect individual judicial independence by providing that a judge's compensation may not be diminished during his term of office. Some countries require judges to write reasoned opinions explaining their decisions as a method of protecting the integrity of the decision-making process. Others provide in their Constitutions that judges may not be transferred against their will. At the 1989 session of the Sub-Commission, Mr. van Boven emphasized various measures to avoid political interference in judicial appointments, including allowing members of the Bar to submit nominations and having nominees screened by a judicial and Bar Council (E/CN.4/Sub.2/1989/SR.12, para. 79). Mr. Fix-Zamudio suggested better education for judges (para. 33).

B. Promotion: training courses, seminars, education

46. The Procedures for the effective Implementation of the Basic Principles on the Independence of the Judiciary call on States to "promote or encourage seminars and courses at the national and regional levels on the role of the judiciary in society and the necessity for its independence".

47. Many States appear to be organizing such courses. Here we will look at the work being done on an international level. A more complete examination of this work is contained in Picken, "A Review of the UN Advisory and Technical Assistance Programs for Human Rights" in UN Assistance for Human Rights (Rädda Barnen, Swedish Section of the ICJ, 1988).

1. Advisory services in the field of human rights

48. The Centre for Human Rights in Geneva administers a programme of advisory services. The most recent report of the Secretary-General on this programme (E/CN.4/1990/43) lists its activities. It would appear that several, including seminars and the provision of the advisory services of experts, are intended to strengthen the judiciary of the target countries although none appears to focus primarily on the independence of the judiciary or the protection of practising lawyers.

2. Crime Prevention Branch

49. The Criminal Justice and Crime Prevention Branch in Vienna also has an advisory services programme, carried out by the interregional Advisor in Crime Prevention and Criminal Justice. In 1988-1989 the Advisor provided advice in the implementation of the Basic Principles on the Independence of the Judiciary to Argentina, Brazil, Egypt, Malawi, Mauritius, Paraguay and Poland.

3. United Nations institutes

50. United Nations institutes are also active in this area. The United Nations Asia and Far East Institute for the Prevention of Crime and the Treatment of Offenders (UNAFEI), for instance, regularly conducts international seminars or training courses for practitioners at all levels of the administration of justice. The United Nations Latin American Institute for the Prevention of Crime and the Treatment of Offenders (ILANUD) organized a meeting of the Presidents of the Latin American Supreme Courts in December 1988, at which the independence of the judiciary was a key topic.

4. Non-governmental organizations

51. Non-governmental organizations have also taken on this work. In 1986, the Centre for the Independence of Judges and Lawyers began a series of regional seminars at which judges and lawyers were provided with the Basic Principles and other international standards and asked to discuss the extent to which the principles and standards were actually adhered to in their regions. Seminars have now been held in 1986 in San José (Costa Rica) for Central America and the Dominican Republic; in 1986 in Lusaka (Zambia) for

0020

anglophone East Africa; in 1987 in Banjul (Gambia) for anglophone West Africa; in 1987 in Kathmandu (Nepal) for South Asia; in 1988 in Buenos Aires (Argentina) for Argentina, Brazil, Uruguay and Paraguay; in 1988 in Tagaytay City (Philippines) for South-East Asia; and in 1988 in Tobago for the Commonwealth Caribbean.

52. The seminars reportedly provide an opportunity for frank debates and also allow the participants - judges, lawyers, attorneys-general and academics - to work out recommendations for the steps that need to be taken in their regions to further strengthen the independence of the judiciary and the legal profession. Typically, the participants divide into working groups which discuss and formulate recommendations on such topics as courts and society, the judiciary as an independent branch of government, the organization and jurisdiction of the courts, the status and rights of judges and the independence of the legal profession. These recommendations are then discussed and adopted in a plenary of all the participants. A follow-up committee is generally established, consisting of one representative from each country to press for implementation at the national level.

53. The CIJL has also held national seminars in co-operation with the United Nations Advisory Services Programme in Nicaragua (1989), Pakistan (1989) and India (1990) and with local human rights groups in Paraguay (1988) and Peru (1989).

C. International intra-professional solidarity

54. In his study, Dr. Singhvi wrote that "an important factor in ensuring the independence of the legal profession is its sense of solidarity. The profession is able to preserve its dignity, ideals. Sometimes when the independence of the legal profession is besieged within a country and internal protests prove to be of little avail, the solidarity of the international community in general and of the legal profession in other countries of the world can prove to be important factors" (para. 364).

1. Interventions

55. Over the past decade, a number of international bodies have begun to organize interventions by international, regional, national and local bar associations with local authorities in specific cases of harassment or persecution of judges and lawyers. These organizations have come to recognize that it is their professional responsibility to speak out on behalf of colleagues being persecuted at home or abroad and that such interventions are not "political" but are vital if a system of justice based on the rule of law is to be protected.

56. The forerunner of these programmes was that of the CIJL, which has built up a network of hundreds of organizations of judges and lawyers willing to respond to CIJL requests for action. The CIJL intervenes in cases involving harassment, persecution or threats directed against individual judges or lawyers or their associations, as well as more subtle pressures such as the use of transfer to punish a judge for having rendered a decision unfavourable to the Government. In addition, the CIJL intervenes in matters such as amendments to the Constitution or legal codes of a country, affecting the judiciary or bar as a whole.

57. More recently, the International Bar Association (IBA), a federation of 115 bar associations and law societies from 69 countries, themselves representing more than 2.5 million lawyers, has begun to regularly intervene with Governments to protest the harassment or persecution of judges and lawyers, and encourages its member bar associations to do the same. In 1989-1900, the President of the IBA wrote to 14 heads of State to protest the harassment of lawyers. Forty-seven member organizations have appointed members or committees to receive and review IBA protests for their support.

58. In 1987, the New York-based Lawyers Committee for Human Rights launched the "Lawyer-to-Lawyer Network" to involve the legal community of the United States in seeking protection for colleagues abroad. Two or more monthly appeals to its network of 1,300 lawyers and 90 state and local bar associations are designed to inform and mobilize United States lawyers and bar groups to write to government officials on behalf of their colleagues. The appeals are also circulated to members of Congress, diplomats, representatives of the department of State and the news media. In 1989, the Lawyers Committee expanded its network to include foreign lawyers.

59. Over the past year the Committee has issued appeals on behalf of 32 lawyers and related professionals. The Network has generated letters from individuals at more than 48 law firms and other organizations on behalf of these attorneys.

60. Amnesty International, as part of its regular practice of sending "Urgent Agent" appeals to its members to protest the detention of persons considered to be "prisoners of conscience," alerts its lawyers' groups worldwide when the appeal involves a member of the legal profession.

61. Other lawyers groups which regularly intercede on behalf of persecuted colleagues include Magistrats Européens pour la Démocratie et les Libertés, the Bureau de Liaison de Défense des Droits de la Défense de la Conférence des Grands Barreaux d'Europe and the Netherlands Bar Association.

2. Co-ordinated action

62. In addition, interprofessional solidarity can extend to other concrete forms of support.

63. In late 1989, for instance, the head of the Colombian judges' association, Asonal Judicial, was invited to Europe by Magistrats Européens pour la Démocratie et les Libertés to inform European lawyers about the difficult situation which Colombian judges face. He was received by lawyers' associations in Belgium, France, Italy, the Federal Republic of Germany, Netherlands, Portugal and Spain and received material contributions to protect Colombian judges.

64. Another model of co-ordinated action was the July 1988 "International Lawyers Forum" in the Philippines, at which 20 international legal organizations met to develop a common response to the increasing violence and intimidation against human rights lawyers in that country.

0022

IV. CONCLUSIONS

65. Since 1989, the Commission on Human Rights has adopted a double approach:

(a) On the one hand, by using the services of the Crime Prevention and Criminal Justice Branch of the Centre for Social Development and Humanitarian Affairs of the United Nations Office at Vienna and the organs which it services, i.e. the Committee on Crime Prevention and Control and the United Nations Congress on the Prevention of Crime and the Treatment of Offenders;

(b) On the other hand, by addressing itself to technical and political expert bodies in Geneva for monitoring those standards, with particular reference to specific cases and situations.

66. This was the sense of Commission resolution 1989/32, which both:

(a) Transferred the Singhvi draft declaration to the Crime Branch, asking that it be taken into account in completing work on the draft basic principles on the role of lawyers;

(b) Called on the Sub-Commission to consider effective means of monitoring the independence of the judiciary and the protection of practising lawyers.

67. The Commission suggested this dichotomy again in its resolution 1990/33 when it:

(a) Noted with satisfaction that the Committee on Crime Prevention and Control had taken into account the Singhvi draft declaration in completing its work on the basic principles on the role of lawyers, as requested in Commission resolution 1989/32, and recommended that the Eighth United Nations Congress consider, as a matter of priority, the draft basic principles on the role of lawyers, with a view to their adoption;

(b) Endorsed the decision of the Sub-Commission to prepare the current working paper and requested the Sub-Commission to study the working paper with a view to recommending to the Commission any initiatives which could be taken to effectuate the implementation of the Basic Principles on the Independence of the Judiciary and the protection of practising lawyers.

68. In both resolutions, the Commission welcomed the close co-operation between the Centre for Human Rights and the Centre for Social Development and Humanitarian Affairs on matters relating to human rights in the administration of justice.

69. To be consistent, therefore, with the Commission's guidance, the Sub-Commission should leave the areas of standard-setting and reporting to the United Nations Crime Branch and should focus its efforts on monitoring. Indeed, this is the sense of the Sub-Commission's request, in resolution 1989/22, that the present report suggest means "in the area of monitoring" by which it could assist in ensuring respect for the independence of the judiciary and the protection of practising lawyers.

70. The Commission's 1989 and 1990 resolutions should serve to rectify an overlap which had previously existed, at least in the area of standard-setting. As will be recalled, in 1980 the Economic and Social Council authorized Dr. Singhvi to begin his study. In the same year, the Sixth United Nations Congress, in its resolution 16, called on the Committee on Crime Prevention and Control to give priority to "the elaboration of guidelines relating to the independence, selection, professional training and status of judges and prosecutors." By the time Dr. Singhvi had presented his draft declaration on the independence and impartiality of the Judiciary, Jurors and Assessors and the Independence of Lawyers to the Sub-Commission in 1985, however, the Seventh United Nations Congress was approving the Basic Principles on the Independence of the Judiciary which had been prepared by the Committee on Crime Prevention and Control, thus somewhat duplicating the principles elaborated by Dr. Singhvi. The Commission, at its forty-fifth session, in 1989, resolved this duplication by calling on States to take into account Dr. Singhvi's detailed principles on the judiciary in implementing the more general Basic Principles on the Independence of the Judiciary and asking the Committee and the Congress to take Dr. Singhvi's principles on lawyers into account in completing its elaboration of the basic principles on the role of lawyers.

71. It can be seen that current United Nations activity relating to standard-setting and reporting is now carried out through the Crime Branch and the organs it services and that the standard-setting task is well underway. The Basic Principles on the Independence of the Judiciary, adopted in 1985, will most likely be matched later this year by approval of the basic principles on the role of lawyers. These general documents are complemented by the more detailed draft declaration on the independence and impartiality of the judiciary, jurors and assessors and the independence of lawyers prepared by Dr. Singhvi.

72. It will also be seen in the above survey that violations of international norms are widespread, as are the means being employed to prevent or combat these violations. Many States have implemented constitutional, legislative and practical protection. A future report might examine types of legislation and other measures which have been taken and their practical effect on judicial independence, and might propose other measures for States to consider.

73. Another principal means of strengthening the independence of judges and lawyers consists of promotional activities such as training courses, seminars and other forms of education. The United Nations Centre for Human Rights, the Centre for Social Development and Humanitarian Affairs and various regional United Nations institutes are providing advisory services and technical co-operation in helping countries strengthen the independence of the judiciary. It might be useful for the Sub-Commission to examine the methodology, practice and resources of these different programmes, propose means by which the co-operation between them could be enhanced and also set forth guidelines and criteria to be taken into account in the provision of these services.

74. The element missing from the above activities is international monitoring (contrôle).

0024

75. As regards the judiciary, as recalled by the Commission in its resolution 1990/33, the Committee on Crime Prevention and Control has established, through the Procedures for the Effective Implementation of the Basic Principles on the Independence of the Judiciary, a system of quinquennial reporting on the implementation of the Basic Principles. However, this system must, by its nature, be limited to collecting reports provided be those States which respond, as well as reports provided by other sources. It cannot exercise a true monitoring function, nor can it bring to the attention of the international community cases in which legislative or practical measures have served to strengthen the independence of the judiciary (and the protection of practising lawyers) or, on the contrary, measures or situations which constitute extreme violations of these principles.

V. RECOMMENDATIONS

76. This paper was commissioned in order to recommend "means in the area of monitoring by which the Sub-Commission could assist in ensuring respect for the independence of the judiciary and the protection of practising lawyers, as requested in Commission resolution 1989/32." It is recommended that the Sub-Commission ask one of its members to prepare a report which would:

(a) Make a system-wide analysis of the advisory service and technical assistance programmes of the United Nations as regards the independence of the judiciary and the protection of practising lawyers, propose means by which the co-operation between the programmes could be enhanced and set forth guidelines and criteria to be taken account in the provision of these services;

(b) Bring to the attention of the Sub-Commission cases in which legislative or practical measures have served to strengthen the independence of the judiciary and the protection of practising lawyers or, on the contrary, measures or situations which constitute extreme violations of these norms.

OFFICE DES NATIONS UNIES A GENÈVE

CENTRE POUR LES DROITS DE L'HOMME

UNITED NATIONS OFFICE AT GENEVA

CENTRE FOR HUMAN RIGHTS

Téléfax: (022) 733 98 79
Télégrammes: UNATIONS, GENÈVE
Télex: 28 96 96
Téléphone: 734 60 11   731 02 11

Palais des Nations
CH-1211 GENÈVE 10

RÉF. Nº: G/SO 234 (19-2)
(à rappeler dans la réponse)

The Secretary-General of the United Nations presents his compliments to the Minister for Foreign Affairs of the Republic of Korea and has the honour to refer to Sub-Commission on Prevention of Discrimination and Protection of Minorities resolution 1990/5 of 23 August 1990, entitled "Possible ways and means of facilitating the peaceful and constructive solution of problems involving minorities". A copy of the resolution is enclosed.

The attention of His Excellency's Government is drawn to paragraph 4 of the resolution, which calls on the Secretary-General to transmit the questionnaire annexed to the Special Rapporteur's progress report (E/CN.4/Sub.2/1990/46), as it might be supplemented and amended by the Special Rapporteur, to Governments for their comments, views and relevant information, and paragraph 6 of the resolution, which requests the Special Rapporteur to submit a preliminary report to the Sub-Commission at its forty-third session including an analysis of information obtained in replies, inter alia, from Governments. A copy of the amended questionnaire is enclosed.

The Secretary-General would appreciate it if any information which His Excellency's Government wished to submit pursuant to the above-mentioned request could be sent to the Centre for human Rights, United Nations Office at Geneva, CH-1211 Geneva 10, no later, if possible, than 15 March 1991.

25 January 1991

0026

1990/5. Possible ways and means of facilitating the peaceful and constructive solution of problems involving minorities

The Sub-Commission on Prevention of Discrimination and Protection of Minorities,

Recalling, its resolution 1988/36 of 1 September 1988, by which it invited Mrs. Claire Palley to prepare a working paper on possible ways and means to facilitate the peaceful and constructive resolution of situations involving racial, national, religious and linguistic minorities,

Recalling also its resolution 1989/44 of 1 September 1989, by which it expressed appreciation to Mrs. Palley for her proposals, and entrusted Mr. Asbjørn Eide with the preparation of a further report on national experience in this field,

Expressing concern that throughout the world there are serious problems arising from inter-ethnic and inter-group conflicts,

Convinced that the Sub-Commission can best contribute to preventing large-scale human rights problems in situations involving minorities by studying and promoting positive measures for the protection of minorities and for the peaceful and constructive solution of problems concerning them within the States in which they live,

Having considered the progress report submitted by Mr. Asbjørn Eide at its forty-second session (E/CN.4/Sub.2/1990/46),

Conscious of the complexity and diversity of national experience with minorities, the magnitude of the task of collecting and evaluating this experience, and the limited extent to which such information is currently available within the United Nations system,

1. Expresses its deep appreciation to the Special Rapporteur, Mr. Asbjørn Eide, for his informative and useful progress report;

2. Endorses the research methods proposed by Mr. Eide for the study in chapter V of his progress report;

3. Affirms the need to assign a high priority and adequate resources to the collection and evaluation of relevant information;

4. Requests the Secretary-General to transmit the questionnaire annexed to the above-mentioned report, as it might be supplemented and amended by the Special Rapporteur, on the basis of the views and comments made by the members of the Sub-Commission, to Governments, specialized agencies, regional intergovernmental organizations and non-governmental organizations for their comments, views and relevant information;

5. Requests also the Secretary-General to give the Special Rapporteur all the assistance he may require to enable him to carry out his study and to accomplish his work successfully;

6. Requests further the Special Rapporteur to submit a preliminary report to the Sub-Commission at its forty-third session on the progress made in his study, and to consider including an analysis of information obtained in replies from Governments, specialized agencies, regional intergovernmental organizations, as well as from State reports submitted under international and regional human rights instruments, and to take into account also relevant decisions and recommendations by human rights bodies, in particular the decisions of the Human Rights Committee;

RES/HR/90/35
GE.90-18676

0027

7. *Recommends* to the Commission on Human Rights the following draft resolution for adoption:

The Commission on Human Rights,

Taking into account resolution 1990/5 of 23 August 1990 of the Sub-Commission on Prevention of Discrimination and Protection of Minorities,

1. *Expresses its deep appreciation* to the Special Rapporteur, Mr. Asbjørn Eide, for his progress report on possible ways and means of facilitating the peaceful and constructive solution of problems involving minorities (E/CN.4/Sub.2/1990/46);

2. *Endorses* the methods proposed by the Special Rapporteur for the further study of facilitating the peaceful and constructive solution of problems involving minorities;

3. *Requests* the Special Rapporteur to submit to the Sub-Commission a preliminary report at its forty-third session, taking into account, among other information, the comments and suggestions made by the members of the Sub-Commission as well as replies from Governments, specialized agencies, regional intergovernmental and non-governmental organizations;

4. *Requests* the Secretary-General to give the Special Rapporteur all the assistance he may require, including a technical meeting of experts for three days, to enable him to carry out his work successfully.

0028

1487Q

Questionnaire

Introduction

1. The Sub-Commission on Prevention of Discrimination and Protection of Minorities, in its resolution 1989/44, entrusted Mr. Asbjørn Eide with the preparation of a report on national experience regarding peaceful and constructive solutions of situations involving minorities. The resolution was endorsed by the Commission on Human Rights in its decision 1990/105.

2. In its resolution 1990/5, the Sub-Commission expressed its deep appreciation to the Special Rapporteur for his progress report (E/CN.4/Sub.2/1990/46), endorsed the research methods proposed by him for the study and requested the Secretary-General to transmit the present questionnaire to Governments, specialized agencies, regional intergovernmental agencies and non-governmental organizations for their comments, views and relevant information.

3. The questionnaire is transmitted pursuant to the above mandate.

4. In responding to the questionnaire, Governments are not requested to duplicate information they have submitted under one of the reporting procedures within the United Nations system. Where relevant information has already been submitted in this way, it will suffice for them to make a reference to the appropriate report. It should be noted, however, that most of the questions below differ from those listed for the submission of State reports under existing treaty provisions, and it will therefore be appreciated if each question is studied carefully to provide responses which may be of use in completing this study.

5. While the main purpose of the study is to explore positive and constructive solutions, it is essential that the responses under each question also indicate the obstacles encountered, if any, and ways in which these have been overcome. This will facilitate the understanding of the best ways to handle such situations.

6. The study does not make use of a precise definition of "minorities". The term is used here in a very broad sense, meaning nationalities, ethnic, linguistic or cultural groups which in significant respects are different from other groups inside a sovereign State.

7. A distinction is made here between "settled minorities" and "recent immigrant groups". The latter is understood to mean aliens in general, immigrants who have not yet become citizens, refugees and asylum seekers, and migrant workers. Please indicate if distinctions are made along these lines regarding the recognition of all or any rights and in the granting of access to procedures and mechanisms for the enjoyment thereof.

8. Wherever there is a question related to the enjoyment by the minority groups of their own cultural institutions and practices, it is understood that such institutions must always operate within the limits of the internationally recognized fundamental freedoms and human rights of the individual.

0029

Questions related to minority groups

(i) Do minority groups, as understood in this questionnaire (see introduction) exist in your country/in the country concerned? Please indicate whether these are settled minorities or recent immigrant groups.

(ii) Are they recognized as separate minorities, or as national, ethnic or linguistic groups, in the legal and political institutions of the country? What obstacles have been encountered, if any, concerning such recognition?

(iii) Does such recognition consist in a federal structure, devolution of power, local autonomy, or does it take other forms? Please describe, and indicate the obstacles encountered, if any.

(iv) Do minority groups maintain or enjoy cultural and/or educational institutions specifically devoted to meet their needs?

(v) Do linguistic minorities, including recent immigrant groups, have the freedom and possibility to receive any part of their education in their own language?

(vi) Do such groups or their representatives have the right and possibility to participate in the planning, implementation and benefits of development policies?

(vii) In regard to the economic conditions of minority groups, is their average standard of living, life expectancy and child mortality rate approximately the same as that of the national average? If not, is it lower or higher than the national average?

Where federal structures exist based on criteria of nationality, the response to question (vii) should compare both the situation among the different nationalities within the federation and that of the different ethnic, cultural and linguistic groups inside each of the member States, or republics, of the federation.

(viii) If some minority groups are disadvantaged relative to the national average, have they been provided with the opportunity to improve their situation by their own efforts?

(ix) Have disadvantaged minority groups benefited from policies of affirmative action?

(x) Do minority groups have direct representation in national legislatures?

(xi) Have members of minority groups benefited from agrarian reform measures or resettlement programmes?

(xii) Do members of minority groups have unimpeded possibility of contact with related ethnic, cultural or linguistic groups in other states?

0030

(xiii) What steps have been taken, and what obstacles have been encountered in ensuring that recent immigrant groups (as understood in this study, see introduction) are not subjected to racial discrimination and that they are ensured equality in the enjoyment of human rights and fundamental freedoms.

0031

OFFICE DES NATIONS UNIES A GENÈVE

CENTRE POUR LES DROITS DE L'HOMME

UNITED NATIONS OFFICE AT GENEVA

CENTRE FOR HUMAN RIGHTS

Téléfax: (022) 733 98 79
Télégrammes: UNATIONS, GENÈVE
Télex: 28 96 96
Téléphone: 734 60 11 731 02 11

Palais des Nations
CH-1211 GENÈVE 10

RÉF. Nº: G/SO 214 (16-5)
(à rappeler dans la réponse)

The Secretary-General of the United Nations presents his compliments to the Minister for Foreign Affairs of the Republic of Korea and has the honour to draw the attention of His Excellency's Government to General Assembly resolution 44/148 of 15 December 1989 entitled "Human Rights based on solidarity" and Commission on Human Rights resolution 1990/15 of 23 February 1990 entitled "Human Rights and extreme poverty". A copy of both resolutions is attached.

By paragraph 1 of resolution 44/148, the Commission on Human Rights is requested to obtain the views of, inter alia, States, on the question of severe suffering of human beings through the world particularly those in conditions of extreme poverty, which calls for the strengthening of a common sense of human solidarity.

By paragraph 1 of resolution 1990/15, the Commission on Human Rights reaffirms that extreme poverty and exclusion from society constitute a violation of human dignity and that urgent national and international action is required to eliminate them. By paragraph 2, States, inter alia, are requested to give the necessary attention to this problem when they make known their views on human rights based on solidarity.

Also in view of the recent decision of the Sub-Commission on Prevention of Discrimination and Protection of Minorities (decision 1990/119) to appoint one of its members to prepare the method and plan of work for the study on human rights and extreme poverty, as was requested by the Commission on Human Rights in paragraph 5 of its resolution 1990/15, the Secretary-General would be grateful if His Excellency's Government could forward its comments and views on the subjects of human rights based on solidarity and human rights and extreme poverty to the Centre for Human Rights, United Nations Office at Geneva, CH-1211 Geneva 10, by 15 March 1991 in order that they may be taken into consideration at the forty-third session of the Sub-Commission and the forty-sixth session of the General Assembly.

28 January 1991

0032

GENERAL ASSEMBLY
FORTY-FOURTH SESSION

44/148. Human rights based on solidarity

The General Assembly,

Reaffirming the Universal Declaration of Human Rights, the International Covenant on Civil and Political Rights, the International Covenant on Economic, Social and Cultural Rights, and other international instruments adopted by the United Nations concerning human rights,

Stressing that respect for the inherent dignity and for the equal and inalienable rights of all members of the human family is the foundation of freedom, justice and peace in the world,

Convinced that the severe suffering of innumerable human beings throughout the world, particularly those in conditions of extreme poverty, calls for the strengthening of a common sense of human solidarity,

1. *Requests* the Commission on Human Rights to obtain from States, the specialized agencies and organizations of the United Nations system, as well as from other international organizations, including non-governmental organizations, their views and to study the question;

2. *Decides* to include in the provisional agenda of its forty-sixth session an item entitled "Human rights based on solidarity".

82nd plenary meeting
15 December 1989

RES/HR/90/36
GE.90-18723

0033

COMMISSION ON HUMAN RIGHTS
FORTY-SIXTH SESSION

1990/15. Human rights and extreme poverty

The Commission on Human Rights,

Recalling that the peoples of the United Nations have reaffirmed in the Charter their faith in fundamental human rights and in the dignity and worth of the human person,

Mindful that the Universal Declaration of Human Rights provides that everyone has the right to a standard of living adequate for the health and well-being of himself and of his family,

Recalling that, in accordance with the Universal Declaration of Human Rights, the International Covenants on Human Rights recognize that the ideal of free human beings enjoying freedom from fear and want can only be achieved if conditions are created whereby everyone may enjoy his economic, social and cultural rights, as well as his civil and political rights,

Reaffirming that all human rights and fundamental freedoms are indivisible and interrelated and that the promotion and protection of one category of rights should never exempt or excuse States from the promotion and protection of other rights,

Recalling that the elimination of widespread poverty and the full enjoyment of economic, social and cultural rights remain interrelated goals,

Deeply concerned by the fact that, despite the progress achieved by the international community in ensuring the effective enjoyment of the rights of the person, extreme poverty continues to spread throughout the world, seriously affecting the most vulnerable and disadvantaged individuals, families and groups in all countries, who are thus hindered in the exercise of their human rights and their fundamental freedoms,

Recognizing, moreover, that respect for and promotion of human rights are essential if individuals are to participate freely and responsibly in the development of the society in which they live,

Recalling its resolution 1989/10 of 2 March 1989, in which it requested the Sub-Commission on Prevention of Discrimination and Protection of Minorities to give particular attention to extreme poverty and exclusion from society and to examine the feasibility of a study of this question,

Recalling General Assembly resolution 44/148 of 15 December 1989, entitled "Human rights based on solidarity",

Recalling resolution 1989/8, "Reaching the poorest", adopted by the Executive Board of the United Nations Children's Fund at its first regular session of 1989, in which it is emphasized, inter alia, that a more thorough knowledge of the situation of the poorest, of their living conditions and the pre-conditions for their partnership would make it easier to reach the groups in question,

RES/HR/90/37
GE.90-18726

0034

Recalling resolution 1989/20 of 31 August 1989 of the Sub-Commission on Prevention of Discrimination and Protection of Minorities, in which the Sub-Commission endorsed the preliminary conclusions of the Special Rapporteur on the realization of economic, social and cultural rights (E/CN.4/Sub.2/1989/19, para. 94),

Bearing in mind the action already taken in the relevant forums to ensure the realization of economic, social and cultural rights,

Aware of the necessity of a better understanding of the causes of extreme poverty, including the causes connected with the problems of development, and its interaction with the enjoyment of human rights,

1. Reaffirms that extreme poverty and exclusion from society constitute a violation of human dignity and that urgent national and international action is therefore required to eliminate them;

2. Requests States, United Nations bodies, the specialized agencies and other international organizations, including non-governmental organizations, to give the necessary attention to this problem when they make known their views on human rights based on solidarity, pursuant to General Assembly resolution 44/148;

3. Draws the attention of the General Assembly and all United Nations bodies to the contradiction between the existence of situations of extreme poverty and exclusion from society, which must be overcome, and the ability to enjoy human rights fully;

4. Urges the Committee on Economic, Social and Cultural Rights to give the necessary attention, in its work, to the question of extreme poverty and exclusion from society;

5. Requests the Sub-Commission on Prevention of Discrimination and Protection of Minorities when giving attention, in accordance with its resolution 1989/20, to problems, policies and progressive measures relating to more effective realization of economic, social and cultural rights, to examine the question of extreme poverty and exclusion from society in greater depth and to carry out a specific study of this question.

38th meeting
23 February 1990

[Adopted without a vote. See chap. VII.]

0035

OFFICE DES NATIONS UNIES A GENÈVE

CENTRE POUR LES DROITS DE L'HOMME

UNITED NATIONS OFFICE AT GENEVA

CENTRE FOR HUMAN RIGHTS

Téléfax: (022) 733 98 79
Télégrammes: UNATIONS, GENÈVE
Télex: 412 962 UNO CH
Téléphone: 734 60 11 731 02 11

Palais des Nations
CH-1211 GENÈVE 10

RÉF. N°: G/SO 214 (3-3-15)
(à rappeler dans la réponse)

11 February 1991

Sir,

At the request and on behalf of Mr. Theo van Boven, Special Rapporteur of the Sub-Commission on Prevention of Discrimination and Protection of Minorities entrusted with the task of undertaking a study concerning the right to restitution, compensation and rehabilitation for victims of gross violations of human rights and fundamental freedoms, I have the honour to draw the attention of His Excellency's Government to the preliminary report on this subject (E/CN.4/Sub.2/1990/10), a copy of which is attached hereto.

I wish to refer to the tentative outline of the study which is contained in an annex to the report, and in particular to items IV, V and VI of this outline which relate to national law and practice and inter-State practice on questions of restitution, compensation and rehabilitation as well as to some basic issues that need to be further studied, including those regarding the obligation to grant compensation, entitlements to compensation, various types of compensation and others.

I would appreciate it if any relevant information which His Excellency's Government may wish to submit on this subject-matter, could be communicated to the Centre for human Rights, United Nations Office at Geneva, CH-1211 Geneva 10, if possible by 15 April 1991, in order to enable the Special Rapporteur to take that information into account in his progress report which will be submitted to the forty-third session of the Sub-Commission scheduled for August 1991, in accordance with the mandate entrusted to him by Sub-Commission resolution 1990/6 of 30 August 1990, a copy of which is attached for ease of reference.

Accept, Sir, the assurances of my highest consideration.

John Pace
Chief, Legislation and Prevention
of Discrimination Branch
Centre for Human Rights

H.E. the Minister for Foreign Affairs
77 Sejong-Ro
Chongro-ku
Seoul
Republic of Korea

0036

1990/6. Compensation for victims of gross violations of human rights

The Sub-Commission on Prevention of Discrimination and Protection of Minorities,

Recalling its resolution 1989/13 of 31 August 1989, by which it entrusted Mr. Theo van Boven with the task of undertaking a study concerning the right to restitution, compensation and rehabilitation for victims of gross violations of human rights and fundamental freedoms,

Recalling further Commission on Human Rights resolution 1990/35 of 2 March 1990 and Economic and Social Council resolution 1990/36 of 25 May 1990, authorizing the Sub-Commission to entrust Mr. van Boven with the task of preparing his study,

1. *Takes note with appreciation* of the preliminary report, including the tentative outline annexed thereto, submitted by Mr. van Boven in accordance with the above-mentioned resolutions (E/CN.4/Sub.2/1990/10);

2. *Requests* Mr. van Boven to prepare for the Sub-Commission, at its forty-third session, a progress report on the subject matter, taking into account comments made in the discussion on the preliminary report, including the provisional plan for the study, at its forty-second session, as well as the relevant work and recommendations of the Committee on Crime Prevention and Control, as requested in Economic and Social Council resolution 1990/22 of 24 May 1990, and whatever relevant decisions which might be adopted by the Eighth United Nations Congress on the Prevention of Crime and the Treatment of Offenders, and for this purpose to undertake the necessary consultations with the United Nations Centre for Social Development and Humanitarian Affairs;

3. *Requests* the Secretary-General to provide all assistance required by the Special Rapporteur to carry out his study.

33rd meeting
30 August 1990

RES/HR/91/1
GE.91-15225

0037

UNITED
NATIONS

Economic and Social Council

Distr.
GENERAL

E/CN.4/Sub.2/1990/10
26 July 1990

Original: ENGLISH

COMMISSION ON HUMAN RIGHTS

Sub-Commission on Prevention of Discrimination and Protection of Minorities

Forty-second session
Item 4 of the provisional agenda

REVIEW OF FURTHER DEVELOPMENTS IN FIELDS WITH WHICH THE SUB-COMMISSION HAS BEEN CONCERNED

Study concerning the right to restitution, compensation and rehabilitation for victims of gross violations of human rights and fundamental freedoms

Preliminary report submitted by Mr. Theo van Boven, Special Rapporteur

CONTENTS

GE.90-12528/2195B

0038

CONTENTS (continued)

0039

INTRODUCTION

1. In its resolution 1988/11 of 1 September 1988, the Sub-Commission on Prevention of Discrimination and Protection of Minorities recognized that all victims of gross violations of human rights and fundamental freedoms should be entitled to restitution, a fair and just compensation and the means for as full a rehabilitation as possible for any damage suffered by such victims, either individually or collectively. The Sub-Commission decided to discuss the matter of compensation at its forty-first session with a view to considering the possibility of developing some basic principles and guidelines in this respect.

2. At its forty-first session, in resolution 1989/13, the Sub-Commission, considering the importance of further developing international standards and of filling remaining gaps in order to ensure that victims of gross violations of human rights and fundamental freedoms have an enforceable right to restitution, compensation and rehabilitation, as appropriate, fully recognized at the international level, decided to entrust one of its members, Mr. Theo van Boven, with the task of undertaking a study concerning the right to restitution, compensation and rehabilitation for victims of gross violations of human rights and fundamental freedoms, taking into account relevant existing international human rights norms on compensation and relevant decisions and views of international human rights organs, with a view to exploring the possibility of developing some basic principles and guidelines in this respect; the Sub-Commission requested Mr. van Boven to submit a preliminary report for consideration by the Sub-Commission at its forty-second session.

3. The Commission on Human Rights, by its resolution 1990/35 of 2 March 1990, endorsed the above-mentioned resolutions of the Sub-Commission. Upon the recommendation of the Commission on Human Rights, the Economic and Social Council, in its resolution 1990/36 of 25 May 1990, authorized the Sub-Commission to entrust Mr. Theo van Boven with the task of undertaking a study concerning the right to restitution, compensation and rehabilitation for victims of gross violations of human rights and fundamental freedoms, taking into account, inter alia, relevant existing international human rights norms on compensation and judgements by courts, decisions and views of international human rights organs and bodies, with a view to exploring the possibility of developing basic principles and guidelines in this respect, and requested the Secretary-General to provide Mr. van Boven with all the assistance that he may require for the completion of his task.

4. In the discussion on this question, the Sub-Commission highlighted, inter alia, the following aspects: (a) a right for which there was no remedy is of no practical use to anyone (E/CN.4/Sub.2/1989/SR.6, para. 38); (b) the complex issue of compensation should be studied in greater detail, and on the basis of such a study, thought could be given to formulating basic principles and guidelines (E/CN.4/Sub.2/1989/SR.7, para. 28); (c) basic principles for redress and compensation for victims of human rights violations are lacking under the current system of international instruments (E/CN.4/Sub.2/1989/SR.15, para. 60). It was generally felt that the issue of compensation merited further reflection on the part of the Sub-Commission.

5. The Economic and Social Council, upon the recommendation of the Committee on Crime Prevention and Control, requested in its resolution 1990/22 of 24 May 1990 that the Special Rapporteur of the Sub-Commission takes into account, in his study of compensation to victim of gross violations of human rights, the relevant work and recommendations of the Committee on Crime Prevention and Control.

6. The present preliminary report is prepared pursuant to paragraph 2 of Sub-Commission resolution 1989/13. An interim report on the subject will be submitted to the Sub-Commission at its forty-third session in 1991, and a final report will be submitted in 1992 to the forty-fourth session of the Sub-Commission.

7. It is the intention of the Rapporteur to prepare a questionnaire on the issue of the right to restitution, compensation and rehabilitation for victims of gross violations of human rights and transmit it to Governments and competent international organizations.

8. The purpose of this preliminary report is to outline the main questions to be considered in the study and thus to provide a basis for discussion by the Sub-Commission at its forty-second session. It is expected that this discussion will assist the Rapporteur in determining the framework of the study and identifying the problems to be analysed. In the Annex of the report, the Rapporteur presents a tentative outline for the study; when the study will be in further progress, the outline may need adaptation.

I. RELEVANT EXISTING INTERNATIONAL NORMS

A. International human rights norms (global and regional human rights instruments)

9. A number of both universal and regional human rights instruments contain express provisions relating to the right of every individual to an "effective remedy" by competent national tribunals for acts violating human rights which are granted to him by the constitution or by law. Such formulation is contained in article 8 of the Universal Declaration of Human Rights. The notion of an "effective remedy" is also included in article 2 (3) (a) of the International Covenant on Civil and Political Rights and in article 6 of the Declaration on the Elimination of All Forms of Racial Discrimination.

10. Some human rights instruments refer to a more particular "right to be compensated in accordance with the law" (art. 10 of the American Convention on Human Rights) or the "right to an adequate compensation" (art. 21 (2) of the African Charter on Human and Peoples' Rights).

11. Even more specific are the provisions of article 9 (5) of the International Covenant on Civil and Political Rights and of article 5 (5) of the European Convention for the Protection of Human Rights and Fundamental Freedoms which refer to the "enforceable right to compensation". Similarly, the Convention against Torture and Other Cruel, Inhuman or Degrading Treatment or Punishment contains a provision providing for the victim of torture a redress and "an enforceable right to fair and adequate compensation, including the means for as full rehabilitation as possible" (art. 14 (1)).

0041

12. In some instruments, a specific provision is contained indicating that compensation is due _in accordance with law_ or with _national law_ (art. 14 (6) of the International Covenant on Civil and Political Rights and art. 11 of the Declaration on the Protection of All Persons from Being Subjected to Torture and Other Cruel, Inhuman or Degrading Treatment or Punishment).

13. Provisions relating to reparation or satisfaction of damages are contained in the International Convention on the Elimination of All Forms of Racial Discrimination, article 6 of which provides for the right to seek "_just and adequate reparation or satisfaction for any damage suffered_". The ILO Convention concerning Indigenous and Tribal Peoples in Independent Countries also refers to "_fair compensation for damages_" (art. 15 (2)), to "_compensation in money_" and "_under appropriate guarantees_" (art. 16 (4)), and to full compensation "_for any loss or injury_" (art. 16 (5)).

14. The American Convention on Human Rights speaks of "_compensatory damages_" (art. 68) and provides that the consequences of the measure or situation that constituted the breach of the right or freedom "_be remedied_" and that "_fair compensation be paid to the injured party_" (art. 63 (1)).

15. The Convention on the Rights of the Child contains a provision to the effect that States Parties shall take all appropriate measures to promote "_physical and psychological recovery and social reintegration of a child victim_ ..." (art. 39).

B. _Norms in the area of crime prevention and criminal justice_

16. Substantial provisions relating to various questions of restitution, compensation and assistance for victims of crime are contained in the Declaration of Basic Principles of Justice for Victims of Crime and Abuse of Power (General Assembly resolution 40/34 of 29 November 1985). The Declaration provides for the following:

(a) Victims are entitled to prompt redress for the harm that they have suffered;

(b) They should be informed of their rights in seeking redress;

(c) Offenders or third parties should make fair restitution to victims, their families or dependents. Such restitution should include the return of property or payment for the harm or loss suffered, reimbursement of expenses incurred as a result of the victimization, the provision of services and the restoration of rights;

(d) When compensation is not fully available from the offender or other sources, States should endeavour to provide financial compensation;

(e) Victims should receive the necessary material, medical, psychological and social assistance and support.

The Declaration also provides that Governments should review their practices, regulations and laws to consider restitution as an available sentencing option in criminal cases, in addition to other criminal sanctions (principle 9).

0042

17. The United Nations Standard Minimum Rules for the Administration of Juvenile Justice ("The Beijing Rules") contains a specific provision to the effect that "in order to facilitate the discretionary disposition of juvenile cases, efforts shall be made to provide for community programmes, such as temporary supervision and guidance, restitution, and compensation of victims".

C. International humanitarian law norms

18. Article 3 of the Hague Convention Regarding the Laws and Customs of Land Warfare provides for the obligation of the contracting party to pay indemnity in case of violation of the regulations. Article 41 of the IV Hague Convention also provides for the right to demand an indemnity for the losses sustained in cases of violations of the clauses of the armistice by individuals.

19. The Four Geneva Conventions of 12 August 1949 contain similar articles providing that "No High Contracting Party shall be allowed to absolve itself or any other High Contracting Party of any liability incurred by itself or another High Contracting Party" in respect of grave breaches involving such acts as "wilful killing, torture or inhuman treatment, including biological experiments, wilfully causing great suffering or serious injury to body or health, and extensive destruction and appropriation of property, not justified by military necessity and carried out unlawfully and wantonly". 1/

20. Article 68 of the Geneva Convention Relative to the Treatment of Prisoners of War contains specific provisions with regard to claims for compensation by a prisoner of war.

21. Article 55 of the Geneva Convention Relative to the Protection of Civilian Persons in Time of War provides that the Occupying Power "shall make arrangements to ensure that fair value is paid for any requisitioned goods".

22. Finally, Protocol I (Protocol additional to the Geneva Conventions of 12 August 1949, and Relating to the Protection of Victims of International Armed Conflicts), states in its article 91 that a Party to the conflicts which violates the provisions of the Conventions or of this Protocol "shall ... be liable to pay compensation".

II. THE RIGHT TO RESTITUTION, COMPENSATION AND REHABILITATION UNDER CUSTOMARY INTERNATIONAL LAW

23. The right to restitution, compensation and rehabilitation is intimately linked with the concept of State responsibility. It is interesting to note that the significance of the well-established international law of State responsibility for the international law of human rights has so far received only scant attention. In the following paragraphs, some important aspects of the international law of State responsibility will be highlighted, with a particular focus on the question of reparation. In this regard it is, of course, relevant to refer to the codification efforts of the International Law Commission. This Commission has so far adopted 35 draft articles on State responsibility.

24. State responsibility is the obligation of a State to make reparation arising from a failure to comply with an obligation under international law. State responsibility applies in the case of an act or omission in violation of

an international legal obligation, attributable to the delinquent State, resulting in injury to the claimant State (see also draft article 3, International Law Commission). In the judgement on the Chorzów Factory (Indemnity) Case, the Permanent Court of International Justice ruled:

> "It is a principle of international law, and even a general conception of law, that any breach of an engagement invokes an obligation to make reparation. [...] reparation is the indispensable complement of a failure to apply a convention, and there is no necessity for this to be stated in the convention itself." 2/

State responsibility can result from actions directly attributable to the State through its agents (original responsibility) or from actions that only indirectly involve the State (vicarious responsibility).

Reparation

25. The basic principles governing reparations for breaches of international obligations were established by the Permanent Court of International Justice in the Chorzów Factory (Indemnity) Case as follows:

> "The essential principle contained in the actual notion of an illegal act - a principle which seems to be established by international practice and in particular by the decisions of arbitral tribunals - is that reparation must, as far as possible, wipe out all consequences of the illegal act and re-establish the situation which would, in all probability, have existed if that act had not been committed. Restitution in kind, or, if this is not possible, payment of a sum corresponding to the value which a restitution in kind would bear; the award, if need be, of damages for loss sustained which would not be covered by restitution in kind or payment in place of it - such are the principles which should serve to determine the amount of compensation due for an act contrary to international law". 3/

The four main forms of reparation are restitution, indemnity, satisfaction and declaratory judgement.

A. Restitution

26. Restitution in kind is designed to re-establish the situation which would have existed if the wrongful act or omission had not taken place, by performance of the obligation which the State failed to discharge: revocation of the unlawful act, return of property wrongfully removed or abstention from further wrongful conduct. The Permanent Court of International Justice implied in its decision in the Chorzów Factory (Indemnity) Case, that restitution is the normal form of reparation and indemnity could only take place if restitution in kind is not possible.

B. Indemnity

27. This is in practice the most usual form of reparation. The indemnity should compensate for all damage which results from the unlawful act, including a profit which would have been possible in the ordinary course of events, but not prospective gains which are highly problematical, too remote or speculative. The basic test is the certainty of the damage. It is not

0044

essential that the damage should have already taken place for compensation to be recoverable. The possibility of punitive or exemplary damages is a matter of some debate in international law. It is generally believed, however, that the imposition of such damages would go beyond the jurisdiction conferred on the International Court of Justice and beyond the jurisdiction normally attributed to arbitral tribunals.

C. Satisfaction

28. Satisfaction may be defined as any measure which the author of a breach of duty is bound to take under customary law or under an agreement by the parties to a dispute, apart from restitution or compensation. There are three objects of satisfaction which are often cumulative: (a) apologies or other acknowledgement of wrongdoing, e.g. by means of payment of an indemnity; (b) the prosecution and punishment of the individuals concerned; and (c) the taking of measures to prevent a recurrence of the harm. There is no evidence under international law of a rule that provides that satisfaction is alternative to and, on being given, exclusive of a right to compensation for the breach of duty.

D. Declaratory judgement

29. A declaratory judgement of a court as to the illegality of the act of the defendant State constitutes in some cases a measure of satisfaction (or reparation in the broad sense). In various instances, the International Court of Justice has been willing to give declaratory judgements, using such formulas as that a State " ... is under a duty immediately to cease and refrain from all such acts as may constitute breaches of the foregoing legal obligations". 4/

30. In his next report, the Special Rapporteur will study in detail the significance of the various forms of reparation under customary international law as briefly described above, with particular reference to compensation for victims of gross violations of human rights. The work of the International Law Commission on the codification and progressive development of the international law of State responsibility will then be duly taken into account.

III. BASIC QUESTIONS AND ISSUES

31. The study entrusted to the Special Rapporteur raises questions and issues which are of considerable legal and moral interest and importance. These questions and issues touch upon the responsibility of States. At the same time they relate to individuals, groups and communities who are victims of gross violations of human rights and who are entitled to remedial justice. The Rapporteur wishes to recall that Sub-Commission resolution 1989/14 of 31 August 1989 which defined his mandate, expressed its deep concern over the substantial damages and acute sufferings caused to these victims. It is therefore the Rapporteur's view that his mandate requires him to be particularly mindful of the perspective of the rights and interests of the victims.

32. Before embarking upon an in-depth analysis of the various aspects of the subject matter of the study, the Rapporteur feels the need of seeking guidance on matters of general orientation and approach. To this end, he has

0045

identified some questions and issues which he would like to discuss in a preliminary and summary fashion. He hopes that the comments he may receive will assist him in setting forth the framework of the study. Among the questions and issues that need to be further discussed and reviewed are the following:

(a) The obligation to grant compensation under international law;

(b) Entitlements to compensation (in particular the scope of the term "victims of gross violations of human rights and fundamental freedoms");

(c) Various types of compensation;

(d) From whom can compensation be sought?

(e) Does a period of limitation apply?

A. The obligation to grant compensation under international law

33. There is no doubt that the obligation to provide for compensation as a means to repair a wrongful act or a wrongful situation is a well established principle in international law. This principle was reaffirmed many times by international tribunals, notably by the Permanent Court of International Justice in the Chorzów Factory Case referred to above (paras. 24-25).

34. In the area of humanitarian law, the obligation of States to pay compensation for breaches of the laws and customs of war was already recognized in Article 3 of Hague Convention No. IV (1907), which is literally reproduced in Article 91 of Additional Protocol I (1977) to the Geneva Conventions of 1949. Related to these articles is the common provision in the four Geneva Conventions to the effect that no State shall be allowed to absolve itself or any other State of any liability incurred by itself or by another State with respect to grave breaches listed in the Geneva Conventions (common Article 51/52/131/148). There are strong arguments for assuming that the obligation to pay compensation for violations of basic rules of humanitarian law has become a part of customary international law.

35. As is clear from the survey of relevant existing international norms (see paras. 9-22 above), many human rights conventions adopted at global and regional levels require States to provide remedies for victims of violations of norms recognized in these conventions. Moreover, some treaties grant victims an enforceable right to fair and adequate compensation. Fully in line with these provisions, international bodies entrusted with the task to supervise the observance of these human rights treaties held that States Parties to whom violations of human rights can be attributed are liable to pay compensation to the victims or to their relatives. The relevant case law will be examined in a next phase of this study.

36. The obligation to pay compensation is evidently an important aspect of the law of State responsibility which is the subject of a comprehensive study of the International Law Commission as part of the United Nations work of codification and progressive development of international law. The recent second report on State Responsibility of the Special Rapporteur of the International Law Commission (document A/CN.4/425 and Add.1) deals with the

0046

substantive consequences of an internationally unlawful act, in particular with the areas of injury covered respectively by compensation and satisfaction. In the further stages of preparation of his study, the Special Rapporteur will take into account the work of the International Law Commission relevant to his mandate.

B. Entitlements to compensation

37. For purposes of the present study Sub-Commission resolution 1989/14 provides some useful guidance with respect to the question of who is entitled to compensation. Ratione personae, the resolution mentions in its first preambular paragraph "individuals, groups and communities". This would imply that the study should not exclusively deal with individuals, but that in appropriate cases the entitlement to compensation of collectivities should also be considered. That collectivities are not excluded is confirmed in Sub-Commission resolution 1988/11 of 1 September 1988 which, in its first operative paragraph, refers to "victims, either individually or collectively".

38. Another indication as regards the categories of victims who fall under the scope of this study is the repeated reference in Sub-Commission resolution 1989/14 to "gross violations of human rights and fundamental freedoms". While under certain international instruments any violation of provisions of these instruments may entail a right to an appropriate remedy, the present study focuses on gross violations of human rights and fundamental freedoms. Many authors have given their views as to what acts and practices would constitute gross violations of human rights as distinct from other violations. The Special Rapporteur is ready to consider in this respect various formulas and options; however, at this preliminary stage, he feels that useful, albeit not conclusive, guidance can be found in the following formula, as a description of the types of violations of human rights which may be considered as falling within the ambit of this study:

> "[A State, violates international law if, as a matter of State policy, it practices, encourages or condones]
>
> (a) genocide,
>
> (b) slavery or slave trade,
>
> (c) the murder or causing the disappearance of individuals,
>
> (d) torture or other cruel, inhuman or degrading treatment or punishment,
>
> (e) prolonged arbitrary detention,
>
> (f) systematic racial discrimination, or
>
> (g) a consistent pattern of gross violations of internationally recognized human rights." 5/

39. It is generally recognized that victims who are entitled to compensation - and this may also include their relatives and survivors - have suffered substantial damages and harm. This is also reflected in the first preambular paragraph of Sub-Commission resolution 1989/14 which refers to

"substantial damages and acute sufferings". In this regard the notion of "victims", spelled out in paragraph 18 of the Declaration of Basic Principles of Justice for Victims of Crime and Abuse of Power, has to be taken into account. The paragraph reads in part:

> "Victims means persons who, individually or collectively, have suffered harm, including physical or mental injury, emotional suffering, economic loss or substantial impairment of their fundamental rights, through acts or omissions that [...] constitute violations [...] of internationally recognized norms relating to human rights".

C. <u>Various types of compensation</u>

40. It is quite clear from the wording of the Sub-Commission resolution 1989/14 that the notion of compensation should be understood in a wider sense than in pecuniary terms. The fourth preambular paragraph and operative paragraph 1 refer to the right to restitution, compensation and rehabilitation. Similar wording was also used in Sub-Commission resolution 1988/11. In this respect, the Declaration of Basic Principles of Justice for Victims of Crime and Abuse of Power may again serve as a helpful frame of reference. In paragraph 19 of this Declaration, dealing in particular with remedies to victims of abuses of power, it is stated that "... such remedies should include restitution and/or compensation, and necessary material, medical, psychological and social assistance and support".

41. It should be recalled that the international law of State responsibility envisages reparation for the wrongful act. While reparation usually takes the form of restitution and/or compensation, there may be other means of granting satisfaction to the victims, for instance in the form of injunctive relief with a view to preclude the further continuation or repetition of the breach of law or by establishing accountability for such breaches. Furthermore, it should not be overlooked that the disclosure of the truth after an official and thorough investigation of the facts and circumstances in connection with gross violations of human rights and fundamental freedoms may constitute another important means of providing satisfaction to the victims. Although the Special Rapporteur is aware that his mandate has as a main focus the right of victims to restitution, compensation and rehabilitation, he is not unmindful of the fact that granting just satisfaction to those victims individually and collectively may have broader implications, pertaining to matters of political, social and criminal justice.

D. <u>From whom can compensation be sought</u>?

42. The question arises whether the present study should deal with the responsibility of States to grant compensation in appropriate cases, or whether, in addition, other entities, for instance industrial concerns and other corporate enterprises in so far as they can be held accountable for causing serious human suffering, should be brought within the scope of the study. With regard to this question, the Special Rapporteur is inclined to interpret his mandate solely from the point of view of the responsibility of States which, to the extent that serious breaches of human rights are imputable to them, are under an obligation to grant compensation to the victims. This approach should, however, in no way be considered as detracting from a victim's right to bring in appropriate cases civil action against non-State entities.

0048

43. It is therefore proposed that for the purpose of this study the State is envisaged as the instance to which claims for compensation should be addressed. The next question is how far the imputability of States extends with regard to serious breaches of basic human rights. The Special Rapporteur will have to examine the relevant doctrine and practice in order to further define the imputability of States. In this connection, the recent judgement of the Inter-American Court of Human Rights in the Velásquez Rodriguez Case 6/ may prove to be of major importance. In this judgement, the Court stated that violations of human rights carried out by an act of public authority or by persons who use their position of authority is imputable to the State, the Court stated in addition that an illegal act which violates human rights and which is initially not imputable to the State can entail the international responsibility of the State if the latter has failed to exercise due diligence because of failure to take the necessary preventive and repressive measures.

E. Does a period of limitation apply?

44. Statutory limitations are applied in the area of criminal justice. The applicability of statutory limitations is generally based on the assumption that passage of time has the effect of gradually erasing the infraction of the legal order and that it may diminish the reliability of evidence. However, important sectors of legal opinion oppose the application of a period of limitation with regard to the most serious crimes. This principle is reflected in the Convention on the Non-Applicability of Statutory Limitations to War Crimes and Crimes against Humanity.

45. The question now arises to what extent a period of limitation applies to the exercise of the right to restitution, compensation and rehabilitation by or on behalf of victims of gross violations of human rights and fundamental freedoms. The Special Rapporteur believes that weighty arguments can be adduced against a short, finite statutory period for the filing of claims. He favours an open-ended or very long period. First of all, it should be taken into account that this study is concerned with the effects of gross violations of human rights, which have much in common with the most serious crimes of the nature of crimes against humanity. A second, no less important consideration, is that on the part of many victims of gross violations, passage of time has often no attenuating effect, but on the contrary an increase in post-traumatic stress, requiring all necessary material, medical, psychological and social assistance and support over a long period of time.

Notes

1/ See articles 50 and 51 of the Geneva Convention for the Amelioration of the Condition of the Wounded and Sick in Armed Forces in the Field; articles 51 and 52 of the Geneva Convention for the Amelioration of the Condition of Wounded, Sick and Shipwrecked Members of Armed Forces at Sea; articles 130 and 131 of the Geneva Convention Relative to the Treatment of Prisoners of War; and articles 147 and 148 of the Geneva Convention Relative to the Protection of Civilian Persons in Time of War.

2/ P.C.I.J., Collection of Judgements, Series A, No. 17, p. 29.

3/ P.C.I.J. op. cit., p. 47.

4/ Case Concerning Military and Paramilitary Activities Against Nicaragua, Merits, ICJ Reports of Judgements, Advisory Opinions and Orders (1986), p. 149, para. 12.

5/ Section 702 of the Third Restatement of the Foreign Relations Law of the United States (1987).

6/ Judgement of 29 July 1988, Inter-American Court of Human Rights, Series C: Decisions and Judgements No. 4, in particular paras. 172-174.

Annex

Tentative Outline of the study

Introduction

Description of the mandate

I. Relevant existing international norms

A. International human rights norms (global and regional human rights instruments)

B. Norms in the area of crime prevention and criminal justice

C. International humanitarian law norms

II. The right to restitution, compensation and rehabilitation under customary international law

III. Relevant decisions and views of international human rights organs

A. Pronouncements of the United Nations General Assembly, the Economic and Social Council, the Commission on Human Rights, the Committee on Crime Prevention and Control

B. Views and recommendations of Charter based human rights organs, such as the United Nations Ad Hoc Working Group of Experts on Southern Africa, the Special Committee to Investigate Israeli Practices Affecting the Human Rights of the Population of the Occupied Territories, the Working Group and Special Rapporteur on Chile, the Working Group on Enforced or Involuntary Disappearances, the Special Rapporteur on Summary or Arbitrary Executions, the Special Rapporteur on Torture

C. Views and decisions of treaty based human rights organs, such as the Human Rights Committee, the Committee against Torture, the Committee on the Elimination of Racial Discrimination and the Committee on the Elimination of Discrimination against Women, the European Court of Human Rights, the Inter-American Court of Human Rights

IV. Inter-State law and practice

(NB Wiedergutmachung)

V. National law and practice

VI. Basic questions and issues

A. The obligation to grant compensation under international law

B. Entitlements to compensation (in particular the scope of the term "victims of gross violations of human rights and fundamental freedoms")

C. Various types of compensation

D. From whom can compensation be sought?

E. Does a period of limitation apply?

VII. Suggested basic principles and guidelines

OFFICE DES NATIONS UNIES À GENÈVE

CENTRE POUR LES DROITS DE L'HOMME

UNITED NATIONS OFFICE AT GENEVA

CENTRE FOR HUMAN RIGHTS

Téléfax: (022) 733 98 79
Télégrammes: UNATIONS, GENÈVE
Télex: 412 962 UNO CH
Téléphone: 734 60 11 731 02 11

Palais des Nations
CH-1211 GENÈVE 10

RÉF. N°: G/SO 214 (12-4-1)
(à rappeler dans la réponse)

The Secretary-General of the United Nations presents his compliments to the Minister for Foreign Affairs of the Republic of Korea and has the honour to transmit to His Excellency's Government the questionnaire prepared by Mr. Varela-Quiros, Special Rapporteur of the Sub-Commission on Prevention of Discrimination and Protection of Minorities, in accordance with decision 1990/118 of 30 August 1990, on a study on problems and causes of discrimination against HIV-infected people or people with AIDS.

The Secretary-General would appreciate receiving soonest any comments His Excellency's Government may wish to provide in this connection by 30 April 1991, if possible, and that they be forwarded to the Centre for Human Rights, United Nations Office at Geneva, CH-1211 Geneva 10, to assist the Special Rapporteur in the preparation of his progress report.

25 February 1991

0053

STUDY ON AIDS AND HUMAN R

Questionnaire for Governments

General discrimination

1. What measures have been adopted by States to provide redress for persons with HIV/AIDS who have suffered discrimination?

2. To what extent is non-discrimination stressed in public information and education programmes?

3. Does national legislation provide for the protection of the human rights of persons suffering from HIV/AIDS?

Screening/testing

4. Do States have policies of compulsory screening/testing for certain individuals or groups of individuals? If so, for whom and with what kind of follow-up?

Public health/AIDS policy

5. Are blood donors tested for HIV? If so, is confidentiality respected?

6. Are certain persons who are more vulnerable to HIV infection excluded from donating blood? If so, who?

7. Are blood supplies regularly screened for HIV?

8. Are disposable syringes available at hospitals, health centres?

9. Is reporting/notification of HIV/AIDS a common public health procedure? If so, is this done on an anonymous basis? If not, is confidentiality strictly adhered to?

10. How is HIV/AIDS classified (sexually transmitted/communicable/contagious/infectious/viral/occupational)? What type of public health policy does this imply?

11. What is the Government's policy concerning the treatment of HIV-infected persons by medical personnel?

12. Is testing being carried out within the health care setting?

13. Are health workers, doctors and dentists informed as to the necessary precautions to protect themselves against HIV/AIDS?

14. What is the Government policy with regard to access to therapeutic drugs and experimental treatments?

15. What HIV/AIDS-related public health legislation has been enacted? What are the enforcement procedures and to what extent is it complied with?

0054

16. What is the AIDS policy towards certain population groups (immigrants/refugees/tourists/prostitutes/homosexuals)?

17. What form of HIV/AIDS-related entry restrictions, if any, exist in the country concerned? What categories of person are most affected by these (tourists/short-term visitors/immigrants/migrant workers/refugees)?

Prenatal transmission

18. Are pregnant women systematically tested for HIV?

19. Is testing done on an anonymous basis? If not, are confidentiality procedures strictly adhered to?

20. Is their consent obtained?

21. Is information and education about AIDS available at ante-natal clinics, child-care facilities, family planning clinics, elsewhere?

Children and AIDS

22. How many children are HIV-infected?

23. What is the most common form of HIV transmission (from the mother to the child/through infected blood or blood products)?

24. What are the figures for AIDS orphans?

25. What form of social, educational or financial support, if any, is provided to children with AIDS?

26. What care is provided to children with AIDS?

Information and education

27. What is the content of AIDS information provided by the Government?

28. How is the information tailored to prevailing cultural, religious and moral norms?

29. Which target groups receive significantly less information about HIV/AIDS (women/minorities/prostitutes/homosexuals/immigrants)?

30. Are human rights issues, particularly the right to non-discrimination, discussed in HIV/AIDS information/education campaigns?

Special institutions

31. Is screening/testing usual policy in prisons or other closed institutions? If so, are all inmates tested or only persons belonging to certain population groups? If the latter is the case, which population groups?

32. When is testing done (on entry/exit; during confinement)?

33. Who is notified of test results (staff, others)?

0055

34. What kind of action, if any, is taken upon positive test results?

35. Is counselling available?

36. Are inmates with HIV/AIDS segregated or prohibited from engaging in certain activities in community life (work/recreation/cooking/other)?

37. Are persons with HIV/AIDS in prisons or other closed institutions allowed to have visitors, access to health care, etc., or is their freedom of movement restricted in any way?

<u>Hospitals</u>

38. Are incoming patients tested for HIV?

39. Are patients having to undergo invasive procedures such as operations required to be tested? If so, is their consent obtained? Are they provided pre- and post-test counselling, and to whom are test results communicated?

40. Are HIV-positive patients isolated?

41. What precautions are hospital staff advised to take to prevent transmission of HIV?

0056

OFFICE DES NATIONS UNIES GENÈVE

CENTRE POUR LES DROITS DE L'HOMME

UNITED NATIONS OFFICE AT GENEVA

CENTRE FOR HUMAN RIGHTS

Téléfax: (022) 733 98 79
Télégrammes: UNATIONS, GENÈVE
Télex: 412 962 UNO CH
Téléphone: 734 60 11 731 02 11

Palais des Nations
CH-1211 GENÈVE 10

RÉF. N°: G/SO 237/41 (3)
(à rappeler dans la réponse)

The Secretary-General of the United Nations presents his compliments to the Minister for Foreign Affairs of the Republic of Korea and has the honour to refer to Sub-Commission on Prevention of Discrimination and Protection of Minorities resolution 1990/2 of 20 August 1990, entitled "Measures to combat racism and racial discrimination and the role of the Sub-Commission". A copy of the resolution is attached.

The attention of His Excellency's Government is drawn to paragraph 4 of the resolution which requests the Secretary-General to prepare, on the basis of replies obtained, inter alia, from Governments an overview of current trends of racism, discrimination, intolerance and xenophobia affecting the groups mentioned in the resolution (ethnic, national, religious and linguistic minorities, indigenous peoples, migrant workers and other vulnerable groups), as well as of measures taken by Governments against those phenomena and the effects of such measures and to submit the overview for consideration by the Sub-Commission at its forty-third session.

The Secretary-General would appreciate it if any information which His Excellency's Government wished to submit pursuant to the above-mentioned request could be sent to the Centre for Human Rights, United Nations Office at Geneva, CH-1211 Geneva 10, no later, if possible, than 1 May 1991.

28 February 1991

0057

1990/2. <u>Measures to combat racism and racial discrimination and the role of the Sub-Commission</u>

<u>The Sub-Commission on Prevention of Discrimination and Protection of Minorities</u>,

<u>Recalling</u> its resolution 1989/19 of 31 August 1989,

<u>Recalling further</u> Commission on Human Rights resolutions 1990/13 of 23 February 1990, and 1990/44, 1990/45 and 1990/46 of 6 March 1990,

<u>Having considered</u> Mr. Asbjørn Eide's study on the achievements made and obstacles encountered during the Decades to Combat Racism and Racial Discrimination, particularly its conclusions and recommendations (E/CN.4/Sub.2/1989/8 and Add.1),

<u>Conscious</u> of its special responsibility to give due regard to new developments in the field of human rights,

<u>Deeply concerned</u> that there are signs of an upsurge of racism, with accompanying manifestations of prejudice, discrimination, intolerance and xenophobia in many parts of the world directed against ethnic, national, religious and linguistic minorities, indigenous peoples, migrant workers and other vulnerable groups,

<u>Firmly determined</u> to do its utmost to contribute to eradicating these dangerous manifestations which affect the basic human rights and fundamental freedoms of the above-mentioned groups,

<u>Taking into account</u>, in this light, the recommendation of the Special Rapporteur to update the study on racial discrimination prepared by Mr. Hernán Santa Cruz in 1976 (E/CN.4/Sub.2/370 and Add.1-6 and Add.6/Corr.1),

1. <u>Expresses again its appreciation</u> to the Special Rapporteur, Mr. Asbjørn Eide, for his valuable, wide-ranging and useful study on the achievements made and obstacles encountered during the Decades to Combat Racism and Racial Discrimination;

2. <u>Decides</u> to transmit the recommendations contained in his study, as revised in the light of the discussion at the present session of the Sub-Commission, to the Secretary-General so that they may be taken into account in further efforts to combat racism and racial discrimination;

3. <u>Emphasizes</u> the need to give an additional thrust towards the achievement of the goals of the Second Decade to Combat Racism and Racial Discrimination and to contribute to the eradication of the recent upsurge of racist, prejudicial, discriminatory, intolerant and xenophobic attitudes and actions against vulnerable human groups in various parts of the world;

0058

4. Requests the Secretary-General to prepare, on the basis of replies obtained from Governments, specialized agencies and other intergovernmental organizations, as well as from non-governmental organizations, an overview of current trends of racism, discrimination, intolerance and xenophobia affecting the above-mentioned groups, as well as of measures taken by Governments against those phenomena and the effects of such measures and to submit the overview for consideration by the Sub-Commission at its forty-third session, under item 5 (a) of its agenda;

5. Decides to give thorough consideration at its forty-third session, under agenda item 5 (a), and in the light of these new trends, to the recommendation of the Special Rapporteur to update the study on racial discrimination prepared in 1976 by Mr. Hernán Santa Cruz.

18th meeting
20 August 1990

[Adopted without a vote. See chap. V.]

OFFICE DES NATIONS UNIES A GENÈVE

CENTRE POUR LES DROITS DE L'HOMME

UNITED NATIONS OFFICE AT GENEVA

CENTRE FOR HUMAN RIGHTS

Téléfax: (022) 733 98 79
Télégrammes: UNATIONS, GENÈVE
Télex: 412 962 UNO CH
Téléphone: 734 60 11 731 02 11

Palais des Nations
CH-1211 GENÈVE 10

RÉF. N°: G/SO 234 (16)
(à rappeler dans la réponse)

The Secretary-General of the United Nations presents his compliments to the Minister for Foreign Affairs of the Republic of Korea and has the honour to draw the attention of His Excellency's Government to Commission on Human Rights resolutions 1991/1 A and B entitled "Question of the violation of human rights in the occupied Arab territories, including Palestine" and 1991/2 entitled "Human rights in the occupied Syrian Arab territory" adopted by the Commission on 15 February 1991. Copies of these resolutions are attached.

The Commission on Human Rights requested the Secretary-General to bring the above-mentioned resolutions to the attention of all Governments, the competent United Nations organs, the specialized agencies, regional intergovernmental organizations, international humanitarian organizations and non-governmental organizations, and to report to the Commission at its forty-eighth session. Any information His Excellency's Government might wish to submit in this connection should be addressed to the Under-Secretary-General for Human Rights, United Nations Office at Geneva, CH-1211 Genève 10, by 1 November 1991.

25 March 1991

0060

COMMISSION ON HUMAN RIGHTS

Forty-seventh session

1991/1. Question of the violation of human rights in the occupied Arab territories, including Palestine

A

The Commission on Human Rights,

Guided by the purposes and principles of the Charter of the United Nations as well as the provisions of the Universal Declaration of Human Rights,

Guided by the provisions of the International Covenant on Economic, Social and Cultural Rights and the International Covenant on Civil and Political Rights,

Taking into consideration the provisions of the Fourth Geneva Convention relative to the Protection of Civilian Persons in Time of War, of 12 August 1949, and the provisions of the First Protocol annexed to it, and The Hague Convention IV of 1907, as well as the principles of international law affirmed by the General Assembly in its resolutions 3 (I) of 13 February 1946, 95 (I) of 11 December 1946, 260 A (III) of 9 December 1948 and 2391 (XXIII) of 26 November 1968,

Recalling the relevant Security Council resolutions, in particular resolutions 252 (1968) of 25 May 1968, 267 (1969) of 3 July 1969, 298 (1971) of 25 September 1971, 446 (1979) of 22 March 1979, 465 (1980) of 1 March 1980, 471 (1980) of 5 June 1980, 476 (1980) of 30 June 1980, 478 (1980) of 20 August 1980, 605 (1987) of 22 December 1987, 607 (1988) of 5 January 1988, 608 (1988) of 14 January 1988, and 672 (1990) of 12 October 1990.

Recalling the General Assembly resolutions on Israeli violations of human rights in occupied Palestine, since 1967 and until now,

Taking note of the reports of the Special Committee to Investigate Israeli Practices Affecting the Human Rights of the Palestinian People and Other Arabs of the Occupied Territories submitted to the General Assembly since 1968, in particular the report of 1990 (A/45/576).

Expressing its deep concern at the contents of the report by the Special Rapporteur, Mr. Amos Wako, regarding execution by summary means or indiscriminate execution (E/CN.4/1990/22 and Corr.1), and what is committed by Israel in this respect,

Recalling all its previous resolutions on the subject,

The final edited text of this resolution will be published in the report of the Commission on Human Rights to the Economic and Social Council.

RES/HR/91/3
GE.91-15592

0061

1. Condemns the policies and practices of Israel, which violate the human rights of the Palestinian people in the Palestinian territory occupied by Israel with military force, including Jerusalem, and, in particular, such acts as the opening of fire by the Israeli army and settlers on Palestinian civilians that results in killing and wounding them, as has happened continuously since the eruption of the Palestinian people's intifada against Israeli military occupation and as took place in the massacres of 20 May 1990 in Rishon Letzion and in the Al-Aqsa Mosque on 8 October 1990; the imposition of restrictive economic measures; the demolition of houses; the ransacking of real or personal property belonging individually or collectively to private persons; collective punishment; arbitrary and administrative detention of thousands of Palestinians; the confiscation of the property of Palestinians, including their bank accounts; the expropriation of land; the prevention of travel; the closure of universities and schools; the perpetration of crimes of torture in prisons and detention centres; and the establishment of Jewish settlements in the occupied Palestinian territory;

2. Affirms the right of the Palestinian people to resist the Israeli occupation by all means, in accordance with the relevant United Nations resolutions, consistent with the purposes and principles of the Charter of the United Nations, as has been expressed by the Palestinian people in their brave intifada since December 1987;

3. Calls once more upon Israel to desist from all forms of violations of human rights in the Palestinian and other occupied Arab territories and to respect the principles of international law, and its commitments to the provisions of the Charter;

4. Calls upon Israel to withdraw from the Palestinian territory, including Jerusalem, and other occupied Arab territories in accordance with the resolutions of the United Nations and the Commission on Human Rights in this regard;

5. Requests the Secretary-General to bring the present resolution to the attention of all Governments, the competent United Nations organs, the specialized agencies, regional intergovernmental organizations and international humanitarian organizations, to disseminate it on the widest possible scale, and to report on its implementation to the Commission on Human Rights at its forty-eighth session;

6. Further requests the Secretary-General to provide the Commission with all United Nations reports issued between sessions of the Commission that deal with the conditions in which the population of the Palestinian and other occupied Arab territories is living;

0062

7. Decides to consider the question at its forty-eighth session as a matter of priority.

28th meeting
15 February 1991

B

The Commission on Human Rights,

Recalling Security Council resolutions 446 (1979) of 22 March 1979, 465 (1980) of 1 March 1980, 497 (1981) of 17 December 1981, 592 (1986) of 8 December 1986, and 605 (1987) of 22 December 1987, as well as all its previous resolutions on the application of the Geneva Conventions of 12 August 1949 to the Palestinian and other Arab territories occupied by Israel and the refusal of Israel to abide by those Conventions,

Recalling all relevant General Assembly resolutions on the applicability of the Fourth Geneva Convention relative to the Protection of Civilian Persons in Time of War, of 12 August 1949, to the occupied Palestinian territory, and the necessity of Israel abiding by their provisions,

Recalling the decisions of the International Conference of the Red Cross in respect of the application of the Fourth Geneva Convention,

Recalling its previous resolutions on this question,

Recalling the different appeals and statements of the International Committee of the Red Cross which point to the continuing Israeli violations of the provisions of the Fourth Geneva Convention and which call upon those authorities to respect the provisions of the Convention and abide by them,

Taking into account that the States parties to the Fourth Geneva Convention undertake, in accordance with article 1 thereof, to respect, and ensure respect for, the Convention in all circumstances,

1. Reaffirms that the Fourth Geneva Convention relative to the Protection of Civilian Persons in Time of War, of 12 August 1949, is applicable to all Palestinian and other Arab territories occupied by Israel since 1967, including Jerusalem, and calls upon Israel to comply with its international commitments, to respect the Fourth Geneva Convention relative to the Protection of Civilian Persons in Time of War and to apply it in the occupied Palestinian territory, including Jerusalem;

0063

2. Urges once more all States parties to the Fourth Geneva Convention to make every effort to ensure the Israeli occupation authorities' respect for, and compliance with, the provisions of that Convention in all the Palestinian and other Arab territories occupied by Israel since 1967, including Jerusalem, and to undertake the necessary practical measures to ensure the provision of international protection for the Palestinian people under occupation in accordance with the provisions of the first article and other relevant articles of the Fourth Geneva Convention;

3. Strongly condemns once more the refusal of Israel to apply the Fourth Geneva Convention to Palestine and the Arab territories occupied since 1967 and to their inhabitants, and Israel's policies of ill-treatment and torture of Palestinian detainees and prisoners in Israeli prisons and concentration camps, and its continued deliberate disregard for the provisions of the Fourth Geneva Convention, in contravention of the resolutions of the Security Council, the General Assembly and the Commission on Human Rights;

4. Strongly condemns Israel for its grave violations of article 49 of the Fourth Geneva Convention, for its continuation of a policy of deportation of Palestinian citizens and their expulsion outside their homeland, as recently happened to the Palestinian citizens Imad Khaled Al-Alami, Fadel Khaled Zuheir Al-Zaamout, Mustafa Yusef Abdallah Al-Lidawi and Mustafa Ahmed Jamil Al-Qanouh, and calls upon Israel to comply with the resolutions of the Security Council, the General Assembly and the Commission on Human Rights which provide for their return to their homeland, and to desist forthwith from this policy;

5. Requests the Secretary-General to bring the present resolution to the attention of all Governments, the competent United Nations organs, the specialized agencies, regional intergovernmental organizations, international humanitarian organizations and non-governmental organizations, and to submit a report on progress in its implementation to the Commission on Human Rights at its forty-eighth session;

6. Decides to consider the question at its forty-eighth session as a matter of high priority.

28th meeting
15 February 1991

0064

COMMISSION ON HUMAN RIGHTS

Forty-seventh session

1991/2. Human rights in the occupied Syrian Arab territory

The Commission on Human Rights,

Deeply concerned by the suffering of the population of the Syrian and other Arab territories occupied by Israel since 1967 and by continued Israeli military occupation and that the human rights of the population continue to be violated,

Recalling Security Council resolution 497 (1981) of 17 December 1981, in which the Council, inter alia, decided that the Israeli decision to impose its laws, jurisdiction and administration in the occupied Syrian Arab Golan was null and void and without international legal effect, and demanded that Israel should rescind forthwith its decision,

Recalling General Assembly resolutions 36/226 B of 17 December 1981, ES-9/1 of 5 February 1982, 37/88 E of 10 December 1982, 38/79 F of 15 December 1983, 39/95 F of 14 December 1984, 40/161 F of 16 December 1985, 41/63 F of 3 December 1986, 42/160 F of 8 December 1987, 43/21 of 3 November 1988, 43/58 F of 6 December 1988, 44/2 of 6 October 1989, and 45/74 F of 11 December 1990,

Recalling General Assembly resolution 3414 (XXX) of 5 December 1975 and other relevant resolutions in which the Assembly, inter alia, demanded the immediate, unconditional and total withdrawal of Israel from all the Arab territories occupied since 1967,

Recalling General Assembly resolution 3314 (XXIX) of 14 December 1974, in which it defined an act of aggression,

Reaffirming once more the illegality of Israel's decision of 14 December 1981 to impose its laws, jurisdiction and administration on the Syrian Arab Golan, which has resulted in the effective annexation of that territory,

Reaffirming that the acquisition of territories by force is inadmissible under the principles of international law and under the Charter of the United Nations and the relevant resolutions of the Security Council and General Assembly, and that all territories thus occupied by Israel must be returned,

---

The final edited text of this resolution will be published in the report of the Commission on Human Rights to the Economic and Social Council.

RES/HR/91/4
GE.91-15595

0065

Taking note with deep concern of the report of the Special Committee to Investigate Israeli Practices Affecting the Human Rights of the Palestinian People and Other Arabs of the Occupied Territories (A/45/576) and in this connection deploring Israel's constant refusal to co-operate with and to receive the Committee,

Expressing its grave alarm, after considering the above-mentioned report of the Committee, over Israel's flagrant and persistent violations of human rights in the Syrian and other Arab territories occupied since 1967, despite the resolutions of the General Assembly and the Security Council which repeatedly called upon Israel to put an end to such occupation,

Reaffirming its previous relevant resolutions, the most recent of which being resolution 1990/3 of 16 February 1990,

Guided by the provisions of the Charter of the United Nations and the Universal Declaration of Human Rights, with particular reference to the Fourth Geneva Convention relative to the Protection of Civilian Persons in Time of War, of 12 August 1949, and relevant provisions of The Hague Conventions of 1899 and 1907,

1. Strongly condemns Israel, the occupying Power, for its refusal to comply with the relevant resolutions of the General Assembly and the Security Council, particularly resolution 497 (1981), in which the Council, inter alia, decided that the Israeli decision to impose its laws, jurisdiction and administration on the occupied Syrian Arab Golan was null and void and without international legal effect, and demanded that Israel, the occupying Power, should rescind forthwith its decision;

2. Condemns the persistence of Israel in changing the physical character, demographic composition, institutional structure and legal status of the occupied Syrian Arab Golan and emphasizes that the displaced persons of the population of the occupied Syrian Arab Golan must be allowed to return to their homes and to recover their properties;

3. Determines that all legislative and administrative measures and actions taken or to be taken by Israel, the occupying Power, that purport to alter the character and legal status of the Syrian Arab Golan are null and void, constitute a flagrant violation of international law and of the Geneva Convention relative to the Protection of Civilian Persons in Time of War, of 12 August 1949, and have no legal effect;

0066

4. *Strongly condemns* Israel for its attempt to impose forcibly Israeli citizenship and Israeli identity cards on the Syrian citizens in the occupied Syrian Arab Golan and for its practices of annexation, establishment of settlements, confiscation of lands and diversion of water resources, and imposing a boycott on their agricultural products; and calls upon Israel to desist from its settlement designs and policies aimed against academic institutions with the goal of distorting the historic facts and serving the objectives of occupation, and to desist from its repressive measures against the population of the Syrian Arab Golan;

5. *Calls once again upon* Member States not to recognize any of the legislative or administrative measures and actions referred to above;

6. *Requests* the Secretary-General to bring the present resolution to the attention of all Governments, the competent United Nations organs, the specialized agencies, the regional intergovernmental organizations and international humanitarian organizations and to give it the widest possible publicity, and to report to the Commission on Human Rights at its forty-eighth session;

7. *Decides* to include in the provisional agenda of its forty-eighth session, as a matter of high priority, the item "Question of the violation of human rights in the occupied Arab territories, including Palestine".

28th meeting
15 February 1991

0067

OFFICE DES NATIONS UNIES A GENÈVE

CENTRE POUR LES DROITS DE L'HOMME

UNITED NATIONS OFFICE AT GENEVA

CENTRE FOR HUMAN RIGHTS

Télé́fax: (022) 733 98 79
Télégrammes: UNATIONS, GENÈVE
Télex: 412 962 UNO CH
Téléphone: 734 60 11 731 02 11

Palais des Nations
CH-1211 GENÈVE 10

RÉF. N°: G/SO 234 (16)
(à rappeler dans la réponse)

The Secretary-General of the United Nations presents his compliments to the Minister for Foreign Affairs of the Republic of Korea and has the honour to refer to General Assembly resolutions 45/74 A to G of 11 December 1990. Copies of these resolutions are attached.

The Secretary-General wishes to draw the attention of His Excellency's Government in particular to paragraph 19 of resolution A, paragraph 4 of resolution B and paragraph 5 of resolution C.

In order to carry out the reporting responsibilities entrusted to him under those resolutions, the Secretary-General would be grateful if His Excellency's Government would inform him, through the Under-Secretary-General for Human Rights, United Nations Office at Geneva, CH-1211 Genève 10, by 1 August 1991, of any steps His Excellency's Government has taken or envisages taking concerning the implementation of the relevant provisions of the resolutions.

25 March 1991

0068

UNITED
NATIONS

A

General Assembly

Distr.
GENERAL

A/RES/45/74
28 February 1991

Forty-fifth session
Agenda item 75

RESOLUTIONS ADOPTED BY THE GENERAL ASSEMBLY

[on the report of the Special Political Committee (A/45/823)]

45/74. Report of the Special Committee to Investigate Israeli Practices Affecting the Human Rights of the Palestinian People and Other Arabs of the Occupied Territories

A

The General Assembly,

Guided by the purposes and principles of the Charter of the United Nations and by the principles and provisions of the Universal Declaration of Human Rights, 1/

Aware of the uprising (intifadah) of the Palestinian people since 9 December 1987 against Israeli occupation, which has received significant attention and sympathy from world public opinion,

Deeply concerned at the alarming situation in the Palestinian territory occupied since 1967, including Jerusalem, as well as in the other occupied Arab territories, as a result of the continued occupation by Israel, the occupying Power, and of its persistent policies against the Palestinian people,

Bearing in mind the provisions of the Geneva Convention relative to the Protection of Civilian Persons in Time of War, of 12 August 1949, 2/ as well as of other relevant conventions and regulations,

---

1/ Resolution 217 A (III).

2/ United Nations, Treaty Series, vol. 75, No. 973.

91-06810 3206Z (E) /...

GE.91-15655

Taking into account the need to consider measures for the impartial protection of the Palestinian people under Israeli occupation,

Recalling the relevant resolutions of the Security Council, in particular resolutions 605 (1987) of 22 December 1987, 607 (1988) of 5 January 1988, 608 (1988) of 14 January 1988, 636 (1989) of 6 July 1989, 641 (1989) of 30 August 1989, 672 (1990) of 12 October 1990 and 673 (1990) of 24 October 1990,

Recalling also all its resolutions on the subject, in particular resolutions 32/91 B and C of 13 December 1977, 33/113 C of 18 December 1978, 34/90 A of 12 December 1979, 35/122 C of 11 December 1980, 36/147 C of 16 December 1981, ES-9/1 of 5 February 1982, 37/88 C of 10 December 1982, 38/79 D of 15 December 1983, 39/95 D of 14 December 1984, 40/161 D of 16 December 1985, 41/63 D of 3 December 1986, 42/160 D of 8 December 1987, 43/21 of 3 November 1988, 43/58 A of 6 December 1988, 44/2 of 6 October 1989 and 44/48 A of 8 December 1989,

Recalling further the relevant resolutions adopted by the Commission on Human Rights, in particular its resolutions 1983/1 of 15 February 1983, 3/ 1984/1 of 20 February 1984, 4/ 1985/1 A and B and 1985/2 of 19 February 1985, 5/ 1986/1 A and B and 1986/2 of 20 February 1986, 6/ 1987/1, 1987/2 A and B and 1987/4 of 19 February 1987, 7/ 1988/1 A and B and 1988/2 of 15 February 1988 and 1988/3 of 22 February 1988, 8/ 1989/1 and 1989/2 of 17 February 1989 and 1989/19 of 6 March 1989, 9/ 1990/1, 1990/2 and 1990/3 of 16 February 1990 and 1990/6 of 19 February 1990, 10/

3/ See _Official Records of the Economic and Social Council, 1983, Supplement No. 3_ and corrigendum (E/1983/13 and Corr.1), chap. XXVII, sect. A.

4/ _Ibid_., _1984, Supplement No. 4_ and corrigendum (E/1984/14 and Corr.1), chap. II, sect. A.

5/ _Ibid_., _1985, Supplement No. 2_ (E/1985/22), chap. II, sect. A.

6/ _Ibid_., _1986, Supplement No. 2_ (E/1986/22), chap. II, sect. A.

7/ _Ibid_., _1987, Supplement No. 5_ and corrigenda (E/1987/18 and Corr.1 and 2), chap. II, sect. A.

8/ _Ibid_., _1988, Supplement No. 2_ (E/1988/12), chap. II, sect. A.

9/ _Ibid_., _1989, Supplement No. 2_ (E/1989/20), chap. II, sect. A.

10/ _Ibid_., _1990, Supplement No. 2_ and corrigenda (E/1990/22 and Corr.1 and 2), chap. II, sect. A.

/...

Having considered the reports of the Special Committee to Investigate Israeli Practices Affecting the Human Rights of the Palestinian People and Other Arabs of the Occupied Territories, 11/ which contain, inter alia, self-incriminating public statements made by officials of Israel, the occupying Power,

Having also considered the reports of the Secretary-General of 21 January 1988, 12/ 15 October 1990 13/ and 31 October 1990, 14/

1. Commends the Special Committee to Investigate Israeli Practices Affecting the Human Rights of the Palestinian People and Other Arabs of the Occupied Territories for its efforts in performing the tasks assigned to it by the General Assembly and for its impartiality;

2. Deplores the continued refusal by Israel to allow the Special Committee access to the occupied Palestinian territory, including Jerusalem, and other Arab territories occupied by Israel since 1967;

3. Demands that Israel allow the Special Committee access to the occupied territories;

4. Reaffirms the fact that occupation itself constitutes a grave violation of the human rights of the Palestinian people in the occupied Palestinian territory, including Jerusalem, and other Arab territories occupied by Israel since 1967;

5. Condemns the continued and persistent violation by Israel of the Geneva Convention relative to the Protection of Civilian Persons in Time of War, of 12 August 1949, 2/ and other applicable international instruments, and condemns in particular those violations which the Convention designates as "grave breaches" thereof;

6. Declares once more that Israel's grave breaches of that Convention are war crimes and an affront to humanity;

7. Reaffirms, in accordance with the Convention, that the Israeli military occupation of the Palestinian territory, including Jerusalem, and other Arab territories is of a temporary nature, thus giving no right whatsoever to the occupying Power over the territorial integrity of the occupied territories;

11/ A/45/84, A/45/306 and A/45/576.

12/ S/19443.

13/ A/45/608.

14/ S/21919 and Corr.1.

/...

0071

8. Strongly condemns the following Israeli policies and practices:

(a) Annexation of parts of the occupied Palestinian territory, including Jerusalem;

(b) Imposition of Israeli laws, jurisdiction and administration on the Syrian Arab Golan, which has resulted in the effective annexation of that territory;

(c) Illegal imposition and levy of taxes and dues;

(d) Establishment of new Israeli settlements and expansion of the existing ones on private and public Palestinian and other Arab lands, and transfer of an alien population thereto;

(e) Eviction, deportation, expulsion, displacement and transfer of Palestinians and other Arabs from the occupied territories and denial of their right to return;

(f) Confiscation and expropriation of private and public Palestinian and other Arab property in the occupied territories and all other transactions for the acquisition of land by Israeli authorities, institutions or nationals;

(g) Excavation and transformation of the landscape and the historical, cultural and religious sites, especially at Jerusalem;

(h) Pillaging of archaeological and cultural property;

(i) Destruction and demolition of Palestinian and other Arab houses;

(j) Collective punishment, mass arrests, administrative detention and ill-treatment of Palestinians and other Arabs;

(k) Torture of Palestinians and other Arabs;

(l) Interference with religious freedoms and practices, as well as family rights and customs;

(m) Interference with the system of education and with the social and economic development and health of the Palestinians and other Arabs in the occupied territories;

(n) Interference with the freedom of movement of individuals within the occupied Palestinian territory, including Jerusalem, and other Arab territories occupied by Israel since 1967;

(o) Illegal exploitation of the natural wealth, resources and labour of the occupied territories;

/...

0072

9. Also strongly condemns, in particular, the following Israeli policies and practices:

(a) Implementation of an "iron-fist" policy against the Palestinian people in the occupied Palestinian territory;

(b) Escalation of Israeli brutality since the beginning of the uprising (intifadah) on 9 December 1987;

(c) Ill-treatment and torture of children and minors under detention and/or imprisonment;

(d) Closure of headquarters and offices of trade unions and social organizations and harassment of their leaders, including through expulsion, as well as attacks on hospitals and their personnel;

(e) Interference with the freedom of the press, including censorship, detention or expulsion of journalists, closure and suspension of newspapers and magazines, as well as denial of access to international media;

(f) Killing and wounding of defenceless demonstrators;

(g) Breaking of bones and limbs of thousands of civilians;

(h) House and/or town arrests;

(i) Use of toxic gas, which has resulted, inter alia, in the killing of many Palestinians;

10. Condemns the Israeli repression against and closing of the educational institutions in the occupied Syrian Arab Golan, particularly prohibiting Syrian textbooks and the Syrian educational system, preventing Syrian students from pursuing their higher education in Syrian universities, denying the right of return to Syrian students receiving their higher education in the Syrian Arab Republic, forcing Hebrew on Syrian students, imposing courses that promote hatred, prejudice and religious intolerance, and dismissing teachers, all in clear violation of the Geneva Convention;

11. Strongly condemns the arming of Israeli settlers in the occupied territories to perpetrate and commit acts of violence against Palestinians and other Arabs, causing deaths and injuries;

12. Requests the Security Council to ensure Israel's respect for and compliance with all the provisions of the Geneva Convention relative to the Protection of Civilian Persons in Time of War, of 12 August 1949, in the occupied Palestinian territory, including Jerusalem, and other Arab territories occupied by Israel since 1967, and to initiate measures to halt Israeli policies and practices in those territories;

/...

13. _Urges_ the Security Council to consider the current situation in the Palestinian territory occupied by Israel since 1967, taking into account the recommendations contained in the reports of the Secretary-General, and with a view to securing international protection for the defenceless Palestinian people until the withdrawal of Israel, the occupying Power, from the occupied Palestinian territory;

14. _Reaffirms_ that all measures taken by Israel to change the physical character, demographic composition, institutional structure or legal status of the occupied territories, or any part thereof, including Jerusalem, are null and void, and that Israel's policy of settling parts of its population and new immigrants in those occupied territories constitutes a flagrant violation of the Geneva Convention 2/ and of the relevant resolutions of the United Nations;

15. _Demands_ that Israel desist forthwith from the policies and practices referred to in paragraphs 8, 9, 10 and 11 above;

16. _Calls upon_ Israel, the occupying Power, to allow the reopening of the Roman Catholic Medical Facility Hospice at Jerusalem in order to continue to provide needed health and medical services to the Palestinians in the city;

17. _Also calls upon_ Israel, the occupying Power, to take immediate steps for the return of all displaced Arab and Palestinian inhabitants to their homes or former places of residence in the territories occupied by Israel since 1967, in implementation of Security Council resolution 237 (1967) of 14 June 1967;

18. _Urges_ international organizations, including the specialized agencies, in particular the International Labour Organisation, the United Nations Educational, Scientific and Cultural Organization and the World Health Organization, to continue to examine the educational and health conditions in the occupied Palestinian territory, including Jerusalem, and other Arab territories occupied by Israel since 1967;

19. _Reiterates its call_ upon all States, in particular those States parties to the Geneva Convention, in accordance with article 1 of that Convention, and upon international organizations, including the specialized agencies, not to recognize any changes carried out by Israel, the occupying Power, in the occupied territories and to avoid actions, including those in the field of aid, that might be used by Israel in its pursuit of the policies of annexation and colonization or any of the other policies and practices referred to in the present resolution;

20. _Requests_ the Special Committee, pending early termination of the Israeli occupation, to continue to investigate Israeli policies and practices in the occupied Palestinian territory, including Jerusalem, and other Arab territories occupied by Israel since 1967, to consult, as appropriate, with the International Committee of the Red Cross in order to ensure that the welfare and human rights of the peoples of the occupied territories are safeguarded and to report to the Secretary-General as soon as possible and whenever the need arises thereafter;

/...

21. *Also requests* the Special Committee to submit regularly to the Secretary-General periodic reports on the present situation in the occupied Palestinian territory;

22. *Further requests* the Special Committee to continue to investigate the treatment of prisoners in the occupied Palestinian territory, including Jerusalem, and other Arab territories occupied by Israel since 1967;

23. *Condemns* Israel's refusal to permit persons from the occupied Palestinian territory to appear as witnesses before the Special Committee and to participate in conferences and meetings held outside the occupied Palestinian territory;

24. *Requests* the Secretary-General:

(*a*) To provide all necessary facilities to the Special Committee, including those required for its visits to the occupied territories, so that it may investigate the Israeli policies and practices referred to in the present resolution;

(*b*) To continue to make available such additional staff as may be necessary to assist the Special Committee in the performance of its tasks;

(*c*) To circulate regularly and periodically the reports mentioned in paragraph 21 above to the States Members of the United Nations;

(*d*) To ensure the widest circulation of the reports of the Special Committee and of information regarding its activities and findings, by all means available, through the Department of Public Information of the Secretariat and, where necessary, to reprint those reports of the Special Committee which are no longer available;

(*e*) To report to the General Assembly at its forty-sixth session on the tasks entrusted to him in the present resolution;

25. *Decides* to include in the provisional agenda of its forty-sixth session the item entitled "Report of the Special Committee to Investigate Israeli Practices Affecting the Human Rights of the Palestinian People and Other Arabs of the Occupied Territories".

65th plenary meeting
11 December 1990

B

The General Assembly,

Recalling Security Council resolution 465 (1980) of 1 March 1980, in which, *inter alia*, the Council affirmed that the Geneva Convention relative to the Protection of Civilian Persons in Time of War, of 12 August 1949, 2/ is applicable to the Arab territories occupied by Israel since 1967, including Jerusalem,

/...

<u>Recalling also</u> Security Council resolutions 672 (1990) of 12 October 1990 and 673 (1990) of 24 October 1990,

<u>Recalling further</u> its resolutions 3092 A (XXVIII) of 7 December 1973, 3240 B (XXIX) of 29 November 1974, 3525 B (XXX) of 15 December 1975, 31/106 B of 16 December 1976, 32/91 A of 13 December 1977, 33/113 A of 18 December 1978, 34/90 B of 12 December 1979, 35/122 A of 11 December 1980, 36/147 A of 16 December 1981, 37/88 A of 10 December 1982, 38/79 B of 15 December 1983, 39/95 B of 14 December 1984, 40/161 B of 16 December 1985, 41/63 B of 3 December 1986, 42/160 B of 8 December 1987, 43/58 B of 6 December 1988 and 44/48 B of 8 December 1989,

<u>Taking note</u> of the reports of the Secretary-General of 21 January 1988, 12/ 15 October 1990 15/ and 31 October 1990, 14/

<u>Considering</u> that the promotion of respect for the obligations arising from the Charter of the United Nations and other instruments and rules of international law is among the basic purposes and principles of the United Nations,

<u>Bearing in mind</u> the provisions of the Geneva Convention, 2/

<u>Noting</u> that Israel and the concerned Arab States whose territories have been occupied by Israel since June 1967 are parties to that Convention,

<u>Taking into account</u> that States parties to the Convention undertake, in accordance with article 1 thereof, not only to respect but also to ensure respect for the Convention in all circumstances,

1. <u>Reaffirms</u> that the Geneva Convention relative to the Protection of Civilian Persons in Time of War, of 12 August 1949, is applicable to the occupied Palestinian territory, including Jerusalem, and other Arab territories occupied by Israel since 1967;

2. <u>Condemns once again</u> the failure of Israel, the occupying Power, to acknowledge the applicability of the Convention to the territories it has occupied since 1967, including Jerusalem;

3. <u>Strongly demands</u> that Israel accept the <u>de jure</u> applicability of the Convention and comply with its provisions in the occupied Palestinian territory, including Jerusalem, and other Arab territories occupied by Israel since 1967;

4. <u>Urgently calls upon</u> all States parties to the Convention to exert all efforts in order to ensure respect for and compliance with its provisions in the occupied Palestinian territory, including Jerusalem, and other Arab territories occupied by Israel since 1967;

15/ A/45/609.

/...

5. Requests the Secretary-General to report to the General Assembly at its forty-sixth session on the implementation of the present resolution.

65th plenary meeting
11 December 1990

C

The General Assembly,

Recalling Security Council resolutions 465 (1980) of 1 March 1980, 605 (1987) of 22 December 1987, 672 (1990) of 12 October 1990 and 673 (1990) of 24 October 1990,

Recalling also its resolutions 32/5 of 28 October 1977, 33/113 B of 18 December 1978, 34/90 C of 12 December 1979, 35/122 B of 11 December 1980, 36/147 B of 16 December 1981, 37/88 B of 10 December 1982, 38/79 C of 15 December 1983, 39/95 C of 14 December 1984, 40/161 C of 16 December 1985, 41/63 C of 3 December 1986, 42/160 C of 8 December 1987, 43/58 C of 6 December 1988 and 44/48 C of 8 December 1989,

Expressing grave anxiety and concern at the serious situation prevailing in the occupied Palestinian territory, including Jerusalem, and other Arab territories occupied by Israel since 1967, as a result of the continued Israeli occupation and the measures and actions taken by Israel, the occupying Power, designed to change the legal status, geographical nature and demographic composition of those territories,

Taking note of the reports of the Secretary-General of 21 January 1988, 12/ 15 October 1990 16/ and 31 October 1990, 14/

Confirming that the Geneva Convention relative to the Protection of Civilian Persons in Time of War, of 12 August 1949, 2/ is applicable to all occupied Palestinian territory, including Jerusalem, and other Arab territories occupied by Israel since 1967,

1. Determines that all such measures and actions taken by Israel in the occupied Palestinian territory, including Jerusalem, and other Arab territories occupied by Israel since 1967 are in violation of the relevant provisions of the Geneva Convention relative to the Protection of Civilian Persons in Time of War, of 12 August 1949, constitute a serious obstacle to the efforts to achieve a comprehensive, just and lasting peace in the Middle East and therefore have no legal validity;

16/ A/45/610.

/...

0077

2. Strongly deplores the persistence of Israel in carrying out such measures, in particular the establishment of settlements in the occupied Palestinian territory, including Jerusalem, and other Arab territories occupied by Israel since 1967;

3. Demands that Israel comply strictly with its international obligations in accordance with the principles of international law and the provisions of the Geneva Convention;

4. Demands once more that Israel, the occupying Power, desist forthwith from taking any action that would result in changing the legal status, geographical nature or demographic composition of the occupied Palestinian territory, including Jerusalem, and other Arab territories occupied by Israel since 1967;

5. Urgently calls upon all States parties to the Geneva Convention to respect and to exert all efforts in order to ensure respect for and compliance with its provisions in all occupied Palestinian territory, including Jerusalem, and other Arab territories occupied by Israel since 1967;

6. Requests the Secretary-General to report to the General Assembly at its forty-sixth session on the implementation of the present resolution.

65th plenary meeting
11 December 1990

D

The General Assembly,

Recalling Security Council resolution 605 (1987) of 22 December 1987,

Recalling also its resolutions 38/79 A of 15 December 1983, 39/95 A of 14 December 1984, 40/161 A of 16 December 1985, 41/63 A of 3 December 1986, 42/160 A of 8 December 1987, 43/21 of 3 November 1988, 43/58 D of 6 December 1988, 44/2 of 6 October 1989 and 44/48 D of 8 December 1989,

Taking note of the reports of the Special Committee to Investigate Israeli Practices Affecting the Human Rights of the Palestinian People and Other Arabs of the Occupied Territories, 11/

Taking note also of the reports of the Secretary-General of 21 January 1988, 12/ 15 October 1990 17/ and 31 October 1990, 14/

1. Deplores the arbitrary detention or imprisonment by Israel of thousands of Palestinians as a result of their resistance against occupation in order to attain self-determination;

17/ A/45/611.

/...

0078

2. _Calls upon_ Israel, the occupying Power, to release all Palestinians and other Arabs arbitrarily detained or imprisoned;

3. _Requests_ the Secretary-General to report to the General Assembly as soon as possible but not later than the beginning of its forty-sixth session on the implementation of the present resolution.

65th plenary meeting
11 December 1990

E

The General Assembly,

Recalling Security Council resolutions 605 (1987) of 22 December 1987, 607 (1988) of 5 January 1988, 608 (1988) of 14 January 1988, 636 (1989) of 6 July 1989, 641 (1989) of 30 August 1989, 672 (1990) of 12 October 1990 and 673 (1990) of 24 October 1990,

Taking note of the reports of the Secretary-General of 21 January 1988, 12/ 15 October 1990 18/ and 31 October 1990, 14/

Alarmed by the continuing deportation of Palestinians from the occupied Palestinian territory by the Israeli authorities,

Recalling the Geneva Convention relative to the Protection of Civilian Persons in Time of War, of 12 August 1949, 2/ in particular article 1 and the first paragraph of article 49, which read as follows:

"_Article 1_

"The High Contracting Parties undertake to respect and to ensure respect for the present Convention in all circumstances."

"_Article 49_

"Individual or mass forcible transfers, as well as deportations of protected persons from occupied territory to the territory of the occupying Power or to that of any other country, occupied or not, are prohibited, regardless of their motive ...",

Reaffirming the applicability of the Geneva Convention to the occupied Palestinian territory, including Jerusalem, and other Arab territories occupied by Israel since 1967,

---

18/ A/45/612.

/...

0079

1. Strongly deplores the continuing disregard by Israel, the occupying Power, of the relevant resolutions and decisions of the Security Council and resolutions of the General Assembly;

2. Demands that the Government of Israel, the occupying Power, rescind the illegal measures taken by its authorities in deporting Palestinians and that it facilitate their immediate return;

3. Calls upon Israel, the occupying Power, to cease forthwith the deportation of Palestinians and to abide scrupulously by the provisions of the Geneva Convention relative to the Protection of Civilian Persons in Time of War, of 12 August 1949;

4. Requests the Secretary-General to report to the General Assembly as soon as possible but not later than the beginning of its forty-sixth session on the implementation of the present resolution.

65th plenary meeting
11 December 1990

F

The General Assembly,

Deeply concerned that the Arab territories occupied since 1967 have been under continued Israeli military occupation,

Recalling Security Council resolution 497 (1981) of 17 December 1981,

Recalling also its resolutions 36/226 B of 17 December 1981, ES-9/1 of 5 February 1982, 37/88 E of 10 December 1982, 38/79 F of 15 December 1983, 39/95 F of 14 December 1984, 40/161 F of 16 December 1985, 41/63 F of 3 December 1986, 42/160 F of 8 December 1987, 43/21 cf 3 November 1988, 43/58 F of 6 December 1988, 44/2 of 6 October 1989 and 44/48 F of 8 December 1989,

Having considered the report of the Secretary-General of 15 October 1990, 19/

Recalling its previous resolutions, in particular resolutions 3414 (XXX) of 5 December 1975, 31/61 of 9 December 1976, 32/20 of 25 November 1977, 33/28 and 33/29 of 7 December 1978, 34/70 of 6 December 1979 and 35/122 E of 11 December 1980, in which, inter alia, it called upon Israel to put an end to its occupation of the Arab territories and to withdraw from all those territories,

Reaffirming once more the illegality of Israel's decision of 14 December 1981 to impose its laws, jurisdiction and administration on the Syrian Arab Golan, which has resulted in the effective annexation of that territory,

---

19/ A/45/613.

/...

0080

Reaffirming that the acquisition of territory by force is inadmissible under the Charter of the United Nations and that all territories thus occupied by Israel must be returned,

Recalling the Geneva Convention relative to the Protection of Civilian Persons in Time of War, of 12 August 1949, _2_/

Reaffirming the applicability of that Convention to the occupied Syrian Arab Golan,

Bearing in mind Security Council resolution 237 (1967) of 14 June 1967,

1. _Strongly condemns_ Israel, the occupying Power, for its refusal to comply with the relevant resolutions of the General Assembly and the Security Council, particularly Council resolution 497 (1981), in which the Council, _inter alia_, decided that the Israeli decision to impose its laws, jurisdiction and administration on the occupied Syrian Arab Golan was null and void and without international legal effect and demanded that Israel, the occupying Power, should rescind forthwith its decision;

2. _Condemns_ the persistence of Israel in changing the physical character, demographic composition, institutional structure and legal status of the occupied Syrian Arab Golan;

3. _Determines_ that all legislative and administrative measures and actions taken or to be taken by Israel, the occupying Power, that purport to alter the character and legal status of the Syrian Arab Golan are null and void, constitute a flagrant violation of international law and of the Geneva Convention relative to the Protection of Civilian Persons in Time of War, of 12 August 1949, and have no legal effect;

4. _Strongly condemns_ Israel for its attempts forcibly to impose Israeli citizenship and Israeli identity cards on the Syrian citizens in the occupied Syrian Arab Golan, and calls upon it to desist from its repressive measures against the population of the Syrian Arab Golan;

5. _Deplores_ the violations by Israel of the Geneva Convention;

6. _Calls once again upon_ Member States not to recognize any of the legislative or administrative measures and actions referred to above;

7. _Requests_ the Secretary-General to report to the General Assembly at its forty-sixth session on the implementation of the present resolution.

65th plenary meeting
11 December 1990

/...

G

The General Assembly,

Bearing in mind the Geneva Convention relative to the Protection of Civilian Persons in Time of War, of 12 August 1949, 2/

Deeply concerned at the continued and intensified harassment by Israel, the occupying Power, directed against educational institutions in the occupied Palestinian territory,

Recalling Security Council resolutions 605 (1987) of 22 December 1987, 672 (1990) of 12 October 1990 and 673 (1990) of 24 October 1990,

Recalling also its resolutions 38/79 G of 15 December 1983, 39/95 G of 14 December 1984, 40/161 G of 16 December 1985, 41/63 G of 3 December 1986, 42/160 G of 8 December 1987, 43/21 of 3 November 1988, 43/58 G of 6 December 1988, 44/2 of 6 October 1989 and 44/48 G of 8 December 1989,

Taking note of the reports of the Secretary-General of 21 January 1988, 12/ 15 October 1990 20/ and 31 October 1990, 14/

Taking note also of the relevant decisions adopted by the Executive Board of the United Nations Educational, Scientific and Cultural Organization concerning the educational and cultural situation in the occupied Palestinian territory,

1. Reaffirms the applicability of the Geneva Convention relative to the Protection of Civilian Persons in Time of War, of 12 August 1949, to the occupied Palestinian territory, including Jerusalem, and other Arab territories occupied by Israel since 1967;

2. Condemns Israeli policies and practices against Palestinian students and faculty members in schools, universities and other educational institutions in the occupied Palestinian territory, especially the opening of fire on defenceless students, causing many casualties;

3. Also condemns the systematic Israeli campaign of repression against and closing of universities, schools and other educational and vocational institutions in the occupied Palestinian territory, in large numbers and for prolonged periods, restricting and impeding the academic activities of Palestinian universities by subjecting the selection of courses, textbooks and educational programmes, the admission of students and the appointment of faculty members to the control and supervision of the military occupation authorities, in flagrant contravention of the Geneva Convention;

20/ A/45/614.

/...

0082

4. *Demands* that Israel, the occupying Power, comply with the provisions of that Convention, rescind all actions and measures taken against all educational institutions, ensure the freedom of those institutions and refrain forthwith from hindering the effective operation of the universities, schools and other educational institutions;

5. *Requests* the Secretary-General to report to the General Assembly as soon as possible but not later than the beginning of its forty-sixth session on the implementation of the present resolution.

65th plenary meeting
11 December 1990

OFFICE DES NATIONS UNIES A GENÈVE

CENTRE POUR LES DROITS DE L'HOMME

UNITED NATIONS OFFICE AT GENEVA

CENTRE FOR HUMAN RIGHTS

Téléfax: (022) 733 98 79
Télégrammes: UNATIONS, GENÈVE
Télex: 412 962 UNO CH
Téléphone: 734 60 11 731 02 11

Palais des Nations
CH-1211 GENÈVE 10

RÉF. N°: G/SO 214 (21-2)
(à rappeler dans la réponse)

The Secretary-General of the United Nations presents his compliments to the Minister for Foreign Affairs of the Republic of Korea and has the honour to refer to General Assembly resolution 45/155 of 18 December 1990 and Commission on Human Rights resolution 1991/30 of 5 March 1991, both entitled "World Conference on Human Rights", copies of which are attached.

The attention of His Excellency's Government is drawn to operative paragraph 1 of the General Assembly resolution, in which the Assembly decided to convene at a high level a World Conference on Human Rights in 1993.

The Secretary-General has the honour to notify His Excellency's Government that by operative paragraph 2 of this resolution the Assembly decided to establish a Preparatory Committee for the World Conference on Human Rights, which shall be open to all States Members of the United Nations or members of the specialized agencies, with the participation of observers, in accordance with the established practice of the General Assembly.

The Preparatory Committee will meet from 9 to 13 September 1991, at the United Nations Office in Geneva. If the Economic and Social Council decides to endorse the request of the Commission on Human Rights contained in paragraph 8 of its resolution 1991/30, the Preparatory Committee will meet for 1 additional day, 16 September 1991, with the first day, 9 September 1991, devoted to informal consultations among all Member States of the United Nations in order to prepare for the election of the 5 officers of the Committee.

The attention of His Excellency's Government is also drawn to operative paragraph 10 of the General Assembly resolution, by which the Assembly invites Governments to submit their comments and recommendations on the Conference to the Preparatory Committee through the Secretary-General and to participate actively in the Conference.

The Secretary-General also has the honour, pursuant to the request by the Commission contained in paragraph 14 of its resolution 1991/30, to invite contributions of extra-budgetary resources to meet, inter alia, the costs of participation by representatives of the least developed countries in the preparatory meetings and the Conference itself, in conformity with operative paragraph 7 of General Assembly resolution 45/155.

The Secretary-General would appreciate it if any information or contribution which His Excellency's Government wished to present pursuant to the above-mentioned requests could be sent, if possible, before 1 July 1991, to the Centre for Human Rights, Palais des Nations, 1211 Geneva 10, Switzerland.

29 March 1991

0084

GENERAL ASSEMBLY

Resolution 45/155

World Conference on Human Rights

The General Assembly,

Mindful of the goal of the United Nations to promote and encourage respect for human rights and fundamental freedoms for all without distinction as to race, sex, language or religion, as set out in the Charter of the United Nations and the Universal Declaration of Human Rights, 471/

Recognizing that all human rights and fundamental freedoms are indivisible and interrelated and that the promotion and protection of one category of rights should never exempt or excuse States from the promotion and protection of another,

Bearing in mind that all Member States have pledged themselves to achieve the promotion of universal respect for and observance of human rights and fundamental freedoms in conformity with relevant articles of the Charter,

Noting the progress made by the United Nations towards this goal and the fact that there are areas in which further progress should be made,

Noting also that violations of human rights and fundamental freedoms continue to occur,

Considering that, in view of the progress made, the problems that remain and the new challenges that lie ahead, it would be appropriate to conduct a review of what has been accomplished through the human rights programme and what remains to be done,

Recalling its resolution 44/156 of 15 December 1989, in which it requested the Secretary-General to seek the views of Governments, specialized agencies, non-governmental organizations and United Nations bodies concerned with human rights on the desirability of convening a world conference on human rights for the purpose of dealing at the highest level with the crucial questions facing the United Nations in connection with the promotion and protection of human rights,

Taking note of the report of the Secretary-General containing those views, 472/

Noting the expression of support for the convening of a world conference on human rights from many Governments, specialized agencies and United Nations bodies concerned with human rights and from non-governmental organizations,

Noting also the many views concerning the importance of thorough advance preparation for the success of the conference,

Convinced that the holding of a world conference on human rights could make a significant contribution to the effectiveness of the actions of the United Nations and its Member States in the promotion and protection of human rights,

1. Decides to convene at a high level a World Conference on Human Rights in 1993 with the following objectives:

(a) To review and assess the progress that has been made in the field of human rights since the adoption of the Universal Declaration of Human Rights 473/ and to identify obstacles and ways in which they can be overcome to further progress in this area;

(b) To examine the relation between development and the enjoyment by everyone of economic, social and cultural rights as well as civil and political rights recognizing the importance of creating the conditions whereby everyone may enjoy these rights as set out in the International Covenants on Human Rights; 474/

(c) To examine ways and means to improve implementation of existing human rights standards and instruments;

(d) To evaluate the effectiveness of the methods and mechanisms used by the United Nations in the field of human rights;

(e) To formulate concrete recommendations for improving the effectiveness of United Nations activities and mechanisms in the field of human rights through programmes aimed at promoting, encouraging and monitoring respect for human rights and fundamental freedoms;

(f) To make recommendations for ensuring the necessary financial and other resources for the United Nations activities in the promotion and protection of human rights and fundamental freedoms;

RES/HR/91/2
GE.91-15442

0085

2. _Decides_ to establish a Preparatory Committee for the World Conference on Human Rights, which shall be open to all States Members of the United Nations or members of the specialized agencies, with the participation of observers, in accordance with the established practice of the General Assembly;

3. _Also decides_ that the Preparatory Committee should have the mandate to make proposals for the consideration of the General Assembly regarding the agenda, date, duration, venue of and participation at the Conference, the preparatory meetings and activities at the international, regional and national levels, which should take place in 1992, and on the desirable studies and other documentation;

4. _Further decides_ that the Preparatory Committee, at its first session, shall elect a five-member bureau composed of a chairman, three vice-chairmen and a rapporteur, with due regard to equitable geographic representation;

5. _Instructs_ the Preparatory Committee to deal with the substantive preparation of the Conference in accordance with the goals and objectives of the Conference as set out in paragraph 1 above and bearing in mind the recommendations of the Commission on Human Rights at its forty-seventh session;

6. _Decides_ that the Preparatory Committee shall hold a five-day session at Geneva in September 1991;

7. _Also decides_, in accordance with its resolution 42/211 of 21 December 1987 and without prejudice to the overall level of resources adopted by the General Assembly for the biennium 1990-1991 and the agreed proposed programme budget outline for the biennium 1992-1993, _475_/ that the preparatory process and the Conference itself should be funded through the regular budget of the United Nations, without any implications for the programmes provided for under section 23 of the programme budget, and invites contributions of extrabudgetary resources to meet, _inter alia_, the cost of participation of representatives of least developed countries in the preparatory meetings and the Conference itself;

8. _Requests_ the Commission on Human Rights to make recommendations to the Preparatory Committee on the above issues during those sessions that will take place prior to the Conference;

9. _Encourages_ the Chairman of the Commission on Human Rights, the chairmen or other designated members of human rights expert bodies as well as special and thematic rapporteurs and chairmen or designated members of working groups to take part in the work of the Preparatory Committee;

10. _Requests_ Governments, the specialized agencies, other international organizations, concerned United Nations bodies, regional organizations and non-governmental organizations concerned with human rights to assist the Preparatory Committee and to undertake reviews and submit recommendations on the Conference and its preparation to the Preparatory Committee through the Secretary-General and to participate actively in the Conference;

11. _Requests_ the Secretary-General to submit to the Preparatory Committee a report on the contributions that will be made pursuant to paragraphs 9 and 10 above;

12. _Also requests_ the Secretary-General to appoint a Secretary-General for the Conference from within the Secretariat and to provide the Preparatory Committee with all necessary assistance;

13. _Requests_ the Preparatory Committee to report to the General Assembly at its forty-sixth and forty-seventh sessions on the progress of work of the Committee.

0086

COMMISSION ON HUMAN RIGHTS

Resolution 1991/30

World Conference on Human Rights

The Commission on Human Rights,

Bearing in mind the objectives of the Charter of the United Nations and the Universal Declaration of Human Rights to promote and encourage respect for human rights and fundamental freedoms for all, without distinction as to race, sex or religion,

Guided by the principles governing its mandate as the body responsible, inter alia, for considering all aspects of human rights calling for the active participation of all members of the international community,

Considering that, under the Charter of the United Nations and other international human rights instruments, all States have an obligation to promote international co-operation for the promotion, effective implementation and protection of all human rights and fundamental freedoms and to create the best possible conditions so that everyone may enjoy these rights and freedoms, which are and remain indivisible and interrelated,

Recalling the historic developments which have taken place in international relations since the International Conference on Human Rights held in Tehran in 1968, and in particular the increasing importance that is universally being attached to the promotion, protection and effective realization of all human rights,

Aware that respect for human rights throughout the world calls for further intensification of the efforts of the world community and international bodies and for appropriate initiatives at the international, regional and national levels,

Recalling its decision 1990/110 of 7 March 1990 relating to the World Conference on Human Rights,

Recalling General Assembly resolution 45/155 of 18 December 1990 on the convening in 1993 of a World Conference on Human Rights, in which the General Assembly requested the Commission on Human Rights to make recommendations to the Preparatory Committee for the Conference on issues of concern to it,

1. Welcomes the unanimous decision of the United Nations General Assembly to convene a World Conference on Human Rights at a high level in 1993;

RES/HR/91/5
GE.91-15598

0087

2. Recognizes the importance of the holding of a World Conference on Human Rights for the effectiveness of joint action by the United Nations and Member States to guarantee through international co-operation the promotion, effective implementation, protection and defence of all human rights;

3. Welcomes the appointment of the Under-Secretary-General for Human Rights as Secretary-General of the Conference;

4. Appeals to all States members of the United Nations, Members of the specialized agencies and observers to take part, in accordance with the practice of the General Assembly, in the Preparatory Committee for the World Conference on Human Rights in order to help to create the necessary conditions for the success of the World Conference;

5. Recommends its Chairman, the chairmen or other designated members of human rights bodies including the chairmen of bodies established under international human rights agreements or their designated representatives, as well as special and thematic rapporteurs and the chairmen or designated members of working groups to contribute to the preparations for the World Conference by taking part as appropriate in the work of the Preparatory Committee;

6. Recommends its Chairman to inform the Preparatory Committee of the debate on the World Conference that took place at the forty-seventh session of the Commission, and in particular of the contents of this resolution and its annex, and to make available to it a summary of the discussions;

7. Recommends the Secretary-General of the World Conference on Human Rights to convene the first meeting of the Preparatory Committee in Geneva, from 9 to 13 September 1991;

8. Requests the Secretary-General of the World Conference to arrange for informal consultations among all Member States of the United Nations one working day before the first meeting of the Preparatory Committee in order to prepare for the election of the five officers of the Committee with due regard for equitable geographical representation, in accordance with General Assembly resolution 45/155 of 18 December 1990;

9. Also recommends that the rules of procedure governing the meetings of the Preparatory Committee should in so far as applicable be those of the functional commissions of the Economic and Social Council;

10. Recommends the Preparatory Committee to prepare the draft rules of procedure for the World Conference on the basis of the standard rules of procedure for United Nations conferences;

11. *Recommends* to the Secretary-General to draw up the provisional agenda and the programme of work of the Preparatory Committee on the basis of General Assembly resolution 45/155;

12. *Recommends* the Preparatory Committee, when discussing the agenda for the World Conference, to base its work on the objectives outlined in the first operative paragraph of General Assembly resolution 45/155, the recommendations annexed to this resolution, and any other guidelines that may be adopted by the General Assembly;

13. *Recommends* the Secretary-General of the Conference to make suggestions to the Preparatory Committee as regards background documentation, including reference material on sources of information in the field of human rights;

14. *Requests* the Secretary-General to invite contributions of extra-budgetary resources to meet, *inter alia*, the costs of participation by representatives of the least developed countries in the preparatory meetings and the Conference itself, in conformity with operative paragraph 7 of General Assembly resolution 45/155;

15. *Takes note* with appreciation of the offers made by certain States to host the World Conference;

16. *Requests* the Secretary-General of the United Nations to report to the Commission at its forty-eighth session on progress in the preparations for the World Conference on Human Rights;

17. *Decides* to consider this question at its forty-eighth session, under the agenda item entitled "World Conference on Human Rights".

Annex

Recommendations

1. The Preparatory Committee, being guided by a spirit of consensus, should make suggestions aimed at ensuring the universality, objectivity and non-selectivity of the consideration of human rights issues in United Nations human rights fora;

2. The Preparatory Committee, pursuant to the objectives contained in paragraph 1 of General Assembly resolution 45/155 of 18 December 1990, should keep in view the equal importance and indivisibility of all categories of human rights as well as the interrelationship between human rights, democracy and development in full respect for the Charter of the United Nations, and should take into account relevant resolutions adopted at the forty-seventh session of the Commission on Human Rights;

0089

Annex

Recommendations

1. The Preparatory Committee, being guided by a spirit of consensus, should make suggestions aimed at ensuring the universality, objectivity and non-selectivity of the consideration of human rights issues in United Nations human rights fora;

2. The Preparatory Committee, pursuant to the objectives contained in paragraph 1 of General Assembly resolution 45/155 of 18 December 1990, should keep in view the equal importance and indivisibility of all categories of human rights as well as the interrelationship between human rights, democracy and development in full respect for the Charter of the United Nations, and should take into account relevant resolutions adopted at the forty-seventh session of the Commission on Human Rights;

3. The Preparatory Committee should encourage, by all appropriate means, all States which have not done so, to become parties to international human rights instruments and, in particular, the International Covenants on Human Rights;

4. The Preparatory Committee should consider how the World Conference and its preparatory process can work towards improving implementation of existing human rights standards and instruments, evaluating and formulating concrete recommendations aimed at improving methods and mechanisms used by the United Nations in the field of human rights and ways to minimize duplication wherever possible;

5. The Preparatory Committee should consider the results and further prospects of the World Public Information Campaign for Human Rights;

6. The Preparatory Committee should examine ways and means of evaluating the role of advisory services stressing the need to strengthen the United Nations system of advisory services and technical assistance and emphasizing that these services are based on a co-operative approach aimed at strengthening the respect for human rights and at overcoming obstacles that impede the full enjoyment of human rights. The Preparatory Committee should also recommend ways and means to encourage States to avail themselves of these services;

7. The Preparatory Committee should consider ways and means of promoting a universal culture of human rights by strengthening co-operation through regional meetings and activities and the encouragement of regional institutions, taking into account conditions specific to different regions, as well as by increasing the impact and presence of the United Nations system, bodies and mechanisms in the field of human rights throughout the world;

0090

8. In order to take into account views in different regions regarding the promotion and protection of human rights, including the implementation of international human rights instruments, the Preparatory Committee should promote and consider means of financing regional meetings and activities, and should also encourage various activities at the national level;

9. The Preparatory Committee should examine ways and means by which the World Conference on Human Rights could encourage the establishment or strengthening of governmental and non-governmental institutions at the national level aiming at the promotion of human rights;

10. The Preparatory Committee should make recommendations to the World Conference regarding further possibilities of improving the implementation of applicable international law through national legislation;

11. The Preparatory Committee should examine ways and means for strengthening the Centre for Human Rights including, *inter alia*, increasing financial support and full application of article 101 (3) of the Charter of the United Nations as well as of Commission on Human Rights resolution 1989/54 of 7 March 1989.

~~0091~~
0090-1

OFFICE DES NATIONS UNIES A GENÈVE

CENTRE POUR LES DROITS DE L'HOMME

UNITED NATIONS OFFICE AT GENEVA

CENTRE FOR HUMAN RIGHTS

Téléfax: (022) 733 98 79
Télégrammes: UNATIONS, GENÈVE
Télex: 412 962 UNO CH
Téléphone: 734 60 11 731 02 11

Palais des Nations
CH-1211 GENÈVE 10

RÉF. N°: G/SO 214 (3-3-16)
(à rappeler dans la réponse)

The Secretary-General of the United Nations presents his compliments to the Minister for Foreign Affairs of the Republic of Korea and has the honour to refer to resolution 1991/43 entitled "Right to a fair trial", adopted by the Commission on Human Rights on 5 March 1991. A copy of the resolution is attached.

The particular attention of His Excellency's Government is drawn to paragraphs 1, 3 and 4 of this resolution.

After having endorsed the decision of the Sub-Commission to entrust Mr. Stanislav Chernichenko and Mr. William Treat with the preparation of a study entitled "The right to a fair trial: current recognition and measures necessary for its strengthening" (paragraph 1), the Commission requested the two Special Rapporteurs to draft a questionnaire on the right to a fair trial (paragraph 3).

In paragraph 4, the Secretary-General was requested to transmit the questionnaire with the brief report to, inter alia, Governments for their response and comments, and to transmit the responses to the Special Rapporteurs for consideration in connection with their study.

In accordance with this request, the Secretary-General has the honour to transmit herewith the questionnaire as well as a copy of the brief report on the right to a fair trial (E/CN.4/Sub.2/1990/34) prepared by the two Special Rapporteurs.

The Secretary-General would appreciate it if any response and comments that His Excellency's Government may wish to provide in accordance with paragraph 4 of the above-mentioned resolution, could be forwarded to the Under-Secretary-General for Human Rights, United Nations Office at Geneva, CH-1211 Geneva 10, if possible by 31 May 1991, in order to enable the Special Rapporteurs to take that information into account in their preliminary report on the subject which will be submitted to the forty-third session of the Sub-Commission scheduled for August 1991.

19 April 1991

0091

1991/43. Right to a fair trial

The Commission on Human Rights,

Guided by the Universal Declaration of Human Rights which affirms the right of every individual to a fair and public hearing by an independent and impartial tribunal,

Bearing in mind the International Covenant on Civil and Political Rights which reaffirms the equality of all persons before courts and tribunals and the right of everyone to a fair and public hearing,

Noting the fair trial provisions in the African Charter on Human and Peoples' Rights, the American Convention on Human Rights, the European Convention on Human Rights, the Geneva Conventions Relating to the Protection of Victims of International Armed Conflict, and the Convention against Torture and Other Cruel, Inhuman or Degrading Treatment or Punishment,

Recalling its decision 1990/108 of 7 March 1990, welcoming the appointment of Mr. Stanislav Chernichenko and Mr. William Treat to prepare a report on the right to a fair trial,

Aware of General Assembly resolution 41/120 of 4 December 1986 regarding the development of international standards in the field of human rights,

Considering that the availability of a fair trial is essential for the protection of human rights and fundamental freedoms as well as maintaining respect for the inherent dignity of the human person,

Having examined the work done by the Sub-Commission on Prevention of Discrimination and Protection of Minorities relating to the right to a fair trial,

Having examined also the brief report on the right to a fair trial prepared by Mr. Chernichenko and Mr. Treat in accordance with Sub-Commission resolution 1989/27 of 1 September 1989 (E/CN.4/Sub.2/1990/34),

Welcoming the recommendations made by Mr. Chernichenko and Mr. Treat (ibid., paras. 146-153) and endorsed by the Sub-Commission in its resolution 1990/18,

1. Endorses the decision of the Sub-Commission to entrust Mr. Stanislav Chernichenko and Mr. William Treat with the preparation of a study entitled "The right to a fair trial: current recognition and measures necessary for its strengthening";

2. Requests the Secretary-General to provide the two Special Rapporteurs with all the assistance they may require;

RES/HR/91/6
GE.91-15706

3. Requests the two Special Rapporteurs to draft a questionnaire on the right to a fair trial;

4. Requests the Secretary-General to transmit the questionnaire with the brief report to Governments, the specialized agencies and non-governmental organizations in consultative status with the Economic and Social Council for their response and comments, and to transmit the responses to the Special Rapporteurs for consideration in connection with their study;

Recommends the following draft resolution to the Economic and Social Council for adoption:

"The Economic and Social Council,

Recalling Commission on Human Rights decisions 1990/108 of 7 March 1990 welcoming the appointment of the two Special Rapporteurs on the right to a fair trial, and Commission resolution 1991/43 of 5 March 1991,

Recalling also General Assembly resolution 41/120 of 4 December 1986 regarding the development of international standards in the field of human rights,

Taking into account the brief report on the right to a fair trial prepared by Mr. Stanislav Chernichenko and Mr. William Treat (E/CN.4/Sub.2/1990/34),

1. Endorses Sub-Commission on Prevention of Discrimination and Protection of Minorities resolution 1990/18 of 30 August 1990, by which the Sub-Commission decided to entrust Mr. Stanislav Chernichenko and Mr. William Treat with the preparation of a study entitled 'The right to a fair trial: current recognition and measures necessary for its strengthening' and Commission on Human Rights resolution 1991/43 of 5 March 1991;

2. Requests the Secretary-General to provide the two Special Rapporteurs with all the necessary assistance to carry out the above-mentioned study;

3. Requests the two Special Rapporteurs to draft a questionnaire on the right to a fair trial;

4. Requests the Secretary-General to transmit the questionnaire with the working paper to Governments, the specialized agencies and non-governmental organizations in consultative status with the Economic

0093

and Social Council for their response and comments and requests the Secretary-General to transmit the responses to the Special Rapporteurs for consideration in connection with their study;

5. Requests the Special Rapporteurs to produce a preliminary report based upon their study, the responses to the questionnaire and ways to formulate the basic guarantees necessary for a fair trial into an international standard like a model code, and to submit it to the Sub-Commission for consideration at its forty-third session and for comments to the Commission on Human Rights at its forty-eighth session."

52nd meeting
5 March 1991

0094

Questionnaire on the Right to a Fair Trial

Part I

A. The rapporteurs would be pleased to receive any comments you may wish to make about the brief report contained in E/CN.4/Sub.2/1990/34.

B. Civil Procedure

The rapporteurs would be pleased to receive information about codes, rules, regulations, and/or practices which have been established governing procedures in civil disputes, including: Procedures governing a person's access to the judicial system, the procurement and use of evidence, trial procedures, examination of witnesses, and appeal or other review of trial court decisions.

C. Criminal Procedure

The rapporteurs would be pleased to receive information about codes, rules, regulations, and/or practices which have been established governing criminal procedure, including: Judicial protection from arbitrary arrest; the procurement of, access to, and presentation of evidence; trial procedures; appeal or other review; and post-conviction relief.

D. Administrative Procedure

The rapporteurs would be pleased to receive information about codes, rules, regulations, and/or practices which have been established governing administrative procedures -- in particular those procedures that may have consequences similar to criminal procedures.

D. Military Court Procedure

The rapporteurs would be pleased to receive information about codes, rules, regulations and/or practices which have been established governing military court procedures (including procedures that may affect the rights of civilians) in regard to the issues mentioned above under item C above.

E. Emergency Court Procedures

The rapporteurs would be pleased to receive information about codes, rules, regulations and/or practices which have been established governing emergency court procedures that may have consequences similar to criminal procedures in regard to the issues mentioned in under item C above. Please explain how these emergency court procedures differ from ordinary procedures.

If such codes, rules, or regulations with regard to procedures in civil, criminal, administrative, military, or emergency proceedings have been established, please send a copy of each to the Centre for Human Rights, United Nations, Palais des Nations, CH-1211 Geneva 10, Switzerland. If possible, please send a copy in English, French, Spanish, or one of the other official languages of the United Nations.

M/HR/91/31
GE.91-15695

Part II

Your answers to each of the questions below would be appreciated as to both codes, rules, and regulations as well as actual practices. If it is too difficult or time-consuming to answer all the questions, please give the greatest attention to answering each of the subject heading questions (in **bold** print and preceded by numbers).

A. Treatment during detention prior to and during trial

1. How are detained persons protected from torture and other cruel, inhuman, or degrading treatment?

2. What protection exists for the accused who refuses to confess or testify against himself or herself?

a. Does an accused have the right to remain silent?

b. Can an accused's silence be used against him or her at trial?

c. Can a confession be used against an accused that was obtained without the benefit of counsel or knowledge of the right to counsel?

d. What protections does an accused have from a coerced or otherwise unlawfully obtained confession being used against him or her at trial?

e. Must an accused know the consequences of the confession, such as the potential sentence, before a lawful confession may be taken?

f. If a confession was made as the result of an agreement with the prosecutor, how does an accused enforce the agreement? Can an accused withdraw the confession if the agreement is not fulfilled?

3. How are accused persons in detention treated differently from convicted prisoners?

a. Are accused persons segregated from convicted prisoners?

B. Notice

1. How long can a person be detained without being charged for a criminal offence or without having his case submitted to a court?

2. How is an accused person guaranteed prompt, detailed notice of the charge(s) against him or her?

a. What provisions are made to ensure that the accused is given notice in a language that he or she can understand?

3. How is the accused guaranteed adequate time and facilities to prepare his or her defence?

b. How long before trial does the defence counsel have to prepare for trial?

c. What access does the accused have to the evidence prepared for use against him or her, such as the names of witnesses?

d. What protection does the accused have from surprise evidence being introduced at trial?

C. Counsel

1. Does the accused have access to counsel in preparing his or her defence?

a. If so, is the accused informed that he or she has the right to counsel?

b. What guarantees assure the accused adequate time for consultation?

c. What guarantees does the accused have in exercising his or her free will in choosing counsel?

d. What procedures are established to ensure that a detained person is able to contact counsel?

2. What arrangements are made for accused persons who cannot afford counsel to receive counsel without cost?

a. What remuneration does appointed counsel receive? How does that amount compare with what counsel would normally expect to receive from a paying client?

b. Are there certain kinds of crimes for which counsel is provided without cost to defendants who cannot afford counsel?

c. Under what circumstances is counsel appointed without cost through the appeals and post-conviction processes?

3. What protections does the accused have ensuring the competence of counsel, adequacy of representation, and the adequacy of facilities for the preparation of the defence at all stages of the investigation, trial, appeal, and post-conviction processes?

4. Does a person's right to counsel extend through the post-conviction level, such as habeas corpus or amparo?

5. How is the confidentiality of communication between the accused and counsel guaranteed?

D. Hearing

1. How is the accused's right to be tried without undue delay guaranteed?

a. Does that protection apply at all stages of the trial process, including the time by which a trial is commenced, completed, decided, and appealed?

b. If possible, please provide statistics for the average amount of time that elapses between:

1. Arrest and formal charging with an offence.

2. Charging with an offence and beginning of the trial.

3. Beginning of the trial and completion of the trial or sentence.

4. Initiation of appeal and the disposition of appeal.

c. What differences are characterized by the delays which occur in trials relating to different sorts of criminal charges?

d. Is there a difference in the amount of time it takes to initiate a trial for a detained defendant and a defendant not in custody?

2. What laws or rules are there mandating that criminal and civil trials be conducted in public?

a. When a trial is conducted in public, what guarantees are there allowing the press to witness and report on the proceedings by television, radio, photographs, and/or print media?

b. How, and under what circumstances, is public or press access to a trial limited? Please describe specific examples of trials which were not held in public during the last two years.

3. What assurances does the accused have that the trial will be conducted in the same geographic locality where the conduct at issue occurred?

a. Under what circumstances might a trial be transferred to another locality?

b. May the court transfer the trial to another locality if it appears that accused would be unable to receive a fair trial due to local bias?

4. Under what circumstances, if any, is a trial in absentia pursued?

a. What protections does the accused have to guarantee that he or she knows all the evidence considered at a trial in absentia?

b. How is a person's right to counsel applied to hearings <u>in absentia</u>?

c. Under what circumstances, if any, is it possible to have a trial of a person who is not living?

5. What protections are afforded the mentally incompetent at criminal trials?

a. How is a person determined to be mentally incompetent for the purposes of trial?

6. How is an accused person's entitlement to the free assistance of an interpreter guaranteed, if he or she does not understand the language of the court?

a. Does the interpreter provide interpretation of the entire proceeding including argument of counsel, all testimony, or only testimony given by the accused?

7. What protections exist to guarantee an accused the right to obtain the attendance and examination of witnesses on the accused's behalf under the same conditions as witnesses against the accused?

8. What guarantees protect the accused's right to examine adverse witnesses?

9. How is the accused's right to the presumption of innocence guaranteed?

a. What protections exist to prevent public authorities from manipulating the media or judicial system so as to prejudge the outcome of a trial?

b. What guarantees does the accused have to a judgment based on the evidence adduced at the hearing?

c. What is the degree of proof required to find a person responsible for criminal conduct?

d. What is the degree of proof required for determining rights and obligations in a civil suit?

10. How is a party to a civil suit guaranteed the opportunity to obtain and examine relevant witnesses at trial?

11. Can evidence be considered against an accused if the evidence is obtained pursuant to an arbitrary or unlawful interference with the accused's privacy, family, home or correspondence?

E. <u>Composition of the Court</u>

1. What protection exists to guarantee the independence and impartiality of judges?[1]

2. In criminal and civil cases, under what circumstances may a person receive a trial by judge(s), jury, and/or by lay assessor(s)?

a. Does a party or accused person have a right to trial by jury or lay assessor?

b. What characteristics must a person have to qualify as a juror or lay assessor?

c. Are there any characteristics that disqualify or excuse a person from being a juror or lay assessor, such as active military service, profession, gender, past criminal record, alien status, membership in a particular political or ethnic group, etc.?

d. How may one of the parties disqualify a judge, juror, or lay assessor who may be biased?

e. Under what circumstances is a trial by jury or lay assessor forbidden? Are there specialized courts that do not permit trials by jury or lay assessor?

F. Decision, Sentencing, and Punishment

1. Under what circumstances must the decision-maker issue a statement of reasons explaining the decision in a criminal case?

2. Under what circumstances must the decision-maker issue a statement of reasons explaining the decision in a civil case?

3. What rights does a person have to avoid being tried or punished again for an offence which he or she has already been lawfully convicted or acquitted?

4. What protection does the accused have from being convicted under ex post facto laws?

a. Where the punishment for an offence has changed, what protections exist to ensure that the accused will not receive a greater punishment than that which applied at the time of the occurrence of the crime, or will receive the lesser punishment if the punishment has since been decreased.

5. What protection is provided against imprisonment for failure to fulfill a contractual obligation?

6. What assurances are given that the judgments rendered in criminal

[1] As to this question respondents are referred to Singhvi, "The administration of justice and the human rights of detainees: study on the independence and impartiality of the judiciary, jurors and assessors and the independence of lawyers," (E/CN.4/Sub.2/1985/18 and Add.1-6, 1985).

cases and civil suits be made public?

7. **Under what conditions are judgments not made public?**

8. **Under what circumstances, if any, is collective punishment permitted?**

9. **Has the country abolished the death penalty? If not:**

a. For what kinds of crimes may the death penalty be imposed?

b. How and when is the person informed of the death sentence?

c. How does a person who is sentenced to death seek pardon or commutation of the sentence?

d. What is the minimum age, if any, below which a person may not be executed?

i. May juveniles (under the age of 18 at the time of the offence) be executed?

a. What is the maximum age, if any, over which a person may not be executed?

10. **What protection does a convicted person have from punishment that is cruel, degrading, or that involves torture or mutilation?**

G. Appeal or Other Review in Higher Courts

1. **How does a person convicted of a crime have his or her sentence reviewed by a higher tribunal?**

a. What limits, if any, are there to the convicted person's right to have the sentence reviewed by a higher tribunal?

b. What kinds of crimes, if any, may not be reviewed by a higher tribunal because they are considered too trivial?

c. May the appeal relate to issues of fact, law, or both?

2. **How does a person appeal a judgment from a civil suit?**

a. What limits, if any, are there to a party's ability to obtain an appeal before a higher tribunal?

b. May the appeal relate to issues of fact, law, or both?

3. **In criminal cases and civil suits, at what point in the trial may a party appeal an intermediate decision rendered prior to the final judgment?**

a. Under what circumstances must a party wait until a final

judgment before an appeal may be made?

H. Pardon

1. What assurances does every convicted person have to the opportunity to seek pardon or commutation of his or her sentence?

I. Other Remedies

1. What judicial or other legal remedies does a person have for a violation of fundamental rights?

2. When a person has been convicted and punished of an offence and that conviction is subsequently reversed, or the person is pardoned due to new evidence showing that there was a miscarriage of justice, what recourse does the convicted person have to receive compensation for the injury suffered?

3. What remedies are available for a person to vindicate a violation of a fundamental right guaranteed by the constitution or under law?

a. Are remedies similar to or including habeas corpus or amparo available? If so, please specify what provisions of law apply, and include a copy of those provisions.

b. If it is determined that a person's rights have been violated, what compensation is made for damages?

c. Are there certain violations of fundamental rights that may not be raised at trial, after trial, on appeal, by habeas corpus, by amparo, pursuant to other post-conviction procedure, or civil suit?

J. Procedures for Juveniles

1. What special procedures exist for juvenile offenders?

a. How do these special procedures take account of the juvenile offender's age?

b. What special procedures are there for the speedy adjudication of cases against juveniles?

2. What special procedures, if any, apply to juveniles in civil proceedings?

3. What protections does a juvenile offender have from the imposition of corporal punishment?

4. How are accused juveniles treated differently from accused adults?

a. Are accused juveniles in detention segregated from accused adults?

5. Are accused juveniles in detention segregated from juveniles who have been found responsible for criminal conduct?

K. Military Courts

1. How do procedures in military courts differ from the procedures in ordinary criminal courts?

2. To what extent are the procedural protections identified above provided in military courts?

3. Under what circumstances may military courts try civilians for offences or otherwise affect the rights of civilians?

L. Emergency Courts

1. Under what circumstances may emergency court procedures be established or applied?

2. How do procedures in emergency courts differ from the procedures in ordinary criminal courts?

3. To what extent are the procedural protections identified above provided in emergency courts?

M. Administrative Courts

1. How do procedures in administrative proceedings differ from the procedures in ordinary criminal or civil courts?

2. To what extent are parties to administrative proceedings given notice of information that may adversely affect them; a fair and public hearing by a competent, independent, and impartial tribunal established by law; an opportunity to present information supporting their claim or defence; a decision based upon the information adduced at the hearing; and a decision which is made public?

3. To what extent are the other procedural protections identified above in subparts A - J, insofar as relevant, provided in administrative proceedings?

N. Other Questions

1. The rapporteurs would be pleased to receive information about the principal books and articles relating to the right to a fair trial in your country.

2. The rapporteurs would be pleased to receive information about any academic or other views about the brief report contained in E/CN.4/Sub.2/1990/34.

3. The rapporteurs would be pleased to receive any other information you may wish to provide.

5/14 위원회

OFFICE DES NATIONS UNIES A GENÈVE

CENTRE POUR LES DROITS DE L'HOMME

UNITED NATIONS OFFICE AT GENEVA

CENTRE FOR HUMAN RIGHTS

Téléfax: (022) 733 98 79
Télégrammes: UNATIONS, GENÈVE
Télex: 412 962 UNO CH
Téléphone: 734 60 11 731 02 11

Palais des Nations
CH-1211 GENÈVE 10

RÉF. N°: G/SO 219/1
(à rappeler dans la réponse)

The Secretary-General of the United Nations presents his compliments to the Minister for Foreign Affairs of the Republic of Korea and has the honour to draw the attention of His Excellency's Government to Commission on Human Rights resolution 1991/41 of 5 March 1991, entitled "Question of enforced or involuntary disappearances". A copy of the resolution is enclosed.

In paragraph 19 of the resolution, the Commission decided to establish an open-ended inter-sessional working group of the Commission on Human Rights to consider the draft Declaration on enforced or involuntary disappearance submitted by the Sub-Commission, with a view to its adoption by the Commission at its forty-eighth session. Further, it invited, inter alia, all Governments to participate in the activities of the working group. It also requested the working group to meet for a period of two weeks before the forty-eighth session of the Commission.

In paragraph 22 of the resolution, the Secretary-General is requested to invite comments, for consideration by the working group, inter alia, from Governments on the draft declaration. The draft adopted by the Sub-Commission is attached (E/CN.4/Sub.2/1990/32, Annex).

The Secretary-General would be grateful if His Excellency's Government could forward to the Centre for Human Rights, United Nations Office at Geneva, CH-1211 Genève 10, by 1 August 1991, any comments it may wish to submit in accordance with paragraph 22 of Commission resolution 1991/41, including any suggestions for the revision and simplification of the draft as submitted by the Sub-Commission.

24 April 1991

0104

COMMISSION ON HUMAN RIGHTS

Resolution

1991/41. Question of enforced or involuntary disappearances

The Commission on Human Rights,

Bearing in mind General Assembly resolution 33/173 of 20 December 1978, in which the Assembly requested the Commission on Human Rights to consider the question of disappeared persons with a view to making appropriate recommendations, and all other United Nations resolutions concerning missing or disappeared persons,

Convinced of the need to continue the implementation of the provisions of General Assembly resolution 33/173 and of the other United Nations resolutions on the question of enforced or involuntary disappearances,

Recalling its resolution 20 (XXXVI) of 29 February 1980, by which it decided to establish a working group consisting of five of its members, to serve as experts in their individual capacity, to examine questions relevant to enforced or involuntary disappearances, and its resolutions 1987/27 of 10 March 1987, 1988/34 of 8 March 1988, 1989/27 of 6 March 1989 and 1990/30 of 2 March 1990,

Recalling also its decision 1986/106 of 13 March 1986, by which it invited the Sub-Commission on Prevention of Discrimination and Protection of Minorities to reconsider the question of a declaration against unacknowledged detention of persons,

Recalling further its resolution 1990/76 on co-operation with representatives of United Nations human rights bodies,

Recalling General Assembly resolution 45/165 of 18 December 1990,

Profoundly concerned at the fact that the practice of enforced or involuntary disappearances is continuing in various regions of the world,

Concerned also at the reports concerning harassment of witnesses of disappearances or relatives of disappeared persons,

Having considered the report of the Working Group (E/CN.4/1991/20),

1. Expresses its appreciation to the Working Group on Enforced or Involuntary Disappearances for the way in which it has done its work, and thanks the Group for submitting to the Commission at its forty-seventh session a report in accordance with its resolution 1990/30;

2. Takes note of the report of the Working Group, and thanks it for continuing to improve its methods of work and for recalling the humanitarian spirit underlying its mandate;

3. Requests the Working Group to report on its work to the Commission at its forty-eighth session and reminds the Group of the obligation to discharge its mandate in a discreet and conscientious manner;

RES/HR/91/7
GE.91-15711

0105

4. *Further requests* the Working Group, in its efforts to help eliminate the practice of enforced or involuntary disappearances, to present to the Commission all appropriate information it deems necessary and all concrete suggestions and recommendations regarding the fulfilment of its task;

5. *Reminds* the Working Group of the need to observe, in its humanitarian task, United Nations standards and practices regarding the receipt of communications, their consideration, their evaluation, their transmittal to Governments and the consideration of government replies;

6. *Notes with concern* that some Governments have never provided substantive replies concerning disappearances alleged to have occurred in their country;

7. *Deplores* the fact that, as the Working Group points out in its report, some Governments have not acted on the recommendations contained in the Group's reports concerning them or replied to the Group's requests for information on those matters;

8. *Urges* the Governments concerned, particularly those which have not yet responded to communications transmitted to them by the Working Group, to co-operate with and assist the Group so that it may carry out its mandate effectively, and in particular to answer expeditiously requests for information addressed to them by the Group;

9. *Also urges* the Governments concerned to intensify their co-operation with the Working Group in regard to any measure taken in pursuance of recommendations addressed to them by the Group;

10. *Once again urges* the Governments concerned to take steps to protect the families of disappeared persons against any intimidation or ill-treatment to which they might be subjected;

11. *Encourages* the Governments concerned to give serious consideration to inviting the Working Group to visit their country, so as to enable the Group to fulfil its mandate even more effectively;

12. *Urges* Governments to take steps to ensure that, when a state of emergency is introduced, the protection of human rights is guaranteed, particularly as regards the prevention of enforced or involuntary disappearances;

13. *Reminds* Governments of the need to ensure that their competent authorities conduct prompt and impartial inquiries when there is reason to believe that an enforced or involuntary disappearance has occurred in a territory under their jurisdiction;

14. Expresses its profound thanks to the Governments which have co-operated with the Working Group and responded to its requests for information;

15. Also expresses its profound thanks to the Governments which have invited the Working Group to visit their country, asks them to give all necessary attention to its recommendations and invites them to inform the Group of any action they take on the recommendations;

16. Requests the Secretary-General to ensure that the Working Group receives all necessary assistance, in particular the staff and resources it requires to perform its functions, especially in carrying out missions or holding sessions in countries which would be prepared to receive it;

17. Expresses its satisfaction to the Sub-Commission's Working Group on Detention, which has completed preparation of the draft Declaration on enforced or involuntary disappearance;

18. Expresses its thanks to the Sub-Commission, which has finalized the draft and is transmitting it to the Commission;

19. Decides to establish an open-ended inter-sessional working group of the Commission on Human Rights to consider the draft Declaration submitted by the Sub-Commission, with a view to its adoption by the Commission at its forty-eighth session;

20. Invites all Governments, the intergovernmental agencies and the non-governmental organizations to participate in the activities of the working group;

21. Requests the Working Group to meet for a period of two weeks before the forty-eighth session of the Commission on Human Rights;

22. Requests the Secretary-General to invite comments, for consideration by the Working Group, from Governments, intergovernmental agencies and non-governmental organizations on the draft Declaration and to circulate these comments to Governments in advance of the meeting of the Working Group;

23. Requests the Secretary-General to extend all facilities to the Working Group for its meeting prior to the Commission's forty-eighth session;

24. Recommends the following draft resolution to the Economic and Social Council for adoption:

0107

"<u>The Economic and Social Council</u>,

<u>Recalling</u> Commission on Human Rights resolution 1991/41 of 5 March 1991,

1. <u>Authorizes</u> an open-ended working group of the Commission on Human Rights to meet for a period of two weeks prior to the forty-eighth session of the Commission to consider the draft Declaration on the protection of all persons from enforced or involuntary disappearance, submitted by the Sub-Commission on Prevention of Discrimination and Protection of Minorities (see E/CN.4/Sub.2/1990/32, annex), with a view to its adoption by the Commission at its forty-eighth session;

2. <u>Requests</u> the Secretary-General to extend all facilities to the Working Group for its meeting prior to the Commission at its forty-eighth session."

UNITED
NATIONS

Economic and Social Council

Distr.
GENERAL

E/CN.4/Sub.2/1990/32
29 August 1990

ENGLISH
Original: ENGLISH/FRENCH/SPANISH

COMMISSION ON HUMAN RIGHTS
Sub-Commission on Prevention of Discrimination and Protection of Minorities
Forty-second session
Agenda item 10

THE ADMINISTRATION OF JUSTICE AND THE HUMAN RIGHTS OF DETAINEES

QUESTION OF HUMAN RIGHTS OF PERSONS SUBJECTED TO ANY FORM OF DETENTION OR IMPRISONMENT

Report of the Working Group on Detention

Chairman: Mr. Louis Joinet

Rapporteur: Mr. Ribot Hatano

CONTENTS

GE.90-13197/2326B

0109

CONTENTS (continued)

0110

INTRODUCTION

1. By resolution 7 (XXVII) of 20 August 1974, the Sub-Commission on Prevention of Discrimination and Protection of Minorities decided to review every year the situation concerning the rights of persons subjected to any form of detention or imprisonment. At its forty-second session, the Sub-Commission decided to continue the practice of establishing a sessional Working Group on Detention. The existing regional groups nominated the following experts as members of the Working Group, and they were duly appointed by the Sub-Commission at its 2nd meeting, held on 7 August 1990: Mr. El Hadji Guissé (Africa), Mr. Ribot Hatano (Asia), Mr. Louis Joinet (Western Europe and other States), Mr. Eduardo Suescún Monroy (Latin America) and Mr. Danilo Türk (Eastern Europe).

2. The Working Group met on 13, 15, 17, 22 and 24 August 1990. The report of the Working Group was adopted unanimously at its 5th meeting on 24 August.

3. At the first meeting, the outgoing Chairman, Mr. Miguel Alfonso Martínez, suggested that, in accordance with its established practice, the Working Group elect its outgoing Rapporteur Chairman of its present session. The Working Group accordingly elected Mr. Louis Joinet Chairman. On a proposal by Mr. Eduardo Suescún Monroy, the Working Group elected Mr. Ribot Hatano Rapporteur.

4. The following members of the Sub-Commission, who are not members of the Working Group, also took part in the discussions: Mr. Miguel Alfonso Martínez (1st, 2nd, 3rd and 4th meetings), Mrs. Mary Concepción Bautista (4th meeting), Mr. Stanislav Chernichenko (5th meeting), Mr. Leandro Despouy (1st meeting), Mr. Cornelis Flinterman (alternate, 1st, 2nd, 3rd and 5th meetings), Mr. Waleed Sadi (alternate, 1st meeting), Mr. William W. Treat (4th and 5th meetings) and Mr. Yozo Yokota (3rd and 5th meetings).

5. The observer for the Government of the Netherlands also addressed the Group (4th meeting).

6. Statements were made by representatives of the following non-governmental organizations in consultative status with the Economic and Social Council: Amnesty International (3rd and 4th meetings), Andean Commission of Jurists (3rd meeting), American Association of Jurists (1st and 2nd meetings), International Commission of Jurists (1st, 3rd and 5th meetings), Defence for Children International (3rd and 4th meetings), Latin American Federation of Organizations of Relatives of Missing Detainees (1st and 3rd meetings).

7. Upon requests by the Chairman and Mr. Eduardo Suescún Monroy, the secretariat made statements at the 3rd meeting concerning existing international norms relating to the treatment of offenders and detained persons in jails, detention centres and other institutions, and concerning the documents and draft norms which will be presented at the 8th Congress on the Administration of Justice in Havana (27 August - 7 September 1990). At the 5th meeting, the secretariat described the procedure followed for submitting the various chapters of the draft report as and when they were ready for translation and reproduction.

8. The Working Group had before it the following documents submitted under item 10 of the Sub-Commission's agenda:

Report of the Secretary-General containing information received from Governments pursuant to Sub-Commission resolution 7 (XXVII) of 20 August 1974 (E/CN.4/Sub.2/1990/20);

Report of the Secretary-General containing information submitted by specialized agencies and intergovernmental organizations pursuant to Sub-Commission resolution 7 (XXVII) of 20 August 1974 (E/CN.4/Sub.2/1990/21);

Synopsis of material received from non-governmental organizations in consultative status with the Economic and Social Council prepared by the Secretariat (E/CN.4/Sub.2/1990/22);

Report of the Secretary-General on succinct information on developments in the human rights programme and on the activities within the United Nations programme on crime prevention and control as they relate to the question of human rights of persons subjected to any form of detention or imprisonment (E/CN.4/Sub.2/1990/23);

Report of the Secretary-General on the application of international standards concerning the human rights of detained juveniles prepared pursuant to Sub-Commission resolution 1989/31 (E/CN.4/Sub.2/1990/25 and Add.1 and 2);

Report of the Secretary-General on the application of the death penalty to persons under 18 years of age prepared pursuant to Sub-Commission resolution 1989/32 (E/CN.4/Sub.2/1990/26 and Add.1 and 2);

Report of the Secretary-General on comments submitted by Governments and specialized agencies pursuant to General Assembly resolution 44/162 of 15 December 1989, entitled "Human Rights in the administration of justice" (E/CN.4/Sub.2/1990/27);

Working paper presented by Mr. Leandro Despouy, Special Rapporteur appointed pursuant to Economic and Social Council resolution 1985/37, on the question of human rights and states of emergency (E/CN.4/Sub.2/1990/33 and Add.1);

Brief report prepared by Mr. Stanislav Chernichenko and Mr. William Treat in accordance with resolution 1989/27 of the Sub-Commission, concerning the right to a fair trial (E/CN.4/Sub.2/1990/34);

Written statement submitted by the American Association of Jurists, a non-governmental organization in consultative status, containing comments on the latest version of the draft declaration on enforced or involuntary disappearances (Category II) (E/CN.4/Sub.2/1990/NGO/1);

Report of the Working Group on Detention (E/CN.4/Sub.2/1989/29/Rev.1);

General Assembly resolution 41/120, "Setting international standards in the field of human rights".

0112

9. The Working Group also had before it the following documents:

Provisional agenda (E/CN.4/Sub.2/1990/WG.1/L.1);

Note by the Secretary-General containing a revised version of the draft declaration on the protection of persons from enforced or involuntary disappearance (E/CN.4/Sub.2/1990/CRP.1/Rev.1);

Selected United Nations draft instruments relating to the administration of justice and the human rights of detainees which will be submitted to the Eighth United Nations Congress on the Prevention of Crime and the Treatment of Offenders to be held at Havana (27 August - 7 September 1990) (E/CN.4/Sub.2/1990/CRP.2).

I. ADOPTION OF THE AGENDA

10. At its 1st meeting, the Working Group considered the provisional agenda proposed at its 1989 session (cf. E/CN.4/Sub.2/1989/29/Rev.1, para. 50):

(a) Unacknowledged detention, enforced and involuntary disappearance;

(b) Annual review of developments concerning the human rights of persons subjected to any form of detention or imprisonemnt;

(c) Privatization of prisons;

(d) Death penalty, with special reference to its imposition on persons of less than 18 years of age; and

(e) Right to a fair trial.

11. At the same meeting, the Chairman suggested that the Working Group first review the provisional agenda, in order to decide on the items which it would consider in 1990, and those which would be proposed in 1991.

12. Since the adoption of the agenda was dependent upon the decision of the Working Group on whether substantive issues relating to the draft declaration on the protection of all persons from enforced and involuntary disappearance should be discussed or whether discussion should be confined only to drafting improvements, the Chairman opened the discussion to preliminary statements on item 1 of the provisional agenda.

13. The agenda was adopted at the 3rd meeting, on 17 August 1990, as it appears in paragraph 9 above and in document E/CN.4/Sub.2/1990/WG.1/L.1.

II. UNACKNOWLEDGED DETENTION, ENFORCED AND INVOLUNTARY DISAPPEARANCE

(agenda item 1)

14. The Working Group considered this item at its 1st, 2nd and 3rd meetings, on 13, 15 and 17 August 1990, discussing the revised draft declaration on the protection of all persons from enforced or involuntary disappearance.

0113

15. The Chairman recalled that the outgoing Chairman had received a mandate from the Working Group to prepare a revised version of the declaration, taking greater account of the suggestions made at many earlier meetings, especially at the Meeting of Experts held at the Palais des Nations from 21 to 23 March 1990, on the initiative of the International Commission of Jurists, in which some members of the Working Group, some government observers and several non-governmental organizations, in particular, Amnesty International, the International Federation of Human Rights and the Latin American Federation of Associations of Relatives of Disappeared Detainees, actively participated, with a view to facilitating a consensus.

16. In almost all of their statements, the participants, and particularly the members of the Working Group, spoke in favour of adoption by consensus at the present session, subject to some improvements in form.

17. It was decided that Mr. Miguel Alfonso Martínez, in liaison with Mr. Ribot Hatano, Rapporteur, would make the necessary contacts to arrange for the requisite corrections and facilitate, at the 2nd meeting, adoption by consensus on the basis of the draft submitted to the Working Group.

18. At the second meeting, the Chairman gave the floor to Mr. Miguel Alfonso Martínez, who informed the Working Group of the results of his informal discussions and read out his technical amendments to the draft declaration contained in document E/CN.4/Sub.2/1990/CRP.1.

19. Other suggestions for improvements in form were put forward by the participants. The Chairman having noted agreement on the need for a final editorial revision, the Working Group gave the Chairman, the Rapporteur and Mr. Alfonso Martínez, in consultation with the Secretariat, a mandate to put the draft declaration in final form. The Chairman noted that there was consensus and the Working Group then unanimously adopted the text contained in annex I below.

III. ANNUAL REVIEW OF DEVELOPMENTS CONCERNING THE HUMAN RIGHTS OF PERSONS SUBJECTED TO ANY FORM OF DETENTION OR IMPRISONMENT

(agenda item 2)

20. At its 3rd meeting, the Working Group started consideration of item 2. The Chairman opened the debate for discussion of new developments in the field, including an oral report by Mr. El Hadji Guissé on trends appearing in the synopsis prepared by the secretariat of information received from non-governmental organizations in consultative status with the Economic and Social Council (E/CN.4/Sub.2/1990/22) in order to identify specific suggestions concerning future work to be taken into consideration in the draft agenda for next year.

A. Recent trends identified by non-governmental organizations

21. Mr. El Hadji Guissé stressed that, according to the information available in the synopsis, it is during the period of detention by the police that most violations of the human rights of persons subjected to detention occur. He also noted that, in many countries, the death penalty increasingly applies to juveniles under 18 years of age. He stated, regarding the death penalty in general, that people are often executed for having expressed an opposing

0114

political opinion. In addition, he emphasized that cruel treatments are increasingly inflicted on detained persons. He pointed out that by the time detained persons are released, they are often disabled or physically mutilated. In this respect, he mentioned particularly vulnerable groups such as women and children. He praised the role of non-governmental organizations (NGOs) in furnishing the members of the Working Group and the Sub-Commission with information concerning violations of the human rights of detained persons. However, he expressed the view that the reality of the situation was even worse than the description contained in the synopsis, and that NGOs should continue to research and analyse the situation further. The Chairman thanked Mr. El Hadji Guissé and suggested that a member of the Working Group should be asked, every year, to report on the trends and situations identified in the synopsis.

22. At its 5th meeting, the Working Group decided to entrust this task to Mr. El Hadji Guissé and Mr. Cornelis Flinterman.

23. The representative of Amnesty International expressed the view that habeas corpus should be considered as a non-derogable right, basing this view, inter alia, on an advisory opinion of the Inter-American Court of Human Rights. This view was supported by Mr. El Hadji Guissé and Mr. Cornelis Flinterman, as well as by the representative of the International Federation of Human Rights. The representative of the International Commission of Jurists and the Andean Commission of Jurists suggested that one of the members of the Working Group prepare a working paper on habeas corpus as a non-derogable right.

24. At its 5th meeting, the Working Group decided to entrust this task jointly to Mr. John Carey (alternate of Mr. William Treat) with regard to the habeas corpus procedure, and to Mr. Eduardo Suescún Monroy with regard to the amparo procedure.

B. Question of model legislation

25. Mr. Cornelis Flinterman, referring to Commission on Human Rights resolution 1990/81 and to document E/CN.4/Sub.2/1990/27, proposed to elaborate texts for national model legislation in the field of the administration of justice. He suggested that one member of the Working Group of the Sub-Commission consider elements of model texts and write a working paper where model legislation could be indicated. Furthermore, he proposed to ask Mr. William Treat and Mr. Stanislav Chernichenko to include model legislation into their study on the right to a fair trial. Mr. El Hadji Guissé pointed out that the search for model legislation could encounter many problems. In his opinion, it would be more appropriate to conduct a survey of all model elements and to present it to the members of the Working Group as a source of information to be taken into consideration by Governments, but not as model legislation. Mr. Louis Joinet agreed with Mr. El Hadji Guissé and expressed the view that the Working Group should develop principles rather than draft models.

C. Treatment of persons subjected to detention or imprisonment

26. Mr. Eduardo Suescún Monroy suggested that, when the study of habeas corpus is completed, the Working Group should consider the conditions in detention centres and prisons in order to see how institutions of detention

0115

really work. Mr. Yozo Yokota supported this suggestion, noting that developing countries had difficulties in improving the physical conditions of facilities and institutions for detention or imprisonment due to lack or shortage of funds. He stressed the importance of financial and technical assistance for improving such conditions. Mr. Miguel Alfonso Martínez agreed with him and supported the suggestion.

D. Application of international standards concerning the human rights of juveniles subjected to any form of detention or imprisonment

27. Ms. Mary Concepción Bautista explained that in her report, not yet available for the Sub-Commission, on the application of international standards concerning the human rights of juveniles subjected to any form of detention or imprisonment (E/CN.4/Sub.2/1990/28), she suggested, *inter alia*, that the conditions of detention or imprisonment of juveniles be improved and that a system of continuous visits in gaols be established.

28. The representative of Defence for Children International emphasized that, according to international human rights law, the most important right of every child is the right to special protection, including, *inter alia*, the rights not to be tried as an adult and not to be held responsible at all before reaching a certain age. He stressed the need for special courts or procedures for juvenile offenders, as recognized by the International Covenant on Civil and Political Rights, the Convention on the Rights of the Child and the Standard Minimum Rules for the Administration of Juvenile Justice. He mentioned the situation in Bangladesh, Bolivia, Canada, Pakistan, the Philippines and the United Kingdom. He suggested that the Working Group consider again the question of juvenile justice next year.

E. Information on the 8th Congress on the Prevention of Crime and the Treatment of Offenders (Havana, 27 August-7 September 1990) and co-operation with the Vienna Committee

29. The secretariat informed the Working Group of the activities within the United Nations programme, as well as on the relevant programme, documents and draft instruments of the Havana Congress (E/CN.4/Sub.2/1990/23; E/CN.4/Sub.2/1990/CRP.2; see also para. 7 above) on crime prevention and control. The Chairman, referring to the problem of co-ordination between the Working Group and the Vienna Committee, proposed that the secretariat contact the Crime Prevention Branch so that a representative of the Branch might be heard next year on this question.

F. Suggestions for next year's agenda

30. Following the suggestions made at the beginning of consideration of agenda item 2 (see para. 18 above), at the 3rd meeting the Chairman listed the propositions so far mentioned for next year's agenda as follows:

(a) *Habeas corpus*;

(b) Model legislation;

(c) Abuse of preventive detention;

0116

(d) Incommunicado detention;

(e) Juvenile justice;

(f) Treatment of detained or imprisoned persons;

(g) Improvement of the physical conditions of prisons and detention facilities and technical and financial assistance therefore;

(h) Individualization of punishment and crime;

(i) Autopsies of persons having deceased during detention;

(j) Investigation in penal cases;

(k) Impunity of perpetrators of disappearances.

31. The Chairman suggested that non-governmental organizations consider a priority list of the above-mentioned items for next year, since the Working Group would not be able to discuss all of them for lack of time.

IV. PRIVATIZATION OF PRISONS

(agenda item 3)

32. Last year, Mr. Miguel Alfonso Martínez agreed to prepare a working paper dealing with the privatization of prisons. For lack of assistance and time, he has not been able to prepare it this year and, upon his suggestion, this item was postponed until next year.

V. DEATH PENALTY, WITH SPECIAL REFERENCE TO ITS IMPOSITION ON PERSONS OF LESS THAN 18 YEARS OF AGE

(agenda item 4)

A. Persons of less than 18 years of age

33. The Working Group took up, at its 4th meeting, the question of the imposition of the death penalty, particularly on persons of less than 18 years of age. The representative of Amnesty International said that his organization had already provided the Working Group with information on the subject in 1989 (E/CN.4/Sub.2/1989/29/Rev.1, para. 45, and annex V). In Amnesty International's view, this practice violated the international norms that were applicable in this field. Amnesty International had expressed its satisfaction at the adoption by the Sub-Commission of resolution 1989/33 in which the Sub-Commission appealed to Member States to stop this practice, but it expressed its deep concern at the reports on the subject which it had received in 1989 regarding the following countries: Barbados, Iran, Nigeria, Saint Vincent and the Grenadines, Union of Myanmar and United States of America. Amnesty International therefore hoped that the Working Group would keep the question on its agenda in 1991.

34. Mr. Miguel Alfonso Martínez supported that suggestion and said that the question, which concerned several countries, would also be discussed at the Havana Congress.

0117

35. Mr. Eduardo Suescún Monroy expressed the hope that the Sub-Commission would recommend that the death penalty should be abolished in the case of persons of less than 18 years of age and that it should be commuted in cases where sentence had been pronounced.

B. Treatment that may cause additional suffering

36. The observer for the Netherlands drew the Working Group's attention to her Government's suggestion in document E/CN.4/Sub.2/1990/27, on the subject of the implementation of norms applicable in the field of administration of justice, that the Working Group should consider rule 9 of the Safeguards guaranteeing protection of the rights of those facing the death penalty. That rule provides that "Where capital punishment occurs, it shall be carried out so as to inflict the minimum possible suffering". The Netherlands Government wished to assess the types of treatment that might cause additional suffering. It pointed out that, in certain cases, long delay between final sentencing and execution of the sentence might constitute inhuman or degrading treatment. The observer for the Netherlands therefore suggested that the Working Group should consider the question in 1991. This suggestion was endorsed by Mr. El Hadji Guissé and Mr. Miguel Alfonso Martínez.

37. Mr. Eduardo Suescún Monroy considered that the question might be examined in conjunction with the study of the treatment of prisoners.

C. Documentation required

38. Mr. El Hadji Guissé briefly outlined the issues raised by imposition of the death penalty and pointed out that a study of the question would require considerable time. He thanked Amnesty International and the other non-governmental organizations which sent members of the Working Group reports on the question and asked them to provide fuller and more factual information to enable the Working Group to be as objective and juridical as possible.

39. It was agreed that the question of the imposition of the death penalty, particularly on persons of less than 18 years of age, should be included in the Working Group's 1991 provisional agenda. The secretariat would provide the Working Group in 1991 with information on the existing international norms and their application. At the suggestion of Mr. Miguel Alfonso Martínez, supported by Mr. Louis Joinet, the Working Group agreed that a member should be asked to submit in 1991 a brief document on world trends in that field. The member of the Working Group having to report on the synopsis of material received from non-governmental organizations would therefore not have to deal with that question.

40. At its 5th meeting, the Working Group decided to entrust this task to Mr. El Hadji Guissé.

VI. RIGHT TO A FAIR TRIAL

41. The Working Group considered this item of its agenda at its 5th meeting. At the invitation of the Working Group, Mr. Treat and Mr. Chernichenko briefly outlined what they considered to be the most important points of their report (E/CN.4/Sub.2/1990/34), in order to prepare for its discussion in plenary meeting.

0118

42. Mr. Treat raised the question how one could arrive at an ultimate document that could serve as a model for legislation.

43. Mr. Chernichenko drew the attention of the Working Group to the fact that there were already a number of existing international standards that could serve as models to the appreciation of States and that could be compiled in a codex of internatinal standards concerning trial procedures.

44. Mr. Joinet expressed his remarks about the report on the right to a fair trial, including the question of whether or not to include this right among the intangible rights to which no derogation is authorized, including during states of emergency. He referred, in this respect, to the studies on states of emergency and human rights prepared by Ms. Nicole Questiaux and Mr. Leandro Despouy. In his view, the list of intangible rights should be limited to the _hard core_ ("noyau dur") of human rights. If the right to a fair trial was to be thought of in this respect, may be only the essential principles of this right should be taken into consideration.

45. Mr. El Hadji Guissé expressed the view that a study on non-derogable minimum trial standards would demand a lengthy work and he invited all NGOs to contribute to this work.

46. Mr. Cornelis Flinterman suggested that the right to a fair trial, considered as a non-derogable right, might be the subject of an additional optional protocol to the International Covenant on Civil and Political Rights. At the present stage, he would prefer a set of principles rather than a declaration. He hoped that the aspects of the right to a fair trial relating to rights and obligations of a civil character, and aspects concerning administrative law, would be taken into consideration.

47. Mr. Yozo Yokota endorsed the objective of a long-term work referred to by previous speakers, considering it preferable not to adopt new international standards hastily. He suggested that an in-depth comparative study should be undertaken, in order to arrive at a universally accepted standard, thus supporting the suggestion made by Mr. Chernichenko and Mr. Treat in their report that a questionnaire should be sent to Governments and interested NGOs in consultative status with the Economic and Social Council. The questionnaire would cover not only existing standards, but also practice.

48. The representative of the International Commission of Jurists also endorsed the idea of a questionnaire. He emphasized that attention should be given to military courts and emergency courts, which rarely met the guarantees required by article 14 of the Covenant.

49. Mr. Louis Joinet agreed that an in-depth study was necessary; he preferred the idea of drafting guiding principles, which might later be used in a convention or protocol. He emphasized that the Commission on Human Rights had expressed the view that the Sub-Commission already sent out too many questionnaires. And in his own experience as Special Rapporteur, he had found that few replies to questionnaires were received from Governments. In his view, the questionnaire should initially be addressed to competent NGOs, in order that they might indicate the most relevant rules of procedure.

0119

VII. PROVISIONAL AGENDA FOR THE NEXT SESSION

50. At the 4th meeting, the Chairman recalled the suggestions made at the 3rd meeting regarding the items which might be included in the agenda of the Sessional Working Group on Detnetion which the Sub-Commission might decide to convene at its forty-third session. He emphasized that these items were suggestions only and that the provisional agenda remained open for discussion.

51. At its 5th meeting, the Working Group adopted the following provisional agenda for the next session:

1. Election of a Chairman and a Rapporteur

2. Adoption of the agenda

3. Annual review of developments concerning the human rights of persons subjected to any form of detention or imprisonment

4. Privatization of prisons

5. The death penalty, with special reference to its imposition on persons of less than 18 years of age

6. *Habeas corpus*, as a non-derogable right

7. Juvenile justice

8. Subsidiary list of questions for possible consideration:

    (a) Model legislation on detention

    (b) Forms of abuse of preventive detention and remedial measures

    (c) Detention in solitary confinement or incommunicado and human rights

    (d) Treatment of persons subjected to any form of detention or imprisonment

    (e) Improvement of the physical conditions of prisons and detention facilities and technical and financial assistance therefore

    (f) Individualization of proceedings and punishment

    (g) Problems raised by suspicious deaths in detention

    (h) Judicial police inquiries in criminal cases

    (i) Impunity of authors of disappearances

9. Provisional agenda for the next session

10. Adoption of the report of the Working Group to the Sub-Commission.

0120

Annex I

DRAFT DECLARATION ON THE PROTECTION OF ALL PERSONS FROM ENFORCED OR INVOLUNTARY DISAPPEARANCE

Preamble

The General Assembly,

Considering that, in accordance with the principles proclaimed in the Charter of the United Nations and other international instruments, recognition of the inherent dignity and of the equal and inalienable rights of all members of the human family is the foundation of freedom, justice and peace in the world,

Considering that these rights derive from the inherent dignity of the human person,

Bearing in mind the obligation of States under the Charter, in particular, Article 55, to promote universal respect for, and observance of, human rights and fundamental freedoms,

Deeply concerned that in many countries, persons are arrested, detained or abducted against their will or otherwise deprived of their liberty by officials of different branches or levels of Government, or by organized groups or private individuals acting on behalf of, or with the support or acquiescence, direct or indirect, of the Government, followed by a refusal to disclose the fate or whereabouts of the persons concerned or a refusal to acknowledge the deprivation of their liberty, thereby placing such persons outside the protection of the law,

Considering that enforced or involuntary disappearance undermines the deepest values of any society committed to respect for the rule of law, human rights and fundamental freedoms,

Recalling resolution 33/173 of 20 December 1978, by which the General Assembly expressed concern about the reports from various parts of the world relating to enforced or involuntary disappearances, as well as about the anguish and sorrow caused by these disappearances, and called upon Governments to hold law enforcement and security forces legally responsible for excesses which might lead to enforced or involuntary disappearances,

Recalling also the protection afforded to victims of armed conflict by the Geneva Conventions of 12 August 1949 and the Additional Protocols of 1977,

Having regard to Articles 3, 5, 6 and 9 of the Universal Declaration of Human Rights and Articles 6, 7, 9 and 16 of the International Covenant on Civil and Political Rights, which protect the right to life, the right to liberty and security of the person, the right not to be subjected to torture and the right to recognition as a person before the law,

0121

Having regard further to the Convention Against Torture and Other Cruel, Inhuman or Degrading Treatment or Punishment, which provides that States Parties shall take effective measures to prevent and punish acts of torture,

Bearing in mind the Code of Conduct for Law Enforcement Officials, the Declaration of Basic Principles of Justice for Victims of Crime and Abuse of Power and the Standard Minimum Rules for the Treatment of Prisoners,

Affirming that, in order to prevent enforced or involuntary disappearances, it is necessary to ensure strict compliance with the Body of Principles for the Protection of All Persons under Any Form of Detention or Imprisonment, contained in its resolution 43/173 of 9 December 1988, and with the Principles on the Effective Prevention and Investigation of Extra-legal, Arbitrary and Summary Executions, contained in Economic and Social Council resolution 1989/65 of 24 May 1989 and endorsed by General Assembly resolution 44/162 of 15 December 1989,

Bearing in mind that, while the acts which comprise enforced or involuntary disappearance constitute a violation of the prohibitions found in the aforementioned international instruments, it is none the less important to devise an instrument which characterizes the enforced or involuntary disappearance of persons as a specific crime in and of itself, setting forth standards designed to punish and prevent its commission,

Proclaims the present Declaration on the Protection of All Persons from Enforced or Involuntary Disappearance, as a body of principles for all States, for any other public authorities, as well as for organized groups or private individuals acting on behalf of, or with the support or acquiescence, direct or indirect, of States or public authorities,

Urges that all efforts be made so that this Declaration becomes generally known and respected.

Article 1

1. Enforced or involuntary disappearance practised, permitted or tolerated by a Government is an offence to human dignity and shall be condemned as a flagrant and grave violation of the purposes of the Charter of the United Nations and of the human rights and fundamental freedoms proclaimed in the Universal Declaration of Human Rights and reaffirmed and developed in international instruments in this field.

2. Such enforced or involuntary disappearance inflicts severe suffering on the persons subjected thereto, as well as on their families, and places them outside the protection of the law. It violates the rules of international law guaranteeing, _inter alia_, the right to recognition everywhere as a person before the law, the right to liberty and security of the person and the right not to be subjected to torture. It also violates or constitutes a grave threat to the right to life.

3. The systematized practice of such enforced or involuntary disappearance is a crime against humanity.

Article 2

1. No State shall practice, permit or tolerate enforced or involuntary disappearances.

2. States shall act jointly and in co-operation with the United Nations to contribute by all means to prevent and eradicate enforced or involuntary disappearance.

Article 3

Each State shall take effective legislative, administrative, judicial or other measures to prevent and terminate enforced or involuntary disappearances in any territory under its jurisdiction.

Article 4

Each State shall ensure that all forms of participation in enforced or involuntary disappearance by, or with the acquiescence of, a public official or anyone acting in an official capacity are specific crimes of the gravest kind under its criminal law, including complicity in, incitement to or an attempt to cause enforced or involuntary disappearance.

Article 5

Enforced or involuntary disappearances engage the personal responsibility of their perpetrators as well as the responsibility of the State whose authorities carried out, acquiesced in, or tolerated them.

Article 6

1. No order or instruction of any public authority, civilian, military or other, shall ever justify or be invoked to excuse enforced or involuntary disappearance.

2. Each State shall ensure that orders or instructions directing, ordering, authorizing or encouraging any enforced or involuntary disappearance are explicitly prohibited. Any person receiving such an order or instruction shall have the right and duty not to obey it.

3. Training of law enforcement officials shall emphasize the above provisions.

Article 7

At no time nor in any place whatsoever shall any exceptional circumstances, such as a state or threat of war or other armed conflict or any other public emergency, justify or be invoked to excuse enforced or involuntary disappearance.

0123

Article 8

No State shall expel, return ("refouler") or extradite a person to any State where there are grounds to believe that the person would be in danger of enforced or involuntary disappearance.

Article 9

1. Each State shall ensure under all circumstances, including those referred to in Article 7, the right to an effective judicial remedy, including habeas corpus, as a means of determining the whereabouts or the state of health of persons deprived of their liberty and/or identifying the authority ordering or carrying out the deprivation of liberty.

2. In such proceedings, competent authorities, national or international, shall have access to all places holding persons deprived of their liberty and to each part thereof, as well as to any place in which there are grounds to believe that such persons may be found.

Article 10

1. Each State shall ensure that persons deprived of their liberty are held in officially recognized places of detention and are brought before a judicial authority promptly after detention. Accurate information on their detention and whereabouts, including transfers, shall be made promptly available to their family members and counsel, anyone designated by them or other persons having a legitimate interest in the information.

2. Each State shall ensure the establishment of an official updated register at each place of detention existing in any territory under its jurisdiction, of all persons deprived of their liberty. Additionally, each State shall, to the extent possible, take steps to establish similar centralized registers. The information contained in these registers shall be made available to the persons mentioned in paragraph 1 above and to any judicial or other competent and independent authority seeking to trace the whereabouts of a detained person.

Article 11

Each State shall ensure that persons deprived of their liberty are released in a manner permitting reliable verification that the persons have actually been released and, further, that they have been released into conditions in which their physical integrity is assured and which enable them to exercise fully the rights to which they are entitled.

Article 12

Each State shall establish rules under its domestic law indicating those officials authorized to order detentions, the conditions under which detention may be ordered, as well as sanctions for those officials who wilfully refuse to provide information on a person's detention. Each State shall likewise ensure strict control, including a clear chain-of-command, over all law enforcement officials and other persons authorized by law to use force and firearms.

Article 13

1. Each State shall ensure that anyone having knowledge or a legitimate interest who alleges that a person has been subjected to enforced or involuntary disappearance in any territory under its jurisdiction has the right to complain to a competent and independent authority, and to have the complaint promptly, thoroughly and impartially investigated by that authority. Whenever there are reasonable grounds to believe that an enforced or involuntary disappearance has been committed, the State shall promptly refer the matter to that authority for such an investigation, even if there has been no formal complaint. No measures shall be taken to curtail or impede the investigation.

2. Each State shall ensure that the authority shall have the necessary powers and resources to conduct the investigation effectively, including powers to compel attendance of witnesses and production of relevant documents and to make immediate on-site visits.

3. Steps shall be taken to ensure that all involved in the investigation, including the complainant, counsel, witnesses and those conducting the investigation, are protected against ill-treatment, intimidation or reprisal.

4. The findings of such an investigation shall be made available upon request, unless doing so would jeopardize a disappeared person, any other innocent person or an ongoing criminal investigation or trial of an individual who is suspected of responsibility for an enforced or involuntary disappearance.

5. The obligations laid down in this Article are not subject to any limitation of time.

Article 14

Each State shall ensure that, when an individual alleged to have committed an offence referred to in Article 4 is found in any territory under its jurisdiction, that individual shall either be brought before its competent authorities for the purpose of investigation and, where the facts disclosed thereby so warrant, prosecution and trial, or be extradited to any State requesting extradition for the purpose of bringing the individual to justice. This provision shall apply regardless of the individual's nationality or the place where the offence was committed.

Article 15

Enforced or involuntary disappearance shall not be considered a political crime for the purpose of extradition. Participation in enforced or involuntary disappearance shall be treated as being included among extraditable offences in extradition treaties entered into by States.

0125

Article 16

1. No State shall grant asylum or refugee status to individuals who have participated in acts of enforced or involuntary disappearance, regardless of the motives of such participation. However, asylum may be granted to such individuals for the sole purpose of allowing them to be instrumental in bringing the victims forward alive or in providing voluntarily information which would contribute to resolve cases of disappearance.

2. Mitigating circumstances may be established in national legislation for individuals who, having participated in enforced or involuntary disappearances, are instrumental in bringing the victims forward alive or in providing voluntarily information which would contribute to resolve cases of disappearance.

Article 17

1. Individuals alleged to have committed any of the acts referred to in Article 4 shall be suspended from any official duties during the investigation referred to in Article 13.

2. Such individuals shall be guaranteed fair treatment at all stages of the investigation and eventual prosecution and trial.

3. Penal liability shall be effective independently of any immunities enjoyed by the individuals responsible.

Article 18

The prosecution and punishment of offences of enforced or involuntary disappearance referred to in Article 4 shall not be subject to a statute of limitations.

Article 19

Individuals who have, are alleged to have, or may have committed offences referred to in Article 4 shall not benefit from any amnesty, pardon or other measure that might have the effect of exempting such individuals from criminal responsibility.

Article 20

Each State shall ensure in its legal system that the person subject to an enforced or involuntary disappearance and the person's family obtain redress and have an enforceable right to fair and adequate compensation, including the means for as full a rehabilitation as possible. In the event of the death of a person as a result of an enforced or involuntary disappearance, the person's family shall be entitled to further compensation.

0126

Article 21

1. States shall prevent and suppress the appropriation of children of parents subjected to enforced or involuntary disappearance and of children born during the mother's deprivation of liberty, and shall devote their efforts to the search, identification and, following a judicial decision, the restitution of the children to their families of origin.

2. States shall provide in their national legislation for the judicial review of the adoption of children referred to in paragraph 1. This judicial review may determine the restitution of the children to their family of origin. States shall also punish the crimes of abduction of children and the alteration and suppression of their true identity.

3. For these purposes, States shall conclude, where appropriate, bilateral or multilateral agreements.

Article 22

Nothing in the present Declaration shall be construed as restricting or derogating from any human right defined in the Universal Declaration of Human Rights or in any other international instrument or as limiting the obligation of States to ensure respect for such rights."

0127

OFFICE DES NATIONS UNIES A GENÈVE

CENTRE POUR LES DROITS DE L'HOMME

UNITED NATIONS OFFICE AT GENEVA

CENTRE FOR HUMAN RIGHTS

Palais des Nations
CH-1211 GENÈVE 10

Téléfax: (022) 733 98 79
Télégrammes: UNATIONS, GENÈVE
Télex: 412 962 UNO CH
Téléphone: 734 60 11 731 02 11

RÉF. N°: G/SO 216/3 (34)
(à rappeler dans la réponse)

The Secretary-General of the United Nations presents his compliments to the Minister for Foreign Affairs of the Republic of Korea and has the honour to draw the attention of His Excellency's Government to resolutions 45/168, adopted by the General Assembly on 18 December 1990 and 1991/28, adopted by the Commission on Human Rights on 5 March 1991, entitled "Regional arrangements for the promotion and protection of human rights in the Asian-Pacific region". Copies of these resolutions are attached.

In paragraph 3 of resolution 45/168, the General Assembly renewed its invitation to States members of the Economic and Social Commission for Asia and the Pacific that have not yet done so to communicate to the Secretary-General as soon as possible their comments on the report of the Seminar on National, Local and Regional Arrangements for the Promotion and Protection of Human Rights in the Asian Region and, in particular, to address themselves to the conclusions and recommendations in the report concerning the development of regional arrangements in Asia and the Pacific. A copy of the report is attached.

The attention of His Excellency's Government is also drawn to paragraph 9 of resolution 1991/28, in which the Commission on Human Rights requested the Secretary-General to consult the countries of the Asian-Pacific region on the widest possible basis in the implementation of the resolution. In this connection, the Secretary-General suggests that His Excellency's Government might with to consider some proposals concerning the implementation of the resolution, such as: (a) organization of national training courses in the field of human rights; (b) assistance of experts in the strengthening of national infrastructures; (c) revising and adapting domestic legal texts to the norms contained in international instruments on human rights promulgated by the United Nations; (d) assisting in the establishment or development of regional human rights institutions and mechanisms established under regional arrangements.

The Secretary-General would like to inform His Excellency's Government that appropriate materials in the field of human rights will continue to be sent to the library, as mentioned in the above resolution. The creation of regional arrangements for the promotion and protection of human rights in the Asian-Pacific region will also be considered.

The Secretary-General would be grateful if His Excellency's Government's views in this respect could be forwarded to the Centre for Human Rights, United Nations Office at Geneva, CH-1211 Geneva 10, by 15 September 1991.

25 April 1991

0128

1991/28. Regional arrangements for the promotion and protection of human rights in the Asian-Pacific region

The Commission on Human Rights,

Recalling that the General Assembly, in its resolutions 41/153 of 4 December 1986, 43/140 of 8 December 1988, and 45/168 of 18 December 1990, affirmed the value of regional arrangements for the promotion and protection of human rights in the Asian-Pacific region,

Recalling also its resolutions 1988/73 of 10 March 1988, 1989/50 of 7 March 1989 and 1990/71 of 7 March 1990,

Noting Economic and Social Commission for Asia and the Pacific resolution 45/2 of 5 April 1989,

Bearing in mind that intergovernmental arrangements for the promotion and protection of human rights have been established in other regions,

Recognizing the valuable contribution that could be made by national institutions in the field of human rights to the concept of regional arrangements,

Recognizing also that non-governmental organizations may have a valuable role to play in this process,

Noting the value of the Seminar on national, local and regional arrangements for the promotion and protection of human rights in the Asian region, held at Colombo in 1982 (A/37/422, annex), and the training course of human rights teaching held at Bangkok in 1987 under the United Nations programme of advisory services in the field of human rights (E/CN.4/1988/39/Add.1),

1. Takes note of the report of the Secretary-General (E/CN.4/1991/21);

2. Requests the Secretary-General to ensure a continuing flow of human rights materials to the library of the Economic and Social Commission for Asia and the Pacific;

3. Encourages all Economic and Social Commission for Asia and the Pacific Member States, associate Members and other parties to make full use of the depositary centre of that organization;

4. Encourages once again United Nations development agencies in the Asian-Pacific region to co-ordinate with the Economic and Social Commission for Asia and the Pacific in their efforts to promote the human rights dimension in their activities;

0129

5. Welcomes the holding of the first Asian-Pacific regional workshop on various human rights issues, including regional and national institutions and arrangements for the promotion and protection of human rights, held in Manila from 7 to 11 May 1990, the Seminar/Workshop on Human Rights for public officials of the countries of the South Pacific held in Rarotonga, the Cook Islands, from 21 to 23 November 1990, the World Congress on Human Rights held in New Delhi from 10 to 15 December 1990 and the National Seminar on Human Rights held in Jakarta on 21 and 22 January 1991;

6. Encourages all States in the region to consider further the establishment of regional arrangements for the promotion and protection of human rights in the Asia and Pacific region and, in this regard, requests the Secretary-General to organize, within existing resources, a seminar to discuss this matter;

7. Appeals to all Governments in the region to consider making use of the possibility offered by the United Nations of organizing, under the programme of advisory services and technical assistance in the field of human rights, information and/or training courses at the national level for appropriate government personnel on the application of international human rights standards and the experience of relevant international organs;

8. Encourages all States in the region to consider ratifying or acceding to the various human rights instruments;

9. Requests the Secretary-General to consult the countries of the Asian-Pacific region on the widest possible basis in the implementation of the present resolution;

10. Requests also the Secretary-General to submit a further report incorporating information on the progress achieved in the implementation of the present resolution to the Commission at its forty-eighth session;

11. Decides to continue its consideration of the question under the agenda item entitled "Further promotion and encouragement of human rights and fundamental freedoms, including the question of the programme and methods of work of the Commission" at its forty-eighth session.

0130

45/168. Regiona[illegible]rangements for the promotion [illegible] protection of human rights in the Asian and Pacific region

The General Assembly,

Recalling its previous resolutions, in particular resolution 43/140 of 8 December 1988, on regional arrangements for the promotion and protection of human rights in the Asian and Pacific region,

Recognizing that regional arrangements make a major contribution to the promotion and protection of human rights and that non-governmental organizations may have a valuable role to play in this process,

Bearing in mind that intergovernmental arrangements for the promotion and protection of human rights have been established in other regions,

Reiterating its appreciation for the report of the Seminar on National, Local and Regional Arrangements for the Promotion and Protection of Human Rights in the Asian Region, held at Colombo from 21 June to 2 July 1982, the comments on the report of the Seminar received from the Economic and Social Commission for Asia and the Pacific and from States members of the Commission, and the report of the Secretary-General on the training course on human rights teaching held at Bangkok from 21 June to 2 July 1987 under the United Nations programme of advisory services in the field of human rights,

Noting also the designation of the Social Development Division of the Economic and Social Commission for Asia and the Pacific as a regional human rights focal point,

Recalling Commission on Human Rights resolution 1989/50 of 7 March 1989 and taking note of Commission resolution 1990/71 of 7 March 1990,

1. Takes note of the report of the Secretary-General;

2. Welcomes the designation of the library of the Economic and Social Commission for Asia and the Pacific as a depository centre for United Nations human rights materials within the Commission at Bangkok, the functions of which would include the collection, processing and dissemination of such materials in the Asian and Pacific region;

3. Renews its invitation to States members of the Economic and Social Commission for Asia and the Pacific that have not yet done so to communicate to the Secretary-General as soon as possible their comments on the report of the Seminar on National, Local and Regional Arrangements for the Promotion and Protection of Human Rights in the Asian Region and, in particular, to address themselves to the conclusions and recommendations in the report concerning the development of regional arrangements in Asia and the Pacific;

4. Requests the Secretary-General to ensure a continuing flow of human rights material to the library of the Economic and Social Commission for Asia and the Pacific at Bangkok for appropriate dissemination in the region;

5. Notes the efforts of United Nations development agencies in the Asian and Pacific region to promote the human rights dimension more actively and systematically in their development activities;

6. Encourages United Nations development agencies in the Asian and Pacific region to co-ordinate with the Economic and Social Commission for Asia and the Pacific their efforts to promote the human rights dimension in their activities;

0131

7. *Notes* that an Asian-Pacific Workshop for Administrators of Justice on international human rights issues, including regional and national institutions and arrangements for the promotion and protection of human rights, was held at Manila from 7 to 11 May 1990, within the framework of the advisory services and technical assistance programme and the world public information campaign on human rights;

8. *Requests* the Secretary-General to submit a report to the General Assembly at its forty-seventh session, through the Economic and Social Council, incorporating information on progress achieved in the implementation of the present resolution;

9. *Decides* to continue its consideration of the question at its forty-seventh session.

0132

OFFICE DES NATIONS UNIES A GENÈVE

CENTRE POUR LES DROITS DE L'HOMME

UNITED NATIONS OFFICE AT GENEVA

CENTRE FOR HUMAN RIGHTS

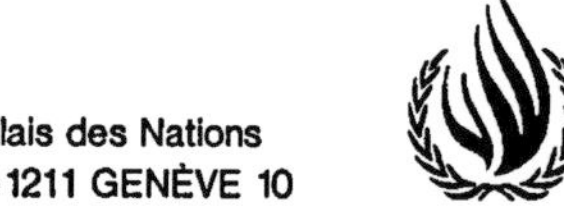

Téléfax: (022) 733 98 79
Télégrammes: UNATIONS, GENÈVE
Télex: 28 96 96
Téléphone: 734 60 11 731 02 11

Palais des Nations
CH-1211 GENÈVE 10

RÉF. N°: G/SO 221 (1)
(à rappeler dans la réponse)

The Secretary-General of the United Nations presents his compliments to the Minister for Foreign Affairs of the Republic of Korea and has the honour to refer to resolution 45/85 of 14 December 1990, by which the General Assembly endorsed the recommendations of the persons chairing the human rights treaty bodies aimed at streamlining, rationalizing and otherwise improving reporting procedures. Pursuant to that resolution, the Secretary-General transmits herewith the consolidated guidelines relating to the preparation of State party reports under the relevant international human rights instruments, namely: the International Covenant on Economic, Social and Cultural Rights, the International Covenant on Civil and Political Rights, the International Convention on the Elimination of All Forms of Racial Discrimination, the International Convention on the Suppression and Punishment of the Crime of Apartheid, the Convention against Torture and Other Cruel, Inhuman or Degrading Treatment or Punishment and the Convention on the Elimination of All Forms of Discrimination against Women.

As indicated in the Explanatory Note attached to the guidelines, the single consolidated text has been approved by all of the relevant treaty bodies. The "core document" containing the information and data supplied by each State party in accordance with the consolidated guidelines will be submitted by the Secretariat to the respective treaty bodies whenever they consider a substantive report from the State party concerned.

The Secretary-General would greatly appreciate it if the above-mentioned document would be submitted by 31 December 1991 to the Centre for Human Rights, Palais des Nations, CH-1211 Geneva, Switzerland.

26 April 1991

0133

Explanatory note

Each of the bodies established under the various human rights instruments to monitor State party compliance with treaty obligations has adopted guidelines concerning the form and content of State party reports. Since a large number of States are parties to several human rights instruments, it has been an added burden for them to provide certain information of a general character to the various treaty bodies in the form requested by each of them. The General Assembly has repeatedly urged that the reporting burdens of States parties, and duplication, be reduced as much as possible.

In the light of the foregoing, and with the agreement of all of the treaty bodies, the guidelines of the various treaty bodies relating to the part of State reports containing general information have now been consolidated into a single text, as attached.

It will be noted that these consolidated guidelines provide for the preparation of basic information and data on each country in a "core document", to be submitted to the Secretariat for distribution to each of the treaty bodies, together with the substantive report of the concerned State party, when future reports from that State party are to be considered. The "core document" will be updated periodically by the Secretariat as needed, based upon information that may be received from States parties from time to time.

M/CCPR/91/10
GE.91-15812

2510Q

0134

UNITED
NATIONS

INTERNATIONAL HUMAN RIGHTS INSTRUMENTS

Distr.
GENERAL

HRI/1991/1
27 February 1991

Original: ENGLISH

Consolidated guidelines for the initial part of the reports of States parties

Land and people

1. This section should contain information about the main ethnic and demographic characteristics of the country and its population, as well as such socio-economic and cultural indicators as per capita income, gross national product, rate of inflation, external debt, rate of unemployment, literacy rate and religion. It should also include information on the population by mother tongue, life expectancy, infant mortality, maternal mortality, fertility rate, percentage of population under 15 and over 65 years of age, percentage of population in rural areas and in urban areas and percentage of households headed by women. As far as possible, States should make efforts to provide all data disaggregated by sex.

General political structure

2. This section should describe briefly the political history and framework, the type of government and the organization of the executive, legislative and judicial organs.

General legal framework within which human rights are protected

3. This section should contain information on:

(a) Which judicial, administrative or other competent authorities have jurisdiction affecting human rights;

(b) What remedies are available to an individual who claims that any of his rights have been violated; and what systems of compensation and rehabilitation exist for victims;

(c) Whether any of the rights referred to in the various human rights instruments are protected either in the constitution or by a separate bill of rights and, if so, what provisions are made in the constitution or bill of rights for derogations and in what circumstances;

2484Q

GE.91-15807

0135

(d) How human rights instruments are made part of the national legal system;

(e) Whether the provisions of the various human rights instruments can be invoked before, or directly enforced by, the courts, other tribunals or administrative authorities or whether they must be transformed into internal laws or administrative regulations in order to be enforced by the authorities concerned;

(f) Whether there exist any institutions or national machinery with responsibility for overseeing the implementation of human rights.

Information and publicity

4. This section should indicate whether any special efforts have been made to promote awareness among the public and the relevant authorities of the rights contained in the various human rights instruments. The topics to be addressed should include the manner and extent to which the texts of the various human rights instruments have been disseminated, whether such texts have been translated into the local language or languages, what government agencies have responsibility for preparing reports and whether they normally receive information or other inputs from external sources, and whether the contents of the reports are the subject of public debate.

0136

OFFICE DES NATIONS UNIES A GENÈVE

CENTRE POUR LES DROITS DE L'HOMME

UNITED NATIONS OFFICE AT GENEVA

CENTRE FOR HUMAN RIGHTS

Téléfax: (022) 733 98 79
Télégrammes: UNATIONS, GENÈVE
Télex: 412 962 UNO CH
Téléphone: 734 60 11 731 02 11

Palais des Nations
CH-1211 GENÈVE 10

RÉF. N°: G/SO 214 (38-10)
(à rappeler dans la réponse)

The Secretary-General of the United Nations presents his compliments to the Minister for Foreign Affairs of the Republic of Korea and has the honour to refer to General Assembly resolution 45/153 of 18 December 1990 and to Commission on Human Rights resolution 1991/73 of 6 March 1991, both entitled "Human rights and mass exoduses". Copies of these resolutions are attached.

The attention of His Excellency's Government is drawn in particular to paragraphs 2 and 3 of General Assembly resolution 45/153 and paragraphs 1 and 2 of Commission on Human Rights resolution 1991/73.

In paragraph 13 of resolution 45/153, the General Assembly requests the Secretary-General to report to its forty-sixth session on the strengthened role that he is playing in undertaking early warning activities, especially in the humanitarian area, as well as on any further developments relating to the recommendations contained in the report of the Group of Governmental Experts on International Co-operation to Avert New Flows of Refugees. A copy of the recommendations is enclosed for easy reference.

The Secretary-General would be grateful to receive from His Excellency's Government any information and views it may wish to submit relating to the recommendations contained in the report of the Group of Governmental Experts on International Co-operation to Avert New Flows of Refugees. Such views or information should reach the Centre for Human Rights, United Nations Office at Geneva, CH-1211 Genève 10, prior to 15 August 1991.

26 April 1991

0137

UNITED
NATIONS

General Assembly

Distr.
GENERAL

A/RES/45/153
1 March 1991

Forty-fifth session
Agenda item 12

RESOLUTION ADOPTED BY THE GENERAL ASSEMBLY

[on the report of the Third Committee (A/45/838)]

45/153. Human rights and mass exoduses

The General Assembly,

Mindful of its general humanitarian mandate under the Charter of the United Nations to promote and encourage respect for human rights and fundamental freedoms,

Deeply disturbed by the continuing scale and magnitude of exoduses of refugees and displacements of population in many regions of the world and by the human suffering of millions of refugees and displaced persons,

Conscious of the fact that human rights violations are one of the multiple and complex factors causing mass exoduses of refugees and displaced persons, as indicated in the study of the Special Rapporteur of the Commission on Human Rights on this subject 1/ and also in the report of the Group of Governmental Experts on International Co-operation to Avert New Flows of Refugees, 2/

Aware of the recommendations concerning mass exoduses made by the Commission on Human Rights to its Sub-Commission on Prevention of Discrimination and Protection of Minorities and to special rapporteurs to be taken into account when studying violations of human rights in any part of the world,

---

1/ E/CN.4/1503.

2/ A/41/324, annex.

91-07168 3217Z (E)
GE.91-15803

/...

0138

Deeply preoccupied by the increasingly heavy burden being imposed, particularly upon developing countries with limited resources of their own and upon the international community as a whole, by these sudden mass exoduses and displacements of population,

Stressing the need for international co-operation aimed at averting new massive flows of refugees while providing durable solutions to actual refugee situations,

Reaffirming its resolution 41/70 of 3 December 1986, in which it endorsed the conclusions and recommendations contained in the report of the Group of Governmental Experts on International Co-operation to Avert New Flows of Refugees,

Bearing in mind its resolution 44/164 of 15 December 1989 and Commission on Human Rights resolution 1990/52 of 6 March 1990, 3/ as well as all previous relevant resolutions of the General Assembly and the Commission on Human Rights,

Welcoming the steps taken so far by the United Nations to examine the problem of massive outflows of refugees and displaced persons in all its aspects, including its root causes,

Noting that the Executive Committee of the Programme of the United Nations High Commissioner for Refugees has specifically acknowledged the direct relationship between observance of human rights standards, refugee movements and problems of protection,

1. *Reaffirms* its support for the recommendation of the Group of Governmental Experts on International Co-operation to Avert New Flows of Refugees that the principal organs of the United Nations should make fuller use of their respective competencies under the Charter of the United Nations for the prevention of new massive flows of refugees and displaced persons;

2. *Again invites* all Governments and intergovernmental and humanitarian organizations concerned to intensify their co-operation with and assistance to world-wide efforts to address the serious problems resulting from mass exoduses of refugees and displaced persons, and also the causes of such exoduses;

3. *Requests* all Governments to ensure the effective implementation of the relevant international instruments, in particular in the field of human rights, as this would contribute to averting new massive flows of refugees and displaced persons;

4. *Invites* the Commission on Human Rights to keep the question of human rights and mass exoduses under review with a view to supporting the early-warning arrangement instituted by the Secretary-General to avert new massive flows of refugees and displaced persons;

3/ See *Official Records of the Economic and Social Council, 1990, Supplement No. 2* and corrigendum (E/1990/22 and Corr.1), chap. II, sect. A.

/...

5. _Takes note_ of the establishment by the Executive Committee of the Programme of the United Nations High Commissioner for Refugees of the Working Group on Solutions and Protection; _4_/

6. _Also takes note_ of the report of the Secretary-General on human rights and mass exoduses, _5_/ and invites him to inform the General Assembly in future reports of the modalities of early-warning activities to avert new and massive flows of refugees;

7. _Welcomes_ the report of the Joint Inspection Unit entitled "The co-ordination of activities related to early warning of possible refugee flows"; _6_/

8. _Specially encourages_ the Secretary-General to continue to discharge the task described in the report of the Group of Governmental Experts on International Co-operation to Avert New Flows of Refugees, including the continuous monitoring of all potential outflows, keeping in mind the recommendations of the Joint Inspection Unit; _7_/

9. _Requests_ the Secretary-General to intensify his efforts to develop the role of the Office for Research and the Collection of Information of the Secretariat as a focal point for the operation of an effective early-warning system and the strengthening of co-ordination of information-gathering and analysis among United Nations agencies with a view to preventing new massive flows of refugees and displaced persons;

10. _Urges_ the Secretary-General to allocate the necessary resources to consolidate and strengthen the system for undertaking early-warning activities in the humanitarian area by, _inter alia_, the computerization of the Office for Research and the Collection of Information and strengthened co-ordination among the relevant parts of the United Nations system, especially the Office for Research and the Collection of Information, the Office of the United Nations High Commissioner for Refugees, the Centre for Human Rights of the Secretariat and the relevant specialized agencies;

11. _Requests_ the Secretary-General to make the necessary information available to the competent United Nations organs, bearing in mind the recommendations of the Joint Inspection Unit;

_4_/ See A/45/12/Add.1, sect. III.A.

_5_/ A/45/607.

_6_/ A/45/649 and Corr.1, annex.

_7_/ _Ibid_., sect. VI.B.

/...

0140

12. Invites bodies of the United Nations system to consider the most expedient ways and means of following up the recommendations of the Joint Inspection Unit on co-ordination; 7/

13. Requests the Secretary-General to report to the General Assembly at its forty-sixth session on the strengthened role that he is playing with regard to early-warning activities, especially in the humanitarian area, as well as on any further developments relating to the recommendations contained in the report of the Group of Governmental Experts on International Co-operation to Avert New Flows of Refugees;

14. Invites the Secretary-General to keep the General Assembly informed of the efforts to follow up recommendations of the Joint Inspection Unit;

15. Decides to continue consideration of the question of human rights and mass exoduses at its forty-sixth session.

69th plenary meeting
18 December 1990

0141

COMMISSION ON HUMAN RIGHTS

Forty-seventh session

1991/73. Human rights and mass exoduses

The Commission on Human Rights,

Mindful of its general humanitarian mandate under the Charter of the United Nations to promote and encourage respect for human rights and fundamental freedoms,

Deeply disturbed by the continuing scale and magnitude of exoduses of refugees and displacements of population in many regions of the world and by the human suffering of millions of refugees and displaced persons,

Conscious of the fact that human rights violations are one of the multiple and complex factors causing mass exoduses of refugees and displaced persons, as indicated in the study of the Special Rapporteur on this subject (E/CN.4/1503) and also in the report of the Group of Governmental Experts on International Co-operation to Avert New Flows of Refugees (A/41/324, annex),

Recalling the recommendations concerning mass exoduses which it has made to the Sub-Commission on Prevention of Discrimination and Protection of Minorities and to the Special Rapporteurs when studying violations of human rights in any part of the world,

Deeply preoccupied by the increasingly heavy burden being imposed, particularly upon developing countries with limited resources of their own, and upon the international community as whole, by these sudden mass exoduses and displacements of population,

Stressing the need for international co-operation aimed at averting new massive flows of refugees in parallel with the provision of durable solutions to actual refugee situations,

Taking note once again of the report of the Secretary-General on human rights and mass exoduses (A/38/538),

Welcoming the endorsement by the General Assembly, at its forty-first session, of the recommendations and conclusions contained in the report of the Group of Governmental Experts on International Co-operation to Avert New Flows of Refugees,

Recalling General Assembly resolution 44/164 of 15 December 1989, by which the Assembly endorsed the recommendation of the Group of Governmental Experts that the principal organs of the United Nations should make fuller use of their respect competencies under the Charter of the United Nations for the prevention of new massive flows of refugees and displaced persons,

Recalling also its resolution 1990/52 of 6 March 1990 and its previous relevant resolutions as well as those of the General Assembly,

---

The final edited text of this resolution will be published in the report of the Commission on Human Rights to the Economic and Social Council.

RES/HR/91/8
GE.91-15797

0142

Noting that the General Assembly, in its resolution 45/153 of 18 December 1990, welcomed the report of the Joint Inspection Unit on the co-ordination of activities related to early warning of possible refugee flows (A/45/649, annex),

Welcoming the steps taken so far by the United Nations to examine the problem of massive outflows of refugees and displaced persons in all its aspects, including its root causes,

Bearing in mind the statement made by the United Nations High Commissioner for Refugees at its 35th meeting, held on 22 February 1990, which drew attention to the complexity of the global refugee problem, the need for a comprehensive approach addressing the concerns of all the different groups involved and the important role to be played in this regard by human rights institutions,

Noting that the Executive Committee of the Programme of the United Nations High Commissioner for Refugees has specifically acknowledged the direct relationship between observance of human rights standards, refugee movements and problems of protection,

Recalling that the General Assembly, in its resolution 45/153, invited the Commission to keep the questions of human rights and mass exoduses under review with a view to supporting the early warning arrangement instituted by the Secretary-General to avert new massive flows of refugees and displaced persons,

1. Invites again all Governments and intergovernmental and humanitarian organizations concerned to intensify their co-operation and assistance in world-wide efforts to address the serious problems resulting from mass exoduses of refugees and displaced persons, and also the causes of such exoduses;

2. Requests all Governments to ensure the effective implementation of the relevant international instruments, in particular in the field of human rights, as this would contribute to averting new massive flows of refugees and displaced persons;

3. Takes note of the report of the Secretary-General on human rights and mass exoduses (A/44/622);

4. Welcomes the report of the Joint Inspection Unit on the co-ordination of activities related to early warning of possible refugee flows;

0143

5. *Invites* the Secretary-General, all intergovernmental agencies and offices, as well as international agencies concerned, speedily to implement the recommendations contained in the report of the Joint Inspection Unit, particularly with regard to the establishment of a working group and of a consultative machinery within the United Nations system for early warning of possible refugee flows and displaced persons;

6. *Encourages* the Secretary-General to continue to take the necessary steps to discharge the function and responsibilities described in the report of the Group of Governmental Experts on International Co-operation to Avert New Flows of Refugees, including the continuous monitoring of all potential outflows, keeping in mind the recommendations of the Joint Inspection Unit;

7. *Welcomes* the establishment by the Executive Committee of the Programme of the United Nations High Commissioner for Refugees of the Working Group on Solutions and Protection;

8. *Requests* the Secretary-General to intensify his efforts to develop the role of the Office for Research and the Collection of Information to strengthen the co-ordination of information-gathering and analysis with agencies so as to provide early warning of developing situations requiring the attention ofthe Secretary-General, as well as to provide a focal point within the United Nations system for policy response, including identification of the policy options for the Secretary-General;

9. *Also requests* the Secretary-General to make the necessary information available to the competent United Nations organs bearing in mind the recommendations of the Joint Inspection Unit;

10. *Urges* the Secretary-General to allocate the necessary resources to consolidate and strengthen the system for undertaking early warning activities in the humanitarian area by, *inter alia*, computerization of the Office for Research and the Collection of Information and strengthened co-ordination among the relevant parts of the United Nations system, especially the Office for Research and the Collection of Information, the Office of the United Nations High Commissioner for Refugees, the Centre for Human Rights and the relevant specialized agencies, and ensuring that data collection and information handling processes are harmonized and, where possible, that use be made of computerized systems;

11. Looks forward to the report of the Secretary-General to the General Assembly at its forty-sixth session on the strengthened role that the Secretary-General could play in undertaking early warning activities, especially in the humanitarian area, as well as any further developments relating to the recommendations contained in the report of the Group of Governmental Experts on International Co-operation to Avert New Flows of Refugees;

12. Decides to continue consideration of the question of human rights and mass exoduses at its forty-eighth session.

54th meeting
6 March 1991

0145

A. Conclusions

63. The analysis of causes and factors showed that the emergence of massive flows of refugees is a result of a number of complex and often interrelated political, economic and social problems related to, and influenced by, the overall international situation. It may affect the political and social stability, as well as the economic development, of the receiving States, and also carry adverse consequences for the economies of the countries of origin and entire regions, thus endangering international peace and security. Moreover, in view of its complex nature and magnitude, as well as its potentially destabilizing effects, averting massive flows of refugees is a matter of serious concern to the international community as a whole. In the first instance, dealing with this problem is the responsibility of the States directly concerned. Given the character of the problem, the task of averting massive flows of refugees requires improved international co-operation at all levels, in particular in the framework of the United Nations, in full observance of the principle of non-intervention in the internal affairs of sovereign States.

64. The Group felt that measures aimed at the strengthening of international security, the development of good-neighbourly relations and the creation of an atmosphere of confidence would contribute to improving international co-operation to avert massive flows of refugees. In order to be appropriate and effective, this co-operation must address all the complex political, economic and social causes and factors of massive flows of refugees with a view to eliminating them, and it must, while this is being undertaken, contribute to the solution of those problems which are the direct cause of such flows. This co-operation should also address natural causes with a view to contributing to reducing and, where possible, even to preventing the consequences of natural disasters. In addition, measures of improving international co-operation must be taken in order to be prepared for the requirements of each specific situation.

65. For these purposes, the Group presents the following recommendations.

B. Recommendations

66. The General Assembly should call upon Member States, for the purpose of averting new massive flows of refugees, to respect in particular the following obligations:

(a) States should respect the principles contained in the Charter of the United Nations and, in particular, refrain from the threat or use of force against the territorial integrity or political independence of any State, or in any other manner inconsistent with the purposes of the United Nations, and from intervention in matters within the domestic jurisdiction of any State, in accordance with the Charter, since the violation of the aforementioned principles is particularly prone to cause new massive flows of refugees;

(b) States should use peaceful means to resolve international disputes in such a manner that international peace and security as well as justice are not

/...

jeopardized and thus improve situations that suggest a danger of future flows of refugees, in accordance with the provisions of the Charter of the United Nations and the Declaration on Principles of International Law concerning Friendly Relations and Co-operation among States in accordance with the Charter of the United Nations;

(c) In view of their responsibilities under the Charter of the United Nations and consistent with their obligations under the existing international instruments in the field of human rights, States, in the exercise of their sovereignty, should do all within their means to prevent new massive flows of refugees. Accordingly, States should refrain from creating or contributing by their policies to causes and factors which generally lead to massive flows of refugees;

(d) States should promote civil, political, economic, social and cultural rights and accordingly refrain from denying them to, and from discriminating against, groups of their population because of their nationality, ethnicity, race, religion or language, thus directly or indirectly forcing them to leave their country;

(e) States should co-operate with one another in order to prevent future massive flows of refugees. They should promote international co-operation in all its aspects, in particular at the regional and subregional levels, as an appropriate and important means to avert such flows;

(f) States should, wherever new massive flows of refugees occur, respect the existing generally recognized norms and principles of international law governing the rights and obligations of States and refugees directly concerned, including those pertaining to the rights of refugees to be facilitated in returning voluntarily and safely to their homes in their homelands and to receive adequate compensation therefrom, where so established, in cases of those who do not wish to return;

(g) States, individually and collectively, should make provisions and take appropriate measures to avert new flows of refugees which may be caused by natural disasters, as appropriate with the support of the relevant international organizations. In the event these natural disasters or other similar situations occur, States should assist the States concerned to the best of their abilities in order to alleviate the situation, as well as to avert new massive flows of refugees.

67. Taking into account the foregoing, the General Assembly should call upon Member States to co-operate with one another and with the Security Council, the General Assembly, the Economic and Social Council, the Secretariat and other relevant organs of the United Nations in a fuller and more timely manner for the prevention of new massive flows of refugees and to turn to these organs at the earliest possible stage of the development of such situations.

68. The main organs of the United Nations are urged to make fuller use of their respective competences under the Charter for the prevention of new massive flows of refugees, with a view to considering at the earliest possible stage situations and problems which could give rise to massive flows of refugees.

/...

0147

69. Furthermore, the General Assembly should consider calling upon Member States to comply vigorously with the decisions of the Security Council and to respect the decisions and recommendations of the General Assembly, the Economic and Social Council and other organs pertaining to the prevention of massive flows of refugees.

70. With a view to improving international co-operation for the prevention of new massive flows of refugees, the General Assembly should encourage the Secretary-General to make full use of his competences. To this effect, he should, in particular, in accordance with the Charter of the United Nations, as well as the relevant mandates of the competent United Nations organs:

(a) Give continuing attention to the question of averting new massive flows of refugees;

(b) Ensure that timely and fuller information relevant to the matter is available within the Secretariat;

(c) Improve co-ordination within the Secretariat for analysing the information, so as to obtain an early assessment on the situations which might give rise to new massive flows of refugees, and to make the necessary information available to the competent United Nations organs in consultation with the States directly concerned;

(d) Help improve the co-ordination, within the Secretariat, of the efforts of United Nations organs and specialized agencies and of Member States concerned for timely and more effective action;

(e) Consider taking such measures as are necessary for the purposes enumerated in this paragraph.

71. In the fulfilment of his mandate in the area of international co-operation to avert new massive flows of refugees, the Secretary-General should act within the limits of financial and personnel resources available to the Secretariat. In doing so, he should bear in mind the ongoing efforts to improve the efficiency of the administrative and financial functioning of the United Nations and, without prejudice to his administration competences and functions, should refrain from creating new divisions or posts for this purpose.

72. In the selection of projects, the relevant economic assistance agencies and other bodies of the United Nations should consider, in consultation with the States directly concerned, giving greater support to those projects that directly or indirectly could help avert new massive refugee flows resulting from the impact of social and economic factors or natural causes in a given region.

***

0148

주 제 네 바 대 표 부

제네(정) 2031-404　　　　　　1991. 4. 26

수신 : 장 관

참조 : 국제기구조약국장

제목 : 신앙문제 특별 보고관 설문서

Ribeiro 유엔 신앙문제 특별 보고관은 별첨 당관앞 공한을 통해 사상, 양심, 신앙의 자유 보장과 관련한 각국의 법률 규정, 행정적, 사법적 관행 및 판결에 관한 설문서에 대해 아국 정부가 91. 9. 30. 까지 회답하여 줄 것을 요청하여 온 바, 검토후 처리 지침을 회시하여 주시기 바랍니다.

첨 부 : 상기 공한 1부. 끝.

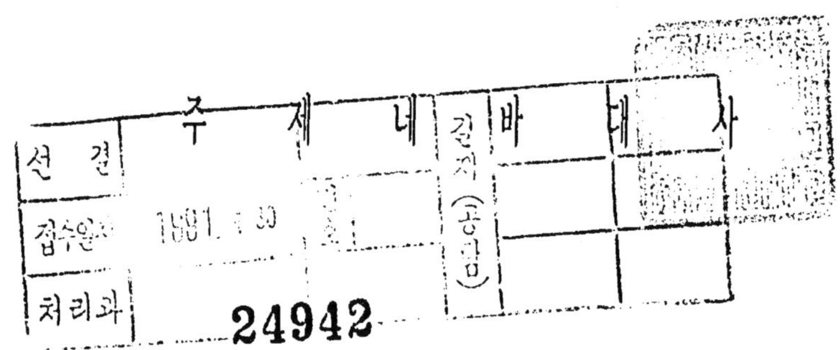

0149

OFFICE DES NATIONS UNIE GENÈVE

CENTRE POUR LES DROITS DE L'HOMME

UNITED NATIONS OFFICE AT GENEVA

CENTRE FOR HUMAN RIGHTS

Téléfax: (022) 733 98 79
Télégrammes: UNATIONS, GENÈVE
Télex: 28 96 96
Téléphone: 734 60 11 731 02 11

Palais des Nations
CH-1211 GENÈVE 10

RÉF. Nº: G/SO 214 (56-5)
(à rappeler dans la réponse)

10 April 1991

Dear Mr. Ambassador,

I have the honour to communicate to you, on behalf of the Under-Secretary-General for Human Rights, the following letter addressed to you by the Special Rapporteur of the Commission on Human Rights on religious intolerance:

"Sir,

I should like to refer to the questionnaire I sent to governments on 25 July 1990 requesting up-to-date and complete information on the most recent legislation, administrative practices and court rulings connected with the exercise of the freedom of thought, conscience, religion and belief and on measures taken to combat incidents which might be inconsistent with the Declaration on the Elimination of All Forms of Intolerance and of Discrimination Based on Religion or Belief.

You may have noticed in my report to the Commission on Human Rights at its 47th session (E/CN.4/1991/56) that a number of countries have sent replies to the questionnaire. It would be my intention to make a final analysis of the information gathered in the report I will present to the 48th session of the Commission on Human Rights. Should your Government wish to provide me with replies to the questionnaire, I would be most grateful if it could do so before 30 September 1991. For ease of reference, please find attached a copy of the questionnaire.

Accept, Sir, the assurances of my highest consideration.

Angelo Vidal d'Almeida Ribeiro
Special Rapporteur
of the Commission on Human Rights
on religious intolerance"

I remain, dear Mr. Ambassador,
Yours sincerely,

Georg Mautner-Markhof
Chief
Special Procedures Section
Centre for Human Rights

His Excellency
Mr. Sang Ock Lee
Ambassador
Permanent Observer of the Republic of Korea to
the United Nations Office at Geneva
20 route de Pré-Bois
Case postale 566
1215 Genève 15

0150

Questionnaire

(a) In national legislation or practice, is a distinction made between religion, religious sects and religious associations? If so, what criteria are used for determining which ones are legal or illegal?

(b) Does your country afford equal protection both to believers of all faiths and to non-believers (free thinkers, agnostics and atheists)? If not, in what way is the treatment different?

(c) How does your country protect the right of its citizens to practice their faith when they constitute a religious minority?

(d) Does your country apply the principle of reciprocity as regards the practice of religion by foreigners?

(e) How does your country deal with conscientious objection to compulsory military service?

(f) Do clashes occur with some frequency between members of different religious denominations in your country? If so, what is the Government's position? What kinds of preventive measures have been adopted?

(g) Has your country taken any steps against the expression or of extremist or fanatical opinions which may lead to religious intransigence or intolerance?

(h) In cases of intolerance or discrimination based on religion or belief, are any effective remedies available to the victims to assert their rights? If so, please specify what type of judicial and administrative remedies are available.

(i) Does your country have conciliation arrangements (for example, a national human rights commission, an ombudsman, etc.) to which a victim of religious intolerance can turn for protection?

(j) In general, does your Government think it would be desirable to revise national legislation to bring it more into line with the principles set forth in the Declaration on the Elimination of All Forms of Intolerance and of Discrimination based on Religion or Belief? If so, would your Government welcome appropriate technical assistance from the Centre for Human Rights?

(k) Does your country think it desirable to receive advisory assistance from the Centre for Human Rights to organize courses and seminars to train selected officials from your country (legislators, judges, lawyers, educators, law enforcement officials, etc.) in the principles, rules and remedies applicable to freedom of religion and belief?

0151

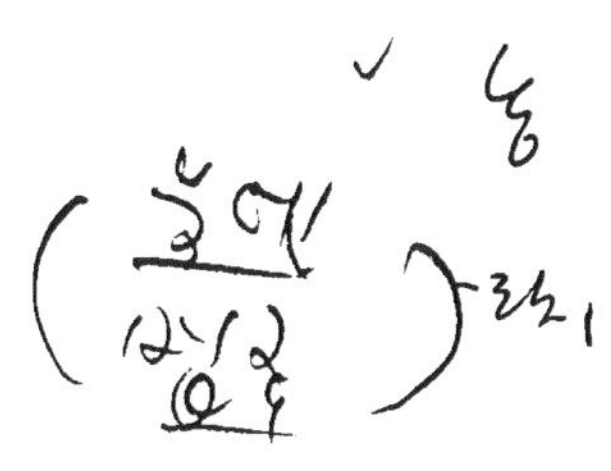

주 제 네 바 대 표 부

제네(정) 2031-405 1991. 4. 26.

수신 : 외무부장관

참조 : 국제기구조약국장

제목 : 공정한 재판을 받을 권리에 관한 자료 요청

유엔 사무총장은 별첨 외무장관 앞 공한을 통해 공정한 재판을 받을 권리에 관한 아국의 입법 내용 및 정책등에 대한 설문 자료를 가급적 91. 5. 31 까지 제출하여 줄 것을 요청하여 온 바, 검토후 처리 지침을 회시하여 주시기 바랍니다.

첨 부 : 상기 공한 1부. 끝.

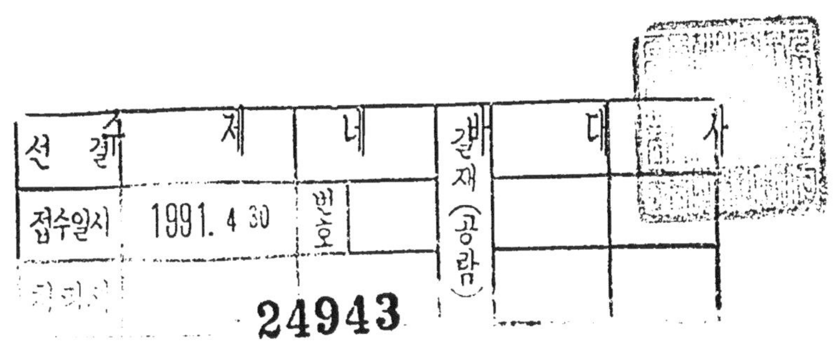

선 결	주 제 네 바 대 사			결재 (공람)
접수일시	1991. 4 30	번호		
처리과				

24943

0152

UNITED NATIONS OFFICE AT GENEVA

CENTRE POUR LES DROITS DE L'HOMME

CENTRE FOR HUMAN RIGHTS

Télétax: (022) 733 98 79
Télégrammes: UNATIONS, GENÈVE
Télex: 412 962 UNO CH
Téléphone: 734 60 11 731 02 11

Palais des Nations
CH-1211 GENÈVE 10

COPIE - COPY

RÉF. Nº: G/SO 214 (3-3-16)
(à rappeler dans la réponse)

The Secretary-General of the United Nations presents his compliments to the Minister for Foreign Affairs of the Republic of Korea and has the honour to refer to resolution 1991/43 entitled "Right to a fair trial", adopted by the Commission on Human Rights on 5 March 1991. A copy of the resolution is attached.

The particular attention of His Excellency's Government is drawn to paragraphs 1, 3 and 4 of this resolution.

After having endorsed the decision of the Sub-Commission to entrust Mr. Stanislav Chernichenko and Mr. William Treat with the preparation of a study entitled "The right to a fair trial: current recognition and measures necessary for its strengthening" (paragraph 1), the Commission requested the two Special Rapporteurs to draft a questionnaire on the right to a fair trial (paragraph 3).

In paragraph 4, the Secretary-General was requested to transmit the questionnaire with the brief report to, inter alia, Governments for their response and comments, and to transmit the responses to the Special Rapporteurs for consideration in connection with their study.

In accordance with this request, the Secretary-General has the honour to transmit herewith the questionnaire as well as a copy of the brief report on the right to a fair trial (E/CN.4/Sub.2/1990/34) prepared by the two Special Rapporteurs.

The Secretary-General would appreciate it if any response and comments that His Excellency's Government may wish to provide in accordance with paragraph 4 of the above-mentioned resolution, could be forwarded to the Under-Secretary-General for Human Rights, United Nations Office at Geneva, CH-1211 Geneva 10, if possible by 31 May 1991, in order to enable the Special Rapporteurs to take that information into account in their preliminary report on the subject which will be submitted to the forty-third session of the Sub-Commission scheduled for August 1991.

19 April 1991

0153

1991/43. Right to a fair trial

The Commission on Human Rights,

Guided by the Universal Declaration of Human Rights which affirms the right of every individual to a fair and public hearing by an independent and impartial tribunal,

Bearing in mind the International Covenant on Civil and Political Rights which reaffirms the equality of all persons before courts and tribunals and the right of everyone to a fair and public hearing,

Noting the fair trial provisions in the African Charter on Human and Peoples' Rights, the American Convention on Human Rights, the European Convention on Human Rights, the Geneva Conventions Relating to the Protection of Victims of International Armed Conflict, and the Convention against Torture and Other Cruel, Inhuman or Degrading Treatment or Punishment,

Recalling its decision 1990/108 of 7 March 1990, welcoming the appointment of Mr. Stanislav Chernichenko and Mr. William Treat to prepare a report on the right to a fair trial,

Aware of General Assembly resolution 41/120 of 4 December 1986 regarding the development of international standards in the field of human rights,

Considering that the availability of a fair trial is essential for the protection of human rights and fundamental freedoms as well as maintaining respect for the inherent dignity of the human person,

Having examined the work done by the Sub-Commission on Prevention of Discrimination and Protection of Minorities relating to the right to a fair trial,

Having examined also the brief report on the right to a fair trial prepared by Mr. Chernichenko and Mr. Treat in accordance with Sub-Commission resolution 1989/27 of 1 September 1989 (E/CN.4/Sub.2/1990/34),

Welcoming the recommendations made by Mr. Chernichenko and Mr. Treat (ibid., paras. 146-153) and endorsed by the Sub-Commission in its resolution 1990/18,

1. Endorses the decision of the Sub-Commission to entrust Mr. Stanislav Chernichenko and Mr. William Treat with the preparation of a study entitled "The right to a fair trial: current recognition and measures necessary for its strengthening";

2. Requests the Secretary-General to provide the two Special Rapporteurs with all the assistance they may require;

RES/HR/91/6
GE.91-15706

0154

3. Requests the two Special Rapporteurs to draft a questionnaire on the right to a fair trial;

4. Requests the Secretary-General to transmit the questionnaire with the brief report to Governments, the specialized agencies and non-governmental organizations in consultative status with the Economic and Social Council for their response and comments, and to transmit the responses to the Special Rapporteurs for consideration in connection with their study;

Recommends the following draft resolution to the Economic and Social Council for adoption:

"The Economic and Social Council,

Recalling Commission on Human Rights decisions 1990/108 of 7 March 1990 welcoming the appointment of the two Special Rapporteurs on the right to a fair trial, and Commission resolution 1991/43 of 5 March 1991,

Recalling also General Assembly resolution 41/120 of 4 December 1986 regarding the development of international standards in the field of human rights,

Taking into account the brief report on the right to a fair trial prepared by Mr. Stanislav Chernichenko and Mr. William Treat (E/CN.4/Sub.2/1990/34),

1. Endorses Sub-Commission on Prevention of Discrimination and Protection of Minorities resolution 1990/18 of 30 August 1990, by which the Sub-Commission decided to entrust Mr. Stanislav Chernichenko and Mr. William Treat with the preparation of a study entitled 'The right to a fair trial: current recognition and measures necessary for its strengthening' and Commission on Human Rights resolution 1991/43 of 5 March 1991;

2. Requests the Secretary-General to provide the two Special Rapporteurs with all the necessary assistance to carry out the above-mentioned study;

3. Requests the two Special Rapporteurs to draft a questionnaire on the right to a fair trial;

4. Requests the Secretary-General to transmit the questionnaire with the working paper to Governments, the specialized agencies and non-governmental organizations in consultative status with the Economic

0155

and Social Council for their response and comments and requests the Secretary-General to transmit the responses to the Special Rapporteurs for consideration in connection with their study;

5. Requests the Special Rapporteurs to produce a preliminary report based upon their study, the responses to the questionnaire and ways to formulate the basic guarantees necessary for a fair trial into an international standard like a model code, and to submit it to the Sub-Commission for consideration at its forty-third session and for comments to the Commission on Human Rights at its forty-eighth session."

52nd meeting
5 March 1991

0156

Questionnaire on the Right to a Fair Trial

Part I

A. The rapporteurs would be pleased to receive any comments you may wish to make about the brief report contained in E/CN.4/Sub.2/1990/34.

B. Civil Procedure

The rapporteurs would be pleased to receive information about codes, rules, regulations, and/or practices which have been established governing procedures in civil disputes, including: Procedures governing a person's access to the judicial system, the procurement and use of evidence, trial procedures, examination of witnesses, and appeal or other review of trial court decisions.

C. Criminal Procedure

The rapporteurs would be pleased to receive information about codes, rules, regulations, and/or practices which have been established governing criminal procedure, including: Judicial protection from arbitrary arrest; the procurement of, access to, and presentation of evidence; trial procedures; appeal or other review; and post-conviction relief.

D. Administrative Procedure

The rapporteurs would be pleased to receive information about codes, rules, regulations, and/or practices which have been established governing administrative procedures -- in particular those procedures that may have consequences similar to criminal procedures.

D. Military Court Procedure

The rapporteurs would be pleased to receive information about codes, rules, regulations and/or practices which have been established governing military court procedures (including procedures that may affect the rights of civilians) in regard to the issues mentioned above under item C above.

E. Emergency Court Procedures

The rapporteurs would be pleased to receive information about codes, rules, regulations and/or practices which have been established governing emergency court procedures that may have consequences similar to criminal procedures in regard to the issues mentioned in under item C above. Please explain how these emergency court procedures differ from ordinary procedures.

If such codes, rules, or regulations with regard to procedures in civil, criminal, administrative, military, or emergency proceedings have been established, please send a copy of each to the Centre for Human Rights, United Nations, Palais des Nations, CH-1211 Geneva 10, Switzerland. If possible, please send a copy in English, French, Spanish, or one of the other official languages of the United Nations.

M/HR/91/31
GE.91-15695

Part II

Your answers to each of the questions below would be appreciated as to both codes, rules, and regulations as well as actual practices. If it is too difficult or time-consuming to answer all the questions, please give the greatest attention to answering each of the subject heading questions (in **bold** print and preceded by numbers).

A. Treatment during detention prior to and during trial

1. How are detained persons protected from torture and other cruel, inhuman, or degrading treatment?

2. What protection exists for the accused who refuses to confess or testify against himself or herself?

a. Does an accused have the right to remain silent?

b. Can an accused's silence be used against him or her at trial?

c. Can a confession be used against an accused that was obtained without the benefit of counsel or knowledge of the right to counsel?

d. What protections does an accused have from a coerced or otherwise unlawfully obtained confession being used against him or her at trial?

e. Must an accused know the consequences of the confession, such as the potential sentence, before a lawful confession may be taken?

f. If a confession was made as the result of an agreement with the prosecutor, how does an accused enforce the agreement? Can an accused withdraw the confession if the agreement is not fulfilled?

3. How are accused persons in detention treated differently from convicted prisoners?

a. Are accused persons segregated from convicted prisoners?

B. Notice

1. How long can a person be detained without being charged for a criminal offence or without having his case submitted to a court?

2. How is an accused person guaranteed prompt, detailed notice of the charge(s) against him or her?

a. What provisions are made to ensure that the accused is given notice in a language that he or she can understand?

3. How is the accused guaranteed adequate time and facilities to prepare his or her defence?

b. How long before trial does the defence counsel have to prepare for trial?

c. What access does the accused have to the evidence prepared for use against him or her, such as the names of witnesses?

d. What protection does the accused have from surprise evidence being introduced at trial?

C. Counsel

1. Does the accused have access to counsel in preparing his or her defence?

a. If so, is the accused informed that he or she has the right to counsel?

b. What guarantees assure the accused adequate time for consultation?

c. What guarantees does the accused have in exercising his or her free will in choosing counsel?

d. What procedures are established to ensure that a detained person is able to contact counsel?

2. What arrangements are made for accused persons who cannot afford counsel to receive counsel without cost?

a. What remuneration does appointed counsel receive? How does that amount compare with what counsel would normally expect to receive from a paying client?

b. Are there certain kinds of crimes for which counsel is provided without cost to defendants who cannot afford counsel?

c. Under what circumstances is counsel appointed without cost through the appeals and post-conviction processes?

3. What protections does the accused have ensuring the competence of counsel, adequacy of representation, and the adequacy of facilities for the preparation of the defence at all stages of the investigation, trial, appeal, and post-conviction processes?

4. Does a person's right to counsel extend through the post-conviction level, such as habeas corpus or amparo?

5. How is the confidentiality of communication between the accused and counsel guaranteed?

D. Hearing

1. How is the accused's right to be tried without undue delay guaranteed?

a. Does that protection apply at all stages of the trial process, including the time by which a trial is commenced, completed, decided, and appealed?

b. If possible, please provide statistics for the average amount of time that elapses between:

1. Arrest and formal charging with an offence.

2. Charging with an offence and beginning of the trial.

3. Beginning of the trial and completion of the trial or sentence.

4. Initiation of appeal and the disposition of appeal.

c. What differences are characterized by the delays which occur in trials relating to different sorts of criminal charges?

d. Is there a difference in the amount of time it takes to initiate a trial for a detained defendant and a defendant not in custody?

2. What laws or rules are there mandating that criminal and civil trials be conducted in public?

a. When a trial is conducted in public, what guarantees are there allowing the press to witness and report on the proceedings by television, radio, photographs, and/or print media?

b. How, and under what circumstances, is public or press access to a trial limited? Please describe specific examples of trials which were not held in public during the last two years.

3. What assurances does the accused have that the trial will be conducted in the same geographic locality where the conduct at issue occurred?

a. Under what circumstances might a trial be transferred to another locality?

b. May the court transfer the trial to another locality if it appears that accused would be unable to receive a fair trial due to local bias?

4. Under what circumstances, if any, is a trial *in absentia* pursued?

a. What protections does the accused have to guarantee that he or she knows all the evidence considered at a trial *in absentia*?

b. How is a person's right to counsel applied to hearings _in absentia_?

c. Under what circumstances, if any, is it possible to have a trial of a person who is not living?

5. What protections are afforded the mentally incompetent at criminal trials?

a. How is a person determined to be mentally incompetent for the purposes of trial?

6. How is an accused person's entitlement to the free assistance of an interpreter guaranteed, if he or she does not understand the language of the court?

a. Does the interpreter provide interpretation of the entire proceeding including argument of counsel, all testimony, or only testimony given by the accused?

7. What protections exist to guarantee an accused the right to obtain the attendance and examination of witnesses on the accused's behalf under the same conditions as witnesses against the accused?

8. What guarantees protect the accused's right to examine adverse witnesses?

9. How is the accused's right to the presumption of innocence guaranteed?

a. What protections exist to prevent public authorities from manipulating the media or judicial system so as to prejudge the outcome of a trial?

b. What guarantees does the accused have to a judgment based on the evidence adduced at the hearing?

c. What is the degree of proof required to find a person responsible for criminal conduct?

d. What is the degree of proof required for determining rights and obligations in a civil suit?

10. How is a party to a civil suit guaranteed the opportunity to obtain and examine relevant witnesses at trial?

11. Can evidence be considered against an accused if the evidence is obtained pursuant to an arbitrary or unlawful interference with the accused's privacy, family, home or correspondence?

E. Composition of the Court

1. What protection exists to guarantee the independence and impartiality of judges?[1]

2. In criminal and civil cases, under what circumstances may a person receive a trial by judge(s), jury, and/or by lay assessor(s)?

a. Does a party or accused person have a right to trial by jury or lay assessor?

b. What characteristics must a person have to qualify as a juror or lay assessor?

c. Are there any characteristics that disqualify or excuse a person from being a juror or lay assessor, such as active military service, profession, gender, past criminal record, alien status, membership in a particular political or ethnic group, etc.?

d. How may one of the parties disqualify a judge, juror, or lay assessor who may be biased?

e. Under what circumstances is a trial by jury or lay assessor forbidden? Are there specialized courts that do not permit trials by jury or lay assessor?

F. Decision, Sentencing, and Punishment

1. Under what circumstances must the decision-maker issue a statement of reasons explaining the decision in a criminal case?

2. Under what circumstances must the decision-maker issue a statement of reasons explaining the decision in a civil case?

3. What rights does a person have to avoid being tried or punished again for an offence which he or she has already been lawfully convicted or acquitted?

4. What protection does the accused have from being convicted under ex post facto laws?

a. Where the punishment for an offence has changed, what protections exist to ensure that the accused will not receive a greater punishment than that which applied at the time of the occurrence of the crime, or will receive the lesser punishment if the punishment has since been decreased.

5. What protection is provided against imprisonment for failure to fulfill a contractual obligation?

6. What assurances are given that the judgments rendered in criminal

---

[1] As to this question respondents are referred to Singhvi, "The administration of justice and the human rights of detainees: study on the independence and impartiality of the judiciary, jurors and assessors and the independence of lawyers," (E/CN.4/Sub.2/1985/18 and Add.1-6, 1985).

cases and civil suits be made public?

7. Under what conditions are judgments not made public?

8. Under what circumstances, if any, is collective punishment permitted?

9. Has the country abolished the death penalty? If not:

a. For what kinds of crimes may the death penalty be imposed?

b. How and when is the person informed of the death sentence?

c. How does a person who is sentenced to death seek pardon or commutation of the sentence?

d. What is the minimum age, if any, below which a person may not be executed?

i. May juveniles (under the age of 18 at the time of the offence) be executed?

a. What is the maximum age, if any, over which a person may not be executed?

10. What protection does a convicted person have from punishment that is cruel, degrading, or that involves torture or mutilation?

G. Appeal or Other Review in Higher Courts

1. How does a person convicted of a crime have his or her sentence reviewed by a higher tribunal?

a. What limits, if any, are there to the convicted person's right to have the sentence reviewed by a higher tribunal?

b. What kinds of crimes, if any, may not be reviewed by a higher tribunal because they are considered too trivial?

c. May the appeal relate to issues of fact, law, or both?

2. How does a person appeal a judgment from a civil suit?

a. What limits, if any, are there to a party's ability to obtain an appeal before a higher tribunal?

b. May the appeal relate to issues of fact, law, or both?

3. In criminal cases and civil suits, at what point in the trial may a party appeal an intermediate decision rendered prior to the final judgment?

a. Under what circumstances must a party wait until a final

judgment before an appeal may be made?

H. Pardon

1. **What assurances does every convicted person have to the opportunity to seek pardon or commutation of his or her sentence?**

I. Other Remedies

1. **What judicial or other legal remedies does a person have for a violation of fundamental rights?**

2. **When a person has been convicted and punished of an offence and that conviction is subsequently reversed, or the person is pardoned due to new evidence showing that there was a miscarriage of justice, what recourse does the convicted person have to receive compensation for the injury suffered?**

3. **What remedies are available for a person to vindicate a violation of a fundamental right guaranteed by the constitution or under law?**

a. Are remedies similar to or including habeas corpus or amparo available? If so, please specify what provisions of law apply, and include a copy of those provisions.

b. If it is determined that a person's rights have been violated, what compensation is made for damages?

c. Are there certain violations of fundamental rights that may not be raised at trial, after trial, on appeal, by habeas corpus, by amparo, pursuant to other post-conviction procedure, or civil suit?

J. Procedures for Juveniles

1. **What special procedures exist for juvenile offenders?**

a. How do these special procedures take account of the juvenile offender's age?

b. What special procedures are there for the speedy adjudication of cases against juveniles?

2. **What special procedures, if any, apply to juveniles in civil proceedings?**

3. **What protections does a juvenile offender have from the imposition of corporal punishment?**

4. **How are accused juveniles treated differently from accused adults?**

a. Are accused juveniles in detention segregated from accused adults?

5. **Are accused juveniles in detention segregated from juveniles who have been found responsible for criminal conduct?**

K. Military Courts

1. How do procedures in military courts differ from the procedures in ordinary criminal courts?

2. To what extent are the procedural protections identified above provided in military courts?

3. Under what circumstances may military courts try civilians for offences or otherwise affect the rights of civilians?

L. Emergency Courts

1. Under what circumstances may emergency court procedures be established or applied?

2. How do procedures in emergency courts differ from the procedures in ordinary criminal courts?

3. To what extent are the procedural protections identified above provided in emergency courts?

M. Administrative Courts

1. How do procedures in administrative proceedings differ from the procedures in ordinary criminal or civil courts?

2. To what extent are parties to administrative proceedings given notice of information that may adversely affect them; a fair and public hearing by a competent, independent, and impartial tribunal established by law; an opportunity to present information supporting their claim or defence; a decision based upon the information adduced at the hearing; and a decision which is made public?

3. To what extent are the other procedural protections identified above in subparts A - J, insofar as relevant, provided in administrative proceedings?

N. Other Questions

1. The rapporteurs would be pleased to receive information about the principal books and articles relating to the right to a fair trial in your country.

2. The rapporteurs would be pleased to receive information about any academic or other views about the brief report contained in E/CN.4/Sub.2/1990/34.

3. The rapporteurs would be pleased to receive any other information you may wish to provide.

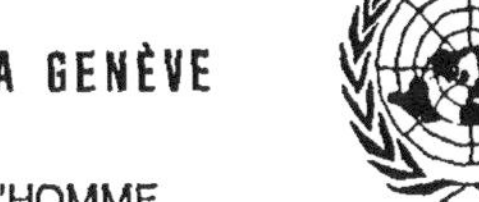

OFFICE DES NATIONS UNIES A GENÈVE

CENTRE POUR LES DROITS DE L'HOMME

UNITED NATIONS OFFICE AT GENEVA

CENTRE FOR HUMAN RIGHTS

Palais des Nations
CH-1211 GENÈVE 10

Téléfax: (022) 733 98 79
Télégrammes: UNATIONS, GENÈVE
Télex: 412 962 UNO CH
Téléphone: 734 60 11 731 02 11

RÉF N°: G/SO 252/2 (4)
(à rappeler dans la réponse)

The Secretary-General of the United Nations presents his compliments to the Minister for Foreign Affairs of the Republic of Korea and has the honour to draw the attention of His/Her Excellency's Government to resolution 1991/54 entitled "Sale of children, child prostitution and child pornography, and the exploitation of child labour" and resolution 1991/55 entitled "Programme of action for the elimination of the exploitation of child labour", both adopted by the Commission on Human Rights on 6 March 1991.

In paragraph 10 of resolution 1991/54 the Commission on Human Rights endorsed the "Programme of action for the elimination of the exploitation of Child Labour" proposed by the Sub-Commission on Prevention of Discrimination and Protection of Minorities.

In paragraph 2 of resolution 1991/55 the Commission on Human Rights decided to transmit the draft programme of action for comments to Governments, specialized agencies and other intergovernmental organizations, as well as non-governmental organizations.

A copy of the Programme of action for the elimination of the exploitation of child labour is attached.

The Secretary-General would appreciate it if any information on the Programme that His/Her Excellency's Government may wish to submit for consideration by the Working Group on Contemporary Forms of Slavery, could be forwarded to the Under-Secretary-General for Human Rights, United Nations Office at Geneva, CH-1211 Genève 10, if possible by 15 July 1991.

2 May 1991

0166

OFFICE DES NATIONS UNIES ≡NÈVE

CENTRE POUR LES DROITS DE L'HOMME

UNITE ⎯TIONS OFFICE AT GENEVA

CENTRE FOR HUMAN RIGHTS

Téléfax: (022) 733 98 79
Télégrammes: UNATIONS, GENÈVE
Télex: 412 962 UNO CH
Téléphone: 734 60 11 731 02 11

Palais des Nations
CH-1211 GENÈVE 10

RÉF. Nº: G/SO 214 (50)
(à rappeler dans la réponse)

The Secretary-General of the United Nations presents his compliments to the Minister for Foreign Affairs of the Republic of Korea and has the honour to refer to General Assembly resolutions 45/101 and 45/102 adopted on 14 December 1990 and entitled, respectively, "New international humanitarian order" and "Promotion of international co-operation in the humanitarian field". Copies of these two resolutions are enclosed.

In resolution 45/101, the Assembly, inter alia, encouraged Governments as well as governmental and non-governmental organizations that have not yet done so to provide their comments and expertise to the Secretary-General regarding the humanitarian order and the report of the Independent Commission on International Humanitarian Issues. Furthermore, the Assembly invited Governments to make available to the Secretary-General, on a voluntary basis, information and expertise on humanitarian issues of concern to them, in order to identify opportunities for future action.

Finally, the Assembly requested the Secretary-General to remain in contact with Governments as well as governmental and non-governmental organizations and the Independent Bureau for Humanitarian Issues and to report on the progress made by them to the General Assembly at its forty-seventh session.

In resolution 45/102, the Assembly, inter alia, called upon Governments further to develop international co-operation in the humanitarian field and invited Governments to promote, within existing mechanisms, regular exchanges of information and of national experience in addressing humanitarian problems.

Pursuant to these two resolutions the Assembly at its forty-seventh session will review the question of a new international humanitarian order and it will consider the question of international co-operation in the humanitarian field.

The Secretary-General will be preparing a report on the progress made in the humanitarian field for submission to the General Assembly at its forty-seventh session pursuant to paragraphs 5 and 6 of resolution 45/101. In that regard the Secretary-General would appreciate receiving any information which His/Her Excellency's Government might wish to provide in connection with the preparation of the report. The Secretary-General would be grateful if that information could be sent to the Centre for Human Rights, United Nations Office at Geneva, CH-1211 Geneva 10, if possible by 1 October 1991.

3 May 1991

0167

45/101. New international humanitarian order

The General Assembly,

Recalling its resolutions 36/136 of 14 December 1981, 37/201 of 18 December 1982, 38/125 of 16 December 1983, 40/126 of 13 December 1985, 42/120 and 42/121 of 7 December 1987 and 43/129 of 8 December 1988 relating to the promotion of a new international humanitarian order,

Taking note of the report of the Secretary-General 1/ and the comments made by various Governments regarding the humanitarian order and the work done in this regard by the Independent Commission on International Humanitarian Issues,

Noting the actions being taken by the specialized agencies and programmes of the United Nations system with regard to the humanitarian issues, examined by the Independent Commission, that fall within their respective mandates,

Recognizing with concern the continuing need further to strengthen international responses to growing humanitarian challenges and to adjust actions of governmental and non-governmental organizations to new realities in a fast-changing world,

Bearing in mind the importance of creative humanitarian action at both the international as well as the regional and national levels to alleviate human suffering and to promote durable solutions to humanitarian problems,

Convinced of the need for active follow-up to the recommendations and suggestions made by the Independent Commission and of the role being played in this regard by the Independent Bureau for Humanitarian Issues set up for the purpose,

1. Expresses its appreciation to the Secretary-General for his continuing active support to the efforts to promote a new international humanitarian order;

2. Encourages Governments as well as governmental and non-governmental organizations that have not yet done so to provide their comments and expertise to the Secretary-General regarding the humanitarian order and the report of the Independent Commission on International Humanitarian Issues;

3. Invites the Independent Bureau for Humanitarian Issues to continue and further strengthen its essential role in following up the work of the Independent Commission;

4. Invites Governments to make available to the Secretary-General, on a voluntary basis, information and expertise on humanitarian issues of concern to them in order to identify opportunities for future action;

5. Requests the Secretary-General to remain in contact with Governments as well as governmental and non-governmental organizations and the Independent Bureau for Humanitarian Issues and to report on the progress made by them to the General Assembly at its forty-seventh session;

6. Decides to review at its forty-seventh session the question of a new international humanitarian order.

1/ A/45/524.

45/102. Promotion of international co-operation in the humanitarian field

The General Assembly,

Recalling its resolutions 42/121 of 7 December 1987 and 43/130 of 8 December 1988,

Noting that one of the purposes of the United Nations, set forth in its Charter, is to achieve international co-operation in solving international problems of a humanitarian character,

Recalling the Universal Declaration of Human Rights, 1/ which proclaims, inter alia, that recognition of the inherent dignity and of the equal and inalienable rights of all members of the human family is the foundation of freedom, justice and peace in the world,

Recalling also that everyone is entitled to a social and international order in which universally recognized human rights and fundamental freedoms can be fully realized,

Mindful of the fact that unresolved humanitarian problems may impede the effective realization of human rights and even lead to violations of these rights,

Convinced that solving humanitarian problems requires co-operation and harmonization of actions taken by Governments, international bodies, non-governmental organizations and individuals,

Mindful of the significance of the existing workable system to promote, facilitate and co-ordinate humanitarian activities carried out by Governments, the United Nations system and intergovernmental and non-governmental organizations,

1. Calls upon Governments, the United Nations system and intergovernmental and non-governmental organizations further to develop international co-operation in the humanitarian field;

2. Reiterates that international co-operation in the humanitarian field will facilitate better understanding, mutual respect, confidence and tolerance among countries and peoples, thus contributing to a more just and non-violent world;

3. Notes the need to identify humanitarian problems of the highest priority and to develop a universal strategy of action in the humanitarian field;

4. Invites Governments to promote, within existing mechanisms, regular exchanges of information and of national experience in addressing humanitarian problems;

5. Calls for the broadening of the concept of international co-operation in the humanitarian field through effective bilateral dialogue and activities pertaining to specific humanitarian issues;

1/ Resolution 217 A (III).

0169

6. Encourages the international community to contribute substantially and regularly to international humanitarian activities;

7. Invites all non-governmental organizations concerned with the humanitarian issues examined by the Independent Commission on International Humanitarian Issues and working with strictly humanitarian motives to bear in mind the recommendations and suggestions made in the report 2/ of the Independent Commission in the context of their policies and actions in the field;

8. Decides to consider this issue at its forty-seventh session under the item entitled "New international humanitarian order".

2/ Winning the Human Race? The Report of the Independent Commission on International Humanitarian Issues (London and New Jersey, Zed Books Ltd., 1988).

0170

OFFICE DES NATIONS UNIES A GENÈVE

CENTRE POUR LES DROITS DE L'HOMME

UNITED NATIONS OFFICE AT GENEVA

CENTRE FOR HUMAN RIGHTS

Téléfax: (022) 733 98 79
Télégrammes: UNATIONS, GENÈVE
Télex: 412 962 UNO CH
Téléphone: 734 60 11   731 02 11

Palais des Nations
CH-1211 GENÈVE 10

RÉF. N°: G/SO 252/2 (4)
(à rappeler dans la réponse)

The Secretary-General of the United Nations presents his compliments to the Minister for Foreign Affairs of the Republic of Korea and has the honour to refer to resolution 1991/58 entitled "Report of the Working Group on Contemporary Forms of Slavery of the Sub-Commission on Prevention of the Discrimination and Protection of Minorities", adopted by the Commission on Human Rights on 6 March 1991. A copy of the resolution is attached.

The particular attention of His/Her Excellency's Government is drawn to paragraphs 2 and 3 of this resolution.

In paragraph 2, the Commission requested the Secretary-General to invite States parties to the Slavery Convention of 1926, the Supplementary Convention on the Abolition of Slavery, the Slave Trade, and Institutions and Practices Similar to Slavery of 1956 and the Convention for the Suppression of the Traffic in Persons and of the Exploitation of the Prostitution of Others of 1949 to submit to the Sub-Commission on Prevention of Discrimination and Protection of Minorities regular reports on the situation in their countries, as provided for under the conventions and in Economic and Social Council decision 16 (LVI) of 17 May 1974, which contains the mandate of the Working Group on Contemporary Forms of Slavery.

In paragraph 3, the Commission invited those eligible States that have not ratified the relevant conventions to consider doing so as soon as possible, or to explain in writing why they feel unable to do so, and invites them to consider providing information regarding their national legislation and practices in this field.

The Secretary-General would appreciate it if any information that His/Her Excellency's Government may wish to provide in accordance with paragraphs 2 and 3 of the above-mentioned resolution, could be forwarded to the Under-Secretary-General for Human-Rights, United Nations Office at Geneva, CH-1211 Genève 10, if possible by 15 July 1991, in order that it can be submitted to the Working Group on Contemporary Forms of Slavery.

6 May 1991

0171

COMMISSION ON HUMAN RIGHTS

Forty-seventh session

1991/58. *Report of the Working Group on Contemporary Forms of Slavery of the Sub-Commission on Prevention of Discrimination and Protection of Minorities*

The Commission on Human Rights,

Recalling the provisions of the Slavery Convention of 1926, the Supplementary Convention on the Abolition of Slavery, the Slave Trade, and Institutions and Practices Similar to Slavery of 1956 and the Convention for the Suppression of the Traffic in Persons and of the Exploitation of the Prostitution of Others of 1949,

Having noted the report of the Working Group on Contemporary Forms of Slavery submitted to the Sub-Commission on Prevention of Discrimination and Protection of Minorities at its forty-second session (E/CN.4/Sub.2/1990/44),

Having considered Sub-Commission resolutions 1987/31 and 1987/32 of 4 September 1987, 1988/31 of 1 September 1988, 1989/41 of 1 September 1989 and 1990/30 of 31 August 1990,

Recalling its resolutions 1982/20 of 10 March 1982 on the question of slavery and the slave trade in all their practices and manifestations and 1988/42 of 8 March 1988, 1989/35 of 6 March 1989 and 1990/63 of 7 March 1990 on the report of the Working Group on Contemporary Forms of Slavery of the Sub-Commission,

Recalling Economic and Social Council resolutions 1982/20 of 4 May 1982 and 1983/30 of 26 May 1983 on the suppression of the traffic in persons and of the exploitation of the prostitution of others,

Recalling also Economic and Social Council resolutions 1988/34 of 27 May 1988, 1989/74 of 24 May 1989 and 1990/46 of 25 May 1990,

Recalling further General Assembly resolutions 38/107 of 16 December 1983 and 40/103 of 13 December 1985 on the prevention of prostitution,

Gravely concerned that slavery, the slave trade, slavery-like practices and even modern manifestations of this phenomenon still exist, representing some of the gravest violations of human rights,

1. *Expresses its appreciation* to the Working Group on Contemporary Forms of Slavery of the Sub-Commission on Prevention of Discrimination and Protection of Minorities for its valuable work, in particular the progress made at its fifteenth session in executing its programme of work, and for its continued broad approach and flexible methods of work;

RES/HR/91/11
GE.91-15883

0172

2. Requests the Secretary-General to invite States parties to the Slavery Convention of 1926, the Supplementary Convention on the Abolition of Slavery, the Slave Trade, and Institutions and Practices Similar to Slavery of 1956 and the Convention for the Suppression of the Traffic in Persons and of the Exploitation of the Prostitution of Others of 1949 to submit to the Sub-Commission on Prevention of Discrimination and Protection of Minorities regular reports on the situation in their countries, as provided for under the conventions and in Economic and Social Council decision 16 (LVI) of 17 May 1974, which contains the mandate of the Working Group on Contemporary Forms of Slavery;

3. Invites those eligible States that have not ratified the relevant conventions to consider doing so as soon as possible, or to explain in writing why they feel unable to do so, and invites them to consider providing information regarding their national legislation and practices in this field;

4. Also invites intergovernmental organizations, relevant organizations of the United Nations system, including the International Labour Organisation, the World Health Organization, the World Bank, the International Monetary Fund, the Food and Agriculture Organization of the United Nations, the United Nations Educational, Scientific and Cultural Organization, the United Nations Development Programme, the United Nations Children's Fund and the United Nations University, the International Criminal Police Organization and non-governmental organizations concerned, to continue to supply relevant information to the Working Group;

5. Encourages the Sub-Commission, including its Working Group, once again to elaborate recommendations on the ways and means of establishing an effective mechanism for the implementation of the Slavery Conventions on the basis of the study prepared by the Secretary-General on this issue (E/CN.4/Sub.2/1989/37);

6. Takes note with appreciation of the assignment by the Secretary-General of a part-time professional staff member to serve the Working Group and undertake other activities relating to contemporary forms of slavery under the post which has been included in the budget of the Centre for Human Rights for questions relating to slavery and slavery-like practices and requests the Secretary-General to assign this staff member on a full-time basis;

7. Recalls once again its request to the Secretary-General to designate the Centre for Human Rights as the focal point for the co-ordination of activities in the United Nations for the suppression of contemporary forms of slavery;

0173

8. Calls upon all relevant non-governmental organizations in consultative status with the Economic and Social Council, including those interested in the rights of children and women, to attend the sessions of the Working Group;

9. Recommends that the General Assembly establish a voluntary fund on contemporary forms of slavery and requests the Economic and Social Council to take further action on this matter;

10. Recommends that the supervisory bodies of the International Labour Organisation give particular attention in their work to the implementation of provisions and standards designed to ensure protection of children and other persons exposed to contemporary forms of slavery;

11. Recommends that the Human Rights Committee, the Committee on Economic, Social and Cultural Rights, the Committee on the Elimination of Discrimination against Women and the Committee on the Rights of the Child, when examining periodic reports of the States parties, give particular attention to the implementation of, respectively, articles 8 and 24 of the International Covenant on Civil and Political Rights, articles 10, 12 and 13 of the International Covenant on Economic, Social and Cultural Rights and article 6 of the Convention on the Elimination of All Forms of Discrimination against Women, and articles 32, 34, 35 and 36 of the Convention on the Rights of the Child with a view to combating contemporary forms of slavery;

12. Invites the Special Rapporteur on sale of children, child prostitution and child pornography to examine ways and means of co-operating with the Working Group on Contemporary Forms of Slavery;

13. Recalls its request to the Secretary-Général to report to the Economic and Social Council on the steps taken by Member States, organizations of the United Nations system and intergovernmental organizations to implement the recommendations contained in Council resolution 1983/30 of 26 May 1983 and requests the Secretary-General to report on the comments received to the Council at its first regular session of 1991, and to make this report available to the Working Group;

14. Invites all Member States to consider the possibility of taking appropriate action for the protection of children and migrant women against exploitation by prostitution and other slavery-like practices, including the possibility of establishing national bodies to achieve these objectives;

15. Requests Governments to pursue a policy of information, prevention and rehabilitation of women victims of the exploitation of prostitution and to take the appropriate economic and social measures deemed necessary to that effect;

16. Recommends that these concerns are fully considered by the Working Group at its sixteenth session, when its main theme of work will be the prevention of the traffic in persons and the exploitation of the prostitution of others.

53rd meeting
6 March 1991

0175

Annex

Programme of action for the elimination of the exploitation of child labour

General

1. In spite of the progress made in combating the exploitation of child labour, in particular through the development of national and international norms which have defined the bases of legal protection, and of mechanisms for monitoring their application, the exploitation of child labour still remains a current and widespread phenomenon of a serious nature in various parts of the world.

2. This phenomenon, which is both complex and world-wide, varies from one country to another. Although the industrialized countries are not spared, it affects the developing countries more particularly, and within each country the more vulnerable groups of the population. Poverty is often the main cause of child labour, but generations of children should not be condemned to exploitation until poverty is overcome. Underdevelopment cannot justify the exploitation of which children are the victims. The Governments concerned and the international community as a whole must not wait for development problems to be adequately solved before attacking the phenomenon of the exploitation of child labour. Besides the long-term action which should be initiated with a view to treating the deep causes underlying the exploitation of child labour, it is essential that urgent measures and medium- and short-term action be taken to meet the immediate needs of the children who are exposed to the gravest dangers, while making sure that such action is integrated into economic and social development strategies.

3. High priority should be given to the eradication of the most odious forms of child exploitation, in particular child prostitution, pornography, the sale of children, the employment of children in dangerous occupations and debt bondage.

4. The international community should place particular emphasis on the new phenomena of the exploitation of child labour, such as the use of children for illegal, clandestine or criminal purposes, including their implication in the narcotic drugs traffic or in armed conflicts or military activities.

5. The action should be directed, first, towards the most dangerous forms of child labour and the elimination of work by children under 10 years of age, with a view to the total eradication of child labour as prohibited by the provisions of the relevant international instruments.

0176

6. Special attention should be paid to the most vulnerable categories of children: children of immigrants, street children, children of minority groups, indigenous children, refugee children, children in occupied territories and those under the apartheid régime.

7. In order to reach the core of one of the prime causes of exploitation of child labour, which is poverty, increased resources should be made available through bilateral and multilateral channels for the elimination of the exploitation of child labour. Eradication of the phenomena linked with the exploitation of child labour calls for social measures and development assistance. Their prevention will require deep structural reforms in the economic, social and cultural spheres.

8. Particular attention should also be given to social rehabilitation, education and information. It is important that the means of protecting children should be strengthened by development, the reinforcement of legislation and proper application of the relevant laws.

9. Adequate means and concerted measures are necessary at the local, national, regional and international levels.

Information

10. The public could be made aware of the problem and the different aspects of the exploitation of child labour by national and international information campaigns. The extent of the problem cannot be accurately defined by reference to the statistics from various sources. The sectors favouring the exploitation of child labour should be specially targeted (agriculture, non-structured urban sector and domestic service). It is important to reach the children who are the invisible victims of parallel employment networks. At the national level it is necessary to develop means of investigation and supervision by labour inspectors in order to detect and prosecute cases of exploitation of child labour, so as to break up the clandestine employment networks. The information campaign should also be able to reach children direct, in order to inform them of their rights and make them aware of the risks they run.

Education and vocational training

11. There is undoubtedly a link between child labour, illiteracy, school failure and the lack of vocational training. Massive literacy programmes, combined with legislation making basic training obligatory and free, as well as measures to combat school wastage and develop vocational training, are extremely necessary. Such programmes could be supported by community campaigns to increase the awareness and motivation of families.

Social action

12. The economic and social causes of the persistence of child labour, including the fact that it is seen in many cases as a means of survival for the children and their families, should be taken up in order to offer an alternative that will take the children out of the circle of poverty and exploitation. Urgent measures could be taken on behalf of children who are subjected to high physical and moral risks. It is important to give them protection and assistance, including social and medical assistance, while at the same time pursuing the objective of eradication of child labour. These urgent measures should be backed up by programmes of social rehabilitation.

Development aid

13. For many countries, the implementation of local, regional and national programmes on behalf of children requires appropriate international aid and a deeper commitment of the international community, whether through specific projects or through development assistance.

Labour standards and their application

14. States should adhere to the international standards in force and ensure that they are rigorously applied. It is important that, in accordance with article 1 of ILO Convention No. 138, States should undertake "to pursue a national policy designed to ensure the effective abolition of child labour and so to raise progressively the minimum age of admission to employment or work to a level consistent with the fullest physical and mental development of young person". National legislation should explicitly prohibit dangerous or high-risk employment and prescribe penalties for employers who break this law. In at least three cases the exploitation of child labour is no less than a flagrant crime which violates the Charter of the United Nations, the principles of the Charter and the Universal Declaration of Human Rights, the most elementary principles of morality and all positive laws. Energetic repressive action is called for in these cases, namely:

(a) Sale and similar practices (serfdom, bond service, fake adoption, abandonment);

(b) Child prostitution, trafficking in pornography, involving the sexuality of children, and international traffic in girls and boys for immoral purposes;

(c) Under-age maidservants in a position of servitude.

Duties of States

15. States should fully apply the provisions of the Declaration of the Rights of the Child of 20 November 1959 (General Assembly resolution 1386 (XIV)), and more particularly:

Principle 2, according to which "The child shall enjoy special protection, and shall be given opportunities and facilities, by law and by other means, to enable him to develop physically, mentally, morally, spiritually and socially in a healthy and normal manner and in conditions of freedom and dignity".

Principle 9, according to which "The child shall be protected against all forms of neglect, cruelty and exploitation. He shall not be the subject of traffic, in any form".

16. States should consider the possibility of ratifying the Convention on the Rights of the Child as soon as possible and in this context should fully implement, in particular, article 32, which reads as follows:

"1. States parties recognize the right of the child to be protected from economic exploitation and from performing any work that is likely to be hazardous or to interfere with the child's education, or to be harmful to the child's health or physical, mental, spiritual, moral or social development.

2. States parties shall take legislative, administrative, social and educational measures to ensure the implementation of the present article. To this end, and having regard to the relevant provisions of other international instruments, States parties shall in particular:

(a) Provide for a minimum age or minimum a[illegible] for admission to employment;

(b) Provide for appropriate regulation of the hours and conditions of employment;

(c) Provide for appropriate penalties or other sanctions to ensure the effective enforcement of the present article."

17. Noting that over 40 countries have ratified ILO Convention No. 138, those that have not done so should take appropriate steps to ratify this Convention. In this connection, greater assistance from ILO should be extended to the developing countries to facilitate their increased participation in standard-setting activities and in the implementation of ratified conventions.

0179

18. States should sign and implement policies and programmes to narrow the gap between legislation and its implementation in practice.

19. States which have not already done so should review their legislation in the field of child labour with a view to absolute prohibition of employment of children in the following cases:

(a) Employment before the normal age of completion of primary schooling in the country concerned;

(b) Under-age maid service;

(c) Night work;

(d) Work in dangerous or unhealthy conditions;

(e) Work concerned with trafficking in and production of illicit drugs;

(f) Work involving degrading or cruel treatment.

20. States should take preventive and curative measures, including the strengthening of their legislation, to combat the phenomena of the exploitation of child labour, such as the use of children for illegal, clandestine or criminal purposes, including the traffic in narcotic drugs or in armed conflicts or military activities, or any other form of conflict.

21. States should, where necessary, undertake development programmes with a view to:

(a) Making primary education compulsory and available free to all;

(b) Assisting and encouraging families in order that their children may continue their education, in order to combat the phenomenon of school drop-outs;

(c) Adapting school curricula to the preparation of a child for a career;

(d) Improving the training programmes of professional workers dealing with child labour, in particular labour inspectors, social workers and magistrates, with a view, in particular, to making them more sensitive to the needs of children;

(e) Establishing or improving medical services for children.

22. States should ensure the availability of a sufficient number of work inspectors and train them systematically to deal with cases of exploitation of child labour. Particular attention should be given to national and regional plans for social and economic development to the occupational training of young people. National development plans should also include a section devoted particularly to the employment of young people, and to methods of ensuring that the most deprived have sufficient resources to be able to protect themselves from conditions leading to exploitation.

0180

23. All member States should endeavour to establish national agencies or institutions to promote the rights of children and to protect them from any form of exploitation.

Role of United Nations organs and specialized agencies

24. The International Labour Organisation should be encouraged in its activities within the framework of its work programme relating to child labour. Other specialized agencies and United Nations organs should develop or reinforce their activities in the field of child labour.

25. All competent United Nations agencies, development banks and intergovernmental bodies involved in development projects should ensure that no child is employed either directly or through local sub-contractors.

26. The United Nations and specialized agencies, having regard to their special responsibilities in the field of child labour, should pay special attention to the situation of children in South Africa and in the occupied Arab territories.

27. While the question of exploitation of child labour should primarily be dealt with in the International Labour Organisation, the United Nations human rights organs should continue to be concerned with this question in the framework of the rights of the child in general. The Sub-Commission should continue to have responsibility in this field.

28. The United Nations and the specialized agencies, including the United Nations University, should continue to incorporate in their programmes a series of interdisciplinary and multinational projects for comparative research into the various aspects of the exploitation of child labour throughout the world and in particular in the countries of Africa, Asia and Latin America.

29. The United Nations and the specialized agencies should reinforce their programmes related to the elimination of the exploitation of child labour, and in particular to the study of the economic, social, legal and cultural factors which give rise to it.

Co-operation at the local, national and international levels

30. All principal steps should be taken by Governments, international organizations and non-governmental organizations to increase awareness, amongst children, parents, workers and employers, of the causes and the adverse effects of child labour, and measures to combat its exploitation. Such steps could include the wider dissemination of relevant international instruments translated, where appropriate, into other languages in addition to the official languages of the United Nations.

0181

31. Support should be given to non-governmental organizations concerned with the problem of child labour, particularly at the community level, and a constructive partnership should be evolved between Governments and non-governmental organizations.

32. The United Nations organs and specialized agencies dealing with the problem of child labour should seek the co-operation of national and international trade unions.

33. Appropriate and necessary forms of support should be given to non-governmental organizations at all levels, especially community organizations, concerned with the problem of child labour.

34. Concerned United Nations organs and specialized agencies should examine the possibility of promoting an information campaign among villagers, employers, parents, children and other groups, in countries where child labour exists.

35. Members of the international community should co-operate in order to assist developing countries in creating conditions under which child labour could be entirely eradicated.

<u>53rd meeting</u>
<u>6 March 1991</u>

0182

통
-기록
검사

주 제 네 바 대 표 부

제네(정) 2031-419 1991. 5. 2

수신 : 외무부장관

참조 : 국제기구조약국장

제목 : 유엔 인권위 강제 실종 실무위 관련 자료 요청

발송 91. 5. 3 주제네바 대표부

Ivan Tosevski 유엔 인권위 강제 실종 실무위 의장은 별첨 91. 4. 26자 본직앞 서한을 통해 강제 실종 관련 범법자 비처벌(impunity) 문제에 대한 아국 정부의 입장을 문의하여 온바, 본부 의견 있을 경우 91. 7. 15까지 당관에 송부하여 주시기 바랍니다.

첨 부 : 상기 서한 사본 1부. 끝.

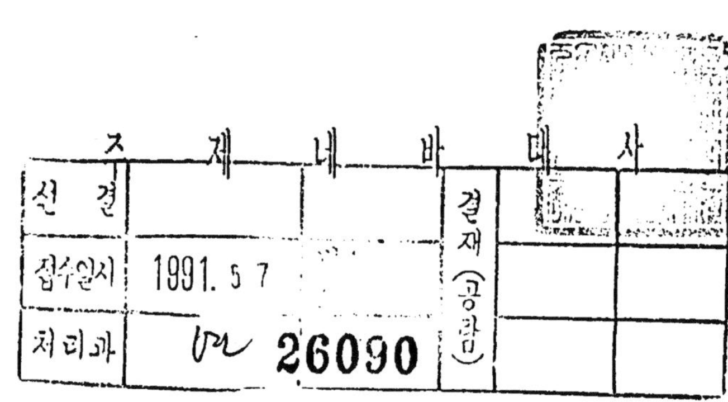

주 제 네 바 대 사

선 결		결재(공람)		
접수일시	1991. 5 7			
처리과	02 26090			

0183

OFFICE DES NATIONS UNIES A GENÈVE

CENTRE POUR LES DROITS DE L'HOMME

UNITED NATIONS OFFICE AT GENEVA

CENTRE FOR HUMAN RIGHTS

Téléfax: (022) 733 98 79
Télégrammes: UNATIONS, GENÈVE
Télex: 28 96 96
Téléphone: 734 60 11 731 02 11

Palais des Nations
CH-1211 GENÈVE 10

RÉF. Nº: G/SO 217/3
(à rappeler dans la réponse)

26 April 1991

Dear Mr. Amb

At its thirty-third session the Working Group on Enforced or Involuntary Disappearances continued its consideration of ways and means that could contribute to eliminating the practice of disappearances, which is one of the tasks entrusted to it by the Commission on Human Rights in successive resolutions regarding this problem.

The Working Group has repeatedly stated in its reports to the Commission that impunity is perhaps the single most important factor contributing to disappearances. This conclusion is supported by a careful analysis of the situation in many countries where disappearances occur. A copy of the relevant parts of the conclusions and recommendations ... relating to the question of impunity contained in the Working Group's most recent report to the Commission is attached for your information.

At its last session, the Working Group considered statements made by Government representatives before the Commission at its forty-seventh session, which further substantiate the views of the Working Group on this matter. It also considered reports submitted by non-governmental organizations which corroborated the Working Group's views and contained a number of suggestions for measures to be taken at the national and international levels to encourage accountability for human rights violations.

The Working Group has consistently requested the co-operation of all Governments concerned, in order to perform more effectively the tasks entrusted to it. For this reason, the Working Group would appreciate receiving from your Government any comments or observations it might wish to make in relation to the question of impunity as it affects the practice of enforced or involuntary disappearances in general and, in particular, in relation to the following tentative considerations:

1. that the investigation of disappearances and the publication of the results of the investigations are perhaps the most important means to establishing accountability for the Government itself. The identity of the victims as well as the identity of those responsible for devising policies and practices, those who carried out disappearances and those who knowingly aided and abetted them, should be made known

.../..2

His Excellency
Mr. Soo Gil Park
Ambassador, Permanent Observer
of the Republic of Korea to
the United Nations Office at Geneva
20 route de Pré-Bois
Case postale 566
1215 Genève 15

0184

to the public. The investigation, prosecution and punishment of those responsible for disappearances should conform to internationally recognized principles of due process of law and should not be subject to any limitation of time;

2. that no laws and decrees should be enacted or maintained which, in effect, immunize the perpetrators of disappearances from accountability;

3. that the duty to investigate, prosecute and punish those responsible for gross abuses such as disappearances is proportionate to the extent and severity of the abuses and the degree of responsibility for such abuses. In making such determinations, it is essential that there should be no granting of impunity either because of the identity of those responsible for gross abuses of human rights or because of the identity of the victims;

4. that the prosecution and punishment of offences involving gross violations of human rights such as disappearances should be dealt with in civilian courts, even if those under prosecution have been or are members of the armed forces;

5. that obedience to orders (in circumstances other than duress) is not a valid defense to charges of responsibility for disappearances. To the extent that obedience to orders is relevant to prosecutions, it should be only as a mitigating circumstance that may be considered by judges according to the facts of each case in determining the appropriate punishment;

Your Government's contribution will be carefully analysed with a view to including in the next report of the Working Group a summary of the positions and suggestions expressed by the international community on this matter.

In view of the fact that the thirty-fourth session of the Working Group will be held from 26 to 30 August 1991 at the United Nations Office at Geneva, it would be greatly appreciated if your contribution could reach the Centre for Human Rights, United Nations Office at Geneva, CH-1211 Genève 10 (cable address UNATIONS GENEVA, telex 412962, telefax 7339879), by 31 July 1991.

I remain, dear Mr. Ambassador
Yours sincerely,

Ivan Tosevski
Chairman
Working Group on Enforced or
Involuntary Disappearnaces

0185

406. As the Working Group indicated in its previous report, impunity is perhaps the single most important factor contributing to the phenomenon of disappearance. Perpetrators of human rights violations, whether civilian or military, become all the more irresponsible if they are not held to account before a court of law. Subversive groups, for their part, may become all the more brazen if their violent acts can be repeated unpunished. Impunity can also induce victims of these practices to resort to self-help, acting as judge and executioner at the same time. The interplay among these various factors may exacerbate the level of violence reigning in a country, and thereby further reinforce impunity.

407. A high level of militarization is often a Government's response to violent action by subversive groups. From the outset, their impact on the enjoyment of human rights and the atrocities they commit have been important factors for the Group in judging the context of violence in which disappearances occur. As soon as a counter-insurgency campaign is launched against such groups, the flow of complaints about human rights abuses often increases. In those circumstances, impunity becomes almost endemic. This is also true for operations conducted by paramilitary forces in various guises. There is a pressing need for those countries where such forces are operating legally, for instance as civil defence groups, to circumscribe their responsibilities as regards maintenance of public order. Where paramilitary forces take the form of death squads and the like, accountability becomes almost illusory, particularly in situations where Governments are unwilling to take decisive action against them.

408. The problem of impunity may be seriously compounded by reticence in the administration of justice. In this sense, the Working Group's experience has shown military courts to contribute significantly to impunity. A recurrent theme in times of internal crisis or under the doctrine of national security is that military personnel attested to have engaged in gross misconduct against civilians hardly ever see their cases investigated in any rigorous manner. In the few cases which are brought to trial, they are almost invariably acquitted or given sentences that, by any standard, are grossly disproportionate to the crime committed. Subsequent promotions are even commonplace. The Working Group continues to be concerned about the widespread tendency to grant jurisdiction over human rights abuses to military courts.

409. Another contributing factor to impunity may likewise be the administration of civilian justice, which is often seen to suffer from institutional paralysis. Prosecutors and judges may find themselves overburdened and over-threatened, making them slow to respond to the need for inquiries. Paralysis may also occur through lack of co-operation by the executive branch. Habeas corpus, a remedy that is the most powerful weapon against unlawful detention, is a case in point. As its success ultimately depends on willingness by the executive to provide information on a disappeared person, habeas corpus is rendered useless if co-operation stops at the barracks' gate. In addition, there are many examples of practical and legal obstacles to its effective use which Governments have seen no reason to remove or which they have purposely put into place. The Working Group feels deeply frustrated that, in this manner, habeas corpus remains virtually inoperative in situations of widespread disappearance. Affected Governments should engage in a systematic revision of habeas corpus procedures, repairing their deficiencies.

410. In certain instances, a pardon or an amnesty is extended to persons suspected of or responsible for human rights violations, including disappearances. Such measures are justified on political and national security grounds or in terms of national reconciliation or peace efforts. Nevertheless, the Working Group finds it hard to accept that a consequence - de facto or de jure - of some of those measures is to prevent investigations being made into the fate or whereabouts of the missing persons. Their relatives, understandably, derive little consolation from such policies, even if they are designed essentially to prevent the recurrence of events such as disappearances.

0186

OFFICE DES NATIONS UNIES A GENÈVE

CENTRE POUR LES DROITS DE L'HOMME

UNITED NATIONS OFFICE AT GENEVA

CENTRE FOR HUMAN RIGHTS

Téléfax: (022) 733 98 79
Télégrammes: UNATIONS, GENÈVE
Télex: 412 962 UNO CH
Téléphone: 734 60 11 731 02 11

Palais des Nations
CH-1211 GENÈVE 10

RÉF. N°: G/SO 234 (18-7)
(à rappeler dans la réponse)

The Secretary-General of the United Nations presents his compliments to the Minister for Foreign Affairs of the Republic of Korea and has the honour to bring to the attention of His Excellency's Government information concerning United Nations activities in connection with indigenous peoples.

On 18 December 1990, the General Assembly adopted resolution 45/164 in which it proclaimed 1993 as International Year of the World's Indigenous People. The Year is intended to strengthen international co-operation for the solution of problems faced by indigenous communities in areas such as human rights, the environment, development, education and health. The resolution invited States to make preparations for the Year. It also authorized the Secretary-General to accept and administer voluntary contributions from Governments and other organizations for the purpose of funding programme activities for the Year.

The Commission on Human Rights in its resolution 1991/57 of 6 March 1991 invited Member States to inform the Secretary-General of their initiatives and to propose themes for the Year. States were also encouraged to consult with indigenous peoples, and non-governmental organizations working with them, regarding possible themes and activities. Both copies of the resolutions are attached.

The Secretary-General would appreciate receiving any information about activities being planned in connection with the International Year of the World's Indigenous People by His Excellency's Government. Such information should be sent to the Centre for Human Rights, United Nations Office at Geneva, CH-1211 Geneva 10, if possible before the end of July, so that it can be reflected in the Secretary-General's report to the forty-sixth session of the General Assembly.

17 May 1991

0187

GENERAL ASSEMBLY

45/164. International Year for the World's Indigenous People

The General Assembly,

Bearing in mind that one of the purposes of the United Nations set forth in the Charter is the achievement of international co-operation in solving international problems of an economic, social, cultural or humanitarian character, and in promoting and encouraging respect for human rights and for fundamental freedoms for all without distinction as to race, sex, language or religion,

Taking note of the recommendation of the Economic and Social Council, in its decision 1990/248 of 25 May 1990, that the General Assembly proclaim 1993 as an international year for the world's indigenous people,

Taking into account the guidelines for international years and anniversaries adopted in its decision 35/424 of 5 December 1980,

1. Proclaims 1993 as International Year for the World's Indigenous People, with a view to strengthening international co-operation for the solution of problems faced by indigenous communities in areas such as human rights, the environment, development, education and health;

2. Invites States to ensure that preparations are made for the Year;

3. Recommends that the specialized agencies, regional commissions and other organizations of the United Nations system consider in their respective forums the contributions that they can make to the success of the Year;

4. Invites organizations of indigenous people and other interested non-governmental organizations to consider the contributions they can make to the success of the Year, with a view to presenting them to the Commission on Human Rights;

5. Requests the Commission on Human Rights to consider at its forty-seventh session possible United Nations activities in connection with the Year;

6. Authorizes the Secretary-General to accept and administer voluntary contributions from Governments and intergovernmental and non-governmental organizations for the purpose of funding programme activities for the Year;

7. Requests the Secretary-General to submit to the General Assembly at its forty-sixth session a draft programme of activities based on the recommendations of the Economic and Social Council and of the specialized agencies;

8. Decides to include in the provisional agenda of its forty-sixth session an item entitled "Preparation and organization of the International Year for the World's Indigenous People".

69th plenary meeting
18 December 1990

0188

OFFICE DES NATIONS UNIES A GENÈVE

CENTRE POUR LES DROITS DE L'HOMME

UNITED NATIONS OFFICE AT GENEVA

CENTRE FOR HUMAN RIGHTS

Téléfax: (022) 733 98 79
Télégrammes: UNATIONS, GENÈVE
Télex: 412 962 UNO CH
Téléphone: 734 60 11 731 02 11

RÉF. N°: G/SO 214 (68-1)
(à rappeler dans la réponse)

Palais des Nations
CH-1211 GENÈVE 10

The Secretary-General of the United Nations presents his compliments to the Minister for Foreign Affairs of the Republic of Korea and has the honour to draw the attention of His Excellency's Government to Commission on Human Rights resolution 1991/29 entitled "Consequences on the enjoyment of human rights of acts of violence committed by armed groups that spread terror among the population and by drug traffickers" adopted by the Commission on 5 March 1991. A copy of the resolution is attached.

In paragraph 4 of this resolution, the Commission on Human Rights requests the Secretary-General to continue collecting information on this question from all relevant sources and to make it available to the special rapporteurs and working groups concerned for their consideration.

In compliance with this request, the Secretary-General would appreciate it if any information His Excellency's Government may deem useful to be made available to the special rapporteurs and working groups concerned could be communicated to the Centre for Human Rights, United Nations Office at Geneva, CH-1211 Geneva 10, if possible before 15 November 1991.

30 May 1991

0189

1991/29. Consequences on the enjoyment of human rights of acts of violence committed by armed groups t spread terror among the pop—ion and drug traffickers

The Commission on Human Rights,

Recalling its resolution 1990/75 of 7 March 1990,

Deeply concerned at the persistent acts of violence committed in many countries by armed groups that spread terror among the population and by drug traffickers, frequently acting together,

Recalling that such acts prevent the unimpeded exercise of civil and political rights, such as participation in free elections, the right to peaceful assembly, freedom of association and trade union rights, as well as the exercise of economic, social and cultural rights, affecting adversely the well-being of peoples and causing severe damage to economic infrastructure and production of countries,

Realizing that the individual, having duties to other individuals and to the community to which he or she belongs, is under a responsibility to strive for the promotion and observance of the rights recognized in the Covenants on human rights,

Acknowledging the invaluable contribution made by non-governmental organizations to the constant monitoring of all matters related to human rights and fundamental freedoms,

Reiterating emphatically that all international obligations relating to the protection and promotion of human rights and fundamental freedoms must be honoured at all times,

1. Reiterates its deep concern at the adverse effect, on the enjoyment of human rights, of persistent acts of violence committed in many countries by armed groups, regardless of their origin, that spread terror among the population, and by drug traffickers;

2. Requests all special rapporteurs and working groups to continue paying particular attention to the adverse effect, on the enjoyment of human rights, of such acts of violence committed by armed groups, regardless of their origin, that spread terror among the population and by drug traffickers, in their forthcoming reports to the Commission on the situation of human rights in those countries where such acts of violence occur;

3. Encourages non-governmental organizations to bear in mind the adverse effect, on the enjoyment of human rights, of the acts of violence committed in many countries by armed groups, regardless of their origin, that spread terror among the population, and by drug traffickers;

4. Requests the Secretary-General to continue collecting information on this question from all relevant sources and to make it available to the special rapporteurs and working groups concerned for their consideration;

5. Decides to continue considering this question as a matter of high priority at its forty-eighth session.

0190

52nd meeting
5 March 1991

/

OFFICE DES NATIONS UNIES A GENÈVE

CENTRE POUR LES DROITS DE L'HOMME

UNITED NATIONS OFFICE AT GENEVA

CENTRE FOR HUMAN RIGHTS

Téléfax: (022) 733 98 79
Télégrammes: UNATIONS, GENÈVE
Télex: 412 962 UNO CH
Téléphone: 734 60 11   731 02 11

Palais des Nations
CH-1211 GENÈVE 10

RÉF. N°: G/SO 216 GEN
(à rappeler dans la réponse)

The Secretary-General of the United Nations presents his compliments to the Minister for Foreign Affairs of the Republic of Korea and has the honour to refer to resolutions 1991/49, entitled "Voluntary Fund for Technical Co-operation in the field of human rights" and 1991/50, entitled "Advisory Services in the field of human rights", both adopted by the Commission on Human Rights on 5 March 1991. Copies of the resolutions are attached for easy reference.

In the above-mentioned resolutions, the Commission on Human Rights encouraged the governments interested in technical co-operation in the field of human rights, particularly those of developing countries, to make use of the Voluntary Fund. The Commission requested the Secretary-General to bring regularly to the attention of all governments and of the competent human rights organs the possibilities that exist under the Voluntary Fund of providing technical co-operation in the field of human rights to governments at their request and encouraged governments to seek contact and to co-operate with non-governmental human rights organizations in formulating and implementing programmes under the Voluntary Fund. The Commission also called upon all governments, intergovernmental and non-governmental organizations and individuals to consider making voluntary contributions for the implementation of projects with the programme of the Voluntary Fund.

In addition, the Commission appealed to all governments to consider making use of the possibility offered by the United Nations of organizing, under the programme of Advisory Services in the field of human rights, information and/or training courses at the national level for appropriate government personnel on the application of international human rights standards and the experience of relevant international organs.

More specifically, the Commission encouraged governments in need of technical assistance in the field of human rights to avail themselves of the advisory services of experts, for example, for drafting basic legal texts in conformity with international conventions on human rights.

In view of the importance of the programme of advisory services and technical assistance in the field of human rights, the Secretary-General would be grateful to receive and consider within available resources any request for assistance that His Excellency's Government may wish to transmit to the Centre for Human Rights. The request should contain specific proposals in order to enable the Secretary-General to co-ordinate, when necessary, with other United Nations bodies and specialized agencies for planning and implementation purposes. An outline of the activities available under the programme of advisory services and technical assistance in the field of human rights is annexed for information. Requests for technical assistance should be addressed to the Under-Secretary-General for Human Rights, United Nations Office at Geneva, CH-1211 Genève 10.

4 June 1991

0191

52nd meeting
5 March 1991

[Adopted without a vote. See chap. XXII.]

1991/49. Voluntary Fund for Technical Co-operation in the Field of Human Rights

The Commission on Human Rights,

Recalling General Assembly resolution 926 (X) of 14 December 1955, by which the Assembly established the United Nations programme of advisory services in the field of human rights,

Recalling the establishment of the Voluntary Fund for Advisory Services and Technical Assistance in the Field of Human Rights by the Secretary-General on 16 November 1987 pursuant to Commission resolution 1987/38 of 10 March 1987 and Economic and Social Council decision 1987/147 of 29 May 1987,

Bearing in mind the appeal made by the Secretary-General on that occasion to Governments and intergovernmental and non-governmental organizations for contributions to the Fund,

Noting with satisfaction that several Governments and non-governmental organizations have responded favourably to this appeal,

Mindful of the provisions of the General Assembly resolution 926 (X) that advisory services shall be rendered by the Secretary-General solely at the request of Governments,

Recalling its resolutions 1990/58 and 1990/59 of 7 March 1990,

Taking note with appreciation of the relevant sections of the annual report of the Secretary-General on advisory services in the field of human rights (E/CN.4/1991/55),

Taking note with interest of the experience gained by the Centre for Human Rights in executing projects under the Voluntary Fund which give

0192

priority to activities aiming at building up or strengthening national and regional institutions and infrastructures in the field of human rights,

Bearing in mind the substantial interrelationship between activities under the regular programme of advisory services and projects of technical co-operation financed under the Voluntary Fund,

Noting with satisfaction that within the comprehensive programme of advisory services and technical co-operation a clear distinction will be made between technical co-operation projects financed under the Voluntary Fund and activities under the regular budget,

Taking note with appreciation of the work of the Advisory Group in the Centre for Human Rights in assisting the Secretary-General to deal with requests submitted by Governments,

Welcoming the fact that the Advisory Group is using project guidelines which have been drawn up in conformity with established practices of the United Nations Development Programme,

Taking note with appreciation that the Centre for Human Rights is assuming functions as a focal point and clearing-house for inter-agency co-ordination with other parts of the United Nations system,

1. *Expresses its appreciation* to the Secretary-General for the projects realized since the establishment of the Voluntary Fund;

2. *Also expresses its appreciation* to those Governments and non-governmental organizations that have made financial contributions to the Voluntary Fund;

3. *Calls upon* all Governments, intergovernmental and non-governmental organizations and individuals to consider making voluntary contributions for the implementation of projects within the programme of the Voluntary Fund;

4. *Emphasizes* that the objective of the Voluntary Fund is to provide financial support for international co-operation aiming at building up and strengthening national and regional institutions and infrastructures which will have a long-term impact on improved implementation of international conventions and other international instruments on human rights promulgated by the United Nations, the specialized agencies or regional organizations;

5. *Requests* the Secretary-General to continue to elaborate comprehensive programmes of advisory services and technical co-operation, maintaining a clear distinction between technical co-operation projects financed under the Voluntary Fund and other activities like seminars, fellowships and dissemination of documentation to be financed under the regular budget and within the World Public Information Campaign for Human Rights;

0193

6. Encourages the Secretary-General in his efforts to attribute to the Centre for Human Rights the functions of a focal point and clearing-house for inter-agency co-ordination with other parts of the United Nations system;

7. Encourages the Secretary-General and the Centre for Human Rights to participate actively in the formulation of projects regarding technical co-operation in the field of human rights, in close consultation with Governments concerned, taking into account relevant suggestions made by human rights treaty bodies, special rapporteurs and non-governmental organizations;

8. Decides to pursue this intensified co-operation in the framework of advisory services in promoting by the Voluntary Fund for Technical Co-operation in the Field of Human Rights;

9. Encourages the Secretary-General to pay due attention to the particular needs of developing countries from all regions and to explore fully the possibilities offered by the co-operation of the relevant specialized agencies with the Centre for Human Rights;

10. Requests the Secretary-General to bring regularly to the attention of all Governments and of the competent human rights organs the possibilities that exist under the Voluntary Fund of providing technical co-operation in the field of human rights to Governments at their request;

11. Encourages Governments interested in technical co-operation in the field of human rights, particularly those of developing countries, to make use of the Voluntary Fund;

12. Also encourages Governments to seek contact and to co-operate with non-governmental human rights organizations in formulating and implementing programmes under the Voluntary Fund;

13. Also requests the Secretary-General to guarantee transparency of the criteria applied and of the rules of procedure to be followed in carrying out technical co-operation in the fields of human rights;

14. Further requests the Secretary-General to report annually to the Commission on Human Rights on the operation and administration of the Voluntary Fund for Technical Co-operation in the Field of Human Rights in a distinct part of his annual report on advisory services and technical Co-operation in the field of human rights.

52nd meeting
5 March 1991

[Adopted without a vote. See chap. XXI.]

0194

1991/50. Advisory services in the field of human rights

The Commission on Human Rights,

Recalling General Assembly resolution 926 (X) of 14 December 1955, by which the Assembly established the United Nations programme of advisory services in the field of human rights,

Recalling also General Assembly resolution 41/154 of 4 December 1986, in which the Assembly requested the Commission on Human Rights to continue to pay special attention to the most appropriate ways of assisting, at their request, countries of the different regions under the programme of advisory services and to make, where necessary, the relevant recommendations,

Recalling also General Assembly resolution 43/90 of 8 December 1988, in which the Assembly invited the Commission on Human Rights to consider a programme of action in the field of human rights, including activities to develop human rights institutions and infrastructures,

Recalling further its resolution 1985/26 of 11 March 1985, in which it encouraged the Secretary-General to continue and enhance his efforts under the programme of advisory services in the field of human rights to provide practical assistance to States in the implementation of international conventions on human rights particularly the International Covenants on Human Rights, and its resolutions 1990/58 and 1990/59 of 7 March 1990,

Mindful of the provisions of General Assembly resolution 926 (X) that advisory services shall be rendered by the Secretary-General solely at the request of Governments,

Taking note with appreciation of the report of the Secretary-General (E/CN.4/1991/55),

Noting with appreciation the enhanced efforts of the Secretary-General to co-ordinate system-wide advisory services and technical assistance in the field of human rights and the foundation of a flexible inter-agency mechanism for human rights activities,

Noting the importance of expert services, fellowships and scholarships, training courses and seminars under the programme of advisory services as forms of practical assistance to States with a view to enabling them to develop the necessary infrastructure to meet international human rights standards,

Supporting, therefore, the general thrust of the plan of activities contained in the report of the Secretary-General,

1. Welcomes the increasing number of requests from Governments for support and technical assistance in the field of human rights;

0195

2. *Reaffirms* that the programme of advisory services in the field of human rights should continue to provide practical assistance in the implementation of international conventions on human rights to those States which indicate a need for such assistance;

3. *Requests* the Secretary-General again to provide urgently more human and financial resources for the enlargement of advisory services, particularly from section 24 of the regular budget of the United Nations concerning technical co-operation, in order to meet the increased demand on this important instrument intended to invigorate the human rights spirit in the world;

4. *Also requests* the Secretary-General to pursue his efforts for a medium-term plan for advisory services and technical assistance in the field of human rights, taking into account the comments and views expressed by Governments at the forty-seventh session of the Commission on Human Rights;

5. *Recommends* to the Secretary-General that the provision of expert assistance and activities to assist Governments in the development of the necessary infrastructures to meet international human rights standards should continue to increase;

6. *Welcomes* the efforts of the Secretary-General to ensure close co-ordination between the activities of the regular programme and those of the voluntary fund and, at the same time, to make a clear distinction between activities under the regular programme of advisory services and technical co-operation projects financed under the voluntary fund;

7. *Requests* the Secretary-General to intensify further co-ordination within the United Nations system for providing advisory services and technical assistance in the field of human rights;

8. *Notes with appreciation* the co-operation between the Centre for Human Rights and the United Nations Development Programme and encourages the leadership of both organizations to further enhance co-ordination and co-operation between them;

9. *Requests* the Secretary-General to explore yet further the possibilities offered by co-operation between the Centre for Human Rights and specialized bodies of the United Nations system, such as the United Nations Development Programme, the United Nations High Commissioner for Refugees, the United Nations Children's Fund, the United Nations Educational, Scientific and Cultural Organization, the International Labour Organisation, the United Nations Institute for Training and Research, the United Nations Interregional Crime and Research Institute and the World Health Organization, as well as the International Committee of the Red Cross;

0196

10. _Also requests_ the Secretary-General to bring the need for further technical assistance in the legal field that has been indicated by a number of States to the attention of the United Nations bodies and agencies that are active in providing assistance in the field of development with a view to promoting human rights in the development strategies and policies of the United Nations;

11. _Invites_ competent United Nations bodies, such as the committees set up under the International Covenants on Human Rights, the Committee on the Elimination of Racial Discrimination, the Committee against Torture and the Committee on the Rights of the Child, to make suggestions and proposals for the implementation of advisory services;

12. _Requests_ its special rapporteurs and representatives, as well as the Working Group on Enforced or Involuntary Disappearances, to inform Governments, whenever appropriate, of the possibility of availing themselves of the services provided for under the programme of advisory services and to include in their recommendations, whenever appropriate, proposals for specific projects to be realized under the programme of advisory services;

13. _Also requests_ the Secretary-General to give special attention to such proposals of special rapporteurs and representatives;

14. _Appeals_ to all Governments to consider making use of the possibility offered by the United Nations of organizing, under the programme of advisory services in the field of human rights, information and/or training courses at the national level for appropriate government personnel on the application of international human rights standards and the experience of relevant international organs:

15. _Encourages_ Governments in need of technical assistance in the field of human rights to avail themselves of the advisory services of experts in the field of human rights, for example, for drafting basic legal texts in conformity with international conventions on human rights;

16. _Requests_ the Secretary-General to report on the progress made in the implementation of the programme of advisory services in the field of human rights to the Commission at its forty-eighth session.

52nd meeting
5 March 1991

[Adopted without a vote. See chap. XXI.]

0197

ANNEX

UNITED NATIONS CENTRE FOR HUMAN RIGHTS

ADVISORY SERVICES AND TECHNICAL ASSISTANCE IN THE FIELD OF HUMAN RIGHTS

The United Nations programme of advisory services in the field of human rights was established pursuant to General Assembly resolution 926 (X) of 14 December 1955 authorizing the Secretary-General to make provision at the request of Governments and with the co-operation of the specialized agencies where appropriate, for the following forms of assistance with respect to the field of human rights: (a) advisory services of experts; (b) fellowships and scholarships; and (c) seminars. Regional and national training courses were added respectively in 1967 and 1986.

On 16 November 1987, the Secretary-General established the United Nations Voluntary Fund for Advisory Services and Technical Assistance in the Field of Human Rights pursuant to Commission on Human Rights resolution 1987/38 and ECOSOC decision 1987/147. The objective of the Voluntary Fund is to provide additional financial support for practical activities focused on the implementation of international conventions and other international instruments on human rights promulgated by the United Nations, its specialized agencies or regional organizations.

The activities undertaken under the programme of advisory services and technical assistance, utilizing the resources of the regular budget and those of the Voluntary Fund as additional support, aim at: (a) furthering knowledge and understanding of international human rights and their normative content, with a view to promoting their widest application; (b) facilitating the implementation of international human rights instruments; (c) providing practical assistance to governments in the establishment and development of national infrastructures for the promotion and protection of internationally recognized human rights norms. Examples of activities that may be provided by the United Nations under the programme of advisory services and technical assistance in the field of human rights are given below. Some of these activities are carried out when necessary in co-operation with other United Nations bodies and specialized agencies.

M/HR/90/44
GE.90-16128

0198

LEGISLATION

- Provision of the advisory services of experts to the States that are not yet parties to the International Covenants on Human Rights and other United Nations conventions on human rights with a view to assisting the States to ratify them or acceed thereto;

- Provision of the advisory services of experts to States to assist national authorities on the legal and technical aspects of the preparations of democratic elections;

- Provision of the advisory services of experts to States to assist the authorities in the elaboration of national constitutions incorporating international human rights standards;

- Provision of the advisory services of experts to States needing to adapt their domestic legislation to international human rights standards. This type of technical assistance may include the drafting of basic legal texts, such as the civil and criminal codes, in conformity with international conventions on human rights;

NATIONAL, REGIONAL
INFRASTRUCTURES

- Provision of technical assistance for the establishment, strengthening and development of regional institutions for the promotion and protection of human rights;

- Provision of technical assistance for the establishment, strengthening and development of national institutions for the promotion and protection of human rights;

- Provision of technical assistance for the establishment and development of basic human rights libraries;

- Provision of technical assistance for the establishment and development of national focal points to liaise with U.N. in the dissemination of information on human rights;

0199

TRAINING AND EDUCATION

- Provision of advisory services of experts to assist States parties in the preparation of their periodic reports under the International Covenants and other U.N. conventions on human rights;

- Provision of fellowships to nationals responsible with the promotion and/or protection of human rights in their respective countries;

- Provision of advisory services of experts to assist States to include in their educational curricula as well as in the training programmes for law enforcement, the armed forces, medicine, diplomacy and other relevant fields materials relevant to a comprehensive understanding of human rights issues.

- Organization of training courses for those States parties experiencing difficulties in meeting reporting obligations under international instruments on human rights;

- Organization of information and/or training courses on the application of international human rights standards and the experience of relevant international organs;

- Organization of workshops for law enforcement officials on issues relevant to the application of the norms contained in the Code of Conduct of Law Enforcement Officials;

INFORMATION

- Provision of technical assistance for the translation and publication in national and local languages of the International Bill of Human Rights and other international human rights instruments.

0200

7/10 유엔과

OFFICE DES NATIONS UNIES A GENÈVE

CENTRE POUR LES DROITS DE L'HOMME

UNITED NATIONS OFFICE AT GENEVA

CENTRE FOR HUMAN RIGHTS

Téléfax: (022) 733 98 79
Télégrammes: UNATIONS, GENÈVE
Télex: 412 962 UNO CH
Téléphone: 734 60 11 731 02 11

Palais des Nations
CH-1211 GENÈVE 10

RÉF. N°: G/SO 214 (26)
(à rappeler dans la réponse)

The Secretary-General of the United Nations presents his compliments to the Minister for Foreign Affairs of the Republic of Korea and has the honour to refer to Commission on Human Rights resolution 1991/25 of 5 March 1991, entitled "Internally displaced persons". A copy of this resolution is attached.

In paragraph 4 of the resolution the Secretary-General is requested to submit to the Commission at its forty-eighth session an analytical report on internally displaced persons, taking into account the protection of human rights of internally displaced persons, based on information submitted by Governments, the specialized agencies, relevant United Nations organs, regional and intergovernmental organizations, the International Committee of the Red Cross and non-governmental organizations.

In order to be able to fulfil the reporting obligation entrusted to him, the Secretary-General would be grateful to receive from His Excellency's Goverment any information and views it may wish to submit in this regard. In formulating the requested information it would be most helpful if His Excellency's Government could follow the outline attached hereto and communicate its reply to the Centre for Human Rights, United Nations Office at Geneva, CH-1211 Genève 10, prior to 31 October 1991.

28 June 1991

0201

1991/25. Internally displaced persons

The Commission on Human Rights,

Mindful of its responsibility under the Charter of the United Nations to promote and encourage respect for human rights and fundamental freedoms,

Welcoming Economic and Social Council resolution 1990/78 of 27 July 1990,

Disturbed by the high numbers of internally displaced persons suffering throughout the world, who have been forced to flee their homes and seek shelter and safety in other parts of their own country,

Concerned at the serious problems encountered by internally displaced persons and the lack of humanitarian assistance,

1. *Invites* all Governments and international organizations to intensify their cooperation and assistance in world-wide efforts to address the serious problems and needs resulting from internal displacement;

2. *Requests* the Secretary-General to take into account the protection of human rights and the needs of internally displaced persons in his system-wide review aimed at ensuring an effective response by the United Nations system to the problems of refugees, displaced persons and returnees;

3. *Stresses* the importance of strict adherence by States parties to their obligations under international human rights instruments and international humanitarian law;

4. *Requests* the Secretary-General to submit to the Commission at its forty-eighth session an analytical report on internally displaced persons, taking into account the protection of human rights of internally displaced persons, based on information submitted by Governments, the specialized agencies, relevant United Nations organs, regional and intergovernmental organizations, the International Committee of the Red Cross and non-governmental organizations;

5. *Decides* to consider this matter at its forty-eighth session under the agenda item "Further promotion and encouragement of human rights and fundamental freedoms.

52nd meeting
5 March 1991

[Adopted without a vote. See chap. XI.]

0202

<u>ANNEX</u>

1. National experiences with the phenomenon of internally displaced persons, its causes and manifestations

2. Human rights and humanitarian law standards applicable in situations of internal displacement and possible needs for their reinforcement

3. Problems in the enjoyment of human rights encountered by internally displaced persons

4. Difficulties encountered in seeking to ensure respect for the human rights of internally displaced persons

5. The issue of access to internally displaced persons for the purposes of providing protection and assistance

6. Specific measures that should be taken nationally, regionally and universally to better protect the human rights of internally displaced persons.

7. Desirability and practical possibility of effective monitoring of situations involving internal displacement by the United Nations, including the utilisation of United Nations human rights procedures.

8. Preventive measures which might be taken in order to avert situations of internal displacement

0203

주 제 네 바 대 표 부

제네(정) 2031-608　　　　　　　　　　　　1991. 7. 5

수신 : 장관

참조 : 국제기구조약국장

제목 : 유엔인권위 아동인신매매 문제 특별보고관 서한

1. Vitit Muntarbhorn 유엔인권위 아동인신매매 문제 특별보고관은 91.6.26자 본직앞 공한을 통해 아국정부가 아동 인신매매와 관련한 별첨 설문 답변서를 작성, 91.9.30까지 제출하여 줄 것을 요청하여왔읍니다.

2. 상기 설문서 답변내용은 92년도 제 48차 유엔인권위에 제출할 동 보고관 보고서에 포함될 예정인바, 아국의 관계법령 및 기본입장을 밝히는 수준에서 답변서를 작성, 제출하는 것이 바람직할 것으로 사료되오니 조치하여 주시기 바랍니다.

첨부 : 상기 서한 및 설문서 사본 1부. 끝.

주 제 네 바 대 사

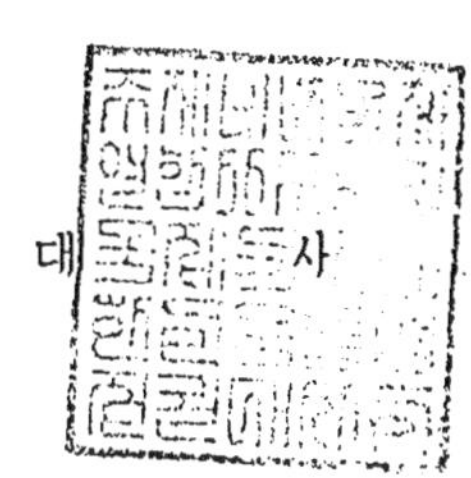

선 결			결재		
접수일시	1991. 7.				
처리과	01/38011				

0204

OFFICE DES NATIONS UNIES GENÈVE

CENTRE POUR LES DROITS DE L'HOMME

UNITED NATIONS OFFICE AT GENEVA

CENTRE FOR HUMAN RIGHTS

Téléfax: (022) 733 98 79
Télégrammes: UNATIONS, GENÈVE
Télex: 28 96 96
Téléphone: 734 60 11 731 02 11

Palais des Nations
CH-1211 GENÈVE 10

RÉF. Nº: G/SO 214 (69-1)
(à rappeler dans la réponse)

26 June 1991

Dear Mr. Ambassador,

I should like, in my capacity as Special Rapporteur, to refer to resolution 1990/68 entitled "Sale of children", adopted by the Commission on Human Rights on 7 March 1990, and to resolutions 1991/53 and 1991/54, entitled respectively "Report of the Special Rapporteur on the sale of children, child prostitution and child pornography" and "Sale of children, child prostitution and child pornography, and the exploitation of child labour", adopted by the Commission on Human Rights on 6 March 1991. Copies of these ... resolutions are attached for ease of reference.

In view of the reporting responsibility entrusted to me in the above-mentioned resolutions, I would be grateful for any relevant information your Government should like to provide. I am attaching ... a questionnaire which I hope will not only facilitate your Government's response to the request formulated by the Commission, but also enable me to make a comparative assessment of the information provided. I would be grateful if the completed questionnaire could be returned to the Centre for Human Rights before 30 September 1991.

In this connection, I may mention that I am also consulting relevant non-governmental organizations in your country on the same question.

I remain, dear Mr. Ambassador,
Yours sincerely,

p.p. Vitit Muntarbhorn
Special Rapporteur
of the Commission on Human Rights
on the sale of children

His Excellency
Mr. Soo Gil Park
Ambassador
Permanent Observer of the Republic of Korea to
the United Nations Office at Geneva
20 route de Pré-Bois
Case postale 566
1215 Genève 15

0205

COMMISSION ON HUMAN RIGHTS

Forty-seventh session

1990/68. Sale of children

The Commission on Human Rights,

Aware of its responsibility to promote and encourage respect for human rights and fundamental freedoms and resolved to remain vigilant with regard to violations of such rights and freedoms wherever they occur,

Recalling the provisions of the Declaration on the Rights of the Child proclaimed by the General Assembly on 20 November 1959 in its resolution 1386 (XIV) and, in particular, Principle 2, whereby the child shall enjoy special protection and shall be given opportunities and facilities, by law and by other means, to enable him to develop physically, mentally, morally, spiritually and socially in a healthy and normal manner and in conditions of freedom and dignity, and Principle 9, whereby the child shall be protected against all forms of neglect, cruelty and exploitation and shall not be the subject of traffic, in any form,

Recalling the provisions of resolution 1989/36 of 6 March 1989, by which the Sub-Commission on Prevention of Discrimination and Protection of Minorities is invited to continue to give due regard to new developments in the field of human rights,

Recalling its resolutions 1982/20 of 10 March 1982, 1988/42 of 8 March 1988 and 1989/34 of 6 March 1989,

Having considered the report of the Working Group on Contemporary Forms of Slavery submitted to the Sub-Commission at its forty-first session (E/CN.4/Sub.2/1989/39),

Deeply concerned about the existence in many parts of the world of cases of serious violations of the rights of children, particularly cases of the sale of children, child prostitution and child pornography,

1. Decides to appoint for a period of one year a Special Rapporteur to consider matters relating to the sale of children, child prostitution and child pornography, including the problem of the adoption of children for commercial purposes;

2. Requests the Chairman of the Commission, following consultations with the other members of the Bureau, to appoint as Special Rapporteur a person of international reputation;

3. Invites the Special Rapporteur to take account, in fulfilling his mandate, of the need to be in a position to use any credible and reliable information made available to him, to request the Governments concerned to state their views and comment on any information he intends to include in his report and to carry out his task with discretion and independence;

The final edited text of this resolution will be published in the report of the Commission on Human Rights to the Economic and Social Council.

RES/HR/91/13
GE.91-16383

4. *Requests* the Secretary-General to urge all Governments to co-operate closely with the Special Rapporteur and to offer their co-operation and assistance so that he may fulfil his mandate effectively;

5. *Also requests* the Secretary-General to give the Special Rapporteur any necessary assistance;

6. *Requests* the Special Rapporteur to submit a comprehensive report to the Commission at its forty-seventh session on his activities relating to these matters, including the frequency and extent of such practices, as well as his conclusions and recommendations;

7. *Decides* to consider the question at its forty-seventh session.

53rd meeting
7 March 1990

[Adopted without a vote]

0207

COMMISSION ON HUMAN RIGHTS

Forty-seventh session

1991/53. Report of the Special Rapporteur on the sale of children, child prostitution and child pornography

The Commission on Human Rights,

Recalling its resolution 1990/68 of 7 March 1990, by which it decided to appoint a special rapporteur to consider matters relating to the sale of children, child prostitution and child pornography,

Recalling Economic and Social Council decision 1990/240 of 25 May 1990, by which the Council extended the mandate of the Special Rapporteur to two years,

Welcoming the appointment of Mr. Vitit Muntarbhorn as Special Rapporteur,

Having considered the report of the Special Rapporteur (E/CN.4/1991/51),

Recognizing the transnational aspects of the sale of children, child prostitution and child pornography,

Recognizing the need to build a network of contacts at both the national and international levels, including the governmental and non-governmental spheres,

1. Welcomes the preliminary assessment by the Special Rapporteur of his task as contained in his report to the Commission on Human Rights (E/CN.4/1991/51);

2. Requests the Special Rapporteur to continue to carry out his work in the light of the mandate as enunciated in resolution 1990/68 and taking into account the conclusions and recommendations in his report;

3. Requests the Secretary-General to provide all necessary assistance to the Special Rapporteur to enable him to submit his report to the Commission on Human Rights at its forty-eighth session;

4. Requests the Special Rapporteur to report on his activities to the Commission on Human Rights at its forty-eighth session;

5. Decides to consider the report of the Special Rapporteur under the agenda item "Rights of the child".

53rd meeting
6 March 1991

[Adopted without a vote]

The final edited text of this resolution will be published in the report of the Commission on Human Rights to the Economic and Social Council.

0208

COMMISSION ON HUMAN RIGHTS

Forty-seventh session

1991/54. Sale of children, child prostitution and child pornography, and the exploitation of child labour

The Commission on Human Rights,

Having considered the report submitted by the Sub-Commission on Prevention of Discrimination and Protection of Minorities (E/CN.4/Sub.2/1991/2),

Taking note of the report by Mr. Vitit Muntarbhorn, Special Rapporteur on the sale of children, child prostitution and child pornography, and of the report of the Secretary-General on comments by Governments, the specialized agencies and non-governmental organizations on the programme of action submitted by the Sub-Commission on the question (E/CN.4/1991/50 and Add.1),

Bearing in mind the UNICEF resolution on children in especially difficult circumstances,

Deeply concerned about the information received on the exploitation of children in its various manifestations, the sale of children, child prostitution, child pornography and the exploitation of child labour,

Also deeply concerned about the consequences for the children who are the victims in all parts of the world, especially in countries of the third world facing development problems,

Having taken note with satisfaction of the intention of the International Labour Organisation to implement a new programme on the elimination of child labour,

Aware of the need to adopt urgent measures to prevent and eliminate these problems,

I.

1. Welcomes with satisfaction the report by Mr. Vitit Muntarbhorn, Special Rapporteur on the sale of children, child prostitution and child pornography (E/CN.4/1991/51);

2. Takes note of the comments by Governments, specialized agencies and non-governmental organizations received by the Secretary-General on the draft programme of action for prevention of sale of children, child prostitution and child pornography (E/CN.4/1991/50 and Add.1);

3. Takes note of the report of the Sub-Commission on Prevention of Discrimination and Protection of Minorities and, in particular, of the report of the Working Group on Contemporary Forms of Slavery contained in Sub-Commission resolution 1990/30 (E/CN.4/Sub.2/1990/44);

0209

4. *Decides* to refer the draft programme of action for prevention of sale of children, child prostitution and child pornography to the Sub-Commission so that it might make the necessary amendments in the light of the opinions of States, specialized agencies and non-governmental organizations interested in the matter;

5. *Requests* the Sub-Commission fully to reflect the 10 points of the plan of action of the World Summit for Children in its reformulation of the programme of action;

6. *Also requests* the Sub-Commission to give the highest priority to the reformulation of this programme of action so that it might be adopted at the forty-eighth session of the Commission on Human Rights;

7. *Requests* the Special Rapporteur, on the basis of his experience, to consider the possibility of submitting his comments and suggestions to the Working Group on Contemporary Forms of Slavery, if possible, by attending its meetings;

8. *Requests* the Under-Secretary-General to provide the Sub-Commission with the necessary co-operation for the fulfilment of this mandate;

9. *Decides* to consider this question at the forty-eighth session under the agenda item "Rights of the child";

II.

10. *Endorses* resolution 1990/VII, entitled "Programme of Action for the Elimination of the Exploitation of Child Labour", and proposed by the Sub-Commission on Prevention of Discrimination and Protection of Minorities;

11. *Decides* to transmit the draft programme of action annexed hereto for their comments to interested Governments, specialized agencies and non-governmental organizations;

12. *Requests* member States to support the programme of the International Labour Organisation on the elimination of child labour through the appropriate means, including financial contributions;

13. *Requests* the Secretary-General to submit an analytical summary of the replies received to the Commission at its forty-eighth session;

14. *Further decides* to examine the draft programme of action and the report of the Secretary-General at its forty-eighth session under the agenda item "Rights of the child".

53rd meeting
6 March 1991

[Adopted without a vote]

The final edited text of this resolution will be published in the report of the Commission on Human Rights to the Economic and Social Council.

0210

QUESTIONNAIRE RELATING TO THE SALE OF CHILDREN, CHILD PROSTITUTION AND CHILD PORNOGRAPHY

Contents

M/HR/91/89
GE.91-16166

0211

INTERPRETATION OF CERTAIN TERMS USED IN THE QUESTIONNAIRE

For the purpose of this questionnare, the term:

"Child" is defined by the United Nations Convention on the Rights of the Child 1990 as meaning "every human being below the age of 18 years unless, under the law applicable to the child, majority is attained earlier";

"Sale of children" should be seen as a flexible term due to the different notions of "sale" and "contracts" in existing municipal systems, noting a definition derived from the 1956 Supplementary Convention on the Abolition of Slavery, as follows: "The transfer of a child from one party (including biological parents, guardians and institutions) to another, for whatever purpose, in exchange for financial or other reward or compensation";

"Child prostitution" refers to the sexual exploitation of a child for remuneration in cash or in kind, usually but not always organized by an intermediary (parent, family member, procurer, teacher, etc.);

"Child pornography" refers to the visual or audio depiction of a child for the sexual gratification of the user, and involves the production, distribution and/or use of such material.

Where those replying to this questionnaire wish to qualify or adjust the interpretation of the words indicated above, kindly indicate accordingly (under Question I).

Question I

1. If you disagree with the interpretations of the words "child", "sale of children", "child prostitution" and "child pornography" given above, please provide your reasons, details and preferred interpretations.

A. International law and co-operation

Question II

1. Is your country a party to the multilateral instruments concerning the prevention and elimination of the sale of children (e.g., the 1956 Supplementary Convention on the Abolition of Slavery, the 1990 Convention on the Rights of the Child, and various instruments of the International Labour Organization)?

2. Is your country a party to the multilateral instruments concerning the prevention and elimination of child prostitution (e.g., the Convention on the Rights of the Child and the 1949 Convention on the Suppression of Traffic in Persons and the Exploitation of the Prostitution of Others)?

3. Is your country a party to the multilateral instruments concerning the prevention and elimination of child pornography (e.g., the Convention on the Rights of the Child and the 1923 International Convention on the Suppression of the Circulation of and the Traffic in Obscene Publications)?

0212

4. How effective is the implementation of these instruments at the local level? Please assess strengths and weaknesses.

5. To what extent is the prevention and elimination of the sale of children, child prostitution and child pornography dependent upon international development strategies and agencies? How should more effective collaboration and interaction be promoted?

Question III

1. Does your country have any bilateral and regional arrangements with other countries to prevent and eliminate the sale of children in relation to adoption? Please give examples.

2. Does your country have any bilateral and regional arrangements with other countries to prevent and eliminate the sale of children in relation to child labour? Please give examples.

3. Does your country have any bilateral and regional arrangements with other countries to prevent and eliminate the sale of children in relation to organ transplantation? Please give examples.

4. Does your country have any bilateral and regional arrangements with other countries to prevent and eliminate child prostitution? Please give examples.

5. Does your country have any bilateral and regional arrangements with other countries to prevent and eliminate child pornography? Please give examples.

B. Sale of children

Question IV

1. The sale of children is mainly carried out for the purposes of:
(a) adoption;
(b) child labour (including sexual exploitation);
(c) organ transplantation.
To what extent, and in what ways and forms, do these violations of children's rights exist in your country? Please describe.

2. What are the root causes of the sale of children in your country, if it exists?

3. What obstacles or problems hamper the prevention and elimination of the sale of children, in particular concerning adoption, child labour, and organ transplantation?

4. What measures and action (e.g., national children's policies; projects to help children and their families; incentives for better law enforcement; community watch; participation of governmental institutions, non-governmental organizations and the private sector, etc.) have been or are being taken to prevent and eliminate the sale of children? Please give examples and assess strengths and weaknesses.

0213

Question V

1. What national laws exist to prevent and eliminate the sale of children in relation to adoption? Please give name of law, date and reference; attach texts if possible.

2. How effective are such laws and what are the sanctions (e.g., maximum/minimum prison sentences, fines. etc.)? Please assess strengths and weaknesses.

3. What national laws exist to prevent and eliminate the sale of children in relation to child labour? Please give name of law, date and reference; attach texts if possible.

4. How effective are such laws and what are the sanctions? Please assess strengths and weaknesses.

5. What national laws exist to prevent and eliminate the sale of children in relation to organ transplantation? Please give name of law, date and reference; attach texts if possible.

6. How effective are such laws and what are the sanctions? Please assess strengths and weaknesses.

7. Have there been any prosecutions where the sale of children relates to adoption, child labour and/or organ transplants? Please give details and statistics.

Question VI

1. Do national development plans, national youth/child policies or other national programmes explicitly mention specific targets and action to prevent and eliminate the sale of children in relation to adoption?

2. How are they implemented? Please assess strengths and weaknesses.

3. Please give examples of measures and action (e.g., programmes, projects) to implement these plans.

4. How much budget is available for these measures and action? Is it sufficient?

5. Who are the counterparts/partners in the implementation of these plans (e.g., governmental, non-governmental, community, children, etc.)?

6. How are these plans evaluated? Who evaluates, and is there follow-up action?

7. What other resources and measures are required to make these plans effective in practice?

0214

Question VII

1. Do national development plans, national youth/child policies or other national programmes explicitly mention specific targets and action to prevent and eliminate the sale of children in relation to child labour?

2. How are they implemented? Please assess strengths and weaknesses.

3. Please give examples of measures and action (e.g., programmes, projects) to implement these plans.

4. How much budget is available for these measures and action? Is it sufficient?

5. Who are the counterparts/partners in the implementation of these plans (e.g., governmental, non-governmental, community, children, etc.)?

6. How are these plans evaluated? Who evaluates, and is there follow-up action?

7. What other resources and measures are required to make these plans effective in practice?

Question VIII

1. Do national development plans, national youth/child policies or other national programmes explicitly mention specific targets and action to prevent and eliminate the sale of children in relation to organ transplantation?

2. How are they implemented? Please assess strengths and weaknesses.

3. Please give examples of measures and action (e.g., programmes, projects) to implement these plans.

4. How much budget is available for these measures and action? Is it sufficient?

5. Who are the counterparts/partners in the implementation of these plans (e.g., governmental, non-governmental, community, children, etc.)?

6. How are these plans evaluated? Who evaluates, and is there follow-up action?

7. What other resources and measures are required to make these plans effective in practice?

C. Child Prostitution

Question IX

1. To what extent, and in what ways and forms, does child prostitution exist in your country? Please describe.

2. What are the root causes of child prostitution in your country, if it exists?

3. What obstacles or problems hamper the prevention and elimination of child prostitution?

4. What measures and action have been or are being taken to prevent and eliminate child prostitution? Please give examples and assess strengths and weaknesses.

5. What national laws exist to prevent and eliminate child prostitution? Under the law in your country, is it an offence for an adult to have sexual intercourse with a child? Until what age is the child protected? Please give name of law, date and reference; attach texts if possible.

6. How effective are such laws, and what are the sanctions? Is tourism regarded as an aggravating factor in the sexual exploitation of children? Please assess strengths and weaknesses.

7. Have there been any prosecutions on child prostitution? Please give details and statistics.

Question X

1. Do national development plans, national youth/child policies or other national programmes explicitly mention specific targets and action to prevent and eliminate child prostitution?

2. How are they implemented? Please assess strengths and weaknesses.

3. Please give examples of measures and action (e.g., programmes, projects) to implement these plans.

4. How much budget is available for these measures and action? Is it sufficient?

5. Who are the counterparts/partners in the implementation of these plans (e.g., governmental, non-governmental, community, children, etc.)?

6. How are these plans evaluated? Who evaluates, and is there follow-up action?

7. What other resources and measures are required to make these plans effective in practice?

D. Child pornography

Question XI

1. To what extent, and in what ways and forms, is child pornography produced, distributed or used in your country? Please describe.?

0216

2. What are the root causes of child pornography in your country, if it exists?

3. What obstacles or problems hamper the prevention and elimination of the production, distribution and use of child pornography?

4. What measures and action have been or are being taken to prevent and eliminate the production, distribution and use of child pornography? Please give examples and assess strengths and weaknesses.

5. What national laws exist to prevent and eliminate the production, distribution and use of child pornography? Is it an offence to produce, distribute and/or possess child pornography? Please give name of law, date and reference; attach texts if possible.

6. What do the laws on child pornography cover: printed matter, films, video, computerized services? How effective are such laws, and what are the sanctions? Please assess strengths and weaknesses.

7. Have there been any prosecutions on the production, distribution and use of child pornography? Please give details and statistics.

Question XII

1. Do national development plans, national youth/child policies or other national programmes explicitly mention specific targets and action to prevent and eliminate child pornography?

2. How are they implemented? Please assess strengths and weaknesses.

3. Please give examples of measures and action (e.g., programmes, projects) to implement these plans.

4. How much budget is available for these measures and action? Is it sufficient?

5. Who are the counterparts/partners in the implementation of these plans (e.g., governmental, non-governmental, community, children, etc.)?

6. How are these plans evaluated? Who evaluates, and is there follow-up action?

7. What other resources and measures are required to make these plans effective in practice?

E. Miscellaneous

Question XIII

1. Are there laws, policies, measures and budgets (e.g., development aid, social welfare) to help those families who are at risk of becoming, unknowingly or involuntarily, involved in the sale of children, child prostitution and/or child pornography?

0217

2. Are there laws, policies, measures and budgets (e.g., development aid, social welfare) to help raise the status of women/girls who would otherwise be involved in the sale of children, child prostitution and/or child pornography?

3. Are there laws, policies, measures and budgets (e.g., development aid, social welfare) to prevent customers/consumers from becoming involved in the sale of children, child prostitution and/or child pornography? Are there sanctions against those who are involved in exploiting children in these ways?

4. Are there laws, policies, measures and budgets to prevent the business sector (e.g., tourist industry, factory owners, film industry, etc.) from undertaking or becoming parties to the sale of children, child prostitution and/or child pornography? Are there sanctions against those who are involved in exploiting children in these ways?

5. Are there laws, policies, measures and budgets to help law enforcement personnel prevent and eliminate the sale of children, child prostitution and child pornography? Are there sanctions against those who abuse their powers? Are there incentives (e.g., better pay) for those who do their duty well?

6. Are there laws, policies, measures and budgets to help non-governmental organizations prevent and eliminate the sale of children, child prostitution and child pornography?

7. Are there laws, policies, measures and budgets to help community institutions and personnel, e.g., religious groups, youth/children's groups, village leaders, prevent and eliminate the sale of children, child prostitution and child pornography?

8. Are there laws, policies, measures and budgets to help the mass media prevent and eliminate the sale of children, child prostitution and child pornography?

9. Are there laws, policies, measures and budgets to help professional groups and associations (e.g., medical associations, law associations) prevent and eliminate the sale of children, child prostitution and child pornography?

Question XIV

1. Are legal aid and assistance available to the families, legal guardians or representatives of child victims of sale, prostitution and pornography, and to the victims themselves? Please give examples and assess strengths and weaknesses.

2. Are there public and/or private rehabilitation programmes and measures for victims of the sale of children, child prostitution and child pornography? Please give examples and assess strengths and weaknesses, including positive and negative effects on the children. Please give suggestions as to how these programmes could be improved.

0218

3. Are there public and/or private rehabilitation programmes and measures for exploiters and abusers of children, especially if there are psychological reasons for their misconduct? Please give examples and assess strengths and weaknesses.

Question XV

1. To what extent is the issue of the sale of children, child prostitution and child pornography dealt with in formal education (e.g., primary, secondary and tertiary levels)? Please describe the substance and form (e.g., whether it is taught as part of existing courses).

2. To what extent is the issue of the sale of children, child prostitution and child pornography dealt with in non-formal education (e.g., out-of-school programmes and via television/radio)? Please give examples.

3. How active are the mass media in collecting and disseminating information on these matters?

4. Is there a data-gathering institution/mechanism on these matters? Please give examples of the types of information gathered, strengths and weaknesses.

5. What is the current state of research on these matters? What has been done and what is needed?

Question XVI

Please add any further suggestions and recommendations. Please supply texts of documents referred to, wherever possible.

0219

2

OFFICE DES NATIONS UNIES A GENÈVE

CENTRE POUR LES DROITS DE L'HOMME

UNITED NATIONS OFFICE AT GENEVA

CENTRE FOR HUMAN RIGHTS

Téléfax: (022) 733 98 79
Télégrammes: UNATIONS, GENÈVE
Télex: 412 962 UNO CH
Téléphone: 734 60 11 731 02 11

Palais des Nations
CH-1211 GENÈVE 10

RÉF. N°: G/SO 234 (18-4)
(à rappeler dans la réponse)

The Secretary-General of the United Nations presents his compliments to the Minister for Foreign Affairs of the Republic of Korea and has the honour to refer to General Assembly resolution 40/131 of 13 December 1985, entitled "United Nations Voluntary Fund for Indigenous Populations". A copy of the resolution is enclosed.

The purpose of the Voluntary Fund, in accordance with General Assembly resolution 40/131, is to provide financial assistance to representatives of indigenous communities and their organizations wishing to attend the annual sessions of the Working Group on Indigenous Populations at Geneva. The Fund is administered by the Secretary-General with the advice of a five-member Board of Trustees.

The attention of His Excellency's Government is drawn, in particular, to sub-paragraph (b) of the resolution which provides that the foreseen financial assistance be funded by voluntary contributions from governments, non-governmental organizations and other private or public entities.

By decision 45/433 entitled "United Nations Voluntary Fund for Indigenous Populations", the General Assembly, taking note of the report of the Secretary-General on the status of the United Nations Voluntary Fund for Indigenous Populations (A/45/698) after the third session of the Board of Trustees of the Fund, held in 1990, decided to call upon governments, non-governmental organizations and other private or public entities to consider contributing to the Fund.

The Commission on Human Rights, in paragraph 9 of its resolution 1991/59, the Sub-Commission on Prevention of Discrimination and Protection of Minorities, in paragraph 5 of its resolution 1991/30 and the Working Group on Indigenous Populations, in Decision/Recommendation 28 contained in Annex I to the report on its ninth session (E/CN.4/Sub.2/1991/40) expressed appreciation to the governments and organizations which had already made contributions to the Fund and encouraged continued support for the activities of the Fund.

The Secretary-General wishes to encourage contributions, preferably prior to the fifth session of the Board of Trustees, scheduled for April 1992, in order to enable the Board to provide representatives of indigenous organizations and communities with relevant financial support to attend the next session of the Working Group on Indigenous Populations in July/August 1992. It would be appreciated if contributions could be addressed to the United Nations General Trust Fund (Account No. 015-004473), Chemical Bank, Branch at the United Nations Headquarters, New York, N.Y. 10017, with a clear indication that the funds are intended for the United Nations Voluntary Fund for Indigenous Populations.

18 October 1991

0220

GENERAL ASSEMBLY

RESOLUTION 40/131 OF 13 DECEMBER 1985

United Nations Voluntary Fund for Indigenous Populations

The General Assembly,

Taking note of Economic and Social Council resolution 1982/34 of 7 May 1982, by which the Council authorized the Sub-Commission on Prevention of Discrimination and Protection of Minorities to establish annually a working group on indigenous populations,

Taking note of Commission on Human Rights resolution 1984/32 of 12 March 1984,

Convinced that the establishment of a voluntary trust fund for indigenous populations would constitute a significant development for the future promotion and protection of the human rights of indigenous populations,

Decides to establish a voluntary trust fund in accordance with the following criteria:

(a) The name of the fund shall be the United Nations Voluntary Fund for Indigenous Populations;

(b) The purpose of the Fund shall be to assist representatives of indigenous communities and organizations to participate in the deliberations of the Working Group on Indigenous Populations by providing them with financial assistance, funded by means of voluntary contributions from Governments, non-governmental organizations and other private or public entities;

(c) The only type of activity to be supported by the Fund is that described in subparagraph (b) above;

(d) The only beneficiaries of assistance from the Fund shall be representatives of indigenous peoples' organizations and communities:

(i) Who are so considered by the Board of Trustees of the United Nations Voluntary Fund for Indigenous Populations described in subparagraph (e) below;

(ii) Who would not, in the opinion of the Board, be able to attend the sessions of the Working Group without the assistance provided by the Fund;

(iii) Who would be able to contribute to a deeper knowledge on the part of the Working Group of the problems affecting indigenous populations and who would secure a broad geographical representation;

(e) The Fund shall be administered in accordance with the Financial Regulations and Rules of the United Nations and other relevant provisions set forth in the annex to the note by the Secretary-General, with the advice of a Board of Trustees composed of five persons with relevant experience on issues affecting indigenous populations, who will serve in their personal capacity; the members of the Board of Trustees shall be appointed by the Secretary-General for a three-year term renewable in consultation with the current Chairman of the Sub-Commission; at least one member of the Board shall be a representative of a widely-recognized organization of indigenous people.

RES/HR/90/33
GE.90-18646

0221

OFFICE DES NATIONS UNIES NÈVE  UNITED IONS OFFICE AT GENEVA

CENTRE POUR LES DROITS DE L'HOMME

CENTRE FOR HUMAN RIGHTS

Téléfax: (022) 733 98 79
Télégrammes: UNATIONS, GENÈVE
Télex: 412 962 UNO CH
Téléphone: 734 60 11 731 02 11

Palais des Nations
CH-1211 GENÈVE 10

RÉF. N°: G/SO 252/2 (4)
(à rappeler dans la réponse)

The Secretary-General of the United Nations presents his compliments to the Minister for Foreign Affairs of the Republic of Korea and has the honour to refer to Economic and Social Council resolution 1991/35 of 31 May 1991, entitled "Suppression of the Traffic in Persons". A copy of the resolution is attached.

The particular attention of His Excellency's Government is drawn to paragraph 1 of this resolution in which the Council reminded States parties to the Slavery Convention of 1926, the Supplementary Convention on the Abolition of Slavery, the Slave Trade and Institutions and Practices Similar to Slavery of 1956, and the Convention for the Suppression of the Traffic in Persons and of the Exploitation of the Prostitution of Others of 1949, of their obligation to submit to the Working Group on Contemporary Forms of Slavery of the Sub-Commission on Prevention of Discrimination and Protection of Minorities regular reports on the situation in their countries, as provided for under the relevant conventions and under Economic and Social Council decision 16 (LVI) of 17 May 1974.

The Secretary-General would appreciate it if any information that His Excellency's Government may wish to provide could be forwarded to the Under-Secretary-General for Human Rights, United Nations Office at Geneva, CH-1211 Genève 10, if possible by 15 March 1992, in order that it can be submitted in time to the Working Group on Contemporary Forms of Slavery at its seventeenth session in 1992.

4 November 1991

0222

1991/35. Suppression of the traffic in persons

The Economic and Social Council,

Recalling Commission on Human Rights resolutions 1982/20 of 10 March 1982 on the question of slavery and the slave trade in all their practices and manifestations, including the slavery-like practices of apartheid and colonialism, and 1988/42 of 8 March 1988, 1989/35 of 6 March 1989, 1990/63 of 7 March 1990 and 1991/58 of 6 March 1991 on the report of the Working Group on Contemporary Forms of Slavery of the Subcommission on Prevention of Discrimination and Protection of Minorities,

Recalling also its resolutions 1982/20 of 4 May 1982 and 1983/30 of 26 May 1983 on the suppression of the traffic in persons and of the exploitation of the prostitution of others, 1988/34 of 27 May 1988 and 1989/74 of 24 May 1989 on the Working Group on Contemporary Forms of Slavery of the Subcommission on Prevention of Discrimination and Protection of Minorities and 1990/46 of 25 May 1990,

Considering that the report of the Special Rapporteur of the Economic and Social Council on the suppression of the traffic in persons and the exploitation of the prostitution of others still constitutes a useful basis for further action,

Noting with appreciation the report of the Secretary-General on the implementation of Economic and Social Council resolution 1983/30 on the suppression of the traffic in persons and of the exploitation of the prostitution of others,

Noting that only a few Member States, United Nations organizations and other intergovernmental organizations have submitted information on the steps taken to implement the recommendations contained in Council resolution 1983/30,

Gravely concerned that slavery, the slave trade and slavery-like practices still exist, that there are modern manifestations of those phenomena and that such practices represent some of the gravest violations of human rights,

Aware of the complexity of the issue of the suppression of the traffic in persons and the exploitation of the prostitution of others, and the need for further coordination and cooperation to implement the recommendations made by the Special Rapporteur and by various United Nations bodies,

1. Reminds States parties to the Slavery Convention of 1926, the Supplementary Convention on the Abolition of Slavery, the Slave Trade and Institutions and Practices Similar to Slavery of 1956, and the Convention for the Suppression of the Traffic in Persons and of the Exploitation of the Prostitution of Others of 1949 that they should submit to the Working Group on Contemporary Forms of Slavery of the Subcommission on Prevention of Discrimination and Protection of Minorities regular reports on the situation in their countries, as provided for under the relevant conventions and under Economic and Social Council decision 16 (LVI) of 17 May 1974;

2. Takes note with appreciation of the report of the Secretary-General on the implementation of Economic and Social Council resolution 1983/30 on the suppression of the traffic in persons and of the exploitation of the prostitution of others;

RES/HR/91/20
GE.91-18045

0223

3. Requests the Secretary-General to submit a further report to the Council, at its regular session of 1992, on the steps taken to implement the recommendations contained in Council resolution 1983/30 by those Member States, United Nations organizations and other intergovernmental organizations that have not yet submitted such information and to make that report available to the Working Group on Contemporary Forms of Slavery of the Subcommission on Prevention of Discrimination and Protection of Minorities;

4. Urges the Secretary-General to ensure effective servicing of the Working Group and of other activities related to contemporary forms of slavery and slavery-like practices, and requests him to report to the Council at its regular session of 1992 on the steps taken;

5. Requests the Secretary-General to designate the Centre for Human Rights as the focal point for the coordination of activities in the United Nations for the suppression of contemporary forms of slavery;

6. Urges the Commission on the Status of Women and the Committee on Crime Prevention and Control to collaborate closely with the Centre for Human Rights on the issue of suppression of contemporary forms of slavery;

7. Endorses the recommendation of the Commission on Human Rights, in its resolution 1991/58, that the supervisory bodies of the International Labour Organisation give particular attention in their work to the implementation of provisions and standards designed to ensure protection of children and other persons exposed to contemporary forms of slavery;

8. Endorses the recommendation of the Commission on Human Rights, in its resolution 1991/58, that the Human Rights Committee, the Committee on Economic, Social and Cultural Rights, the Committee on the Elimination of Discrimination against Women and the Committee on the Rights of the Child, when examining periodic reports of States parties, give particular attention to the implementation of, respectively, articles 8 and 24 of the International Covenant on Civil and Political Rights, articles 10, 12 and 13 of the International Covenant on Economic, Social and Cultural Rights, article 6 of the Convention on the Elimination of All Forms of Discrimination against Women, and articles 32, 34, 35 and 36 of the Convention on the Rights of the Child, with a view to combating contemporary forms of slavery;

9. Decides to consider the question of the suppression of traffic in persons at its regular session of 1992 under the agenda item entitled "Human rights questions".

13th plenary meeting
31 May 1991

0224

facilities necessary for the implementation of the present resolution.

14th plenary meeting
26 May 1983

1983/28. Participation of non-governmental organizations in the preparations for the World Conference to Review and Appraise the Achievements of the United Nations Decade for Women

The Economic and Social Council,

Taking note of the report of the Commission on the Status of Women Acting as the Preparatory Body for the World Conference to Review and Appraise the Achievements of the United Nations Decade for Women,[58]

Bearing in mind the valuable contributions that non-governmental organizations have made to the advancement of women, particularly during the United Nations Decade for Women and especially in the preparation for and follow-up of the World Conference of the International Women's Year, held at Mexico City from 19 June to 2 July 1975, and the World Conference of the United Nations Decade for Women: Equality, Development and Peace, held at Copenhagen from 14 to 30 July 1980,

1. *Requests* the Secretary-General to invite the interested non-governmental organizations in consultative status with the Economic and Social Council to participate actively in the preparations for and in the World Conference to Review and Appraise the Achievements of the United Nations Decade for Women, to be held in 1985;

2. *Further requests* the Secretary-General to invite interested non-governmental organizations in consultative status with the Economic and Social Council to submit to the Commission on the Status of Women Acting as the Preparatory Body for the 1985 World Conference, information, including their views on the progress made and the obstacles still to be overcome towards the attainment of the goals of the Decade, as well as their views on priorities and strategies looking to the year 2000;

3. *Urges* Governments to invite interested non-governmental organizations in their respective countries also to submit views on the progress made at the national level, obstacles remaining and goals to be attained, and to co-operate in the preparation of the national reports to be submitted by them to the Secretary-General;

4. *Requests* the regional commissions to ensure that the interested non-governmental organizations in consultative status with the Economic and Social Council participate in their respective regions in the preparations for and in the intergovernmental preparatory regional meetings for the 1985 World Conference.

14th plenary meeting
26 May 1983

1983/29. International Research and Training Institute for the Advancement of Women

The Economic and Social Council,

Recalling its resolution 1982/27 of 4 May 1982 on the International Research and Training Institute for the Advancement of Women,

[58] A/CONF.116/PC/9 and Corr.1.

Bearing in mind the goals of the United Nations Decade for Women: Equality, Development and Peace,

Having considered the report of the Board of Trustees of the International Research and Training Institute for the Advancement of Women on its third session,[59]

1. *Expresses its satisfaction* with the activities thus far accomplished in the programme of work of the International Research and Training Institute for the Advancement of Women;

2. *Takes note* of the decisions and recommendations made by the Board of Trustees of the Institute at its third session;[60]

3. *Notes with satisfaction* the completion of the first phase of the programme on statistics and indicators on the situation of women and the launching of training and fellowship programmes of the Institute;

4. *Emphasizes* that the work programme of the Institute for the biennium 1984-1985 should continue to focus on research, training and information that would lead to the integration of women in mainstream developmental activities;

5. *Reiterates* the need for support and close co-operation between the Institute and the regional commissions, specialized agencies and other United Nations bodies;

6. *Calls upon* all Member States to contribute to the United Nations Trust Fund for the International Research and Training Institute for the Advancement of Women and to ensure regular and effective financing for its progress and development.

14th plenary meeting
26 May 1983

1983/30. Suppression of the traffic in persons and of the exploitation of the prostitution of others

The Economic and Social Council,

Recalling that the enslavement of women and children subjected to prostitution is incompatible with the dignity and fundamental rights of the human person,

Recalling its resolution 1982/20 of 4 May 1982,

Having taken note of the report prepared by the Special Rapporteur in pursuance of that resolution,[61]

1. *Again invites* Member States to sign, ratify and implement the Convention for the Suppression of the Traffic in Persons and of the Exploitation of the Prostitution of Others;[62]

2. *Also invites* Member States to sign, ratify and implement the International Convention for the Suppression of the Circulation of and Traffic in Obscene Publications, concluded at Geneva on 12 September 1923, as amended by the Protocol signed at Lake Success, New York, on 12 November 1947;[63]

3. *Recommends* that Member States should take account of the report of the Special Rapporteur and draw up, subject to their constitutions and legislation and in consultation with the parties concerned, policies aimed, to the extent possible, at:

[59] E/1983/31.
[60] *Ibid.*, sect. I.
[61] E/1983/7 and Corr.1 and 2.
[62] General Assembly resolution 317 (IV), annex.
[63] United Nations, *Treaty Series*, vol. 46, No. 710, p. 201.

(*a*) Preventing prostitution by moral education and civics training, in and out of school;

(*b*) Increasing the number of women among the State's personnel having direct contact with the populations concerned;

(*c*) Eliminating discrimination that ostracizes prostitutes and makes their reabsorption into society more difficult;

(*d*) Curbing the pornography industry and the trade in pornography and penalizing them very severely when minors are involved;

(*e*) Punishing all forms of procuring in such a way as to deter it, particularly when it exploits minors;

(*f*) Facilitating occupational training for and the reabsorption into society of persons rescued from prostitution;

4. *Further invites* Member States to co-operate closely with one another in the research for missing persons and in the identification of international networks of procurers and, if they are members of the International Criminal Police Organization, to co-operate with that organization, requesting it to make the suppression of the traffic in persons one of its priorities;

5. *Invites* the regional commissions to help Member States and United Nations bodies wishing to organize regional expert meetings, seminars or symposia on the traffic in persons;

6. *Suggests* to the Secretary-General that he designate as a focal point the Centre for Human Rights, specifically the secretariat of the Working Group on Slavery, in close co-operation with the Centre for Social Development and Humanitarian Affairs of the Department of International Economic and Social Affairs;

7. *Requests* the Sub-Commission on Prevention of Discrimination and Protection of Minorities to consider the possibility of inviting the Commission on the Status of Women to designate a representative to participate in all sessions of the Working Group on Slavery, in accordance with Economic and Social Council resolution 48 (IV) of 29 March 1947;

8. *Requests* the Centre for Human Rights to prepare, in liaison with the United Nations agencies and organs concerned and with the competent non-governmental organizations, two complementary studies: one on the sale of children and the other on the legal and social problems of sexual minorities, including male prostitution, and to submit those studies as soon as possible to the Sub-Commission on Prevention of Discrimination and Protection of Minorities;

9. *Encourages* the Centre for Social Development and Humanitarian Affairs of the Department of International Economic and Social Affairs to utilize the available resources of all its branches with a view to undertaking interdisciplinary studies, and to co-operate with the Division of Narcotic Drugs;

10. *Invites* all the organs, organizations and agencies of the United Nations system concerned, particularly the United Nations Children's Fund, the Office of the United Nations High Commissioner for Refugees, the International Labour Organisation and the World Health Organization, to bring the traffic in persons to the notice of their representatives and experts and to transmit their observations and their studies to the focal point designated by the Secretary-General;

11. *Encourages* the United Nations Educational, Scientific and Cultural Organization to draw up, with member States, programmes for use in schools and in the media concerning the image of women in society;

12. *Invites* the World Tourism Organization to place the question of sex-oriented tourism on its agenda;

13. *Requests* the Secretary-General to take the necessary steps to have the report prepared by the Special Rapporteur in pursuance of Council resolution 1982/20 reproduced as a United Nations publication so that it may be widely disseminated;

14. *Also requests* the Secretary-General to report to the Economic and Social Council, at its first regular session of 1985, on the steps taken to implement the present resolution;

15. *Decides* that the activities recommended in the present resolution will be carried out within the limits of the resources provided for by the Secretary-General in the proposed programme budget for the biennium 1984-1985.

14th plenary meeting
26 May 1983

1983/31. Question of the realization in all countries of the economic, social and cultural rights contained in the Universal Declaration of Human Rights and in the International Covenant on Economic, Social and Cultural Rights, and study of special problems which the developing countries face in their efforts to achieve these human rights

The Economic and Social Council,

Recalling its resolution 1929 (LVIII) of 6 May 1975, in which it noted that, to be effective, popular participation should be consciously promoted by Governments with full recognition of civil, political, social, economic and cultural rights and through innovative measures, including structural changes and institutional reform and development, as well as through the encouragement of all forms of education designed to involve actively all segments of society,

Recalling further General Assembly resolutions 32/130 of 16 December 1977, 34/46 of 23 November 1979 and 37/55 of 3 December 1982,

1. *Requests* the Secretary-General to undertake a comprehensive analytical study on the right to popular participation in its various forms as an important factor in the full realization of all human rights, and to submit a preliminary study to the Commission on Human Rights at its fortieth session and the final study at its forty-first session;

2. *Further requests* the Secretary-General in the preparation of the study, to take account of the work on the concept and practice of popular participation that has been carried out by relevant United Nations organs, specialized agencies and other bodies, as well as of the views expressed at the thirty-ninth session of the Commission on Human Rights and such views on, *inter alia*, relevant national experiences as may be submitted by Governments in response to General Assembly resolution 37/55 and the present resolution.

15th plenary meeting
27 May 1983

외교문서 비밀해제: 한국 인권문제 14
한국 인권문제 유엔 반응 및 동향 1

초판인쇄 2024년 03월 15일
초판발행 2024년 03월 15일

지은이 한국학술정보(주)
펴낸이 채종준
펴낸곳 한국학술정보(주)
주 소 경기도 파주시 회동길 230(문발동)
전 화 031-908-3181(대표)
팩 스 031-908-3189
홈페이지 http://ebook.kstudy.com
E-mail 출판사업부 publish@kstudy.com
등 록 제일산-115호(2000. 6. 19)

ISBN 979-11-7217-068-4 94340
979-11-7217-054-7 94340 (set)

책에 대한 더 나은 생각, 끊임없는 고민, 독자를 생각하는 마음으로 보다 좋은 책을 만들어갑니다.